Lecture Notes in Computer Science   10153

Commenced Publication in 1973
Founding and Former Series Editors:
Gerhard Goos, Juris Hartmanis, and Jan van Leeuwen

More information about this series at http://www.springer.com/series/7408

Paul Grünbacher · Anna Perini (Eds.)

Requirements Engineering: Foundation for Software Quality

23rd International Working Conference, REFSQ 2017
Essen, Germany, February 27 – March 2, 2017
Proceedings

 Springer

Editors
Paul Grünbacher
Johannes Kepler University
Linz
Austria

Anna Perini
Fondazione Bruno Kessler
Trento
Italy

ISSN 0302-9743   ISSN 1611-3349 (electronic)
Lecture Notes in Computer Science
ISBN 978-3-319-54044-3   ISBN 978-3-319-54045-0 (eBook)
DOI 10.1007/978-3-319-54045-0

Library of Congress Control Number: 2017931542

LNCS Sublibrary: SL2 – Programming and Software Engineering

Printed on acid-free paper

This Springer imprint is published by Springer Nature
The registered company is Springer International Publishing AG
The registered company address is: Gewerbestrasse 11, 6330 Cham, Switzerland

Preface

It is our great pleasure to welcome you to the proceedings of the 23rd International Working Conference on Requirements Engineering – Foundation for Software Quality! The REFSQ working conference series is a leading international forum for discussing Requirements Engineering (RE) and its many relations to quality. The first REFSQ conference took place in 1994. The conference was organized as a stand-alone meeting since 2010 and is now well established as Europe's premier conference series on RE. This conference publication contains the proceedings of REFSQ 2017, held in Essen, Germany, from February 27 to March 2, 2017.

Requirements Engineering is a crucial factor for developing high-quality software, systems, and services. RE methods, tools, and processes are nowadays expected to support engineering diverse types of systems of different scale and complexity – such as information systems, safety-critical systems, socio-technical systems, service-based applications, apps for mobile devices, or cyberphysical systems – and are applied in diverse domains. The special theme of REFSQ17 was "My RE" to emphasize an important issue: How can RE evolve to deal with this diversity, still keeping its ultimate objective: understanding what is the right software system and helping developing it in the right way.

The exciting program consisted of high-quality contributions selected after a thorough reviewing process. This year we invited four categories of submissions for the main track of the REFSQ conference: (1) technical design papers that describe and explain novel solutions for requirements-related problems or significant improvements of existing solutions; (2) scientific evaluation papers that investigate existing real-world problems, evaluate existing real-world implemented artifacts, or validate newly designed artifacts, e.g., by means such as case studies, experiments, simulation, surveys, systematic literature reviews, mapping studies, or action research; (3) vision papers that state where the research in the field should be heading towards; and (4) research previews that describe well-defined research ideas at an early stage of investigation.

This year, 82 abstracts were submitted to the research track, resulting in 74 submissions. The program chairs desk-rejected two papers violating the formatting instructions or the guidelines stated in the call. The remaining 72 submissions were reviewed by the members of the Program Committee (PC), with each paper receiving at least three reviews. We also had a very active online discussion phase, with many long and detailed discussions among the members of the PC. During a physical PC meeting held at the paluno Ruhr Institute for Software Technology in Essen on December 2, 2016, the members of the Program Committee selected the 24 papers to be presented at REFSQ 2017. Specifically, the research track comprised seven technical design papers, nine scientific evaluation papers, one vision paper, and seven research previews (some of these were recategorized long papers).

The REFSQ 2017 conference was organized as a three-day symposium: Two conference days were devoted to presentations and discussions of research papers. A one-day industry track reported on real-world experiences and applications of RE. In addition, the REFSQ conference program also included a research methodology track as well as posters and tools. Furthermore, several workshops and a doctoral symposium were co-located with the conference. All papers from the Research Track and the Research Methodology Track can be found in the present proceedings. The papers included in the satellite events can be found in the REFSQ 2017 workshop proceedings published with CEUR.

The REFSQ conference program was enriched by two keynote talks: Lionel C. Briand from the University of Luxembourg on "Analyzing Natural-Language Requirements: The Not-Too-Sexy and Yet Curiously Difficult Research that Industry Needs" and Inga Wiele from gezeitenraum on "Design Thinking in a Nutshell-90 Minutes from Idea to Prototype and Back."

REFSQ 2017 would not have been possible without the engagement and support of many individuals who contributed in many different ways. As program co-chairs, we would like to thank the REFSQ Steering Committee members for their help and guidance. We are grateful to all the members of the Program Committee for their timely and thorough reviews of the submissions and for dedicating their time to the online discussion and the face-to-face meeting. In particular, we thank those PC members who volunteered to serve as a shepherd or gatekeeper to authors of conditionally accepted papers. We are grateful to all members of the Organizing Committee, who organized the different tracks and co-located events. Finally, we would like to thank Christina Bellinghoven, Eric Schmieders, and Klaus Pohl for their excellent work in coordinating the background organization, as well as Fitsum Meshesha Kifetew (Fondazione Bruno Kessler) and Anna Kramer (Springer) for their support in preparing this volume.

February 2017

Paul Grünbacher
Anna Perini

Organization

Organizing Committee

Head of Background Organization

Klaus Pohl   paluno, University of Duisburg-Essen, Germany

Local Organization

Christina Bellinghoven paluno, University of Duisburg-Essen, Germany
Eric Schmieders   paluno, University of Duisburg-Essen, Germany

Research Track

Paul Grünbacher   Johannes Kepler University Linz, Austria
Anna Perini   Fondazione Bruno Kessler Trento, Italy

Research Methodology Track

Oscar Dieste   Universidad Politécnica de Madrid, Spain
Fabio Massacci   Università di Trento, Italy

Industry Track

Joerg Doerr   Fraunhofer IESE, Germany
Kim Lauenroth   adesso AG, Dortmund, Germany

Workshops

Eric Knauss   Chalmers | University of Gothenburg, Sweden
Angelo Susi   Fondazione Bruno Kessler Trento, Italy

Doctoral Symposium

Jennifer Horkoff   Chalmers | University of Gothenburg, Sweden
Jolita Ralyté   University of Geneva, Switzerland

Posters and Tools

Fabiano Dalpiaz   Utrecht University, The Netherlands
Patrick Mäder   Ilmenau Technical University, Germany

Social Media and Publicity

Itzel Morales-Ramirez   INFOTEC Center of Research and Innovation in ICT,
                                  Mexico
Norbert Seyff   FHNW and University of Zurich, Switzerland

Proceedings

Fitsum Meshesha Kifetew   Fondazione Bruno Kessler Trento, Italy

Research Track Program Committee

Joao Araujo   Universidade Nova de Lisboa, Portugal
Thorsten Berger   Chalmers | University of Gothenburg, Sweden
Daniel Berry   University of Waterloo, Canada
Sjaak Brinkkemper   Utrecht University, The Netherlands
Eya Ben Charrada   University of Zurich, Switzerland
Nelly Condori-Fernández   VU University of Amsterdam, The Netherlands
Fabiano Dalpiaz   Utrecht University, The Netherlands
Maya Daneva   University of Twente, The Netherlands
Joerg Doerr   Fraunhofer IESE, Germany
Michael Felderer   University of Innsbruck, Austria
Alessio Ferrari   ISTI-CNR Pisa, Italy
Xavier Franch   Universitat Politècnica de Catalunya, Spain
Samuel Fricker   FHNW, Switzerland and Blekinge Institute
                                  of Technology, Sweden
Vincenzo Gervasi   University of Pisa, Italy
Martin Glinz   University of Zurich, Switzerland
Renata Guizzardi   Universidade Federal do Espirito Santo, Brazil
Irit Hadar   University of Haifa, Israel
Patrick Heymans   University of Namur (FUNDP)/PReCISE
                                  research centre, Belgium
Jennifer Horkoff   Chalmers | University of Gothenburg, Sweden
Hermann Kaindl   Vienna University of Technology, Austria
Erik Kamsties   Dortmund University of Applied Sciences and Arts,
                                  Germany
Alessia Knauss   Chalmers | University of Gothenburg, Sweden
Eric Knauss   Chalmers | University of Gothenburg, Sweden
Anne Koziolek   Karlsruhe Institute of Technology, Germany
Kim Lauenroth   adesso AG, Dortmund, Germany
Emmanuel Letier   University College London, UK
Walid Maalej   University of Hamburg, Germany
Patrick Mäder   Ilmenau Technical University, Germany
Nazim Madhavji   Western University, Canada
Raimundas Matulevičus   University of Tartu, Estonia
Raul Mazo   CRI, Université de Paris 1 Panthéon-Sorbonne, France
John Mylopoulos   University of Ottawa, Canada

Andreas L. Opdahl   University of Bergen, Norway
Barbara Paech   Heidelberg University, Germany
Elda Paja   Università di Trento, Italy
Liliana Pasquale   Lero - The Irish Software Engineering Research Centre,
                           Ireland
Oscar Pastor Lopez   Universitat Politécnica de Valéncia, Spain
Klaus Pohl   paluno, University of Duisburg-Essen, Germany
Björn Regnell   Lund University, Sweden
Mehrdad Sabetzadeh   University of Luxembourg, Luxembourg
Camille Salinesi   CRI, Université de Paris 1 Panthéon-Sorbonne, France
Nicolas Sannier   SNT, University of Luxembourg, Luxembourg
Pete Sawyer   Lancaster University, UK
Kurt Schneider   Leibniz Universität Hannover, Germany
Norbert Seyff   FHNW and University of Zurich, Switzerland
Alberto Siena   Delta Informatica S.p.A., Italy
Paola Spoletini   Kennesaw State University, USA
Angelo Susi   Fondazione Bruno Kessler, Italy
Richard Berntsson Svensson Blekinge Institute of Technology, Sweden
Michael Vierhauser   Johannes Kepler University Linz, Austria
Roel Wieringa   University of Twente, The Netherlands
Krzysztof Wnuk   Blekinge Institute of Technology, Sweden
Tao Yue   Simula Research Laboratory and University of Oslo,
                           Norway
Yuanyuan Zhang   University College London, UK
Didar Zowghi   University of Technology, Sydney, Australia

Research Methodology Track Program Committee

Kristian Beckers   Technische Universität München, Germany
Travis Breaux   Carnegie Mellon University, USA
Maya Daneva   University of Twente, The Netherlands
Karen Elliott   Newcastle University Business School, UK
Katsiaryna Labunets   Università di Trento, Italy
Ignacio Panach   Universitat de València, Spain
Lutz Prechelt   Freie Universität Berlin, Germany
Maria Riaz   Google Inc., USA
Riccardo Scandariato   Chalmers | University of Gothenburg, Sweden

Additional Reviewers

David Ameller   Parisa Ghazi
Fatma Başak Aydemir   Emitzá Guzmán
Alejandro Catala   Paul Hübner
Jean-Marc Davril   Anne Hess
Carles Farré   Sofija Hotomski

Timo Johann
Matthias Koch
Martina Kolpondinos-Huber
Christian Kücherer
Zijad Kurtanovic
Yan Li
Grischa Liebel
Johan Linåker
Hong Lu
Dominik Pascal Magin
Salome Maro
Ibtehal Noorwali
Marc Oriol Hilari
Raquel Ouriques

Sietse Overbeek
Thomas Quirchmayr
Raquel Quriques
Manuel Rudolph
Marcela Ruiz
Marcus Seiler
Melanie Stade
Christoph Stanik
Marcus Trapp
Joselaine Valaski
Dirk van der Linden
Gerard Wagenaar
Dustin Wüest
Huihui Zhang

Steering Committee

Björn Regnell (Chair)
Kurt Schneider (Vice Chair)
Daniela Damian
Maya Daneva
Jörg Doerr
Samuel Fricker
Rainer Grau
Paul Grünbacher

Eric Knauss
Andreas L. Opdahl
Oscar Pastor
Anna Perini
Klaus Pohl
Richard Berntsson Svensson
Inge van de Weerd

Sponsors

Partners

JOHANNES KEPLER
UNIVERSITY LINZ

Invited Talks

Analyzing Natural-Language Requirements: The Not-Too-Sexy and Yet Curiously Difficult Research that Industry Needs

Lionel C. Briand

University of Luxembourg, Luxembourg, Luxembourg
lionel.briand@uni.lu

Abstract. While often complemented by models at various degrees of formality and detail, natural-language requirements remain pervasive across all industry sectors. Decades of research on formal methods and model-based development have not made a noticeable dent in this practice, and I do not expect the situation to change in the foreseeable future. The prevalence of natural-language requirements is largely due to the flexibility and understandability of natural language, especially when stakeholders with diverse backgrounds are involved. External factors, such as laws and regulations, further contribute to the popularity of natural language in requirements specifications. Despite inherent challenges and drawbacks associated with natural language, it is imperative to provide scalable support for requirements analysts to be able to handle hundreds and sometimes thousands of natural-language statements. A first question here is to understand what type of support the analysts need. This varies across domains or even specific contexts. The examples I will present include checking in a practical manner the conformance of requirements with pre-defined sentence templates, extracting glossary terms and domain models from requirements, analyzing the impact of requirements changes, and deriving system test cases from requirements. I will report on results obtained from research projects in collaboration with industry, and reflect on our experience at the Software Verification and Validation group, SnT Centre, University of Luxembourg. Providing scalable support for handling natural-language requirements entails, to various degrees, the use of natural-language processing, as well as constraint solving, information retrieval and machine learning. Such research endeavours are therefore fundamentally multidisciplinary. Unfortunately, and probably in part because of such multidisciplinarity, academic research on the management and analysis of natural-language requirements is limited and comparatively dwarfed by the more formal approaches to requirements engineering.

Design Thinking in a Nutshell - 90 Minutes from Idea to Prototype and Back

Inga Wiele

gezeitenraum, Sankt Peter-Ording, Germany
inga@gezeitenraum.com

Abstract. Creating products and services that really suit peoples' lives and needs – that is the goal of Design Thinking. To achieve this goal, you have to observe peoples' lives. Empathy is important to better understand the needs of others. Very often we pass each other without looking or talk without really perceiving what others really feel and what they need. Design Thinking provides a structured approach to innovation processes in which human needs are the focus. You may think to yourself "Are 90 minutes enough to get an understanding of Design Thinking? How good are the results that you achieve in one hour? Is it possible that all participants have their say and have a constructive outcome in the end?" This talk will approach this venture with you. Based on the process model of Design Thinking, you experience the different elements of Design Thinking within 90 minutes and learn how much a team can achieve when expectations follow the motto "Done is better than perfect".

Contents

Use Case Models

Incremental Reconfiguration of Product Specific Use Case Models for Evolving Configuration Decisions

Ines Hajri[1(✉)], Arda Goknil[1], Lionel C. Briand[1], and Thierry Stephany[2]

[1] SnT Centre for Security, Reliability and Trust, University of Luxembourg,
Luxembourg City, Luxembourg
{ines.hajri,arda.goknil,lionel.briand}@uni.lu
[2] International Electronics & Engineering (IEE), Contern, Luxembourg
thierry.stephany@iee.lu

Abstract. *Context and motivation*: Product Line Engineering (PLE) is increasingly common practice in industry to develop complex systems for multiple customers with varying needs. In many business contexts, use cases are central development artifacts for requirements engineering and system testing. In such contexts, use case configurators can play a significant role to capture variable and common requirements in Product Line (PL) use case models and to generate Product Specific (PS) use case models for each new customer in a product family. *Question/Problem*: Although considerable research has been devoted to use case configurators, little attention has been paid to supporting the incremental reconfiguration of use case models with evolving configuration decisions. *Principal ideas/results*: We propose, apply, and assess an incremental reconfiguration approach to support evolving configuration decisions in PL use case models. PS use case models are incrementally reconfigured by focusing only on the changed decisions and their side effects. In our prior work, we proposed and applied Product line Use case modeling Method (PUM) to support variability modeling in PL use case diagrams and specifications. We also developed a use case configurator, PUMConf, which interactively collects configuration decisions from analysts to generate PS use case models from PL models. Our approach is built on top of PUM and PUMConf. *Contributions*: We provide fully automated tool support for incremental configuration as an extension of PUMConf. Our approach has been evaluated in an industrial case study in the automotive domain, which provided evidence it is practical and beneficial.

Keywords: Product Line Engineering · Use case-driven development

1 Introduction

Product Line Engineering (PLE) is becoming common practice in many domains such as automotive and avionics, due to the increasing complexity of software

© Springer International Publishing AG 2017
P. Grünbacher and A. Perini (Eds.): REFSQ 2017, LNCS 10153, pp. 3–21, 2017.
DOI: 10.1007/978-3-319-54045-0_1

systems that warrant better support for reusable software artifacts. In such domains, many business contexts are use case-driven where use cases are the main artifacts driving requirements engineering and system testing practices [1–3]. This is also the case for the industrial context of our work, IEE [4], a leading supplier of embedded systems in the automotive domain. The current development practice at IEE is use case-driven and based on clone-and-own reuse [5]. To develop a new product in a new project, IEE analysts elicit requirements as a use case diagram and its accompanying use case specifications. For each new customer of the product, they need to clone the current models, and negotiate variabilities with the customer to produce new use case models. This is a manual, error prone, and time-consuming practice since variability information is not explicitly represented.

The need for PLE support in the context of use case-driven development has already been acknowledged and several product line use case modeling and configuration approaches have been proposed [6–8]. Existing approaches rely on feature modeling, including establishing and maintaining traces between features and use case models [9]. Due to limited resources, IEE, as well as other software development companies, find such additional traceability and maintainability effort to be impractical. In addition, existing use case configurators (e.g., [6–8]) do not support incremental reconfiguration of use case models resulting from changes in configuration decisions, e.g., a selected variant use case being unselected.

In practice, for example at IEE and for a variety of reasons, analysts manually assign traces from the configured use case models to other software and hardware specifications as well as to the customers' requirements documents for external systems [10]. Furthermore, configuration decisions frequently change, resulting in the reconfiguration of Product Specific (PS) use case models. When the use case models are reconfigured for all decisions, including unchanged and unaffected decisions, manually assigned traces are lost. The analysts need to reassign all the traces after each reconfiguration. It is therefore vital to enable the incremental reconfiguration of use case models focusing only on changed decisions and their side-effects. With such support, the analysts could then reassign traces only for the parts of the reconfigured models impacted by decision changes. Our main motivation is to preserve the unimpacted parts of the PS use case models for evolving configuration decisions, thus avoiding manual effort during reconfiguration such as manual updating of traces from PS models to other documents.

In our previous work [11], we proposed and assessed the Product line Use case modeling Method (PUM) to support variability modeling in Product Line (PL) use case diagrams and specifications, without making use of feature models, thus avoiding unnecessary modeling and traceability overhead. PUM includes existing PL extensions for use case diagrams [12,13] and, for modeling variability in use case specifications, we introduced new extensions for the Restricted Use Case Modeling method (RUCM) [14]. Building on this, we developed a use case-driven configuration approach [15] supporting three crucial activities. First, the analyst is guided to make configuration decisions in an appropriate order. Second, the consistency of configuration decisions is ensured by automatically identifying contradicting decisions. Third, PS use case diagram and specifications are automatically generated from PL models and configuration decisions. Our configuration approach is supported by a tool, *PUMConf*, integrated with IBM DOORS.

In this paper, we propose, apply and assess an incremental reconfiguration approach, based on PUM and PUMConf, to support the evolution of configuration decisions for PL use case models. We do not address here evolving PL use case models, which is an entirely different problem and needs to be treated in a separate approach. In our proposed solution, the PS use case diagram and specifications are incrementally reconfigured by focusing only on the changed configuration decisions and their side effects. To do so, we implemented a model differencing pipeline which identifies decision changes to be used in the regeneration of PS models. There are two sets of decisions: (i) the set of previously made decisions used to initially generate the PS use case models and (ii) the set of decisions including decisions changed after the initial generation of the PS models. Our approach compares the two sets to incrementally regenerate the PS use case models. We extended our configurator, *PUMConf*, to fully automate our approach. We also report an industrial case study demonstrating its applicability and benefits.

This paper is structured as follows. In Sect. 2, we discuss the related work. Section 3 provides a short overview of the background on *PUM* and *PUMConf*, proposed in our previous work, on which this paper builds. In Sect. 4, we provide an overview of the approach. Sections 5 and 6 provide the details of the core technical parts of our approach. Sections 7 and 8 present our tool support and industrial case study along with results and lessons learned. We conclude the paper in Sect. 9.

2   Related Work

Several use case-driven configuration approaches were proposed in the literature (e.g., [6–8]). These approaches do not support incremental reconfiguration of use cases for changes in configuration decisions. There are also more general configuration approaches that can be customized to configure PS use case models. For instance, DOPLER [16] supports capturing variability information as a variability model, and modeling any type of artifact as asset models. Variability and asset models are linked by using trace relations. Heider et al. [17,18] propose an approach as an extension of DOPLER to identify the impact of changes of variability information on products. For a change in a variability model of a product line, the approach identifies whether configuration decisions for the existing products need to be changed as well. Then, it reconfigures all the products in the product line and also compares the reconfigured products with the previous version to inform the analysts about the differences in the products. However, it focuses on changes in variability information, not changes in decisions. It is also not incremental, limiting its applicability, as the reconfiguration encompasses all the decisions, not only the affected ones.

Considerable attention in the model-driven engineering research community has been given to incremental model generation/transformation for model changes (e.g., [19–21]), and this line of work has inspired initiatives in many software engineering domains. For instance, Vogel et al. [22] use incremental model transformation techniques for synchronizing runtime models by integrating a general-purpose model transformation engine into their runtime modeling environment. Bidirectional model transformations are employed by Eramo et al. [23] to support the synchronization and interoperability of architecture models for architecture model changes. Alternatively, we could also have employed a generic model transformation engine and language to implement the incremental generation of PS use case models. Compared to model transformation languages, in terms of loading, matching and editing text in natural language, Java provides much more flexibility for handling plain text use case specifications. As a result, we used Java to implement the generation of PS use case models in our prior work [15], and also to implement the incremental reconfiguration of PS models as a model differencing and reconfiguration pipeline (see Sect. 4). To the best of our knowledge, our approach is the first work which supports incremental reconfiguration of PS use case models for evolving configuration decisions in a product family.

3   Background

In this section we give the background information about elicitation of PL use case diagram and specifications (Sect. 3.1), and our configuration approach (Sect. 3.2).

In the rest of the paper, we use Smart Trunk Opener (STO) as a case study. STO is a real-time automotive embedded system developed by IEE. It provides automatic, hands-free access to a vehicle's trunk, in combination with a keyless entry system. In possession of the vehicle's electronic remote control, the user moves her leg in forward and backward directions at the vehicle's rear bumper. STO recognizes the movement and transmits a signal to the keyless entry system, which confirms that the user has the remote. This allows the trunk controller to open the trunk automatically.

3.1   Elicitation of Variability in PL Use Cases

Elicitation of PL use case models is based on the Product line Use case modeling Method (PUM) [11]. In this section, we give a brief description of the PUM artifacts.

Use Case Diagram with PL Extensions. For use case diagrams, we employ the PL extensions proposed by Halmans and Pohl [12,13] since they support explicit representation of variants, variation points, and their dependencies (Fig. 1). We do not introduce any further extensions.

A use case is either *Essential* or *Variant*. Variant use cases are distinguished from essential (mandatory) use cases, i.e., mandatory for all the products in a product family, by using the 'Variant' stereotype. A variation point given as a triangle is associated

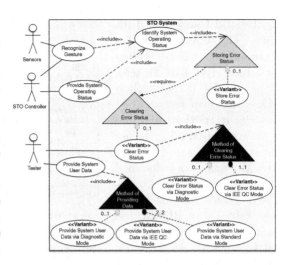

Fig. 1. Part of the PL use case diagram for STO

to one, or more than one use case using the 'include' relation. The mandatory variation points indicate where the customer has to make a selection for a product (the black triangles in Fig. 1). A 'tree-like' relation, containing a cardinality constraint, is used to express relations between variants and variation points, which are called *variability relations*. The relation uses a [min..max] notation in which *min* and *max* define the minimum and maximum numbers of variants that can be selected for the variation point. A variability relation is optional where $(min = 0)$ or $(min > 0$ and $max < n)$; n is the number of variants in a variation point. A variability relation is mandatory where $(min = max = n)$. Optional and mandatory relations are depicted with light-grey and black filled circles, respectively (Fig. 1). For instance, the 'Provide System User Data' essential use case has to support multiple methods of providing data where the methods of providing data via IEE QC mode and Standard mode are mandatory. In addition, the customer can select the method of providing data via diagnostic mode. In STO, the customer may decide the system does not store the errors determined while the operating status is being identified (see the 'Storing Error Status' optional variation point in Fig. 1). The extensions support the dependencies *require* and *conflict* among variation points and variant use cases [13]. Based on *require* in Fig. 1, the selection of the variant use case in 'Storing Error Status' implies the selection of the variant use case in 'Clearing Error Status'. Further variability information is given in PL use case specifications. For instance, only PL use case specifications indicate in which flows of events a variation point is included.

Restricted Use Case Modeling (RUCM) and Its Extensions. This section introduces the RUCM template and its PL extensions which we proposed. RUCM provides restriction rules and keywords constraining the use of natural language [14]. Since RUCM was not designed for PL modeling, we introduced some PL extensions (see Table 1). In RUCM, use cases have basic and alternative flows (Lines 2, 8, 13, 16, 22, 27, 33 and 38). In Table 1, we omit some alternative flows and some basic information such as actors and pre/post conditions.

A basic flow describes a main successful path that satisfies stakeholder interests. It contains use case steps and a postcondition (Lines 3–7, 23–26 and 39–43). A step can be one of the following interactions: an actor sends a request or data to the system (Line 34); the system validates a request or data (Line 4); the system replies to an actor with a result (Line 7). The

Table 1. Some STO use cases in the extended RUCM

1	**USE CASE** Recognize Gesture
2	**1.1 Basic Flow**
3	1. INCLUDE USE CASE Identify System Operating Status.
4	2. The system VALIDATES THAT the operating status is valid.
5	3. The system REQUESTS the move capacitance FROM the sensors.
6	4. The system VALIDATES THAT the movement is a valid kick.
7	5. The system SENDS the valid kick status TO the STO Controller.
8	**1.2 <OPTIONAL>Bounded Alternative Flow**
9	RFS 1-4
10	1. IF voltage fluctuation is detected THEN
11	2. RESUME STEP 1.
12	3. ENDIF
13	**1.3 Specific Alternative Flow**
14	RFS 2
15	1. ABORT.
16	**1.4 Specific Alternative Flow**
17	RFS 4
18	1. The system increments the OveruseCounter by the increment step.
19	2. ABORT.
20	
21	**USE CASE** Identify System Operating Status
22	**1.1 Basic Flow**
23	1. The system VALIDATES THAT the watchdog reset is valid.
24	2. The system VALIDATES THAT the RAM is valid.
25	3. The system VALIDATES THAT the sensors are valid.
26	4. The system VALIDATES THAT there is no error detected.
27	**1.4 Specific Alternative Flow**
28	RFS 4
29	1. INCLUDE <VARIATION POINT: Storing Error Status>.
30	2. ABORT.
31	
32	**USE CASE** Provide System User Data
33	**1.1 Basic Flow**
34	1. The tester SENDS the system user data request TO the system.
35	2. INCLUDE <VARIATION POINT : Method of Providing Data>.
36	
37	**<VARIANT>USE CASE** Provide System User Data via Standard Mode
38	**1.1 Basic Flow**
39	V1. <OPTIONAL>The system SENDS calibration TO the tester.
40	V2. <OPTIONAL>The system SENDS sensor data TO the tester.
41	V3. <OPTIONAL>The system SENDS trace data TO the tester.
42	V4. <OPTIONAL>The system SENDS error data TO the tester.
43	V5. <OPTIONAL>The system SENDS error trace data TO the tester.

system can alter its internal state (Line 18). The inclusion of another use case is given in a step with the keyword '*INCLUDE USE CASE*' (Line 3). The keywords are written in capital letters. '*VALIDATES THAT*' (Line 4) indicates a condition that must be true to take the next step, otherwise an alternative flow is taken.

An alternative flow describes other scenarios, both success and failure. It always depends on a condition in a specific step of the basic flow. RUCM has *specific*, *bounded* and *global* alternative flows. A specific alternative flow refers to a step in the basic flow (Lines 13, 16, and 27). A bounded alternative flow refers to more than one step in the basic flow (Line 8), while a global one refers to any step in the basic flow. '*RFS*' is used to refer to reference flow steps (Lines 9, 14, 17, and 28). Bounded and global alternative flows begin with '*IF .. THEN*' for the conditions under which they are taken (Line 10). Specific alternative flows do not necessarily begin with '*IF .. THEN*' since a guard condition is already indicated in their reference flow steps (Line 4).

Our extensions are (i) new keywords for modeling interactions in embedded systems and (ii) new keywords for modeling variability. The keywords '*SENDS .. TO*' and '*REQUESTS .. FROM*' are to distinguish system-actor interactions (Lines 5, 7, 34, and 39–43). We introduce the notion of variation point and variant, complementary to the extensions in Sect. 3.1, into RUCM. Variation points can be included in basic or alternative flows with the keyword '*INCLUDE <VARIATION POINT : ... >*' (Lines 29 and 35). Variant use cases are given with the keyword '*<VARIANT>*' (Line 37).

Some variability cannot be captured in PL use case diagrams due to the required level of granularity for product configuration. To model such variability, as part of our extensions, we introduce optional steps, optional alternative flows and a variant order of steps. Optional steps and alternative flows begin with '*<OPTIONAL>*' (Lines 8 and 39–43). We use 'V' before any step number to express variant step orders (Lines 39–43).

3.2   Configuration of PS Use Case Models

PUMConf relies on variability information given in the PL use case diagram and specifications. The user selects (1) variant use cases in the PL diagram and (2) use case elements in the PL specifications, to generate the PS models.

The user makes decisions for the variation points in Fig. 1. PUMConf automatically generates the PS use case diagram from the PL diagram and the diagram decisions (see

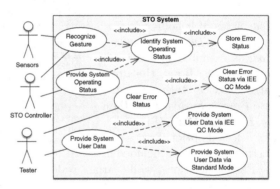

Fig. 2. Generated PS use case diagram

Fig. 2 generated from Fig. 1). For instance, based on the decision for *Method of Providing Data* in Fig. 1, PUMConf creates *Provide System User Data via IEE QC Mode*, *Provide System User Data via Standard Mode* and two *include* relations in Fig. 2.

In Table 1, there are two variation points (Lines 29 and 35), one variant use case (Lines 37–43), five optional steps (Lines 39–43), one optional alternative flow (Lines 8–12), and one variant order group (Lines 39–43). The user selects only three optional steps with the order *V3*, *V1*, and *V5*. The optional alternative flow is not selected.

The PS specifications are automatically generated from the PL specifications and the diagram and specification decisions. (see Table 2 generated from Table 1). For instance, based on the diagram decision for *Method of Providing Data* in Fig. 1, PUMConf creates two include statements for *Provide System User Data via Standard Mode* and *via IEE QC Mode* (Lines 31 and 34 in Table 2), a validation step (Line 30), and a specific alternative flow where *Provide System User Data via IEE QC Mode* is included (Lines 32–35). The validation step checks if the precondition of *Provide System User Data via Standard Mode* holds. If it holds, *Provide System User Data via Standard Mode* is executed in the basic flow (Line 31). If not, the alternative flow is taken to execute *Provide System User Data via IEE QC Mode* (Lines 32–35). Selected optional steps and alternative flows are included in

Table 2. Some of the generated PS specifications

1	**USE CASE** Recognize Gesture
2	**1.1 Basic Flow**
3	1. INCLUDE USE CASE Identify System Operating Status.
4	2. The system VALIDATES THAT the operating status is valid.
5	3. The system REQUESTS the move capacitance FROM the sensors.
6	4. The system VALIDATES THAT the movement is a valid kick.
7	5. The system SENDS the valid kick status TO the STO Controller.
8	**1.2 Specific Alternative Flow**
9	RFS 2
10	1. ABORT.
11	**1.3 Specific Alternative Flow**
12	RFS 4
13	1. The system increments the OveruseCounter by the increment step.
14	2. ABORT.
15	
16	**USE CASE** Identify System Operating Status
17	**1.1 Basic Flow**
18	1. The system VALIDATES THAT the watchdog reset is valid.
19	2. The system VALIDATES THAT the RAM is valid.
20	3. The system VALIDATES THAT the sensors are valid.
21	4. The system VALIDATES THAT there is no error detected.
22	**1.4 Specific Alternative Flow**
23	RFS 4
24	1. INCLUDE USE CASE Store Error Status.
25	2. ABORT.
26	
27	**USE CASE** Provide System User Data
28	**1.1 Basic Flow**
29	1. The tester SENDS the user data request TO the system.
30	2. The system VALIDATES THAT 'Precondition of Provide System User Data via Standard Mode'.
31	3. INCLUDE Provide System User Data via Standard Mode.
32	**1.2 Specific Alternative Flow**
33	RFS 2
34	1. INCLUDE Provide System User Data via IEE QC Mode.
35	2. ABORT.
36	
37	**USE CASE** Provide System User Data via Standard Mode
38	**1.1 Basic Flow**
39	1. The system SENDS the trace data TO the tester.
40	2. The system SENDS the calibration data TO the tester.
41	3. The system SENDS the error trace data TO the tester.

the PS specifications, while variant order groups are ordered (Lines 39–41).

4   Overview of the Approach

The reconfiguration of PS models is implemented as a pipeline (Fig. 3). Configuration decisions are captured in a decision model during the decision-making process. The decision model conforms to a decision metamodel, described in our prior work [11]. PUMConf keeps two decision models, i.e., the decision model

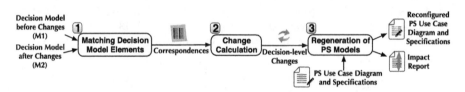

Fig. 3. Overview of the model differencing and regeneration pipeline

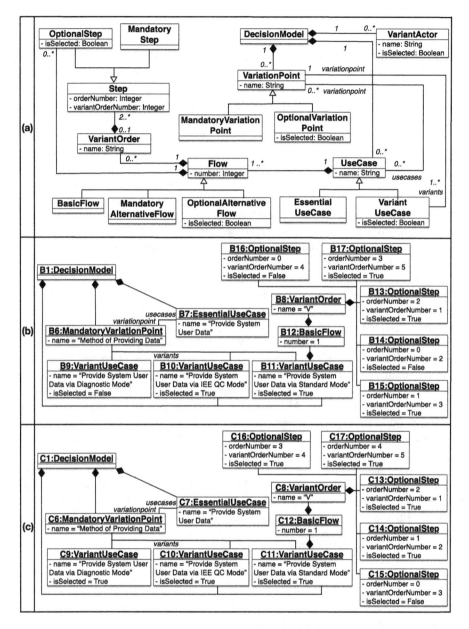

Fig. 4. (a) Decision metamodel, (b) Example *M1*, and (c) Example *M2* (Color figure online)

before changes (*M1* in Fig. 3) and the decision model after changes (*M2* in Fig. 3). Figure 4 provides the decision metamodel and the two input decision models for the PL models in Fig. 1 and Table 1.

The pipeline takes the decision models, and the PS diagram and specifications as input. The PS models are reconfigured, as output, together with an impact report, i.e., list of reconfigured parts of the PS models. The pipeline has three steps given in Fig. 3.

In Step 1, *Matching decision model elements*, the structural differencing of *M1* and *M2* is done by looking for the correspondences in *M1* and *M2*. To that end, we devise an algorithm that identifies the matching model elements in *M1* and *M2*. The output of Step 1 is the corresponding elements, representing decisions for the same variations, in *M1* and *M2* (Sect. 5).

The decision metamodel in Fig. 4(a) includes the main use case elements for which the user makes decisions (i.e., variation point, optional step, optional alternative flow, and variant order). In a variation point, the user selects variant use cases to be included for the product. For PL use case specifications, the user selects optional steps and alternative flows to be included and determines the order of steps (variant order). Therefore, the matching elements in Step 1 are the pairs of variation points and use cases including the variation points, the pairs of use cases and optional alternative flows in the use cases, and the triples of use cases, flows in the use cases, and optional steps in the flows.

In Step 2, *Change calculation*, decision-level changes are identified from the corresponding model elements (see Sect. 5). A set of elements in *M1* which does not have a corresponding set of elements in *M2* is considered to be a deleted decision, which we refer to as *DeleteDecision* in the decision-level changes. Analogously, a set of model elements in *M2* which does not have a corresponding set of elements in *M1* is considered to be added (*AddDecision*). Each set of corresponding model elements with non-identical attribute values (see the red-colored attributes in Fig. 4(c)) is considered to be a decision-level change of the type *UpdateDecision*. Alternatively, we could record changes during the decision-making process. However, the user might make changes cancelling previous changes or implying some further changes. In such a case, we would have to compute cancelled changes and infer new changes.

In Step 3, *Regeneration of PS models*, the PS use case diagram and specifications are regenerated only for the added, deleted and updated decisions (see Sect. 6). For instance, use cases selected in the deleted decisions are removed from the PS models, while use cases selected in the added decisions are added in the PS models.

5   Model Matching and Change Calculation

We devise an algorithm (see Fig. 5) for the first two pipeline steps, *Matching Decision Model Elements* and *Change Calculation*, in Fig. 3. The algorithm calls some *match* functions (Lines 7–9 in Fig. 5) to identify the corresponding model elements, which represent decisions for the same variations, in the input decision models. The *match* functions implement Step 1 in Fig. 3.

– **matchDiagramDecisions** returns the set of pairs (*variation point, use case*) matching in the decision models (*M1* and *M2*), which are capturing which variation points are included in the use cases involved in diagram decisions,

- **matchFlowDecisions** returns the set of pairs (*use case, optional alternative flow*) matching in the input decision models (*M1* and *M2*), which are capturing which optional alternative flows are in the use cases involved in flow decisions,
- **matchStepDecisions** returns the set of triples (*use case, flow, step*) matching in the input decision models (*M1* and *M2*), which are capturing which steps are in the flows of the use cases involved in step decisions.

The corresponding model elements in the example decision models in Fig. 4(b) and (c) are as follows (Lines 7–9 in Fig. 5):

- For decisions in the variation points,
  $U3 = \{(B6, B7), (C6, C7)\}$,
- For decisions in the optional alternative flows, $F3 = \{\emptyset\}$,
- For decisions in the use case steps, $S3 = \{(B11, B12, B13), (B11, B12, B14), (B11, B12, B15), (B11, B12, B16), (B11, B12, B17), (C11, C12, C13), (C11, C12, C14), (C11, C12, C15), (C11, C12, C16), (C11, C12, C17)\}$.

A variant use case in a variation point (vp) may include another variation point (vp'). Changing the decision for vp may imply another decision to be added or deleted for vp'. As part of Step 2, *Change Calculation*, the algorithm first identifies deleted and added diagram decisions by checking the pairs of variation points and use cases which exist only in one of the input decision models (($U1 \setminus U3$) and ($U2 \setminus U3$) in Lines 10–11). Similar checks are done for flow and step decisions in the specifications (Lines 10–11). For the decision models in Fig. 4, there is no deleted or added decision (($U1 \setminus U3 = \emptyset$), ($U2 \setminus U3 = \emptyset$), ($F1 \setminus F3 = \emptyset$), ($F2 \setminus F3 = \emptyset$), ($S1 \setminus S3 = \emptyset$), and ($S2 \setminus S3 = \emptyset$)).

Input: Initial decision model $M1$, New decision model $M2$
Output: Triple of sets of decision-level changes
(ADD, DELETE, UPDATE)

1. Let a pair (vp, uc) denote cases where vp is a variation point and uc is a use case including vp
2. Let a pair (uc, fl) denote cases where uc is a use case and fl is an optional alternative flow in uc
3. Let a triple (uc, fl, st) denote cases where uc is a use case, fl is a flow in uc, and st is a step in fl
4. Let $U1$ and $U2$ be the sets of (vp, uc) in $M1$ and $M2$
5. Let $F1$ and $F2$ be the sets of (uc, fl) in $M1$ and $M2$
6. Let $S1$ and $S2$ be the sets of (uc, fl, st) in $M1$ and $M2$
7. $U3 \leftarrow$ **matchDiagramDecisions**($U1$, $U2$)
8. $F3 \leftarrow$ **matchFlowDecisions**($F1$, $F2$)
9. $S3 \leftarrow$ **matchStepDecisions**($S1$, $S2$)
10. $DELETE \leftarrow (U1 \setminus U3) \cup (F1 \setminus F3) \cup (S1 \setminus S3)$
11. $ADD \leftarrow (U2 \setminus U3) \cup (F2 \setminus F3) \cup (S2 \setminus S3)$
12. **foreach** ($k \in (U3 \cap U1)$) **do**
13. $z \leftarrow$ **getMatchingDecision**(k, $U3$)
14. $SUC1 \leftarrow$ **getSelectedUseCases**(k, $M1$)
15. $SUC2 \leftarrow$ **getSelectedUseCases**(z, $M2$)
16. **if** ($SUC1 \neq SUC2$) **then**
17. $UPDATE \leftarrow UPDATE \cup \{k\}$;
18. **end if**
19. **end foreach**
20. **foreach** ($t \in (F3 \cap F1)$) **do**
21. $y \leftarrow$ **getMatchingDecision**(t, $F3$)
22. **if** ($t.fl.isSelected \neq y.fl.isSelected$) **then**
23. $UPDATE \leftarrow UPDATE \cup \{t\}$
24. **end if**
25. **end foreach**
26. **foreach** ($u \in (S3 \cap S1)$) **do**
27. $m \leftarrow$ **getMatchingDecision**(u, $S3$)
28. **if** ($u.st$ is $OptionalStep$) **and** ($u.st.isSelected \neq m.st.isSelected$) **then**
29. $UPDATE \leftarrow UPDATE \cup \{u\}$
30. **else**
31. **if** ($u.st.orderNumber \neq m.st.orderNumber$)
32. **then** $UPDATE \leftarrow UPDATE \cup \{u\}$
33. **end if**
34. **end if**
35. **end foreach**
36. **return** (*ADD, DELETE, UPDATE*)

Fig. 5. Algorithm for Steps 1 and 2 in Fig. 3

The matching pairs of variation points and their including use cases represent decisions for the same variation point (($B6$, $B7$) and ($C6$, $C7$) in Fig. 4(b) and (c)). If the selected variant use cases for the same variation point are not the same in $M1$ and $M2$, the corresponding decision in $M1$ is considered as updated in $M2$ (Lines 12–19). The variant use case *Provide System User Data via Diagnostic Mode* of the variation point *Method of Providing Data* is unselected in $M1$ ($B6$, $B7$ and $B9$ in Fig. 4(b)), but selected in $M2$ ($C6$, $C7$ and $C9$ in Fig. 4(c)). The diagram decision for the pair ($B6$, $B7$) in $M1$ is identified as updated (Line 17). To identify updated specification decisions, the algorithm compares decisions across $M1$ and $M2$ that involve optional alternative flows, optional steps and steps with a variant order (Lines 22–24, 28–30 and 31–33). In our example, the triples ($B11$, $B12$, $B14$), ($B11$, $B12$, $B15$), ($B11$, $B12$, $B16$), and ($B11$, $B12$, $B17$) in Fig. 4 are identified as updated decisions.

6   Regeneration of PS Use Case Models

After all the changes are calculated by matching the corresponding model elements in the input decision models, the parts of PS use case models affected by the changed decisions are automatically regenerated (Step 3 in Fig. 3).

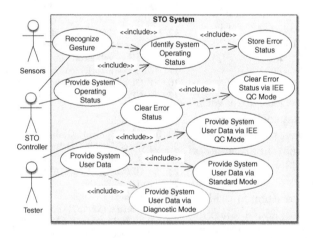

Fig. 6. Regenerated PS use case diagram (Color figure online)

Our approach first handles the diagram decision changes to reconfigure the PS use case diagram. For selected variant use cases in the added diagram decisions (i.e., in the pairs (vp, uc) in ADD in Line 36 in Fig. 5), we generate the corresponding use cases and *include* relations in the PS diagram. For selected variant use cases in deleted diagram decisions (i.e., in the pairs (vp, uc) in $DELETE$ in Line 36), we remove the corresponding use cases and *include* relations from the PS diagram. If a selected variant use case is unselected in an updated diagram decision (i.e., in the pairs (vp, uc) in $UPDATE$ in Line 36), we remove the corresponding use case from the PS diagram. For unselected variant use cases which are selected in the updated diagram decisions, the corresponding use cases and *include* relations are added to the PS diagram. Figure 6 gives the regenerated parts of the PS use case diagram in Fig. 2 for *M1* and *M2* in Fig. 4.

There is no added or deleted diagram decision in *M1* and *M2* in Fig. 4. The decision for the variation point *Method of Providing Data* (i.e., $(B6, B7)$ in *UPDATE* in Line 36) is updated by selecting the variant use case *Provide System User Data via Diagnostic Mode*. Only the corresponding use case and its *include* relation are added to the PS diagram (red-colored in Fig. 6).

Changes for diagram and specification decisions are used to regenerate the PS specifications. For diagram decision changes, we add or delete the corresponding use case specifications. Table 3 provides the regenerated parts of the PS specifications in Table 2, for *M1* and *M2* in Fig. 4.

For the variation point *Method of Providing Data* included by the use case *Provide System User Data* (i.e., $(B6, B7)$), we have one updated diagram decision in which the unselected use case *Provide System User Data via Diagnostic Mode* is selected. The corresponding use case specification is added (Lines 24–29 in Table 3). A new specific alternative flow is also generated for the inclusion of the newly selected use case in the specification of the use case *Provide System User Data* (Lines 12–15, red-colored).

The specification decision changes are about selecting optional alternative flows, optional steps and steps with a variant order (e.g., the triples $(B11, B12, B14)$, $(B11, B12, B15)$, $(B11, B12, B16)$, and $(B11, B12, B17)$ in Fig. 4(b)). The use case *Provide System User Data via Standard Mode* has two new steps in Lines 19 and 21 in Table 3 (i.e., $(B11, B12, B14)$, and

Table 3. Regenerated PS use case specifications

1	**USE CASE** Provide System User Data
2	**1.1 Basic Flow**
3	1. The tester SENDS the user data request TO the system.
4	2. The system VALIDATES THAT 'Precondition of Provide System User Data via Standard Mode'.
5	3. INCLUDE Provide System User Data via Standard Mode.
6	**1.2 Specific Alternative Flow**
7	RFS 2
8	1. IF 'Precondition of Provide System User Data via IEE QC Mode' holds THEN
9	2. INCLUDE Provide System User Data via IEE QC Mode.
10	3. ABORT.
11	4. ENDIF
12	**1.3 Specific Alternative Flow**
13	RFS 2
14	1. INCLUDE Provide System User Data via Diagnostic Mode.
15	2. ABORT.
16	
17	**USE CASE** Provide System User Data via Standard Mode
18	**1.1 Basic Flow**
	1. The system SENDS trace data TO the tester.
19	1. The system SENDS sensor data TO the tester.
20	2. The system SENDS calibration TO the tester.
21	3. The system SENDS error data TO the tester.
22	4. The system SENDS error trace data TO the tester.
23	
24	**USE CASE** Provide System User Data via Diagnostic Mode
25	**1.1 Basic Flow**
26	1. The system SENDS the RAM data TO the tester.
27	2. The system SENDS the NVM data TO the tester.
28	3. The system SENDS the session response TO the tester.
29	4. The system SENDS the message length TO the tester.

$(B11, B12, B16)$ in Fig. 4(b)), while one of the steps (red-colored, strikethrough step) is removed (i.e., $(B11, B12, B15)$ in Fig. 4(b)). The step number of one of the steps is changed (Line 22, blue-colored) due to the change in the order of the steps with a variant order (i.e., $(B11, B12, B17)$ in Fig. 4(b)).

7   Tool Support

We implemented our approach as an extension of PUMConf [24] which has been developed as an IBM DOORS Plug-in. PUMConf uses GATE (http://gate.ac. uk/), an open source NLP framework, to annotate PL use case specifications to be used for (re)configuring PS use case specifications. PUMConf relies upon: (i) *IBM DOORS* to model PL use case specifications and (ii) *Papyrus* to model and save PL use case diagrams as a UML file. To load use cases from IBM DOORS, it uses DOORS Document Exporter, an API that exports the DOORS content as text files. The reconfiguration of PS use case models has been implemented as a Java application. The DOORS eXtension Language (DXL) is employed to load the configured PS specifications into DOORS. PUMConf is approximately 25K lines of code, excluding comments and third-party libraries. Additional details about PUMConf, including executable files and a screencast covering motivations, are available on the tool's website at https://sites.google.com/site/pumconf/.

8   Industrial Case Study

We evaluate our reconfiguration approach via reporting an industrial case study (STO).

Goal: Our goal was to assess, in an industrial context, the feasibility of using our approach. We assessed whether we could improve reuse and reduce manual effort by preserving unimpacted parts of PS use case models, when possible, and their manually assigned traces.

Study Context: STO was selected for the assessment of our approach since it was a relatively new project at IEE with multiple potential customers requiring different features. IEE provided their initial STO documentation, which contained a use case diagram, use case specifications, and supplementary requirements specifications describing non-functional requirements. To model the STO requirements according to our modeling method, PUM, we first examined the initial STO documentation and then worked with IEE engineers to build and iteratively refine our models [11] (see Table 4). Due to the confidentiality concerns, we do not put the entire case study online. However, the reader can download the sanitized example models from the tool's website.

Table 4. Product line use cases in the case study

	# of use cases	# of variation points	# of basic flows	# of alternative flows	# of steps	# of condition steps
Essential use cases	11	6	11	57	192	57
Variant use cases	13	1	13	131	417	130

Table 5. Configuration results for the selected product

Product	# of selected variant use cases	# of selected optional steps	# of selected optional flows	# of decided variant order
P1	6	1	0	0

Table 6. Decision change scenarios

ID	Change scenario	Explanation
S1	Update a diagram decision	Unselecting selected use cases
S2	Update and delete diagram decisions	Unselecting selected use cases, removing other decisions
S3	Update a diagram decision	Selecting unselected use cases
S4	Update and add diagram decisions	Selecting unselected use cases, implying other decisions
S5	Update a specification decision	Selecting unselected optional steps
S6	Update a diagram decision	Selecting unselected use cases
S7	Update a diagram decision	Unselecting selected use cases
S8	Update a specification decision	Updating the order of optional steps

Results and Analysis: By using PUMConf, we, together with the IEE analysts, configured the PS use case models for four products selected among the STO products IEE had already developed [15]. The IEE analysts made the decisions on the PL models using the guidance provided by PUMConf. Among the four products, we chose one product to be used for reconfiguration of PS models (see Table 5) because it was the most recent one in the STO product family with a properly documented change history. The IEE engineers identified 36 traces from the PS use case diagram and 278 traces from the PS use case specifications to other software and hardware specifications as well as to the customers' requirements documents for external systems (see Fig. 7). We considered eight change scenarios derived from the change history of the initial STO documentation for the selected product (see Table 6).

Fig. 7. An example specification with a trace in DOORS

Some change scenarios contain individual decision changes such as selecting unselected use cases in a variation point, while some others contain a series of individual changes applied sequentially (see *S2* and *S4*). For instance, *S2* starts with unselecting *Clear Error Status* in Fig. 1, which automatically deletes the decision for the variation point *Method of Clearing Error Status* and implies another decision change, i.e., unselecting *Store Error Status*.

Table 7. Summary of the reconfiguration of the PS use case models for STO

		Decision Change Scenarios							
		S1	S2	S3	S4	S5	S6	S7	S8
PS Model Changes	# of Added UCs	0	0	1	4	0	1	0	0
	# of Deleted UCs	1	4	0	0	0	0	1	0
	# of Added UC Steps	0	0	53	140	3	85	0	0
	# of Deleted UC Steps	53	140	0	0	0	0	103	0
Traces for the PS Use Case Diagram	# of Initial Traces	36	34	25	27	36	36	38	38
	# of Deleted Traces During Reconfiguration	2	9	0	0	0	0	0	0
	# of Manually Added Traces After Reconfiguration	0	0	2	9	0	2	0	0
	# of Preserved Traces	34	25	25	27	36	36	38	38
	% of Preserved Traces	94.4	73.5	100	100	100	100	100	100
Traces for the PS Use Case Specifications	# of Initial Traces	278	265	218	231	278	287	298	278
	# of Deleted Traces During Reconfiguration	13	47	0	0	0	0	20	0
	# of Manually Added Traces After Reconfiguration	0	0	13	47	9	11	0	0
	# of Preserved Traces	265	218	218	231	278	287	278	278
	% of Preserved Traces	95.3	82.2	100	100	100	100	93.2	100

Table 7 provides a summary of the reconfiguration of the PS models for the change scenarios. After each change scenario, we ran PUMConf and checked the preserved and deleted traces. Our approach preserved all the traces for the unchanged parts of the PS models, while only the traces for the deleted parts of the PS models were removed. We had to manually assign traces only for the new parts of the PS models. In terms of saving traceability effort while reconfiguring, we can look at the percentages of traces from the use case diagram and the use case specifications that were preserved over all the change scenarios. From Table 7, we can see that between 73% and 100% (average ≈96%) of the use case diagram traces were preserved. Similarly, for the use case specifications, trace reuse was between 82% and 100% (average ≈96%). We can therefore conclude that our automated approach to incremental reconfiguration leads to significant reuse and savings when updating traceability to other documents to account for changed configuration decisions.

Discussion: We also had semi-structured interviews with IEE engineers to better assess their perception. All interview participants agreed that the proposed approach could help reduce, by a substantial amount, the manual effort in terms of preserving traces for the unchanged parts of the PS use case models.

Threats to Validity: The main threat to the validity of our case study regards the generalizability of our conclusions. To mitigate this threat, we applied our approach to an industrial case study that includes nontrivial use cases in an application domain with many potential customers and numerous sources of variability. To limit threats to internal validity, we had many interviews with IEE engineers in the STO project to verify the correctness and completeness of the PL models and the reconfigured PS models.

9   Conclusion

Product line requirements need to be configured for each product. This paper presents an incremental reconfiguration approach for use case models in the context of product lines. Our main motivation is to preserve the unimpacted parts of the Product Specific (PS) use case models, when changing their configuration decisions, based on a careful analysis of the Product Line (PL) use case models. Our main goal is to avoid manual effort during reconfiguration due to the manual updating of traceability links from the PS use case models to other documents and artifacts, a common practice and requirement in industry. We therefore need to carefully determine which parts of the PS models remain unchanged and we do so by carefully analysis decision dependencies in PL models. We aim to incrementally reconfigure PS use case models by minimizing their changes based on a careful impact analysis of changed decisions. We performed a case study in the context of automotive embedded system development. The results suggest that our approach is practical and provides significant savings with respect to traceability updates during reconfiguration.

This work is an intermediate step to achieve our long term objective [25], i.e., change impact analysis and regression test selection in the context of use case-driven development and testing. Changes can also emerge in variability aspects of product line models, and they entail impact assessment on decisions for each individual product and may require reconfiguration and regression test selection in several products. Our plan for the next steps is to support change impact analysis to help analysts properly manage changes in PL use case models.

Acknowledgments. Financial support was provided by IEE and FNR under grants FNR/P10/03 and FNR10045046.

References

1. Nebut, C., Fleurey, F., Traon, Y.L., Jezequel, J.-M.: Automatic test generation: a use case driven approach. IEEE TSE **32**(3), 140–155 (2006)
2. Wang, C., Pastore, F., Goknil, A., Briand, L.C., Iqbal, M.Z.Z.: Automatic generation of system test cases from use case specifications. In: ISSTA 2015, pp. 385–396 (2015)
3. Wang, C., Pastore, F., Goknil, A., Briand, L.C., Iqbal, M.Z.Z.: UMTG: a toolset to automatically generate system test cases from use case specifications. In: ESEC/SIGSOFT FSE 2015, pp. 942–945 (2015)

4. IEE (International Electronics & Engineering) S.A. http://www.iee.lu/
5. Clements, P., Northrop, L.: Software Product Lines: Practices and Patterns. Addison-Wesley, Boston (2001)
6. Eriksson, M., Börstler, J., Borg, K.: The PLUSS approach – domain modeling with features, use cases and use case realizations. In: Obbink, H., Pohl, K. (eds.) SPLC 2005. LNCS, vol. 3714, pp. 33–44. Springer, Heidelberg (2005). doi:10.1007/11554844_5
7. Fantechi, A., Gnesi, S., Lami, G., Nesti, E.: A methodology for the derivation and verification of use cases for product lines. In: Nord, R.L. (ed.) SPLC 2004. LNCS, vol. 3154, pp. 255–265. Springer, Heidelberg (2004). doi:10.1007/978-3-540-28630-1_16
8. Czarnecki, K., Antkiewicz, M.: Mapping features to models: a template approach based on superimposed variants. In: Glück, R., Lowry, M. (eds.) GPCE 2005. LNCS, vol. 3676, pp. 422–437. Springer, Heidelberg (2005). doi:10.1007/11561347_28
9. Sepulveda, S., Cravero, A., Cachero, C.: Requirements modeling languages for software product lines: a systematic literature review. IST **69**, 16–36 (2016)
10. Ramesh, B., Jarke, M.: Toward reference models for requirements traceability. IEEE TSE **27**(1), 58–93 (2001)
11. Hajri, I., Goknil, A., Briand, L.C., Stephany, T.: Applying product line use case modeling in an industrial automotive embedded system: lessons learned and a refined approach. In: MODELS 2015, pp. 338–347 (2015)
12. Halmans, G., Pohl, K.: Communicating the variability of a software-product family to customers. SoSyM **2**, 15–36 (2003)
13. Buhne, S., Halmans, G., Pohl, K.: Modeling dependencies between variation points in use case diagrams. In: REFSQ 2003, pp. 59–69 (2003)
14. Yue, T., Briand, L.C., Labiche, Y.: Facilitating the transition from use case models to analysis models: approach and experiments. TOSEM **22**(1), 1–38 (2013)
15. Hajri, I., Goknil, A., Briand, L.C., Stephany, T.: Configuring use case models in product families. SoSyM (2016)
16. Dhungana, D., Grünbacher, P., Rabiser, R.: The DOPLER meta-tool for decision-oriented variability modeling: a multiple case study. ASE **18**, 77–114 (2011)
17. Heider, W., Rabiser, R., Grünbacher, P.: Facilitating the evolution of products in product line engineering by capturing and replaying configuration decisions. STTT **14**(5), 613–630 (2012)
18. Heider, W., Rabiser, R., Lettner, D., Grünbacher, P.: Using regression testing to analyze the impact of changes to variability models on products. In: SPLC 2012, pp. 196–205 (2012)
19. Hearnden, D., Lawley, M., Raymond, K.: Incremental model transformation for the evolution of model-driven systems. In: Nierstrasz, O., Whittle, J., Harel, D., Reggio, G. (eds.) MODELS 2006. LNCS, vol. 4199, pp. 321–335. Springer, Heidelberg (2006). doi:10.1007/11880240_23
20. Kurtev, I., Dee, M., Göknil, A., van den Berg, K.: Traceability-based change management in operational mappings. In: ECMDA-TW 2007, pp. 57–67 (2007)
21. Jahann, S., Egyed, A.: Instant and incremental transformation of models. In: ASE 2004, pp. 362–365 (2004)
22. Vogel, T., Neumann, S., Hildebrandt, S., Giese, H., Becker, B.: Incremental model synchronization for efficient run-time monitoring. In: Ghosh, S. (ed.) MODELS 2009. LNCS, vol. 6002, pp. 124–139. Springer, Heidelberg (2010). doi:10.1007/978-3-642-12261-3_13

23. Eramo, R., Malavolta, I., Muccini, H., Pelliccione, P., Pierantonio, A.: A model-driven approach to automate the propagation of changes among architecture description languages. SoSyM **11**, 29–53 (2012)
24. Hajri, I., Goknil, A., Briand, L.C., Stephany, T.: PUMConf: a tool to configure product specific use case and domain models in a product line. In: FSE 2016, pp. 1008–1012 (2016)
25. Hajri, I.: Supporting change in product lines within the context of use case-driven development and testing. In: Doctoral Symposium - FSE 2016, pp. 1082–1084 (2016)

Aligning the Elements of the RUP/UML Business Use-Case Model and the BPMN Business Process Diagram

Yves Wautelet[(✉)] and Stephan Poelmans

KU Leuven, Leuven, Belgium
{yves.wautelet,stephan.poelmans}@kuleuven.be

Abstract. *Context and Motivation*: The *Business Use Case Model* (*BUCM*) formalized in the *Rational Unified Process* (*RUP*) defines stereotypes of elements refining the UML *Use Case Model* for coarse-grained business processes modeling (BPM). The *Business Process Model and Notation* (*BPMN*) *Business Process Diagram* (*BPD*) is designed for workflow-based (i.e. fine-grained) BPM. These are frameworks that can possibly be complementary for enterprise modeling. *Question/Problem*: The semantically richer BPMN BPD can be used instead of UML activity diagrams for operational BPM when the BUCM is used for tactical BPM. *Principal ideas/results*: The common use of the BUCM and BPMN BPD requires anchoring of elements in between the frameworks to ensure traceability. Traceable models increase their overall consistency. *Contribution*: The paper allowed to set up traceability rules for the combined use of these frameworks.

Keywords: RUP/UML Business Use-Case Model · Business modeling · BPMN

1 Introduction

Within the *Rational Unified Process* (*RUP*) [3], the *Business Use-Case Model*[1] (*BUCM*) offers a syntax and semantic to represent business processes at tactical and strategic[2] levels. The BUCM is an extension of the *Unified Modeling Language* (*UML*) [8] UCM supported by RUP and many *Computer Aided Software Engineering* (*CASE*) tools. In RUP, operational workflows are represented with Activity Diagrams (AD) [8].

The RUP/UML BUCM and the *Business Process Modeling Notation* (*BPMN*) [1,7] *Business Process Diagram* (*BPD*) have in common that they are targeted to pure business process modeling so that they dispose of a rich set

---

[1] We do not refer here to the Use Case Model (UCM) as defined by the OMG in [8] but to the refinement proposed in the business modeling discipline from the RUP (see [3,6]).

[2] The only strategic elements within the BUCM are the business goal and objectives.

© Springer International Publishing AG 2017
P. Grünbacher and A. Perini (Eds.): REFSQ 2017, LNCS 10153, pp. 22–30, 2017.
DOI: 10.1007/978-3-319-54045-0_2

of elements associated with precise semantics for this purpose. Even if they come from different semantic domains, some elements are semantically close enough that they can be used for anchoring (and traceability) among representation levels; this paper studies this.

Once correctly integrated, the BUCM allows to represent the strategic and tactical levels and BPMN BPD to represent the operational level of a business process set; traceability between knowledge representation levels is ensured. The conjunct use of these two frameworks is supported by CASE tools like *Visual Paradigm* [9] (e.g. [11]).

2   Related Work and Positioning

Process Maps (PM) are included in BPMN. A PM is a tactical level model (made of coarse-grained elements) but with limited expressiveness. PM are only constituted by a set of elements representing sets of business processes and the triggering actors represented as lanes. A PM is comparable to a classical use-case model. UML AD define a set of elements for operational level (workflow) modeling but the set of available elements is much poorer for pure business (enterprise) modeling than the ones of BPMN's BPD. AD are mostly oriented on representing software system behavior with user interaction.

[2] suggests to use BPMN BPD instead of UML activity diagrams in the RUP process. Their study showed that the perceived complexity of the BPMN BPD is lower than the one of the activity diagrams. The only guideline given in the paper is the use of one BPMN BPD to depict one particular use-case; no further traceability rules are given. We define anchoring points for traceability between the representation levels.

3   Research Method

We distinguish groups of elements both within the ones defined by the RUP/UML BUCM and BPMN BPD. As presented in Table 1, three categories of elements are distinguished within the RUP/UML BUCM on the basis of the study of the RUP knowledge base (see [4–6]). The business objective and goal have been left out because they are strategic elements and we focus here on the mapping of tactical elements to operational ones. Similarly, as presented in Table 2, four categories of elements are distinguished within the BPMN BPD on the basis of a study of [7].

We start from the categories established for the RUP/UML BUCM to evaluate the semantic mapping to BPMN BPD elements. We take each category of the RUP/UML BUCM and, within these categories, we firstly evaluate the relevance of each element for business process modeling. Once an element of a category is considered relevant, its possible alignment with elements of the BPMN BPD is overviewed on a pure semantic basis. Possible maps are identified and evaluated in practice before being adopted.

Table 1. RUP/UML business use case elements

Inheriting from Use Case (IUC)	Inheriting from the Actor (IA)	Links (UMLLink)
Use case	Business actor	Association
Use case realization	Business worker	Include
Business Use Case (BUC)	Business entity	Extend
BUC realization	Business event	Generalization or specialization

Table 2. Business process modeling notation elements

Events (Evt)	Activity (Act)	Gateway (Gwy)	Connections (Cnt)	Swimlanes and Artifacts (SwA)
Start event	Task	Exclusive	Sequence flow	Pool
Intermediate event	Sub-process	Event based	Message flow	Lane
End event	Transaction	Parallel	Association	Artifacts
	Call activity	Inclusive		Data objects
	Actor boundary	Exclusive event based		Group
		Complex		Annotation
		Parallel event based		

4   Studying the Alignment Between the RUP/UML BUCM's Elements and BPMN BPD's Ones

4.1   Elements of the Use Case Category

The four elements defined in IUC category are the *Use Case (UC)*, *Business Use Case (BUC)*, *Business Use Case Realization (BUC Realization)* and *Use Case Realization (UC Realization)*. Only the BUC and BUC Realization are relevant in the context of general business process modeling since we do not want to describe behavior with respect to a potential system *to-be*. Following the RUP knowledge base, *a Business Use Case (instance) is a sequence of actions that a business performs that **yields an observable result of value** to a particular business actor*. The notion of sequence of actions explicitly refers to a notion of (business) process and to the (added) value it provides to a business actor (i.e. an actor outside the organization interacting with it). Let us further study the *BUC Realization* element; following the RUP knowledge base, *a Business Use-Case Realization describes **how** business workers, business entities, and* *business events collaborate* **to perform a particular business use case.** If we compare both elements, we notice that they refer to business processes but the BUC focuses on a *prescriptive* level – *WHAT is done to obtain value* – while the BUC Realization is on a *descriptive* level *HOW value is achieved.*

Alignment with BPMN BPD Element: Typically, a BPMN BPD represents the description of a business process and the alignment can then be envisaged with the BUC Realization. The latter is a coarse-grained element representing the business process while the BPMN BPD is a fine-grained representation of a process. As illustrated in Fig. 1, a BPMN BPD (as a whole) can thus be encapsulated in a BUC realization for fully documenting how value is achieved so that we dispose of a *tactical* representation – the BUC Realization – and an *operational* one – the BPMN BPD.

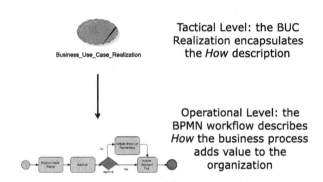

Fig. 1. Tracing business use cases and BPMN BPD.

4.2   Elements of the Actor Category

The Business Actor. The RUP knowledge base defines a business actor (instance) as *someone or something outside the business that interacts with the business.*

Alignment with BPMN BPD Element: Following [7], a Pool ... *represents a Participant in a Collaboration.* [10] argues *BPMN uses Pools when representing the interaction between an organization and participants outside of its control.* It then highlights that *within a company, a single pool covers its own internal operations ... only when it interacts with external participants that additional Pools are required.* Since a business actor represents an actor outside the organization, it could be traced, within the BPMN BPD, as a different pool than the one containing the activities performed by actors inside the organization (the Business Workers). Moreover, [7] highlights that *a Pool is not required to contain a Process, i.e., it can be a "black box"*; the pool corresponding to the business actor can thus be[3] a black box. The left part of Fig. 2 shows an example of how the organization and its identified business actor(s) is/are traced and modeled when interacting with the organization in a *Collaboration* context.

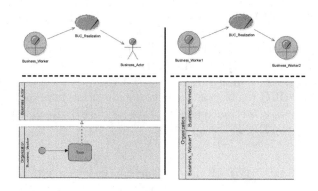

Fig. 2. Business actor interacting with the organization and business workers within it.

The Business Worker. The RUP knowledge base defines a business worker as ... *a role or set of roles in the business. A business worker interacts with other business workers and manipulates business entities while participating in business use-case realizations.*

Alignment with BPMN BPD Element: Following [7], a Lane is *a partition that is used to organize and categorize activities within a Pool*; it then further argues that *Lanes are often used for such things as internal roles (e.g., Manager, Associate), systems (e.g., an enterprise application), or an internal department (e.g., shipping, finance).* Similarly, [10] argues that lanes are *often assumed to represent internal business roles within a Process* .... Since the lane refers to internal roles, each business worker can be envisaged as a lane within the pool representing the modeled organization; this is the closest semantic map we were able to achieve with BPMN BPD elements. The right part of Fig. 2 shows an example of how the organization and its identified business worker(s) is/are traced and modeled within the organization.

The Business Entity. Following the RUP knowledge base, the business entity is *a piece of information that is manipulated by business actors and business workers.* Furthermore, *business entities represent an abstraction of important persistent information within the business. Stakeholders use business entities to*

---

[3] It depends if, from the point of view of the modeler's organization, the business actor is involved in a private or public workflow. Indeed, a process purely within the business actor's organization is private and not documented (this is known as *Collaboration*); a process where realization requires coordination is partially public because the information and objects needed to be exchanged should be documented (this is known as *Choreography*), see [7].

ensure that the information created and required by the organization is present in the Business Analysis Model ....

Alignment with BPMN BPD Element: Following [10], data objects are *used to represent the documents and data that are manipulated by the processes.* [7] argues that data objects *provide information about what Activities require to be performed and/or what they produce, Data Objects can represent a singular object or a collection of objects ....* A business entity can thus be represented as a data object in the BPMN BPD; this is the closest semantic map we were able to achieve with BPMN BPD elements. Due to a lack of space we do not repeat the icons of these elements here.

The Business Event. Following the RUP knowledge base, the business event *... represents a significant occurrence in the activities of the business that requires immediate action.* Furthermore, *a business event describes a significant occurrence in space and time that is of importance to the business. ... Useful when synchronization, interaction, or integration is necessary across business functions, applications, or locations.*

Alignment with BPMN BPD Element: Following [7], an Event is *... something that happens during the course of a Process*; it also highlights that *Events affect the flow of the Process and usually have a cause or an impact.* The BPMN *cause* can be aligned with the *significant occurrence* found in the definition of the RUP/UML business event and the *impact* aligned with the *of importance to the business.* [7] later indicates that *BPMN has restricted the use of Events to include only those types of Events that will affect the sequence or timing of Activities of a Process.* The latter property of the event can be seen as aligned with the business event definition because it is used for synchronization, interaction, or integration across business functions, applications, or locations. We point to the traceability between a RUP/UML business event in the form of a *start, intermediate* or *end* event into the BPMN BPD (depending on its moment of occurrence in the process realization). Indeed, each of those BPMN BPD elements originates from a significant occurrence of activities; this is the closest semantic map we were able to achieve with BPMN BPD elements.

4.3 Links

Association. This association is meant to be the link between an element of the IA category and an element of the IUC one (see Table 1).

Alignment with BPMN BPD Element: Two possibilities can be distinguished:

– If the association link is directed from the element of the IA category to the IUC one, we suggest to interpret this as: *"the IA category element triggers the action so that the Start Event from the BPMN BPD depicting the IUC category element should be placed in the Swimlane corresponding to the IA category element"*;

– If the association link is directed from IUC category to the IA one, we suggest to interpret this as: *"the IA category element is involved in the realization of the process but not triggering the action so that this IA category elements must be found as a swimlane or pool in the BPMN BPD, but does not host the start event (it can possibly host an intermediate or an end event)"*.

Include. [8] emphasizes that *An include relationship defines that a use case contains the behavior defined in another use case.* This definition is extended here to the whole IUC category elements and we highlight that a IUC category element is thus necessarily fulfilled into another one's realization.

Alignment with BPMN BPD: The IUC category element is thus included in another one so that the IUC element representing the "main" process includes as a sub-process in its BPMN BPD the second one; the latter **must be** executed in **any** path of achievement of the main process. Left part of Fig. 3 shows the traceability of an include relationship at business use case level and BPMN BPD.

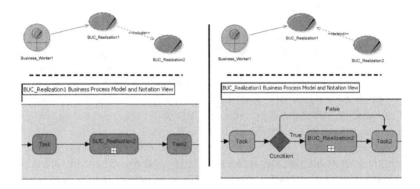

Fig. 3. Traceability of include and extend relationships.

Extend. [8] emphasizes that *A relationship from an extending use case to an extended use case that specifies how and when the behavior defined in the extending use case can be inserted into the behavior defined in the extended use case.* This definition is extended here to the whole IUC category elements and we highlight that a IUC category element is thus possibly fulfilled into another one's realization.

Alignment with BPMN BPD: The IUC category element is thus extended by another one so that the IUC element representing the "main" process includes as a sub-process in its BPMN BPD the second one; the latter **may be** executed in the path of achievement of the main process but not necessarily. Right part of Fig. 3 shows the traceability of an extend relationship at business use case level and BPMN BPD.

Generalization. The RUP knowledge base emphasizes that *A parent use case may be specialized into one or more child use cases that represent more specific forms of the parent. Neither parent nor child is necessarily abstract, although the parent in most cases is abstract. A child inherits all structure, behavior, and relationships of the parent. Children of the same parent are all specializations of the parent.*

Alignment with BPMN BPD Element: A generalization can take place both between elements of IA category or the IUC one in the RUP/UML BUCM. Between 2 elements of the IA category, it cannot be traced at the level of the BPMN BPD. When there is one between two elements of the IUC category and the parent is abstract, only a BPMN BPD is build for the realization of the child IUC category element. If it is not abstract, a BPMN BPD is also associated with the parent IUC category element.

5   Conclusion and Future Work

The BUCM (part of RUP) allows to model business processes at strategic and tactical levels. The operational level – which is represented using UML AD – however fails to furnish anchoring points to ensure traceability with the upper level. For integrated business process modeling – so to increase consistency between modeling levels by giving modeling guidelines – we have envisaged to use the BPMN BPD at operational level instead of UML AD. Even if we face different semantic domains, the RUP/UML BUCM and the BPMN BPD are both made for enterprise modeling; elements constituting the two frameworks have been easily aligned on the basis of their semantic. This allows to build a set of rules to ensure traceability between tactical and operational levels.

The mapping proposal will be further validated in the coming months. Validation will be performed longitudinally and cross-sectionally. Students of a master level project-based course will be made familiar with the traceability rules and apply them onto a real life case. The same case has already been solved by a cohort of former students, 3 years ago. These students were made aware of the importance of traceability, but were not given the specific rules presented in this paper. Students reports will be given a score in function of the (i) the quality of the application of traceability in particular (including the cohort not familiar with the developed rules), and (ii) on the general structural quality and completeness of the models produced. We will then compare the results of the 2 cohorts (without and with knowledge of the transformation rules). Across the cohorts, traceability scores will also be correlated to the general scores.

References

1. Chinosi, M., Trombetta, A.: BPMN: an introduction to the standard. Comput. Stan. Interfaces **34**(1), 124–134 (2012)
2. Herden, A., Farias, P.P.M., Albuquerque, A.B.: An approach based on BPMN to detail use cases. In: Elleithy, K., Sobh, T. (eds.) New Trends in Networking, Computing, E-learning, Systems Sciences, and Engineering, pp. 537–544. Springer, Cham (2015)

3. IBM: The Rational Unified Process, Version 7.0.1 (2007)
4. Johnston, S.: Ration®uml profile for business modeling. Technical report (2004)
5. Kruchten, P.: The rational unified process: an introduction. Longman/Addison-Wesley, Wokingham (2003)
6. Nailburg, E.J., Maksimchuk, R.A.: UML for Database Design, 1st edn. Addison-Wesley Longman Publishing Co., Inc., Boston (2001)
7. OMG: Business process model and notation (BPMN). Version 2.0.1. Technical report (2013)
8. OMG: OMG unified modeling language (OMG UML). Version 2.5. Technical report (2015)
9. Oscar, S.: Visual Paradigm for UML. International Book Market Service Limited, Beau-Bassin Rose-Hill (2013)
10. White, S.A., Miers, D.: BPMN Modeling and Reference Guide. Future Strategies Inc., Lighthouse Point (2008)
11. VisualParadigm: from use case to business process (2012). https://www.youtube.com/watch?v=jkIZuBZ876c

Ecosystems and Innovation

Modeling and Analyzing Openness Trade-Offs in Software Platforms: A Goal-Oriented Approach

Mahsa H. Sadi[1(✉)] and Eric Yu[1,2]

[1] Department of Computer Science, University of Toronto, Toronto, Canada
{mhsadi, eric}@cs.toronto.edu
[2] Faculty of Information, University of Toronto, Toronto, Canada

Abstract. *Context and motivation:* Open innovation is becoming an important strategy in software development. Following this strategy, software companies are increasingly opening up their platforms to third-party products for extension and completion. *Question/problem:* Opening up software platforms to third-party applications often involves difficult trade-offs between openness requirements and critical design concerns such as security, performance, privacy, and proprietary ownership. Deliberate assessment of these trade-offs is crucial to the ultimate quality and viability of an open software platform. *Principal ideas/results:* We propose to treat openness as a distinct class of non-functional requirements, and to model and analyze openness requirements and related trade-offs using a goal-oriented approach. The proposed approach allows to refine and analyze openness requirements in parallel with other competing concerns in designing software platforms. The refined requirements are used as criteria for selecting appropriate design options. We demonstrate our approach using an example of designing an open embedded software platform for the automotive domain reported in the literature. *Contributions:* The proposed approach allows to balance the fulfillment of interacting requirements in opening up platforms to third-party products, and to determine "good-enough" and "open-enough" platform design strategies.

Keywords: Requirements engineering · Software design · Decision making · Open software platforms · Software ecosystems · Open innovation

1 Introduction

"How open is open enough?"–Joel West [1]

Open innovation is becoming an increasingly important strategy in software development. Following this strategy, software development organizations open up their processes and software platforms to external developers and third parties in order to use external ideas and paths to market (as well as the internal ones) to advance their technology [2]. External developers become part of a software ecosystem offering complementary applications and services for the open platforms [3–5]. Google Android, Apple iOS, and Windows Mobile are a few examples of open software platforms.

© Crown Copyright 2017
P. Grünbacher and A. Perini (Eds.): REFSQ 2017, LNCS 10153, pp. 33–49, 2017.
DOI: 10.1007/978-3-319-54045-0_3

However, developing open software platforms that are technically sound, socially sustainable and economically viable is a challenging problem in software development. First, critical decisions need to be taken in opening up software platforms to third-party products that raise serious concerns about proprietary ownership and confidentiality of a platform and its complementary applications. Examples of such decisions include: deciding between the core features and functionalities that build the core competencies of a platform, and those that can be opened up to third-party developers [6, 7]; or identifying the appropriate *degree of openness* for engaging different third-party developers, some of whom are also competitors in the market place [7, 8]. Second, openness introduces a specific set of requirements on the design of a platform which are in competition with crucial requirements such as security, performance, maintainability, and controllability. For example, opening up a platform may urge the need for transparency and visibility of platform functionalities and data to third-party applications. These requirements pose serious risks to the security of the platform. Another example is that distributing platform features among applications from different parties threatens the controllability and maintainability of the overall platform [4, 9].

A successful example of an open software platform is Google Android. Lowering the entry barriers and providing easy access to extend the platform has significantly increased the adoption of Google Android among mobile manufacturers and application developers, introducing this operating system as a leader mobile software platform in the market [10]. However, Google Android and its complementary applications suffer from performance and security issues [11].

It is crucial to clearly understand and analyze the requirements that openness introduces on the design and evolution of a platform, and to carefully assess the related trade-offs before opening up a platform to third-party applications. To model and reason about openness requirements and related trade-offs, we propose a goal-oriented approach. The proposed approach reduces the problem of designing open software platforms to a decision making problem, treats openness requirements as a distinct class of non-functional requirements, refines them in parallel with other important design concerns, and uses the refined requirements as selection criteria to determine an appropriate design strategy from among alternative options for opening up a platform.

In Sect. 2, we identify some requirements and concerns that have been raised in the design of open software platforms. We briefly review the main steps of the Non-Functional Requirement (NFR) engineering approach in Sect. 3. We illustrate how to model and analyze openness requirements using NFR, in Sect. 4. We review the related research in Sect. 5 and conclude the paper in Sect. 6.

2 Requirements and Concerns in Open Software Platforms

An open software platform is a platform on top of which third-party applications can be built [3–5, 12]. Unlike in Free and Open-Source Software (FOSS) [13, 14], the source code of an open software platform is usually not made available to third parties. Instead, there are extension mechanisms, such as Application Programming Interfaces (APIs) or development environments that allow sufficient access to the services and functionalities of the open platform. Moreover, in open software platforms, major players develop purposive strategies attempting to gain competitive advantage [3, 15].

The requirements that need to be considered in opening up software platforms to third-party applications can be categorized into two main groups: (1) *Openness design requirements*: The specific concerns and quality requirements that openness introduces on the design; and (2) *General concerns in designing software platforms*: The requirements that are possibly violated or at risk when opening up platforms to external applications. Often, these requirements cannot be fully fulfilled simultaneously in the design of a platform. A designer may need to compromise between these two types of requirements. In the following, we identify several of these requirements and concerns.

Table 1. Business-level openness requirements

Market-related objectives – market reach, market presence, new markets, standardized market, adoptability, and time to market. A main reason for opening up software platforms is to expand market reach, open up new markets and communities for a platform, increase the adoption of a platform among various users and developers communities, increase the number and variety of innovative and complementary features, and reduce time to market of new and innovative features [15–17].

Customer-related objectives – attracting new customers and developing new customer communities, stickiness of the platform, and customer retention. Growing the network size of complementary applications hardens switching to a different platform, thus increases the stickiness of a platform. Moreover, growing the variety of platform offerings increases attractiveness of the platform for new and potential users, and increases value of the core product to the existing users [15, 16].

Product-related objectives – co-innovation and open-innovation, and variety of software vendor's offerings. Innovative features play an important role in the success of a platform, specifically in knowledge intensive domains. Via growing the network size of developers, the platform owners can benefit from emerging external innovations [15].

Financial-related objectives – revenue stream, sharing the costs of innovation, and decreasing total costs of ownership. Collaborating with partners in ecosystems shares the cost of innovation and decreases the total cost of ownership for commodity and innovative functionality [15, 16].

Network-effect-related objectives – customer and partner ecosystem gravity, and community building. Third-party developers play an important role in the success of an open platform through their contributions and innovations. A larger pool of developers will provide more innovative output. Thus, platform developers aim to attract and engage a large number of developers to contribute and develop applications to their platforms. Factors, such as the degree of openness, low entry barriers of both monetary and technical nature, and the network size of a platform influence the choice of external developers to join a platform [10, 15, 16].

2.1 Openness Design Requirements

Openness introduces two types of requirements on the design of software platforms: (1) *Business-level openness requirements*: These requirements are the main motivations for opening up a software platform to third-party applications. Business-level openness

Table 2. System-level openness requirements

Accessibility. An open software platform needs to be accessible to third-party applications and have access to the features and services of third-party applications. The ease of access to and from a software platform is an important quality requirement for opening up a platform. The accessibility of a platform can be categorized into four levels: (1) accessibility of functionalities and services; (2) accessibility of data; (3) accessibility of platform structure (i.e., access to features and components); (4) accessibility of source code [18].

Extensibility – composability, deployability, stability, configurability, and evolvability. An open software platform needs to be extended and complemented by other software applications and components over time. Extensibility quality attribute identifies how easy a new application or feature can be added to a platform. Various quality criteria contribute to the extensibility of a platform, including: **(1)** *Composability*: Open and seamless integration of external modules is an important requirement for a platform. Factors such as *decoupling* third-party applications from each other, *eliminating the need for development synchronization*, and *independent development, integration, and validation* of third-party applications contribute to the composability of an open platform [12, 19]. Carefully decoupled components with well-defined interfaces enable third-party developers to modify their applications without disrupting the overall correctness. Platform interfaces should decouple the platform organization from the third-party applications. Achieving this objective, allows the platform owner to release new version of the platform or new components without disabling the externally developed applications operating on top of the platform [12, 20]. **(2)** *Deployability*: Third-party applications must be possible to be deployed independently of each other, and the platform behavior must not depend on the order in which applications are deployed [19]. **(3)** *Stability*: Open software platforms and their APIs need to be sufficiently stable over time to provide a stable infrastructure for third-party applications [19]. *Backwards compatibility* is an important quality attribute contributing to the stability of the platform. **(4)** *Configurability*: Open software platforms must support variability in configuring the platform and third-party applications to enable customized products be developed [19]. **(5)** *Evolvability*. In open software platforms, new functionality are continuously added and the size of the platforms continuously grow. To deal with the growth, it is required to proactively refactor platform architecture and standardize platform interfaces [20].

Decentralizability and distributability. The functionalities of an open software platform need to be distributed among several applications, and platform components need to operate in a decentralized environment. Thus, the ease to operate in a decentralized environment is an important quality requirement for an open software platform [13].

Interoperability. An open software platform requires to easily cooperate and interact with third-party applications. Mechanisms are required to coordinate and facilitate the interactions between the platform and third-party applications and to resolve conflicts that arise in coordination [4, 13, 20].

Reusability. An open software platform and its components need to be used and re-used in the development of other software features and applications. The ease to do so is an important design quality in an open platform.

Modifiability. To use the platform in the development of other applications and software features, the platform or some parts of its functionalities or structures may need to be modified and cust?omzied. Thus, the platform should provide mechanisms that enables easy modification of some features.

Visibility or transparency. To be complemented and extended by third-party applications, the platform structure, functionalities, and behavior need to be visible and transparent to external applications to various degrees [21].

requirements are non-technical, related to the social, business, and organizational environment of a software platform, and may indirectly influence the design of an open platform. These requirements often compete or interact with technical quality requirements in the design of open software platforms. Thus, specific attention should be given to this group in choosing effective design strategies for opening up a software platform. These requirements can be categorized into five main groups described in Table 1. (2) *System-level openness requirements*: These requirements are technical, related to the quality of software design, and directly influence the design decisions. The technical quality requirements that need to be considered in opening up software platforms can be classified into seven groups described in Table 2.

2.2   General Concerns in Designing Software Platforms

Aside from openness requirements, there are other considerations applicable to the design of software platforms that are potentially impacted by openness requirements. Several instances of these requirements are identified in Table 3.

Table 3. General design concerns in open software platforms

Security – operational security, integrity, confidentiality, and privacy. The end-users use a composition of the core of platform and various external applications developed on top of it. Security concerns arise as possible defective or malicious code in external applications may disable the overall system [20, 22, 23]. Mechanisms are required: (1) to guarantee the integrity of platform services and data in the presence of access by third-party applications [19]; (2) to preserve the confidentiality and privacy of the end-users' information and platform data when opening up a platform to third-party developers [7, 20]; and (3) to ensure safe and correct operation of features and services developed by multiple parties.

Controllability, maintainability, and centralizability. The development and maintenance of an open platform and its complementary applications is shared among various parties. In this setting, mechanisms are required to manage software enhancements, extensions, and architectural revisions in decentralized projects. Moreover, rules are required to govern and control the applications network [4, 9, 13].

Reliability, trust and accountability. In open software platforms, parties providing and consuming a software service are easily exposed to cheaters. Therefore, mechanisms are required to guarantee trustworthiness and accountability of third-party services and functionalities [13, 23].

Proprietary ownership. The ownership and intellectual property rights of the applications, components and data produced by external developers is a critical concern in open software platforms. Mechanisms are required to ensure responsibility and commitment to updating and supporting third-party modules. Moreover, the alignment of component licenses need to be checked in the usage and composition of open software components and modules at build time and deployment [7, 20, 23].

3   Non-functional Requirements Analysis Method

To deal with interacting and competing requirements, we use the Non-Functional Requirements (NFR) engineering approach [24]. NFR reduces the problem of designing a software system into a decision making problem and a search for satisfactory design options. To identify an appropriate design option, four main steps are performed in NFR: (1) *Characterizing and Prioritizing Design Requirements*: In this step, the requirements and constraints important to a specific design context are identified and characterized in terms of a set of non-functional requirements; i.e., a set of technical and non-technical quality objectives that a design should meet. For this purpose, two main activities are performed: The design requirements are first identified and refined, then they are prioritized based on their importance in the specific design context. (2) *Identifying Alternative Design Options*: The second step is to identify the design objective (i.e., the specific functionality to be designed or implemented) and to explore alternative design options for achieving the specified objective. (3) *Evaluating Design Alternatives against Design Requirements*: To choose an appropriate design option, the design alternatives are evaluated based on the identified design requirements. (4) *Selecting Satisficing Design Options*. The final step is to select the most appropriate design options from among the available alternatives. To select an appropriate design option, it is required to formally describe and prioritize the identified design requirements, and to assess their fulfillment in each design option. For this purpose, NFR provides a goal-oriented modeling and analysis procedure [25]. The modeling procedure has two main steps of *describing a design decision* and *modeling the design decision* (explained in Table 4). To analyze the fulfilment of the identified design requirements in each design option, NFR provides a semi-automatic goal-oriented forward evaluation procedure. Using this approach, all the design alternatives are evaluated against the design requirements, and then the most satisfactory design option is selected. To analyze the impact of each design alternative on the design requirements, a labeling system is used, which is explained in Table 4.

Table 4. Modeling and analyzing design decisions using i* goal-oriented language

---

Modeling. Each design decision is described using three elements: (a) a *design objective*, (b) at least two atomic alternative *design options* (which are non-overlapping and exclusive), and (c) at least one *design requirement* which discriminates between the alternative design options.

A design decision is modeled as follows: (1) The design objective is represented using "*Goal*" element. (2) Alternative design options are modeled using "*Task*" element. (3) The relationship between a design goal and design options are modeled using "*Means-Ends*" link. (4) If design requirements are atomic they are modeled using "*Soft Goal*" element. If design requirements are non-atomic, they need to be refined and modeled using "*Soft Goal Interdependency Graphs (SIG)*". In SIG graphs, refinement of a design requirement is modeled using "*Help*" contribution link. (5) Evaluation of design options against design requirements are modeled using "*Help*" and "*Hurt*" contribution links. (6) Priorities of design requirements are modeled using three types of priorities: *non-critical*, *critical*, and *very critical*.

Analysis. (1) *Label Assignment*. The selection of a design option is described using a label assigned to the "*Task*" element representing the chosen option. (2) *Label Propagation*. The impact of an alternative on immediate design requirements are described using a predefined set of label propagation rules, which can be redefined in a specific evaluation. (3) *Label Resolution*. After each step of performing label propagation, a "*Soft Goal*" might receive a set of labels from the underneath "*Soft Goal*" or "*Task*" elements. A set of predefined label resolution rules determine the final label of the "*Soft Goal*" element, representing a design requirement. Label resolution step requires human input and is semi-automatic.

---

4   Example Modeling and Analysis

To demonstrate our proposed approach, we use the case study of designing the AUTOSAR platform for embedded automotive software reported in [19]. We have chosen this case study for two reasons. First, AUTOSAR is a real-world industrial open platform and its design process is explained in detail in [19]. The design process is explained in terms of the design requirements, the decisions taken in the design, and the final strategies adopted to design the platform. Thus, we add no hypothetical data or assumption to the requirements of this case. We only extract the explanations about platform functionalities (Sect. 4.1) and the related design requirements (Table 5), and then apply our proposed approach. Second, the designers have adopted a structured approach in identifying requirements and decisions, without using modeling for analysis. Using this study, we can show how the proposed modeling and analysis approach might be effective for designing a real-world industrial-scale open platform.

4.1   System Description: An Open Embedded Automotive Platform

The AUTOSAR platform manages the electronic units of a vehicle. Some electronic units control vehicle steering sensors and actuators, and some are responsible for accessory functions such as infotainment modules. Different electronic units communicate via data buses. The platform shares the control of the electronic units with third-party applications. The platform controls most of critical electronic units in charge of basic operations of a vehicle (such as the engine, brakes and forward sensing modules). Less critical functions (such as displaying vehicle speed in the cluster display, locking the doors or infotainment modules) can be controlled either by certified third-party applications or by third-party applications developed by undirected developers. The core of the platform, including the set of software modules providing necessary services to use a vehicle, will be deployed on a car before delivery to the end-user. Less critical functions and accessories can be updated or deployed after delivery on an ongoing basis. The platform should be designed in a way that can accommodate these kinds of extensions and completion.

In the following, we focus on the scenario of designing data provision service to third-party applications from the platform. Third-party applications may require to access to and operate on platform data or data from other third-party applications. Examples of these data include: the speed and lateral acceleration of the vehicle or the speed of nearby cars. These data are aggregated from sensors in the wheels. Third-party applications may require access to platform data such as speed data to simply display it in the speed display or to automatically adjust the speed of a vehicle with respect to nearby cars. It is possible that several third-party applications require access to the same data at the same time. For example, auto-cruise system and direct brake control system may want to adjust the speed at the same time. Therefore, generic mechanisms should be designed in the platform to provide data service to present and future third-party applications. In the following, we demonstrate how to determine an optimal design strategy for opening up AUTOSAR platform data to third-party applications, treating openness requirements as a class of non-functional requirements.

4.2 Modeling and Analysis

Determining the most appropriate design strategy for providing data service to third-party applications consists of four main steps: (1) characterizing and prioritizing design requirements, including *domain-specific requirements* (general design concerns) and the *requirements that openness introduces on the design*; (2) identifying alternative design options for opening up platform data to third-party applications; (3) evaluating the design options against the identified design requirements; and (4) selecting an appropriate design option. To select an appropriate design option, the identified design options are modeled, prioritized and analyzed using NFR goal-oriented modeling and analysis as described in Table 4.

Characterizing domain-specific design requirements. The embedded platform is in charge of controlling automotive electronic units, many of which have safety-critical functionalities such as automatic control of the vehicle speed and brakes. Therefore, the design has to meet stringent *dependability requirements* with high priority. The dependability requirements are of two types: (1) *Performance requirements*: Platform and individual third-party applications must operate in real-time. Therefore, *the response-time* of the platform must be minimized and undesirable interactions between applications should be eliminated. (2) *Security requirements:* including *integrity* and *availability* of services to assure operational security of the platform. Relevant aspects of these requirements need to be fulfilled in the design of data provision service. The details of domain design requirements and their priorities are provided in Table 5.

Characterizing openness design requirements. The platform shares control of the electronic units with third-party applications. Opening up the platform imposes high-priority *extensibility requirements* on the platform including: (1) *Composability*: The automotive platform needs to accommodate and interact with third-party applications. Therefore, the open platform should enable open and seamless integration of external modules. (2) *Deployability*: Third-party applications must be deployed independently of each other. Openness requirements also need to be refined and considered in the design of data provision service. The details of openness design requirements and their priorities are described in Table 5.

Identifying alternative design options. Three alternative design options can be considered to provide data service to third-party developers, including: (1) *centralized data provision*, (2) *semi-centralized data provision* and (3) *decentralized data provision*. In centralized data provision, all data exchange operations between the platform and third-party applications are controlled by the platform. Third-party applications cannot communicate directly with each other. In semi-centralized data provision, third-party applications are allowed to exchange data directly. However, a supervisor (either the platform or the end user) mediate the data interactions between third-party applications. In decentralized data provision, the third-party applications can independently exchange data with each other. Further details about the design options is provided in Table 6.

Evaluating design options against the design requirements. The fulfilment of each domain-specific and openness design requirement (Table 5) should be evaluated in

Table 5. Design requirements important for providing data service to third-party apps

Design requirement	Description
Domain design requirements: security | Priority: high	
Integrity [Platform Data]	Many of platform data are safety critical (such as speed data). The platform must implement necessary mechanisms to ensure the integrity, accuracy and consistency of all the operations performed on safety-critical data.
Availability [Platform] and [Third-Party Applications]	The platform services should correctly operate at any time. Mechanism are required to guarantee high-availability and fast failure recovery of platform operations.
Domain design requirements: performance | Priority: high	
*** Response Time [Platform]	Access-Time [Data]: Platform and third-party applications should operate in real-time. Thus, response-time of the platform and access-time of third-party applications to the required data should be minimized and platform should respond to the data access requests in real-time.
Openness design requirements: composability [Platform] | Priority: high	
Decoupling	(1) [Third-Party Applications]: Third-party applications must be decoupled from each other and work independently.
	(2) [Platform]: Platform and third-party applications development and evolution should be decoupled.
Development Asynchronization [Third-Party Applications]	The design must eliminate the need for development synchronization and enable third-party applications to be developed, integrated and validated independently of other applications. Since non-technical users cannot integrate and validate the composition themselves, this requirement must be supported by the platform.
Openness design requirements: deployability [Platform] | Priority: high	
Independent Deployment [Third-Party Applications]	Third-party applications must be deployed independently from each other.
Independent Behaviour [Third-Party Applications]	Platform behaviour must not depend on the order in which the applications are installed and deployed.

*** Response time and access time design requirements were not explicitly mentioned in [19]. We inferred these requirements from the real-time operations that the automotive platform must perform

each data provision design option. The details of this evaluation is presented in Table 7. In Table 7, the contribution of design options to the refined design requirements are represented by a (+) or (−) label. A (+) indicates that a design option has a positive impact on the fulfilment of a design requirement. A (−) indicates that the design option violates or is negatively co-related with a design requirement. Each evaluation is accompanied with reasons explaining why a positive or negative label has been assigned.

Selecting an appropriate design option. As shown in Table 7, each design option has received a set of (+) and (−) labels in the evaluation against the requirements. This

Table 6. Providing data service to third-party apps: three alternative design options

---

Design objective: To provide data service to third-party applications.

Design option 1: centralized data provision

The platform controls all data interactions between third-party applications and the platform, and between one third-party application and another. In this design alternative, all data is stored and exchanged through the platform, but most data is isolated to a single application through a single API. Data and provided services are accessed through the platform API by either and explicit get/set and/or subscribe, both at run-time. There is also and API to determine the available data set at runtime.

*** Design option 2: semi-centralized data provision

Third-party applications can communicate directly in some cases. Any data access request is initially submitted to a mediator (end-user or the platform). After checking and allowing the request, third-party applications can communicate directly. For this purpose, applications declare what data and information they need at install-time. The platform decides to control data write operations, data read operations or both.

*** Design option 3: decentralized data provision

Third-party applications can directly exchange data and information with each other. Data and information exchange between one third-party application and another is controlled and supervised by the third-party application that provides the requested data. In this design, data access requests are declared at run-time and third-party applications are responsible for managing the data access requests from other third-party applications. Data provider application is in charge of controlling the consistency of data write operations.

*** Design options 2 and 3 did not exist in the original study. They are generated as alternative options for the design strategy that the original designers have adopted (as a part of the proposed analysis approach)

means that in choosing each design option, trade-offs should be made between a set of competing requirements. For example, choosing centralized data provision helps achieve "*Decoupling[TP App]*" (an important design requirement for opening up the platform) but as a result "*Access Time[Data]*" is violated. However, access time is also an important requirement for real-time operations of the automotive platform. To take a final decision between the design options, all the trade-offs between the requirements need to be carefully examined. For this purpose, the identified requirements, their priorities and their trade-offs need to be formally modeled and analyzed. We have modeled the information presented in Tables 5, 6, and 7, and analyzed the impact of each design option on the design requirements using goal-oriented modeling and analysis (explained in Table 4). The results are presented in Fig. 1.

In Fig. 1, the design requirements and their refinements are shown in the upper part, the design options and their evaluation against the immediate refined requirements are shown at the bottom, and the degree of fulfillment of each design requirement in each design option is shown by the colored labels besides the requirements. Moreover, trade-offs points can be recognized in two ways: (1) directly from the "*conflict*" label beside a design requirement. For example, "*Composability [Platform]*" has received a "*conflict*" label from two options. The reason for the conflict can be traced back to the fulfillment of its refinement; i.e., "*Decoupling[Platform]*" and "*Decoupling[TP App]*". "*Centralized data provision*" design option helps decouple third-party applications

Table 7. Evaluating design options against identified design requirements

	Decoupling
Option 1	(1) [Platform] (−): Centralized data provision increases the interactions between third-party applications and the platform since all data access operations should pass through the platform. (2) [Third-Party Applications] (+): Central control by the platform eliminates any one-to-one interaction between third-party applications.
Option 2	(1) [Platform] (−): Platform is involved in data write operations between third-party applications. This increases the interactions between the platform and third-party application. (2) [Third-Party Applications] (−): Since the applications can interact with each other directly, the interactions between third-party applications increase.
Option 3	(1) [Platform] (+). Third-party applications can exchange data without platform control. Application interactions are thus decoupled from the platform. (2) [Third-Party Applications] (−): Applications can interact with each other directly. Thus the interactions between third-party applications increase.
	Development asynchronization [Third-party applications]
Option 1	(+): Prohibiting direct communications between third-party applications separates the integration and validation of third-party application from each other.
Option 2	(−): The correctness of the behavior of third-party applications should be validated in combination with the related third-party applications.
Option 3	(−): This design is similar to Option 2.
	Independent behavior [Third-party applications]
Option 1	(+): Since all the data interactions are controlled by the platform, the behavior of the applications are completely separated and independent from each other.
Option 2	(−): The applications installed later can access the data of the applications that are installed earlier.
Option 3	(−): This design is similar to option 2.
	Independent deployment [Third-party applications]
Option 1	(+): The platform prohibits direct communications between third-party applications. Therefore, third-party applications can be deployed independently of each other.
Option 2	(−): Third-party applications can request access to the data of other third-party applications at install-time. This kind of requests violates the independent deployment of applications.
Option 3	(−): Third-party applications can send data requests to other applications at any time (either at install-time or after that).
	Availability [Third-party application data]: failure recovery
Option 1	(+): The platform is informed if a third-party application becomes unavailable. Therefore, data requests for unavailable data can be mitigated proactively.
Option 2	(+): The supervisor (either platform or end-user) is informed of possible unavailability of third-party applications. Therefore, a data request for an unavailable third-party application can be mitigated proactively.
Option 3	(−): In decentralized communications, the unavailability of applications is not known beforehand. Therefore, a data request for an unavailable third-party application lead to an unmitigated failure.

(*continued*)

Table 7. (*continued*)

	Integrity [Data]: consistency [Data]
Option 1	(+): Platform controls every data access and modifications between third-party applications. This centralized access control reduces the chance of inconsistency in data read and write operations.
Option 2	(+): Data write operation can be supervised by the platform. This supervised access control reduces the chance of inconsistency in data read and write operations.
Option 3	(−): Third-party applications can interact with each other without informing central control. This increases the possibility of data inconsistencies in several data read and write operations by different third-party applications.
	Response time [Platform]: access time [Data]
Option 1	(−): All data operation requests should pass through a central gateway and queue controlled by the platform. Central checking increases the waiting time of third-party applications that require to access data around the same time, even if the requests are for different data from different third-party applications.
Option 2	(+): Many of unwanted waiting time for data requests, specifically data read operations, can be eliminated, because third-party applications can directly request data read from other third-party applications.
Option 3	(+): Data read operations are handled similar to option 2. Moreover, there will be no central queue for data write operations since the third-party application that provides data is responsible for consistency checking.

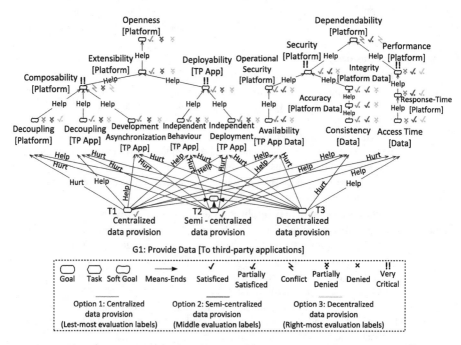

Fig. 1. Modeling and analyzing trade-offs between openness and other requirements in alternative data provision design options using i* goal-oriented language

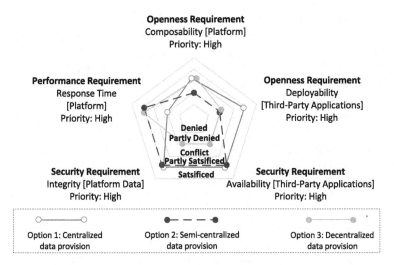

Fig. 2. Comparing design strategies for opening up platform data to third-party applications based on important design requirements for the automotive platform

from each other, but in return, it increases the coupling between the platform and third-party applications. Similarly, *"Decentralized data provision"* design option has this conflict in reverse order; (2) indirectly by comparing the labels of the same color between different design requirements. For example, *"Extensibility [Platform]"* has received a *"partially satisfied"* red label, and *"Performance[Platform]"* has received a *"partially denied"* red label. This difference indicates that by choosing *"Centralized data provision"* option, a designer has to sacrifice some degree of performance in order to gain some degree of extensibility for openness. The fulfillment of the design requirements in each design option is summarized and compared in Fig. 2. In Fig. 2, the nested pentagons represent different degrees of design requirements satisfaction (from denied to satisfied). The nodes of the pentagon depict the main design requirements for the automotive platform. As Fig. 2 shows, *"Centralized data provision"* outperforms other options except in fulfilling *"Performance [Platform]"*.

4.3   Discussion

Our modeling and analysis (Fig. 1) detects two important trade-off points between the requirements: One trade-off is between two openness requirements of *"Decoupling [Platform]"* and *"Decoupling[TP App]"*. This means that in choosing each of the design options, a designer has to comprise between independence of the platform from third-party applications and independence of third-party applications from each other. Both of the requirements are important for the platform and their dissatisfaction may have irreversible impacts. Another trade-off is between the openness requirement of *"Extensibility[Platform]"* and *"Performance[Platform]"*. Performance requirement is of particular importance for the real-time operations of the automotive platform (e.g. the real-time adjustment of speed or the real-time activation of brakes). On the other hand, extensibility is also crucial to accommodate third-party applications. The impact of this trade-off must be carefully assessed before making any final design decision.

In [19], the original designers have implemented "*centralized data provision*" strategy for designing the automotive platform, without acknowledging the above trade-offs. This decision may have two reasons: (1) The designers use an informal and descriptive method for designing the open platform; i.e., they identify the requirements and then explain a set of generic design patterns that fulfill the requirements. Since the design process is comprised of numerous decisions (typical in an industrial-scale design project), it is possible that the designers have lost the track of some requirements in the design. (2) It is also possible that the designers have noticed the above trade-offs, and have decided to sacrifice some degrees of performance to gain higher degrees of extensibility (i.e. deployability and composability) for openness. According to our analysis, to alleviate the performance issue, a combination of centralized and semi-centralized data provision strategies could be considered for providing data to different types of third-party applications in different layers of the platform.

The presented modeling and analysis is only one design scenario among several others that we have investigated in the design of AUTOSAR platform. We aim to confirm our findings with the original designers in a future case study.

5 Related Research

Three groups of research efforts relate to this paper: (1) *Designing open software platforms*: Various efforts have been dedicated to the design and development of software platforms that can smoothly accommodate third-party applications. Most of these efforts focus on providing best practices and techniques for developing APIs that enable seamless and secure communications with third-party applications. (e.g. [21]). Little attention has been given to model-based approaches for designing open software platforms. In a few research works, the need for systematic modeling and analysis in open platforms has been discussed (e.g. [26–29]) However, no validated modeling method has been proposed for this purpose yet. (2) *Requirements engineering in open software platforms:* Many recent research efforts have investigated the practice of requirements engineering in open software platforms (e.g. [7, 8, 30–32]). These efforts either focus on identifying the challenges of requirements engineering practices in the presence of multiple development parties or characterising the multi-faceted nature of requirements in open software platforms. A few research works also emphasize the need for rigorous modeling and checking of the requirements in open platforms (e.g. [22]). To support requirements modeling and analysis in open software platforms, several attempts have been made (e.g. [29, 33, 34]) which are in the early stages of development. (3) *Decision Support for open software platforms.* Another group of research works discuss the need to support systematic decision making of open platforms owners and designers (e.g. [33]). However, these efforts mainly focus on adopting open-source components rather than design reasoning support for opening up platforms.

6 Conclusions

We presented a goal-oriented method to model and analyze openness requirements and related trade-offs in designing software platforms. Modeling and analysis of openness trade-offs allows to formally compare alternative design strategies for opening up a platform to third-party applications. This systematic comparison helps determine "good-enough" and "open-enough" design strategies for opening up a platform to third-party applications. Adopting such balanced design strategies is essential to developing open software platforms that are technically, socially and economically balanced, thus having a higher chance of sustainability.

The proposed approach allows to model the relation between business-level and system-level openness requirements, and provides semi-automated support to assess alternative design options and to spot trade-off points.

To improve the applicability of the presented method for modeling and analyzing openness trade-offs, two issues need to be addressed: (1) *Scalability of modeling*: In this work, we illustrated trade-off modeling in a single design decision in an open software platform. Applying trade-off modeling and analysis at the scale of a design process comprised of numerous interrelated decisions need to be further addressed. (2) *Scalability of analysis*: To find appropriate design options, we used the goal-oriented forward evaluation method, which exhaustively evaluates all the possible options to reach to the best alternative. To improve the efficiency of analysis, algorithms are required which eliminate this exhaustive search.

Moreover, future work is required to compare the proposed method with existing methods for analyzing trade-offs, including Architecture Trade-off Analysis Method (ATAM) [35], and to assess the applicability of the proposed method in real-world open software projects.

This research work is the first step to support design and decision making in open software platforms. The next steps towards this ultimate objective aim to enrich the proposed method in three ways: (1) to provide knowledge support via developing modules for refining openness design requirements as a class of non-functional requirements and developing catalogues of options for designing open platforms; (2) to enrich the analytical and reasoning capabilities of the presented method for incorporating the priorities and preferences of multiple parties in selecting optimal design options in open software platforms; and (3) to provide semi-automated tool support for modeling and analyzing requirements in open software platforms and finding optimal design options.

References

1. West, J.: How open is open enough?: Melding proprietary and open source platform strategies. Res. Policy **32**(7), 1259–1285 (2003)
2. Chesbrough, H.W.: Open Innovation: The New Imperative for Creating and Profiting from Technology. Harvard Business Press, Brighton (2006)
3. Fitzgerald, B.: The transformation of open source software. MIS Q. **30**(3), 587–598 (2006)

4. Boudreau, K.: Open platform strategies and innovation: granting access vs. devolving control. Manag. Sci. **56**(10), 1849–1872 (2010)
5. Jansen, S., Brinkkemper, S., Souer, J., Luinenburg, L.: Shades of gray: opening up a software producing organization with the open software enterprise model. J. Syst. Softw. **85** (7), 1495–1510 (2012)
6. Munir, H., Wnuk, K., Runeson, P.: Open innovation in software engineering: a systematic mapping study. Empirical Softw. Eng. **21**(2), 1–40 (2015)
7. Knauss, E., Yussuf, A., Blincoe, K., Damian, D., Knauss, A.: Continuous clarification and emergent requirements flows in open-commercial software ecosystems. Requirements Eng. **21**, 1–21 (2016)
8. Valenca, G., Alves, C.M., Heimann, V., Jansen, S., Brinkkemper, S.: Competition and collaboration in requirements engineering: a case study of an emerging software ecosystem. In: IEEE 22nd International Requirements Engineering Conference, pp. 384–393 (2014)
9. Ghazawneh, A., Henfridsson, O.: Balancing platform control and external contribution in third-party development: the boundary resources model. Inf. Syst. J. **23**(2), 173–192 (2013)
10. Koch, S., Kerschbaum, M.: Joining a smartphone ecosystem: application developers' motivations and decision criteria. Inf. Softw. Technol. **56**(11), 1423–1435 (2014)
11. Shabtai, A., Fledel, Y., Kanonov, U., Elovici, Y., Dolev, S., Glezer, C.: Google android: a comprehensive security assessment. IEEE Secur. Priv. **2**, 35–44 (2010)
12. Bosch, J., Bosch-Sijtsema, P.: From integration to composition: on the impact of software product lines, global development and ecosystems. J. Syst. Softw. **83**(1), 67–76 (2010)
13. Scacchi, W.: Free/open source software development: recent research results and methods. Adv. Comput. **69**, 243–295 (2007)
14. Feller, J., Fitzgerald, B.: A framework analysis of the open source software development paradigm. In: Proceedings of the Twenty First International Conference on Information Systems, pp. 58–69 (2000)
15. Popp, K.M.: Goals of software vendors for partner ecosystems – a practitioner's view. In: Tyrväinen, P., Jansen, S., Cusumano, Michael, A. (eds.) ICSOB 2010. LNBIP, vol. 51, pp. 181–186. Springer, Heidelberg (2010). doi:10.1007/978-3-642-13633-7_17
16. Bosch, J.: Software ecosystems: taking software development beyond the boundaries of the organization. J. Syst. Softw. **85**(7), 1453–1454 (2012)
17. Jarke, M., Loucopoulos, P., Lyytinen, K., Mylopoulos, J., Robinson, W.: The brave new world of design requirements. Inf. Syst. **36**(7), 992–1008 (2011)
18. Anvaari, M., Jansen, S.: Evaluating architectural openness in mobile software platforms. In: Proceedings of the Fourth European Conference on Software Architecture: Companion Volume, pp. 85–92, August 2010
19. Eklund, U., Bosch, J.: Architecture for embedded open software ecosystems. J. Syst. Softw. **92**, 128–142 (2014)
20. Bosch, J.: Architecture challenges for software ecosystems. In: Proceedings of the Fourth European Conference on Software Architecture: Companion Volume, pp. 93–95 (2010)
21. Cataldo, M., Herbsleb, J.D.: Architecting in software ecosystems: interface translucence as an enabler for scalable collaboration. In: Proceedings of the Fourth European Conference on Software Architecture: Companion Volume, pp. 65–72 (2010)
22. Scacchi, W., Alspaugh, T.A.: Processes in securing open architecture software systems. In: Proceedings of International Conference on Software and System Process (2013)
23. Baresi, L., Di Nitto, E., Ghezzi, C.: Toward open-world software: Issue and challenges. Computer **39**(10), 36–43 (2006)
24. Chung, L., Nixon, B.A., Yu, E., Mylopoulos, J.: Non-functional Requirements in Software Engineering, vol. 5. Springer Science & Business Media, Heidelberg (2012)

25. Horkoff, J., Yu, E.: Comparison and evaluation of goal-oriented satisfaction analysis techniques. Requirements Eng. **18**(3), 199–222 (2013)
26. Christensen, H.B., Hansen, K.M., Kyng, M., Manikas, K.: Analysis and design of software ecosystem architectures–towards the 4S telemedicine ecosystem. Inf. Softw. Technol. **56** (11), 1476–1492 (2014)
27. Boucharas, V., Jansen, S., Brinkkemper, S.: Formalizing software ecosystem modeling. In: Proceedings of the 1st International Workshop on Open Component Ecosystems, pp. 41–50 (2009)
28. Sadi, M.H., Yu, E.: Designing software ecosystems: how can modeling techniques help? In: Gaaloul, K., Schmidt, R., Nurcan, S., Guerreiro, S., Ma, Q. (eds.) CAISE 2015. LNBIP, vol. 214, pp. 360–375. Springer, Heidelberg (2015). doi:10.1007/978-3-319-19237-6_23
29. Sadi, M.H., Dai, J., Yu, E.: Designing software ecosystems: how to develop sustainable collaborations? In: Persson, A., Stirna, J. (eds.) CAISE 2015. LNBIP, vol. 215, pp. 161–173. Springer, Heidelberg (2015). doi:10.1007/978-3-319-19243-7_17
30. Wnuk, K., Runeson, P.: Engineering open innovation–towards a framework for fostering open innovation. In: Herzwurm, G., Margaria, T. (eds.) ICSOB 2013. LNBIP, vol. 150, pp. 48–59. Springer, Heidelberg (2013). doi:10.1007/978-3-642-39336-5_6
31. Linåker, J., Rempel, P., Regnell, B., Mäder, P.: How firms adapt and interact in open source ecosystems: analyzing stakeholder influence and collaboration patterns. In: Daneva, M., Pastor, O. (eds.) REFSQ 2016. LNCS, vol. 9619, pp. 63–81. Springer, Heidelberg (2016). doi:10.1007/978-3-319-30282-9_5
32. Linåker, J., Regnell, B., Munir, H.: Requirements engineering in open innovation: a research agenda. In: Proceedings of the 2015 International Conference on Software and System Process, pp. 208–212 (2015)
33. Franch, X., Susi, A.: Risk assessment in open source systems. In: Proceedings of the 38th International Conference on Software Engineering Companion, pp. 896–897 (2016)
34. Sadi, M.H., Yu, E.: Analyzing the evolution of software development: from creative chaos to software ecosystems. In: 2014 IEEE Eighth International Conference on Research Challenges in Information Science (RCIS), pp. 1–11 (2014)
35. Kazman, R., Klein, M., Barbacci, M., Longstaff, T., Lipson, H., Carriere, J.: The architecture tradeoff analysis method. In: Proceedings of the Fourth IEEE International Conference on Engineering of Complex Computer Systems, ICECCS 1998, pp. 68–78. IEEE (1998)

A Contribution Management Framework for Firms Engaged in Open Source Software Ecosystems - A Research Preview

Johan Linåker[(✉)] and Björn Regnell

Lund University, Lund, Sweden
{johan.linaker,bjorn.regnell}@cs.lth.se

Abstract. *Context and motivation*: Contribution Management helps firms engaged in Open Source Software (OSS) ecosystems to motivate what they should contribute and when, but also what they should focus their resources on and to what extent. Such guidelines are also referred to as contribution strategies. The motivation for developing tailored contribution strategies is to maximize return on investment and sustain the influence needed in the ecosystem. *Question/Problem*: We aim to develop a framework to help firms understand their current situation and create a starting point to develop an effective contribution management process. *Principal ideas/results*: Through a design science approach, a prototype framework is created based on literature and validated iteratively with expert opinions through interviews. *Contribution*: In this research preview, we present our initial results after our first design cycle and consultation with one experienced OSS manager at a large OSS oriented software-intensive firm. The initial validation highlights importance of stakeholder identification and analysis, as well as the general need for contribution management and alignment with internal product planning. This encourages future work to develop the framework further using expert and case validation.

Keywords: Requirements engineering · Open source · Software ecosystem · Open innovation · Co-opetition · Scoping · Contribution strategy · Contribution management

1 Introduction

Requirements Engineering (RE) concerns capturing the needs of the customer and translating these into a product that satisfies the elicited needs [1]. For software-intensive firms, RE can therefore be considered as a pivotal part in the product planning and spans over different time horizons and abstractions, from requirements management, to release-planning, roadmapping and portfolio management [2]. Firms operating in an Open Source Software (OSS) ecosystem have to consider participation in two such RE instances; one that regards the internal product planning facilitated by themselves, and one that regards the

© Springer International Publishing AG 2017
P. Grünbacher and A. Perini (Eds.): REFSQ 2017, LNCS 10153, pp. 50–57, 2017.
DOI: 10.1007/978-3-319-54045-0_4

external product planning of the OSS project facilitated by the OSS ecosystem. In the latter, to impose their own agendas, firms have to collaborate and compete with other actors in the ecosystem that all have a stake in the OSS project that underpins the ecosystem [3].

To gain the influence needed in order to impose their agenda, align their internal RE with the ecosystem's RE and to maximize Return On Investment (ROI), firms need consider how to participate in the OSS ecosystem in terms of what they contribute and when (cf. requirements scoping [4], but also what they should focus their resources on and to what extent. We choose to label this process as *contribution management* and guidelines that come as output *contribution strategies* [4]. To create these strategies, we believe that firms need to understand how they draw value [5] from the OSS project and their ecosystems [3], and identify the related business requirements [6]. Further, firms need to understand the relation between the OSS projects, their ecosystems, and the firms' internal product planning [2], and as a consequence how important is it to be able to influence the RE in the OSS ecosystems [7]. These factors need to align with the reasons for why firms make contributions and dedicate resources to the OSS project and its ecosystem, i.e., the foundations for the contribution management process.

We aim to develop a contribution management framework to help firms understand their current situation and create a starting point that can help them construct guidelines for what they should contribute to the OSS ecosystems and when, i.e., contribution strategies [4]. We apply a design science approach [8] by first building on literature [9], and then consult with experts for opinions in an iterative fashion. In this research preview we present our initial results after our first design cycle and consultation with an experienced OSS manager at a large OSS oriented software-intensive firm.

2   Research Methodology

We consider the problem context of aligning the contribution management with a firm's internal product planning [2] and business requirements [6] as a design problem. We adopt a design science approach [8] and define our design problem to:

– *Improve alignment between a firm's contribution management towards OSS projects with the firm's internal product planning and business requirements, by designing a framework that can help the firm to create guidelines for what should be contributed and when, in order for its developers to better decide what to contribute and how to prioritize their work.*

The treatment addressing the stated design problem includes the framework (i.e., the artifact [8]) as well as the interaction between it and the problem context, which in our case is constituted by firms engaged in an OSS ecosystem.

In our study, we identify and explain the problem based on literature [9] and develop a prototype of an artifact along with a potential interaction set-up. As a validation model, we will use expert opinions where the prototype and interaction set-up is simulated through interviews. Based on the output of each interview, the treatment is refined and again validated in a new cycle. The interviews are semi-structured with introductory questions that covers current involvement in OSS ecosystems, contribution practices, and how internal RE functions relative the ecosystems'. In the second part, the framework is presented for the interviewee with an explanation and open discussion on its structure and content. In the third part, the interviewee and interviewer walk through the framework for an OSS ecosystem of the interviewee's choice. The interview ends with a discussion of usage scenarios, potential improvements and changes of the framework. The interviews are audio-recorded and transcribed.

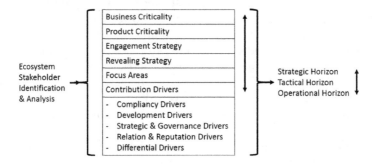

Fig. 1. Overview of the first iteration of the proposed contribution management framework.

In this research preview, the results from the first design cycle is presented where our initial treatment design was validated with an OSS manager of a large OSS oriented software-intensive firm. Based on the output from the first interview, some factors in the original prototype was reordered and made clearer. E.g., the engagement and revealing strategies, originally elicited from Dahlander and Magnusson [10] was made more explicit, while the ecosystem stakeholder analysis and identification was abstracted as a general input to all levels. For the framework, see Fig. 1.

3   Structure of the Framework

In this section we present the structure of the framework. As illustrated in Fig. 1, it consists of six levels: Business Criticality, Product Criticality, Engagement Strategy, Revealing Strategy, Focus Areas, and Contribution Drivers. These levels are used to frame and explain how the firm engages or should engage with a specific OSS ecosystem. Business and Product Criticality represents the role and importance of the OSS project and its ecosystem in relation to the firm's internal business requirements and product planning. Engagement and Revealing Strategy represents the way in to the firm interacts and contributes to OSS project and its ecosystem. Focus areas is used to separate between parts of an OSS project which are valued differently in terms of previous framework levels. Contributions Drivers are what motivate what, when and to whom a software artifact should be revealed, or where resources should be invested and to what extent, i.e., contribution management. The framework presents a list of possible drivers, but not all may be relevant or even listed. These should be identified and be in alignment with previous framework levels. As input to all framework levels, the firm should perform stakeholder identification and analysis on the OSS ecosystem. The output from the framework (i.e., how an OSS project is viewed in terms of Business and Product Criticality, what strategies are used, and what drivers that are relevant for which focus areas) may differ with time and should be in alignment with the firm's internal product planning, why it can be divided into different time horizons (e.g., Strategic, Tactical, and Operational). Below we present the each part of the framework in more detail.

Time Horizons: To capture the short to long-range views, three horizons are defined: (1) the strategic horizon which looks beyond one year, (2) the tactical horizon which looks up to one year ahead, and (3) the operational horizon which is the practice at the current point in time. The precise time intervals are to be adapted relative each firm's internal product planning [2]. The important aspect is how the engagement with the ecosystem should be adapted as time and development progresses.

Ecosystem Stakeholder Population: What stakeholders that are present and what their agendas are may affect how a firm judges the business criticality of the OSS project, to what extent the firm should engage the ecosystem, and what they choose to reveal, and when [9]. E.g., The presence of competitors may affect what is to be considered differential and not. Some stakeholders may be unknown and indirect competitors pending on their agendas [11]. Similarly, the presence of existing and potential partners may offer opportunities for closer collaborations, some of which are too specific or differential to share with the rest of the ecosystem. Knowing who are the most influential and what their interests are may hint how the OSS project's roadmap aligns with the firm's, how easy it is to affect, but also who that should be influenced to create traction in a direction favorable for the firm [7]. Additionally, it may provide an input to if the OSS ecosystem is worth engaging in the first place, and also to help monitor the general health of it [3].

Business Criticality: Refers to how the firm draws value [5] from the OSS project and its ecosystem, and how the related business requirements [6] are defined. From a business model perspective, the business criticality of the OSS may be judged based on the rationale of how it helps the firm to create, deliver, and capture value [12]. E.g., [13,14], as a direct part of the product offering through an open core or platform-extension model, as a basis for support, subscriptions and professional services, or as part of a duel-licensing model. However, it may also be the case that the value comes indirect when the OSS is used as an enabler for the firms' product offerings, e.g., as a development component or as part in the infrastructure supporting the product. It may also a combination of such direct and indirect factors. E.g., in asymmetric business models, software is made OSS to instead capture value from additional products, services and data gathering that is managed through the OSS [15]. Even though considered a difficult process [16], firms must be able to determine the strategic importance of the OSS in regard to differentiation and added value [5] in order to decide if and how much the firm should invest and interact with the ecosystem [4].

Product Criticality: Refers to how the firm uses the OSS project in their future plans and actions in regards to their product over a series of releases, i.e., how integrated the OSS project is with the product and how the internal product planning [2] needs to align with that of the OSS project. This affects what requirements need to be present in both or separately, and therefore what should be contributed or not. Further, if the firm uses a product-line approach with an underlying platform from which it creates its products, there may be an interest to contribute back to the OSS project in order to enable reuse. If they focus on developing single products and reuse more opportunistic, there may be less of a long-term perspective so less may be contributed back.

Engagement Strategy: Pending on the business and product criticality of the OSS project, the firm may need to have an influence on the development going on in the ecosystem. By actively engaging and contributing back to the ecosystem firms can increase their level of influence. Dahlander and Magnusson [17] describes three types of relationships in regards to activity and influence on the ecosystem. Firstly, symbiotic relationships imply giving back to the ecosystem and is associated with a high influence for the firm. Second, commensalistic relationships imply interacting with the ecosystem but to the required minimum, and is associated with a low influence for the firm. Finally, parasitic relationships imply no interaction or giving back to the ecosystem, and is related to no, or very limited influence. Dahlander and Magnusson [17] highlights that these are to be considered as a continuum.

Revealing Strategy: Pending on the business and product criticality, and the level of engagement, different strategies may be enforced in regards of what to reveal. E.g., by selectively revealing, differentiating parts can be kept closed while commodity parts can be made open [11,18]. Further, with licensing schemas (cf. Dual-licensing [13]), parts can be opened fully but under such circumstances that competitors cannot exploit the OSS that may hurt the focal firm [14]. Alternatively, everything may be disclosed under open and transparent conditions [13], or even closed for that matter. Different strategies may be applied to different parts of an OSS project, as well as combined.

Focus Area(s): Areas or modules of strategic importance and/or extra value to the firm. For some OSS projects, it may necessary to consider different parts or sub projects separately in regards to this framework.

Contribution Drivers: Pending on previous levels in the framework, the firm can identify which drivers that motivate what should be contributed and shared with the OSS ecosystem, and when, but also what resources should be dedicated and to what extent. Those listed in Table 1 are not to be considered exhaustive, nor all relevant per default. There may be further drivers which are specific for the focal firm and how it makes use of the OSS project and its ecosystem.

Table 1. Contribution drivers for why to contribute to an OSS project and ecosystem.

Compliancy Drivers
Parts required for compliance with licenses, patents, standards, and law.
Development Drivers
Parts that can ease future maintenance and avoid unnecessary internal patch-work
Parts that may allow for better synced release cycles
Parts that may reduce integration costs
Parts that allows for third party products and services
Parts that would benefit from external development and testing due to lack of internal resources, or a wish for increased quality and innovation
Parts necessary to maintain an absorptive and learning capacity
Parts necessary to keep a low entrance barrier for new developers
Strategic and Governance Drivers:
Parts necessary to maintain a common standard in the ecosystem and at the market
Parts that may allow for a first-mover advantage, if in the interest of the firm
Parts that may force a competitor to adapt
Parts required to maintain or reach a certain level in the ecosystem governance hierarchy
Relation and Reputation Drivers:
Parts that may add to the firm's reputation as a competitive edge
Parts necessary to maintain relationships with ecosystem participants or external partners
Parts needed to maintain an open attitude internally of firm
Parts necessary to maintain interest among ecosystem participants and attract others
Parts necessary to maintain competitive edge to other OSS ecosystems
Parts necessary to maintain legitimacy and goodwill among ecosystem participants
Parts requested by ecosystem participants and customers
Parts that may help to identify potential employees
Differential Drivers:
Parts that may enable internally differential parts
Parts that are non-differentiating for possible competitors in the ecosystem
Parts regarded as commodity

4   Discussion and Conclusions

Target audience for the framework are firms engaged in OSS ecosystems. We believe that the interaction between the firm and the framework should be managed in a workshop format. Further, as in the traditional roadmapping process [16], we believe that the participants should be cross-functional and include those concerned with the use of OSS in the firm, e.g., legal, management, marketing, product managers, project managers, community managers, and developers. In the workshop, each level of the framework should be addressed and discussed to create a unified view of the current state of practice and how it can be optimized in order for the different levels of the framework to align.

By identifying its contribution drivers, firms may understand what the alternative cost is to not contribute back to an OSS project and its ecosystem. By aligning this to their internal product planning and business requirement, we believe that they can motivate what should be contributed and not. For some firms this may be part of an improvement and maturity process in which the firm starts to understand how they should act in order to influence and draw value from the OSS project and its ecosystem. With time firms may realize how they can make use of OSS projects and their ecosystems on a general level, e.g., how to adapt business models, but also to adopt new ones.

Pending on the ecosystem's stakeholder population, there may be multiple agendas present, all of which may not align. The agendas may reveal potential competitors and partners, of which some stakeholders may hold both roles as typical in co-opetition. All these factors impact how an OSS project and its ecosystem should be used and engaged [9]. This highlights the importance for stakeholder identification and analysis processes to be in place in order to provide necessary input when working with the framework and the improvement process. By using the same framework in the analysis to profile other stakeholders, a firm may benchmark and learn more about how they can adjust their requirements scoping, e.g., in order to gain better influence in the ecosystem.

In this paper we have created an initial version of our framework based on one design cycle. The initial validation highlights the importance of stakeholder identification and analysis, the need for suggested alignment as well as for context specific contribution strategies in general.

In future work, we plan to reiterate the framework using further expert validation, and also develop an initial set of workshop guidelines for how the framework may be used in an interactive manner. After stabilization is reached in the structure of the framework, it will be piloted in a workshop format with firms engaged in OSS ecosystems. Consideration will be taken to background of experts and firms to strengthen external validity, e.g., in regards to size of development organization and usage of OSS in relation to the business model of firm, but also type of OSS project and ecosystem population. The long term goal is to create a strategic support for contribution management based on the proposed framework in this research preview. The strategic support should allow for tailored contribution strategies to be created, communicated and followed-up through the development organization. The support should further take input from continuous stakeholder identification and analysis of the concerned ecosystems. The work aims to help firms engaged in OSS ecosystems to gain the influence needed in order to impose their agenda, align their internal RE with the ecosystem's RE and to their maximize ROI.

References

1. Aurum, A., Wohlin, C.: Requirements engineering: setting the context. In: Aurum, A., Wohlin, C. (eds.) Engineering and Managing Software Requirements, pp. 1–15. Springer, Heidelberg (2005)
2. Fricker, S.A.: Software product management. In: Maedche, A., Botzenhardt, A., Neer, L. (eds.) Software for People, pp. 53–81. Springer, Heidelberg (2012)
3. Jansen, S., Brinkkemper, S., Finkelstein, A.: Business network management as a survival strategy: a tale of two software ecosystems. In: Proccedings of the 1st International Workshop on Software Ecosystems, pp. 34–48 (2009)
4. Wnuk, K., Pfahl, D., Callele, D., Karlsson, E.-A.: How can open source software development help requirements management gain the potential of open innovation: an exploratory study. In: Proceedings of the ACM-IEEE International Symposium on Empirical Software Engineering and Measurement, pp. 271–280. ACM (2012)
5. Aurum, A., Wohlin, C.: A value-based approach in requirements engineering: explaining some of the fundamental concepts. In: Sawyer, P., Paech, B., Heymans, P. (eds.) REFSQ 2007. LNCS, vol. 4542, pp. 109–115. Springer, Heidelberg (2007). doi:10.1007/978-3-540-73031-6_8
6. Wiegers, K., Beatty, J.: Software Requirements. Pearson Education, Upper Saddle River (2013)
7. Linåker, J., Rempel, P., Regnell, B., Mäder, P.: How firms adapt and interact in open source ecosystems: analyzing stakeholder influence and collaboration patterns. In: Daneva, M., Pastor, O. (eds.) REFSQ 2016. LNCS, vol. 9619, pp. 63–81. Springer, Heidelberg (2016). doi:10.1007/978-3-319-30282-9_5
8. Wieringa, R.J.: Design Science Methodology for Information Systems and Software Engineering. Springer, Heidelberg (2014)
9. Munir, H., Wnuk, K., Runeson, P.: Open innovation in software engineering: a systematic mapping study. Empir. Softw. Eng. $21(2)$, 1–40 (2015)
10. Dahlander, L., Magnusson, M.: How do firms make use of open source communities? Long Range Plan. $41(6)$, 629–649 (2008)
11. Van der Linden, F., Lundell, B., Marttiin, P.: Commodification of industrial software: a case for open source. IEEE Softw. $26(4)$, 77–83 (2009)
12. Osterwalder, A., Pigneur, Y.: Business Model Generation: A Handbook for Visionaries, Game Changers, and Challengers. Wiley, Hoboken (2010)
13. Chesbrough, H.W., Appleyard, M.M.: Open innovation and strategy. Calif. Manage. Rev. $50(1)$, 57–76 (2007)
14. West, J.: How open is open enough? Melding proprietary and open source platform strategies. Res. policy $32(7)$, 1259–1285 (2003)
15. Schuermans, S., Constantinou, A., Vakulenko, M.: Assymetric business models: the secret weapon of software-driven companies (2014)
16. Komssi, M., Kauppinen, M., Töhönen, H., Lehtola, L., Davis, A.M.: Roadmapping problems in practice: value creation from the perspective of the customers. Requir. Eng. $20(1)$, 45–69 (2015)
17. Dahlander, L., Magnusson, M.G.: Relationships between open source software companies and communities: observations from nordic firms. Res. Policy $34(4)$, 481–493 (2005)
18. Henkel, J.: Selective revealing in open innovation processes: the case of embedded linux. Res. Policy $35(7)$, 953–969 (2006)

Human Factors in Requirements Engineering

Defect Prevention in Requirements Using Human Error Information: An Empirical Study

Wenhua Hu[1], Jeffrey C. Carver[1(⊠)], Vaibhav Anu[2],
Gursimran Walia[2], and Gary Bradshaw[3]

[1] University of Alabama, Tuscaloosa, AL, USA
`carver@cs.ua.edu`
[2] North Dakota State University, Fargo, ND, USA
[3] Mississippi State University, Starkville, MS, USA

Abstract. *Context and Motivation*: The correctness of software requirements is of critical importance to the success of a software project. Problems that occur during requirements collection and specification, if not fixed early, are costly to fix later. Therefore, it is important to develop approaches that help requirement engineers not only detect, but also prevent requirements problems. Because requirements engineering is a human-centric activity, we can build upon developments from the field of human cognition. *Question/Problem*: Human Errors are the failings of human cognition during the process of solving, planning, or executing a task. We have employed research about Human Errors to describe the types of problems that occur during requirements engineering. The goal of this paper is to determine whether knowledge of Human Errors can serve as a fault prevention mechanism during requirements engineering. *Principal ideas/results*: The results of our study show that a better understanding of human errors does lead developers to insert fewer problems into their own requirements documents. Our results also indicate that different types of Human Error information have different impacts on fault prevention. *Contribution*: In this paper, we show that the use of Human Error information from Cognitive Psychology is useful for fault prevention during requirements engineering.

Keywords: Human errors · Software requirements · Fault prevention · Empirical study · Human factors

1 Introduction

The quality of software products largely depends on the quality of the underlying requirements. Prior research has shown the importance of producing correct requirements because requirement faults are more expensive to fix later [8], are among the most severe kinds of faults [6], and cause the majority of software failures [13]. Due to the large expense to find and fix faults after they occur, it is crucial to develop effective defect prevention methods.

The software development process, especially during the requirement phase, is a human-centric activity. As humans are fallible, the potential for error is high.

© Springer International Publishing AG 2017
P. Grünbacher and A. Perini (Eds.): REFSQ 2017, LNCS 10153, pp. 61–76, 2017.
DOI: 10.1007/978-3-319-54045-0_5

As defined by IEEE Standard 24765 [1], an *error* is the failing of human cognition in the process of problem solving, planning, or execution. These cognitive failures can then lead to various types of requirements faults. Cognitive psychologists have long studied these cognitive failures and referred to these cognitive failures as the term *human errors*. By understanding how the human mental process can fail in various situations, *human error* research has been able to support error prevention in fields ranging from medicine to aviation.

Of all the software engineering phases, the requirements engineering phase may be the most human-centric. Therefore the ability to understand and prevent human errors that occur during requirements engineering can be especially beneficial to software projects. To make this human error information tractable, human error researchers develop taxonomies to classify the specific types of errors that occur in each domain. While the underlying theoretical basis is similar across domains, the specific types of errors differ. In our own previous work, we have developed two taxonomies of requirement errors, using different approaches: The Requirement Error Taxonomy (RET) [25] and the Human Error Taxonomy (HET) [15]. Section 2.3 provides more details on these taxonomies)

Because human errors occur while eliciting and formalizing requirements, we anticipate that as requirement engineers better understand specific types of errors, the less likely they will be to make those errors, resulting in higher-quality requirements. Therefore, the goal of this research is to *evaluate whether an understanding of Human Error reduces the likelihood of making errors and the resulting faults during the requirements engineering process.*

The primary contribution of this paper are (1) evaluation of whether the knowledge of error information prevents developers from injecting related errors and faults into a requirements document, (2) comparison the performance of RET and HET in providing guidelines for developers in developing requirements document, and (3) an analysis of contribution of the specific error types in RET and HET in preventing errors and faults.

The remainder of this paper is organized as follows. Section 2 describes related work. Section 3 provides a description of the study conducted to evaluate the utility of error information in preventing errors and faults. Section 4 describes the analysis and results of this study. Section 5 discusses the threats to validity of this study, followed by a brief conclusion of this paper and ideas for future studies in Sect. 6.

2   Background

This section provides background information on topics relevant to our study. Section 2.1 describes previous research about fault prevention. Section 2.2 briefly describes research related to human error. Section 2.3 briefly describes the two kinds of error taxonomies (RET and HET) that we have developed.

2.1   Fault Prevention Techniques

The fault prevention process uses information about the types of problems that are likely to occur (often using historical data, a sample of faults, or expert opinion) to prevent those problems from occurring in the future. Defect prevention methods utilize the fault injection rate in software development processes and provide specific strategies to prevent related faults [12]. Furthermore, training and mentoring can also result in dramatic reductions of fault rates (close to 50%) [4]. There are three types of fault prevention measurement recently applied:

- **Quality improvement techniques** – These techniques, that have seen widespread success [5,10,14,19], focus developers attention on different type of faults (e.g., missing or incorrect functionality) recorded in software artifacts. Because they only deal with the fault itself, these techniques cannot help inspectors understand underlying errors (i.e., source of faults) and prevent the occurrence of these errors.
- **Prevention of faults via process improvement** – These methods focus on determining the causes for commonly identified faults. Examples include:
  - *fault causal analysis* [4] - uses a sample of faults to determine their causes and prevent future faults. An empirical study found that most of the causes of software faults were due to people-related factors;
  - *software failure analysis* [11] - improves the development and maintenance process by analyzing a representative sample of faults to understand the causes of particular classes of faults;
  - *fault prevention process* [20] - determines the source of a fault and suggests preventive actions by classifying faults causes as oversight (e.g., developer overlooked something, or something was not considered thoroughly), education (developer did not understand some aspect), or transcription (developer knew what to do but simply made a mistake).
  - *root cause analysis* [18] - uses a multi-dimensional fault trigger concept to help developers determine the root cause of a fault and help them identify improvement area.
- **Error abstraction approach** – Lanubile et al. proposed the process of analyzing a group of related faults to determine the errors that lead their occurrence [17]. Based on this approach, several fault prevention techniques have been proposed, including: the fault distribution method [21], fault based process improvement (DBPI) technique [16], and fault prevention-based process improvement (DPPI) method [23]. However, these methods lack formal error information to provide guidelines for developers to use. They can only prevent the errors that have been identified, but cannot provide the type of information that developers need to learn from those errors.

While all these methods use some representative faults/problem reports to analyze the root cause, they lack an underlying cognitive theory of how people make errors. Therefore, there was a need to develop more formal taxonomies, like the RET and HET, to address this shortcoming.

2.2 Human Error Research

Human error research focuses on understanding how the psychological processes go awry. For example, choosing an incorrect solution, forgetting to perform a task, or accidentally performing an incorrect task. The process of analyzing human error in a particular domain includes collecting information, finding common failure patterns, and interpreting those patterns in light of the limitations of human information processing facilities and known error patterns. This type of understanding can provide insight into how to prevent similar errors from happening in the future. This approach has been used successfully to improve aviation [26] and medicine [9].

2.3   Error Taxonomies

To make the error information described above useful, researchers classify the errors into taxonomies. A taxonomy provides a logical, hierarchical organization of the error information. Without such an organization, developers will find it difficult to successfully use the information about errors to have a practical impact on their work. Earlier work on using error information to improve software quality [7,17,18] provided developers with ways to use the sources of faults (i.e. errors) to improve software quality. While this work provided a significant step forward, the main weakness was the lack of a formal error taxonomy. To improve upon these methods, we employed two different approaches to create taxonomies of human errors that occur in the requirements phase. The remainder of this section explains each taxonomy in more detail.

Requirement Error Taxonomy (RET). To develop the first taxonomy, we performed a systematic literature review (SLR) to identify and classify requirement errors that were described in the software engineering and cognitive psychology literatures. We developed this taxonomy strictly from the software engineering perspective without input from a human error expert. Therefore, we built it bottom-up, based primarily on the errors identified in the literature, without using a formal human error theory as a driver. Figure 1 provides an overview of the taxonomy, which includes 14 detailed error classes grouped into three high-level error types. The three high-level error types are: *People Errors* (arise from fallibilities of the people involved in the development process), *Process Errors* (arise while selecting the appropriate processes for achieving the desired goals and relate mostly to the inadequacy of the requirements engineering process), and *Documentation Errors* (arise from mistakes in organizing and specifying the requirements) [25]. Initial evaluation of the RET demonstrated that finding more errors during a training exercise resulted in fewer errors during requirements creation [24], suggesting that error information can be helpful for prevention.

Human Error Taxonomy (HET). To more closely tie our work to the concept of human error, we collaborated with a human error expert to develop a new taxonomy. We again performed an SLR to identify specific requirement engineering human errors reported in the literature. But, this time, we classified those detailed errors into a predefined set of high-level error types drawn from human error research [22] (see Fig. 2). Those three high-level error types are:

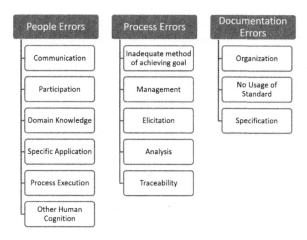

Fig. 1. Requirement Error Taxonomy

Slips (someone carries out a planned task incorrectly or in the wrong sequence), *Lapses* (memory related failures; they occur when someone forgets a goal in the middle of a sequence of actions or omits a step in a routine sequence), and *Mistakes* (planning errors in that someone designed an incorrect plan to achieve the desired goal). The details of the HET are beyond this paper, but have been described elsewhere [2,15].

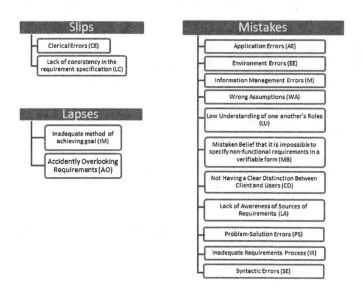

Fig. 2. Human Error Taxonomy

We have conducted a feasibility study to validate the effectiveness of HET for detecting human errors and faults, but not for prevention [15]. The results of this study showed that the use of the HET allowed developers to identify errors in requirements documents and to find additional faults during a reinspection guided by knowledge of the existing errors. Thus, in this study, we plan to evaluate the usefulness of HET in preventing human errors.

3   Experiment Design

The goal of this study is *to evaluate whether an understanding of Human Error helps prevent faults during requirements creation.* The following subsections describe the research questions, the participants, and study procedures.

3.1   Research Hypotheses

To address the overall study goal, we investigate three specific hypotheses. These hypotheses move from human errors in general to more specific aspects of human error. Figure 3 provides an overview of the relationship among the hypotheses.

First, our previous work indicated that knowledge of requirement errors can help in fault prevention (see Sect. 2) [24]. In this study we employ two different methods for understanding requirement errors (the RET and the HET). Based on previous work that the information could be useful, our first hypothesis is:

H1 - The better a developer understands human errors the less likely he/she will be to inject errors and faults into a requirements document

Second, because we built the HET on a stronger cognitive theory of human errors (compared with the RET), it should provide more help with regard to preventing errors and faults. Therefore, our second hypothesis is:

H2 - Knowledge of the HET will provide more benefit for error/fault prevention than knowledge of the RET

Finally, the RET and the HET each have three high-level error types that represent different types of human errors. We anticipate that the better a developer understand each type, the fewer of that type of error he or she will make. Therefore, our third hypothesis is:

H3 - The better a developer understands each error type, the less likely he/she will be to insert errors/faults related to that type into a requirements document

3.2   Variables

For each hypothesis, this section describes the Independent and Dependent variables. Section 4 defines how each variable is measured.

H1   **H2**   **H3**

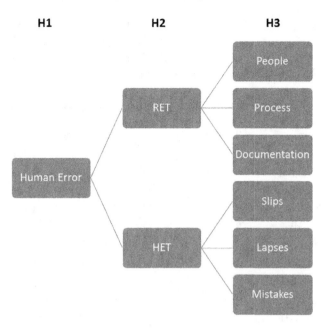

Fig. 3. Research questions

– H1
  - Independent Variables
    Ability to classify errors
    Ability to use error information to find new faults
  - Dependent Variable
    Likelihood of injecting new faults
– H2
  - Independent Variable
    Knowledge of error taxonomy (HET or RET)
  - Dependent Variables
    Number of faults injected into SRS
    Number of errors injected into SRS
– H3
  - Independent Variable
    Level of understanding of each error type in the HET or RET
  - Dependent Variable
    Number of each error type injected into SRS

3.3   Participants

The study included 31 senior-level undergraduate computer science enrolled in the Spring 2016 capstone course at the University of Alabama. In this course, students worked in teams to iterate through the software lifecycle and build a software system. The course instructor, independent of the research team, divided the participants into ten 3- or 4-person teams. To address H2, we randomly assigned each team to either the RET group (control) or the HET group (experimental). Table 1 illustrates the assignment of participant teams to groups.

Table 1. Assignment of participant teams to groups

System	Team members	Pages	Requirements	Group
Color coord	3	13	22	HET
GesConnect	3	17	12	HET
PlayMaker	3	31	25	HET
PoliceVideo	3	15	5	HET
Harmedia	3	11	8	HET
CalPal	3	20	14	RET
Coupon Catcher	4	11	11	RET
EnterntainMe	3	17	20	RET
WhatsKitchen	3	14	12	RET
MansBestFriend	3	11	7	RET

3.4 Experiment Procedure

Figure 4 provides an overview of the study procedure, which included one training session and five experimental steps.

RET or HET Training: We held two training sessions, one for the members of the RET group and one for members of the HET group. In each of these 90-minute sessions, we trained participants on requirements inspections, fault detection, fault classes, and on how to use either the RET or HET (depending upon their group) to abstract and classify requirement errors from faults. We explained the error abstraction process in detail along with the RET or HET error classes. Finally, we trained the participants on how to use the abstracted errors to guide the reinspection of a requirement document.

Step 1 – Error Abstraction and Classification: This step served as a pretest to measure how well the participants understood human errors based on their ability to correctly abstract faults into errors and classify those errors. We gave the participants the SRS for the Parking Garage Control System (PGCS), which has been used in a number of studies. We also gave the participants a list of 10 of the 35 faults seeded in the PGCS SRS document. We chose these faults because they were used in a previous study and represent a cross-section of the error classes [3]. The participants used their knowledge from the RET or HET Training to abstract the faults into errors and classify those errors, into the respective taxonomies. Each participant performed this task independently. The output of this step was 31 **PGCS Error Forms** (15 from subjects who use the HET and 16 from subjects who used the RET).

Step 2 – Error-Based Inspection of PGCS: This step served as a second pretest to measure how well the participants understood human errors based on their ability to use error information to find additional requirement faults. Using the errors identified in Step 1 and their knowledge of the RET or HET, the participants individually inspected the PGCS SRS to identify any additional faults. If the participant identified a fault that was not related to one of the errors from Step 1, he/she abstracted that fault into its underlying error, added that error **PGCS Error Form**, and used that error to identify additional related faults. The output of this step was 31 **PGCS Fault Forms** (one per subject).

Step 3 – Development of SRS: In this step each team developed the SRS for their own respective systems.

Step 4 – Inspection of SRS: Participants individually used the RET or HET to inspect the SRSs developed by two other teams, one from the RET group and one from the HET group. The output of this step was 62 **Individual SRS Fault Forms** (one per subject).

Step 5 – Consolidate Fault Lists and Abstract Errors: Each team consolidated the results from Step 4 into one comprehensive fault list. The team used either the RET or HET to abstract those faults into the underlying errors. The output of this step was 10 **Final Team Fault and Error Forms** (one per team).

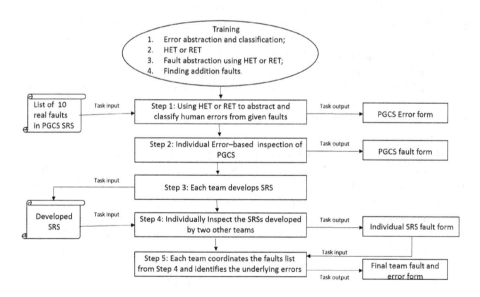

Fig. 4. Experiment procedure

4   Results and Analysis

This section provides a detailed analysis of the data collected during the study organized around the hypotheses posed in Sect. 3.1.

4.1   H1 - The Better a Developer Understands Human Errors the Less Likely He/she Will Be to Inject Errors and Faults into a Requirements Document

To test this hypothesis, we measured **understanding** in two ways: (1) *ability to classify errors* - how accurately participants abstracted faults into errors and classified those errors (Step 1) and (2) *ability to use error information to find new faults* - how effective the participants were at identifying additional faults based on the identified errors (Step 2). We measured **likelihood of injecting errors and faults** as the number faults in each SRS found by inspection (Step 4) and abstracted to errors by the teams (Step 5).

Effect of Correctly Abstracting and Classifying Errors (Step 1). Because the participants performed Step 1 independently but the SRSs were developed as a team, we computed the level of understanding for a team as the average of level of understanding of the team members. Figure 5 plots the average percentage of errors correctly abstracted and classified in Step 1, by each team, against the number of unique errors and faults found during inspection (Step 4) and abstracted to errors (Step 5), for that team's SRS. Figure 5 also shows the results of the linear regression analysis between these pairs of variables. For this analysis, and the remainder in the paper, we used one-tailed significance tests because our hypotheses were for a negative correlation. The results of the linear regressions show a very slight, non-significant correlation in both cases. These results suggest that overall, a developer's ability to correctly abstract faults to errors and classify those errors does not seem to have an impact on the number of faults or errors he/she injects into his/her own SRS document.

Effect of Finding Additional Faults (Step 2). For this analysis, we computed each team's level of understanding by counting the total number of unique faults identified by the team members during Step 2. Figure 6 plots that number against the number of unique faults found during inspection (Step 4) and abstracted to errors (Step 5) for the SRS developed by the team. Figure 6 also shows the results of the regression analysis between each pair of variables. In this case, both linear regression analyses show a strong, significant, negative correlation.

These results suggest that overall, a developer's increased ability to use error information (regardless whether it was learned in the context of the HET or the RET) to find faults during an error-based inspection is related to a decrease in the number of faults and errors he/she injects into his/her own SRS document. Yet, as shown in Fig. 5, the ability to correctly abstract faults to errors and classify those errors does not seem to have an impact on the number of faults and errors injected into the requirements.

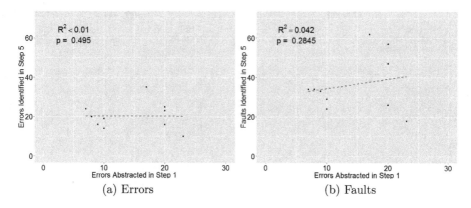

Fig. 5. Comparison between correctly abstracted errors in Step 1 and the number of faults/errors found in Step 5

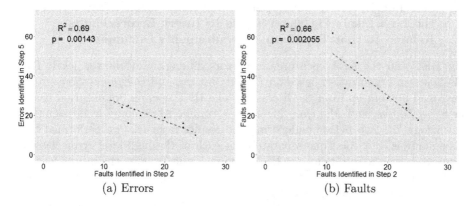

Fig. 6. Comparison between number of faults identified in Step 2 test and the number of faults/errors found in Step 5

4.2 H2: Knowledge of the HET Will Provide More Benefit for Error/Fault Prevention Than Knowledge of the RET

Based on the results of H1, performance on the error-based inspection (Step 2) has a significant, negative correlation with the number of errors/faults inserted into the SRS. To compare the performance of the RET and the HET, we analyzed each approach separately. Figure 7 shows the results for each error taxonomy, along with the linear regression analysis. While teams in both groups exhibit a strong, negative correlation, the correlation for the HET teams is stronger. These results suggest that knowledge of the HET, which is based more closely on the concepts of human error, is more beneficial than knowledge of the RET.

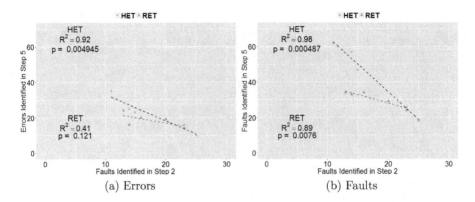

Fig. 7. Comparison of faults identified in Step 2 and faults/errors identified in Step 5, separated by error taxonomy (HET and RET)

4.3   H3: The Better a Developer Understands Each Error Type, the Less Likely He/she Will Be to Insert Errors/Faults Related to that Type into a Requirements Document

The HET and the RET each organize errors differently at the top level. The RET uses an organization based on *People*, *Process*, and *Documentation* errors, developed bottom-up from the literature. The HET uses an organization based on *Slips*, *Lapses*, and *Mistakes*, based on a common taxonomy from cognitive psychology [22]. To better understand the results from H2, we performed the same analysis, but this time separately for each of the high-level error classes. Figure 8 shows the results for the HET groups. Figure 9 shows the results for the RET groups. As before, the figures show the results of the regression analyses performed between the pairs of variables.

We can make a few observations about these results. First, for the HET, *Slips* and *Mistakes* both showed a significant negative correlation. This results is consistent with our previous studies [15]. Our previous work also found that *Mistake* is the most common error type. Therefore, if this approach is able to help prevent those errors, it can be quite beneficial. Second, for the RET, the only error type that showed a strong, significant, negative correlation was *People* errors. Based on the results from H2 (that HET is more helpful than RET), this result is not surprising. When comparing the RET to the HET, the *People* error type contains errors that are most similar to those contained in the HET.

5   Threats to Validity

This section describes the primary threats, along with the steps taken to mitigate them where possible.

Internal Validity. First, even though we have no evidence to the contrary, we have no way of ensuring that the participants followed the specified HET or RET

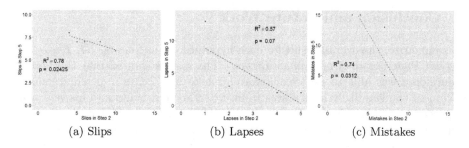

(a) Slips (b) Lapses (c) Mistakes

Fig. 8. HET error details

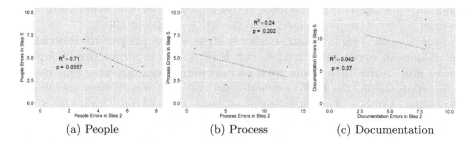

(a) People (b) Process (c) Documentation

Fig. 9. RET error details

processes. Therefore, this threat is minimal. In Step 4, we did have participants inspect the SRS documents from two other groups. Second, it is possible that by the second inspection they became fatigued and did not perform as well. To mitigate this threat, we gave them enough time to perform both inspections.

External Validity. The study participants were undergraduate students. Therefore, the results are not directly applicable in an industrial context. Even so, the students were building a real system, so the activities performed in this study did have relevance to the projects. We will need additional studies to understand how these results apply in industry.

Construct Validity. First, we defined *understanding of human error* in two ways in Sect. 4.1. Based on our study design, these definitions seemed to be the most appropriate. It is possible that other definitions would have provided different results. Second, because the students were building their own systems (rather than using systems with seeded faults/errors) we do not know the total number of errors made during SRS development. Our conclusions are based only on the errors that reviewers identified in Step 4. Third, the students were working on different projects and it is hard to compare the results.

6   Conclusion and Future Work

To summarize, the overall result for each hypothesis is as follows. *H1: Impact of Overall Understanding of Human Errors* - The results showed that the better a developer was able to use error information to find faults in a requirements document the less likely he/she was to insert errors and faults into his/her own requirements document. *H2: Comparison of HET and RET* - The results showed that learning either taxonomy helped the developers insert fewer faults and errors into their requirements documents, those who learned the HET saw a stronger effect than those who learned the RET. *H3: Details of the HET and RET* - The results here showed that (1) for the RET, the high-level error type most closely associated with human errors, *People Errors* was the only one that showed a significant effect; and (2) for the HET, two of the high-level error types, including the most common one of *Mistakes*, also showed a significant effect.

Therefore, the overall finding of this study is that **a proper understanding of human error information can lead a developer to insert fewer errors and faults into their own requirements documents**. This result is important due to the large cost and delay associate with finding and fixing requirements errors and faults, especially at later stages of the software lifecycle. This observation is important for developers and researchers who are interested in understanding how to improve the quality of their software by reducing the number of problems that occur early in the software lifecycle.

The primary contribution of this paper are (1) conclusions about the type of human error knowledge that helps prevent errors and faults during software development, (2) evidence that a taxonomy based directly on human error information (the HET) is more effective in fault prevention, and (3) insight into how the specific error types in each taxonomy contribute to the overall result.

Our future work includes plans to address some limitations of this study. First, we are in the process of conducting surveys and interviews with industrial professionals to gain a deeper understanding of how human error information impacts practice. By doing this study, we hope to ensure that the results from this study are applicable in practice and to evolve our approach based on the findings. Ultimately, our goal is to have a validated error prevention approach that is effective for industrial practice.

Acknowledgments. This work was supported by NSF awards 1421006 and 1423279.

References

1. Systems and software engineering – vocabulary. ISO/IEC/IEEE 24765:2010(E), pp. 1–418, December 2010
2. Anu, V., Hu, W., Carver, J.C., Walia, G.S., Bradshaw, G.: Development of a human error taxonomy for software requirements: a systematic literature review. Technical report NDSU-CS-TR-16-001, North Dakota State University (2016). http://vaibhavanu.com/NDSU-CS/TR-16-001.pdf

3. Anu, V.K., Wali, G.S., Hu, W., Carver, J.C., Bradshaw, G.: Effectiveness of human error taxonomy during requirements inspection: an empirical investigation. In: 2016 International Conference on Software Engineering and Knowledge Engineering, pp. 531–536 (2016)

4. Card, D.N.: Learning from our mistakes with defect causal analysis. IEEE Softw. **15**(1), 56–63 (1998)

5. Carver, J., Nagappan, N., Page, A.: The impact of educational background on the effectiveness of requirements inspections: an empirical study. IEEE Trans. Softw. Eng. **34**(6), 800–812 (2008)

6. Chen, J.C., Huang, S.J.: An empirical analysis of the impact of software development problem factors on software maintainability. J. Syst. Softw. **82**(6), 981–992 (2009)

7. Chillarege, R., Bhandari, I.S., Chaar, J.K., Halliday, M.J., Moebus, D.S., Ray, B.K., Wong, M.Y.: Orthogonal defect classification-a concept for in-process measurements. IEEE Trans. Softw. Eng. **18**(11), 943–956 (1992)

8. Dethomas, A.: Technology requirements of integrated, critical digital flight systems. In: Guidance, Navigation and Control Conference, p. 2602 (1987)

9. Diller, T., Helmrich, G., Dunning, S., Cox, S., Buchanan, A., Shappell, S.: The human factors analysis classification system (HFACS) applied to health care. Am. J. Med. Qual. **29**(3), 1062860613491623 (2013)

10. Freimut, B., Denger, C., Ketterer, M.: An industrial case study of implementing and validating defect classification for process improvement and quality management. In: 11th IEEE International Software Metrics Symposium, 10 p. IEEE (2005)

11. Grady, R.B.: Software failure analysis for high-return process improvement decisions. Hewlett Packard J. **47**, 15–24 (1996)

12. Graham, M.: Software defect prevention using orthogonal defect prevention (2005)

13. Hamill, M., Goseva-Popstojanova, K.: Common trends in software fault and failure data. IEEE Trans. Softw. Eng. **35**(4), 484–496 (2009)

14. Hayes, J.H.: Building a requirement fault taxonomy: experiences from a nasa verification and validation research project. In: 14th International Symposium on Software Reliability Engineering, pp. 49–59. IEEE (2003)

15. Hu, W., Carver, J.C., Anu, V., Walia, G., Bradshaw, G.: Detection of requirement errors and faults via a human error taxonomy: a feasibility study. In: 10th International Symposium on Empirical Software Engineering and Measurement (2016)

16. Kumaresh, S., Baskaran, R.: Experimental design on defect analysis in software process improvement. In: 2012 International Conference on Recent Advances in Computing and Software Systems (RACSS), pp. 293–298. IEEE (2012)

17. Lanubile, F., Shull, F., Basili, V.R.: Experimenting with error abstraction in requirements documents. In: Proceedings of the Fifth International Software Metrics Symposium, Metrics 1998, pp. 114–121. IEEE (1998)

18. Leszak, M., Perry, D.E., Stoll, D.: A case study in root cause defect analysis. In: Proceedings of the 22nd International Conference on Software Engineering, pp. 428–437. ACM (2000)

19. Masuck, C.: Incorporating a fault categorization and analysis process in the software build cycle. J. Comput. Sci. Coll. **20**(5), 239–248 (2005)

20. Mays, R.G., Jones, C.L., Holloway, G.J., Studinski, D.P.: Experiences with defect prevention. IBM Syst. J. **29**(1), 4–32 (1990)

21. Pooley, R., Senior, D., Christie, D.: Collecting and analyzing Web-based project metrics. IEEE Softw. **19**(1), 52 (2002)

22. Reason, J.: Human Error. Cambridge University Press, New York (1990)

23. Terzakis, J.: Reducing requirements defect density by using mentoring to supplement training. Int. Adv. Intell. Sys. **6**(1 & 2), 102–111 (2013)
24. Walia, G.S., Carver, J.C.: Using error abstraction and classification to improve requirement quality: conclusions from a family of four empirical studies. Empir. Softw. Eng. **18**(4), 625–658 (2013)
25. Walia, G.S., Carver, J.C.: A systematic literature review to identify and classify software requirement errors. Inf. Softw. Technol. **51**(7), 1087–1109 (2009)
26. Wiegmann, D., Faaborg, T., Boquet, A., Detwiler, C., Holcomb, K., Shappell, S.: Human error and general aviation accidents: a comprehensive, fine-grained analysis using HFACS. Technical report, DTIC Document (2005)

Requirements Quality Assurance in Industry: Why, What and How?

Michael Unterkalmsteiner[(✉)] and Tony Gorschek

Software Engineering Research Lab Sweden,
Blekinge Institute of Technology, Karlskrona, Sweden
{mun,tgo}@bth.se

Abstract. *Context and Motivation:* Natural language is the most common form to specify requirements in industry. The quality of the specification depends on the capability of the writer to formulate requirements aimed at different stakeholders: they are an expression of the customer's needs that are used by analysts, designers and testers. Given this central role of requirements as a mean to communicate intention, assuring their quality is essential to reduce misunderstandings that lead to potential waste. *Problem:* Quality assurance of requirement specifications is largely a manual effort that requires expertise and domain knowledge. However, this demanding cognitive process is also congested by trivial quality issues that should not occur in the first place. *Principal ideas:* We propose a taxonomy of requirements quality assurance complexity that characterizes cognitive load of verifying a quality aspect from the human perspective, and automation complexity and accuracy from the machine perspective. *Contribution:* Once this taxonomy is realized and validated, it can serve as the basis for a decision framework of automated requirements quality assurance support.

Keywords: Requirements engineering · Requirements quality · Natural language processing · Decision support

1 Introduction

The requirements engineering process and the artefacts used in coordination and communication activities influence the performance of downstream development activities [6]. While research has proposed myriads of formal, semi-formal and informal methods to convey requirements, plain natural language (NL) is the *lingua franca* for specifying requirements in industry [14,17]. One potential reason is that NL specifications are easy to comprehend without particular training [3]. However, NL is also inherently imprecise and ambiguous, posing challenges in objectively validating that requirements expressed in NL represent the customers' needs [1]. Therefore it is common practice to perform some sort of review or inspection [14] to quality assure NL requirements specifications. While there exists a plethora of methods to improve requirements specifications [15], there are no guidelines that would support practitioners in deciding

© Springer International Publishing AG 2017
P. Grünbacher and A. Perini (Eds.): REFSQ 2017, LNCS 10153, pp. 77–84, 2017.
DOI: 10.1007/978-3-319-54045-0_6

which method(s) to adopt for their particular need. We think that a first step to such a decision framework is to characterize the means by which quality attributes in requirements specifications can be affected. Therefore, we initiated an applied research collaboration with the Swedish Transport Administration (STA), the government agency responsible for the rail, road, shipping and aviation infrastructure in Sweden. STA's overall goal is to improve the communication and coordination with their suppliers, mostly handled through NL requirements specifications. Infrastructure projects vary in duration (months to decades) and budget (up to 4 Billion USD), requiring an adaptive quality assurance strategy that is backed by methods adapted to the needs of the particular project. The large number of requirements (several thousands) and the need to communicate them to various suppliers makes specifications in NL the only viable choice. Still, STA needs to quality assure the requirements and decide what level of quality is acceptable. In this paper we present the basic components for a taxonomy that will drive, once the research is completed, a requirements quality assurance decision support framework. To this end, we illustrate a research outline aimed at answering our overall research question: **How can we support practitioners in achieving "good-enough" requirements specification quality?**

2   Related Work

Davis et al. [7] proposed a comprehensive set of 24 attributes that contribute to software requirements specification (SRS) quality. Saavedra et al. [16] compared this set with later contributions that studied means to evaluate these attributes. Similarly, Pekar et al. [15] reviewed the literature and identified 36 studies proposing techniques to improve SRS quality. While Agile software development is notorious for promoting as little documentation as possible [10], Heck and Zaidman [13] identified 28 quality criteria used for Agile requirements, six of them being novel and specifically defined for Agile requirements. All these reviews point to relevant related work potentially contributing to the components of a decision support framework for requirements quality assurance. The importance of providing decision support to practitioners is growing hand-in-hand with the complexity of today's developed software products and the available number of technologies to realize them [12]. To the best of our knowledge, no framework exists to support the selection of requirements quality assurance techniques.

3   Characterizing Requirements Quality Assurance

The purpose of this taxonomy is to characterize the components that are involved in the process to achieve a particular requirements quality (RQ) level (Fig. 1). This systematization then allows to take informed decisions about effort and potential impact for RQ improvement.

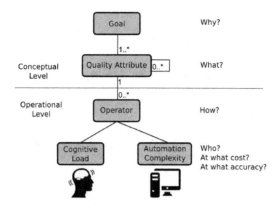

Fig. 1. Requirements quality assurance taxonomy

A *goal* determines what the improvement of RQ should achieve. Typical goals could be to improve the communication between stakeholders, to improve the ability to verify the product, or better cost estimates. Different goals can also contradict each other. Goals are important as they provide a scope that limits the potential actions on the operational level to a set that is economically acceptable - this enables focus of efforts to assure certain quality aspects within the given opportunities of the resources afforded.

Quality attributes describe the favourable properties of a requirement. For example, unambiguity is commonly defined as the quality of a statement being interpretable in a unique way. Quality attributes for requirements have been described in numerous quality models, reviewed by Saavedra et al. [16]. Quality attributes are not independent, i.e. one attribute can positively or negatively influence another. Figure 2 provides an overview of RQ attributes and their relationships to each other. For example, atomicity positively influences design independence, traceability and precision of a requirement, as indicated by the (+) in Fig. 2. On the other hand, unambiguous requirements, often achieved by higher formality, are generally also less understandable.

Goals and quality attributes build the *conceptual level* of the taxonomy. They can help to answer questions pertaining to why an improvement of RQ is necessary, and what quality attributes are associated with that goal. Taking the example from earlier, improving the ability to verify the product based on the stated requirements, one can see in Fig. 2 that many quality attributes influence requirements verifiability. Depending on constraints in the operational level, discussed next, one can decide how to reach the stated goal by choosing a set of quality attributes, which in turn are associated with operators.

Operator is the generic term we use for instruments that tangibly characterize quality attributes. An operator provides a definition of how a requirement is analysed w.r.t. the associated quality attribute. Examples of operators are metrics [8,11], requirement smells [9] or rules and constraints on how to formulate requirements. An operator can be implemented by either a person or a computer program (or both). In either case, we want to characterize the operator

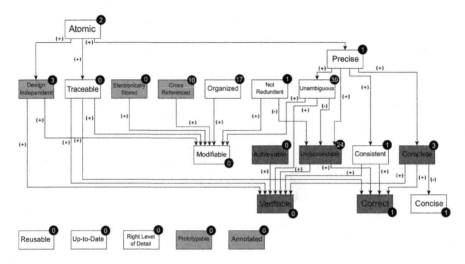

Fig. 2. Quality attributes and their relationships (adapted from Saavedra et al. [16]; color coding and numbers are our addition, and used and explained in Sect. 4)

by some notion of cost and accuracy, providing input for the decision on how and whether at all to realize the operator. We borrow the concept of *cognitive load* from the field of instruction design where cognitive load theory [18] is used to describe and improve learning efficiency. Each operator is associated with a level of intrinsic cognitive load, describing the complexity of applying the operator on a single requirement or a complete specification. For example, if the operator is the ambiguous adverbs requirements smell [9], then the intrinsic cognitive load is determined by the number of ambiguous terms one has to remember to detect these terms in the requirements text. Since cognitive load is additive [18], there are (individual) limits to the efficiency of applying operators, and is therefore one determinant for the effective cost of RQ assurance. If an operator is realized through machine-based processing of information, we characterize this realization by its *automation complexity*. Continuing with the example of ambiguous adverbs, the automation complexity of this operator is low as it can be implemented with a dictionary [9]. On the other hand, some of the requirements writing rules found in STA are rather complex. For example, one rule states that repetition of requirements shall be avoided and a reference to a general requirement shall be made (addressing redundancy). The detection of rule violations requires the analysis of the complete specification, identifying similar phrased statements. While this is certainly possible (e.g. with code clone and plagiarism detection [5]), the analytical complexity is higher than for a dictionary lookup.

4   Research Outline

The taxonomy serves three main purposes which are outlined in this section, together with six research questions and our planned approaches to answer them.

4.1 Prioritize Quality Attributes

We have asked six requirements experts at STA to rank RQ attributes (definitions were extracted from the review by Saavedra et al. [16]) by their importance using cumulative voting [2]. Figure 2 shows the five top and bottom attributes in green and orange respectively. Individual quality attributes have been researched earlier, focusing on ambiguity, completeness, consistency and correctness [15]. While the perceived importance of completeness and correctness is matched by research on these attributes, ambiguity and consistency were ranked by the experts only at position 13 and 16 respectively. At first sight, this might indicate that research focus needs adjustment. However, taking into consideration the relationships between quality attributes, we see a moderate overlap between the needs at STA and past research. Nevertheless, there are certain quality attributes whose evaluation has seen little research, like traceability [15], while being important for STA since they affect verifiability and correctness. The relationships between quality attributes inform us also about potential inconsistencies among the goals of quality improvement. For example, design independence was ranked by STA's experts on position 21 while it affects verifiability, ranked at position 3. This could indicate that, while verifiability is important for STA, design independence as a related aspect has been overlooked as a means to achieve this. These examples show how the relationships between quality attributes can be used to analyse the goals of the company. However, since Saavedra et al. [16] deduced the relationships shown in Fig. 2 by interpreting the quality models they reviewed, these dependencies need further empirical validation, leading to *RQ1: To what extent do requirements quality attributes affect each other?* One approach to address this question, dependent on the answers to the questions in Sect. 4.2, would be to analyse the correlation between operators for different quality attributes. We plan to perform this analysis at STA, which in turn partially answers *RQ2: To what extent can quality attribute rankings be used for planning quality assurance activities?* Further inquiries at STA are needed to identify factors that affect planning, such as timing (does quality attribute importance depend on the project phase?) and implementation cost.

4.2 Determine Operators and Their Accuracy

At STA we have identified 110 *operators* in the form of requirements writing rules. These rules describe how requirements shall be formulated and provide review guidelines. Table 1 shows five examples of writing rules. We have mapped, where the description allowed it, which quality attribute was primarily targeted by each rule. The numbers in Fig. 2 indicate how many operators we identified for each quality attribute. Several quality attributes have no or very few associated operators, leading to the question *RQ3: Which quality attributes can be characterized by an operator?* We plan to answer this question by systematically reviewing the literature, extending the work by Saavedra et al. [16], Pekar et al. [15], and Heck and Zaidman [13]. On the other hand, we have identified

110 operators in STA, leading to the questions *RQ4: How can NL processing be used to implement operators?* and *RQ5: What is the accuracy of these operators in relation to state-of-practice?* We estimated that 40–50% of the writing rules in STA can be implemented with current techniques, e.g. as proposed by Femmer et al. [9]. However, as indicated in the last column of Table 1, techniques to implement rules 4 and 5 still need to be determined. In addition we plan to evaluate the practical benefits of machine-supported RQ assurance compared to the state-of-practice, i.e. manual quality assurance, at STA.

Table 1. Examples of requirements writing rules at STA

Rule	Quality attribute	Implementation
1. No time should be specified in the technical documents. Instead, refer to the Schedule document ◦	Non-redundant	Named entity extraction
2. Numbering of figures, illustrations and tables should be consecutively numbered throughout the document, starting from 1.	Organized	Document meta-data analysis
3. Numbers "1–12" shall be written as shown in the following example, "to be at least two (2)."	Unambiguous	POS Tagging
4. Terms such as "user", "dispatcher", "operator" should be used consistently	Unambiguous	TBD
5. If a functional requirement is supplemented by additional requirements to clarify fulfilment, these must be written as separate requirements	Atomic	TBD

4.3   Estimate Cognitive Load and Automation Complexity

Applying all 110 operators on a specification consisting of thousands of requirements is a cognitively demanding task. For deciding how to implement an operator, it would be useful to be able to estimate the cognitive load each operator will cause and the complexity to implement the operator in a computer-based support system, leading to *RQ6: How can the cognitive load and automation complexity of an operator be estimated?* Cognitive load could be approximated by a heuristic that describes whether the application of the operator requires domain knowledge or not, and to what extent context needs to be considered. Context could be defined as "local", referring to a single requirement, "regional" referring to a section or chapter in the specification, or "global" the whole specification and beyond, e.g. regulations and standards. There exist also multiple approaches to measure cognitive load directly [4]. Automation complexity could be estimated by categorizing operators on the linguistic aspect they address. Operators that require semantic understanding are more complex than operators that require syntactic or lexical analyses of a requirement. The least complex operators are statistical, i.e. analyses that work with letter, word or sentence counts. Since, to the best of our knowledge, no such characterization of operators exists, we plan to collaborate with experts from both neuropsychology and linguistics to perform literature reviews and design experiments.

5   Conclusion

In this paper, we have proposed a requirements quality assurance taxonomy that, once the stated research questions are answered, forms the engine for a decision framework that allows companies to initiate or improve their requirements quality assurance program through (a) realizing the consequences of dependencies between quality attributes in their current manual activities for quality assurance, (b) mapping cognitive load to the prioritized actions for quality assurance, and (c) enabling the decision on the trade-off between manual and machine-supported quality assurance, given cost and accuracy of the choices.

References

1. Ambriola, V., Gervasi, V.: Processing natural language requirements. In: Proceedings of 12th IEEE International Conference on Automated Software Engineering, pp. 36–45. IEEE, Incline Village, USA (1997)
2. Berander, P., Andrews, A.: Requirements prioritization. In: Aurum, A., Wohlin, C. (eds.) Engineering and Managing Software Requirements, Part 1, pp. 69–94. Springer Verlag, Heidelberg (2005)
3. Carew, D., Exton, C., Buckley, J.: An empirical investigation of the comprehensibility of requirements specifications. In: International Symposium on Empirical Software Engineering, p. 10. IEEE, Noosa Heads, Australia (2005)
4. Chen, F., Zhou, J., Wang, Y., Yu, K., Arshad, S., Khawaji, A., Conway, D.: Robust Multimodal Cognitive Load Measurement. Springer, Heidelberg (2016)
5. Chen, X., Francia, B., Li, M., McKinnon, B., Seker, A.: Shared information and program plagiarism detection. IEEE Trans. Inf. Theory **50**(7), 1545–1551 (2004)
6. Damian, D., Chisan, J.: An empirical study of the complex relationships between requirements engineering processes and other processes that lead to payoffs in productivity, quality, and risk management. IEEE Trans. Softw. Eng. **32**(7), 433–453 (2006)
7. Davis, A.M., Overmyer, S., Jordan, K., Caruso, J., Dandashi, F., Dinh, A., Kincaid, G., Ledeboer, G., Reynolds, P., Sitaram, P., Ta, A., Theofanos, M.: Identifying and measuring quality in a software requirements specification. In: Proceedings of 1st Intrnational Software Metrics Symposium, pp. 141–152. IEEE, Baltimore, USA (1993)
8. Fabbrini, F., Fusani, M., Gnesi, S., Lami, G.: An automatic quality evaluation for natural language requirements. In: Proceedings of 7th International Workshop on Requirements Engineering: Foundation for Software Quality. Interlaken, Switzerland (2001)
9. Femmer, H., Méndez Fernández, D., Wagner, S., Eder, S.: Rapid quality assurance with requirements smells. J. Syst. Softw. (2016, in Print)
10. Fowler, M., Highsmith, J.: The agile manifesto. Softw. Dev. **9**(8), 28–35 (2001)

11. Génova, G., Fuentes, J.M., Llorens, J., Hurtado, O., Moreno, V.: A framework to measure and improve the quality of textual requirements. Requir. Eng. **18**(1), 25–41 (2011)
12. Hassan, A.E., Hindle, A., Runeson, P., Shepperd, M., Devanbu, P., Kim, S.: Round-table: what's next in software analytics. IEEE Softw. **30**(4), 53–56 (2013)
13. Heck, P., Zaidman, A.: A systematic literature review on quality criteria for agile requirements specifications. Softw. Q. J. (2016, in Print)
14. Kassab, M., Neill, C., Laplante, P.: State of practice in requirements engineering: contemporary data. Innov. Syst. Softw. Eng. **10**(4), 235–241 (2014)
15. Pekar, V., Felderer, M., Breu, R.: Improvement methods for software requirement specifications: a mapping study. In: Proceedings of 9th International Conference on the Quality of Information and Communicating Technology, pp. 242–245. IEEE, Guimaraes, Portugal (2014)
16. Saavedra, R., Ballejos, L., Ale, M.: Software requirements quality evaluation: state of the art and research challenges. In: Proceedings of 14th Argentine Symposium on Software Engineering, Cordoba, Argentina (2013)
17. Sikora, E., Tenbergen, B., Pohl, K.: Industry needs and research directions in requirements engineering for embedded systems. Requir. Eng. **17**(1), 57–78 (2012)
18. Sweller, J., Ayres, P., Kalyuga, S.: Intrinsic and extraneous cognitive load. In: Sweller, J., Ayres, P., Kalyuga, S. (eds.) Cognitive Load Theory. Explorations in the Learning Sciences, Instructional Systems and Performance Technologies, vol. 1, pp. 57–69. Springer, New York (2011)

The Impact of Specification Structure on Human Memory Performance - Experiences from a First Experiment

Kim Lauenroth[1]([⊠]), Erik Kamsties[2]([⊠]), and Tim Pfeiffer[1,2]

[1] Adesso AG, Stockholmer Allee 20, 44269 Dortmund, Germany
{kim.lauenroth,tim.pfeiffer}@adesso.de
[2] University of Applied Science and Arts Dortmund,
Emil-Figge-Strasse 42, 44227 Dortmund, Germany
erik.kamsties@fh-dortmund.de

Abstract. *Context and motivation*: The major workload in Requirements Engineering lies with those people who create requirements specifications. Inevitably, in doing so people use their memory to store and process related information. *Question/problem*: This paper examines the question: does the underlying structure of a requirements specification (template vs. prose) have an impact on the memory performance of requirements engineers? *Principal ideas/results*: We present results from cognitive psychology that support the assumption that template-based specifications lead to better memory performance and present an experiment to test this assumption. *Contribution*: An initial run of our experiment did not provide sufficient results to support or refute our assumption. In this research preview, we report on the design of experiment, our initial results, and conclusions for future research.

1   Introduction

A core activity of requirements engineering is the documentation of requirements in order to make the requirements available for further development activities [12]. The underlying goal of every kind of requirements specification is storing information independently of the human memory. However, without a certain recollection of the information stored in a requirements specification, there is no anchor in the human mind that points to the stored information. The tools used for making the specification accessible (e.g. tables of content, index, traceability information, or searchable documents) are useless as well because they also require a minimum anchor to the documented information. For example: A person is specifying requirements related to an online payment process. If he does not remember that the existing requirements document already contains requirements related to online payment, he will not search the document for such requirements. It is therefore very likely that he will introduce inconsistent or redundant requirements.

Such examples occur frequently in our industrial practice and motivated us to investigate the performance of human memory in the RE context. Unfortunately,

P. Grünbacher and A. Perini (Eds.): REFSQ 2017, LNCS 10153, pp. 85–91, 2017.
DOI: 10.1007/978-3-319-54045-0_7

our analysis of the related work showed that we are far away from an instrument to measure the capabilities of the human memory with respect to RE-related activities. This research preview is a first step to approach such an instrument: we examine natural language requirements, treat the human memory as a dependent variable in an experimental setting, and discuss how approaches for natural language requirements may have an impact on human memory.

This research preview is structured as follows. Section 2 presents the current state of research on requirements specification and on the human memory from a psychological and a software engineering perspective. The next section provides the theoretical background why specification structures are expected to affect memory performance and how to measure the memory performance. Section 4 discusses the experimental design, Sect. 5 reports on initial results and Sect. 6 closes the paper with our conclusions for future research.

2   Related Work

Human memory performance is one of the core fields of research in cognitive psychology (cf., e.g., [13]). For example, Miller argues that the typical working memory size is about $7+/-2$ information units [9]. Engle [5] shows that there are individual differences in the working memory capacity. If the working memory is stressed during a particular task (e.g. because a person has to keep several information units in the working memory), the performance of the current task is decreased and the probability of mistakes is increased [2].

Storing of information in the short- and the long-term memory is explained by the process of *chunking*: A chunk is defined 'as a familiar collection of more elementary units that have been inter-associated and stored in memory repeatedly and act as a coherent, integrated group when retrieved' [13]. Chunking is then the process of structuring information in a way that support the recall of this information. For example, remembering the following sequence of numbers *2 0 1 6 1 2 2 8* is more difficult than remembering *2016 12 28*. The second way of chunking leads to 3 chunks (instead of 8 chunks) and is thus more memory efficient and easier to remember.

RE literature provides a rich set of techniques for documenting requirements. Typical examples are (a) formal specifications [6], (b) structured requirements documents [1], (c) natural language templates [4], and (d) use cases [3]. However, this work only focuses on the structure of the documentation and does not take into account aspects that are related to human memory performance.

Software engineering research in general provides only a few contributions related to cognitive psychology (cf. [8]). Moody studied approaches for developing visual notations taking the cognitive complexity of models into account (e.g., the ability to remember notation elements) [10]. Some work on human memory in software engineering has been presented in the area of psychology of programming, e.g. [11] examines the relationship between programming tasks, task-switching, human memory, and programming tool support.

From our own research [7] and based on the results of Lenberg et al. [8], we conclude that the human memory has not been taken into account as a factor in software engineering or requirements engineering research. However, according to the results from cognitive psychology, the performance of human memory may have a significant impact on the performance of requirements engineering tasks.

3   Theoretical Background

In the following, we will develop a theory and an experiment to test the relationship between specification types and memory performance. We first present an operationalization of memory performance for requirements specifications that uses the process of chunking as underlying theory.

On a very high abstraction level, a requirements document is a collection of facts concerning the system under development. A given fact can be part of the requirements specification or not. A person can remember a fact or not. These cases can be interpreted as a binary classifier with the classification results *true/false positive* (TP/FP) and *true/false negative* (TN/FN). Several metrics are commonly in use to rate the quality of a binary classifier, we use the *TPR - True Positive Rate (Recall)* to measure memory performance.

Approaches for creating a requirements specification can be subdivided into two types. A *prose* specification (e.g., [1]) presents the requirements in terms of prose text and is structured by headlines for sections and subsections. A *template-based* specification (e.g., [4]) presents the requirements in terms of a structured template. Each requirement is presented by an individual template including content-related information (e.g. the title and a description of the requirement) and administrative information (e.g. the status of the requirement, an identification number, or a change log). A popular example for such templates are use cases [3].

Comparing prose and template approaches for specifications with the process of chunking in mind, one can observe the following: (1) a template can be considered as a chunk that contains a particular requirement, (2) a template provides key information (the title of the requirement) that supports remembering the particular requirement, (3) the template structure of a specification offers predefined chunks to the reader whereas the prose specification requires that the reader performs the chunking of the information on his/her own.

From these observations, we derived the following assumption: *Specifications using templates to structure requirements information provide better chunking of requirements information and will therefore lead to a better memory performance than specifications that use a prose approach.*

4   Experimental Setup

The goal of the experiment is to compare prose and template-based specifications with respect to the memory performance.

Hypothesis and Variables. The main hypothesis of this experiment is that *there is a difference between prose - and template - based specifications with*

respect to the number of correctly remembered facts from the specification.
Independent (controlled) variables are: *Style* (prose, template) - main controlled
variable, *Domain* (library system, vacation tracker) - to make sure that our
results do not depend on a particular domain, *Order* - to control learning effects.
Dependent variables are: *Number of correctly answered questions* (per question
type, per recall, total), *Confidence* of the participant in his answer (to be able
to include only those answers in the analysis, where the participant was more or
less sure).

Design. We use a $2 \times 2 \times 2$ full factorial design to systematically variate the
style, the *domain*, and the *order* (prose $\rightarrow$ template vs. template $\rightarrow$ prose), see
Table 1

Table 1. $2 \times 2 \times 2$ Factorial design of experiment

Group	Run 1	Run 2
A1	Vacation tracker, prose	Library system, template
A2	Library system, template	Vacation tracker, prose
B1	Library system, prose	Vacation tracker, template
B2	Vacation tracker, template	Library system, prose

Specifications. The target audience of the experiment are students and professionals. As the authors have access to students of computer science and young
software development professionals in Germany, we have chosen German as the
language for all experimental material for the first runs of the experiment. By
this decision, we avoid one threat to validity (language barriers), the obvious
drawback is that the ability to replicate the experiment is reduced.

The specifications are 10 pages long and contained 40 requirements artefacts
(30 textual requirements and 10 use cases). In the prose specification, the textual
requirements and use cases were presented in two separate sections. The textual
requirements were documented in individual paragraphs and each use case was
presented in an individual subsection. In the template-based specification, each
requirement was documented with an individual template.

Questionnaire. To measure the recall of facts depending on the specification
style, we defined questions addressing two dimensions, open vs. closed, and positive vs. negative questions. These two dimensions lead to four types of questions:

1. *A positive open question* asks for a fact that is part of the specification
   and is expected to be answered with the corresponding fact. For example:
   What the shortcut for creating a new application for leave? Correct answer:
   Shift + Ctrl + v.
2. *A negative open questions* asks for a fact that is *not* part of the specification and is expected to be answered with the statement *fact not part of
   specification.*

3. *A positive closed question* asks for a fact that is part of the specification and is expected to be answered with *yes* or *true*. For example: *Is it possible to cancel a part of a vacation period?*
4. *A negative closed question* asks for a fact that is *not* part of the specification and is expected to be answered with *no* or *false*.

Additionally, three question types were targeted to the *style* of the specification, e.g. *What was the name of the 3rd use case?*

We developed a questionnaire for each domain with balanced difficulty to avoid a bias towards one of the domains. Finally, a questionnaire contained 20 questions with a balanced set of open and closed, positive and negative questions. It is possible that a participant does not know the answer for sure. To avoid betting and to measure the level of certainty, each question is complemented with a confidence level ranging from 0 ("don't know") to 5 ("sure").

Procedure. The experiment reproduces an artificial project situation based on exemplary specifications. The participants are volunteers and receive an introduction to the motivation and goals of the experiment. No training session takes place as we do not evaluate a particular technique. The participants shall have basic RE knowledge, for instance familiarity with the specification styles. The experiment consists of two runs of several steps each.

(1) Reading. The participant reads the specification. This activity may result in different familiarity with the specification depending on motivation, personal habits and so forth.
(2) Working. The participant derives a class/data model from the specification to acquire a deeper understanding of the requirements. This step helps to harmonize the familiarity with the specification among the participants.
(3) Recall. The last step is to answer questions about the specification. The questions have to be **answered without access to the specification**. The recall is exercised three times over a week. The first recall is requested immediately after working with the specification ("Monday"). The second recall takes places 2 days after the experiment to challenge the long term memory ("Wednesday"). The third recall happens after another two days ("Friday"). The order of questions was randomized for each participant to minimize the effect of particular questions on the result and to minimize the possibility of cheating.

5   Results from a First Run

24 employees from a German software development company (>1000 employees) participated in an initial experiment in May 2016[1]. Participation was voluntary, mostly young software development professionals were involved. They were randomly assigned to the four groups. One participant assigned himself to another group, another one dropped out. This resulted in slightly different group sizes:

---

[1] Please contact the authors if you are interested in getting the experimental material.

A1 (5), A2 (7), B1 (6), B2 (5). The participants were 25 years $(+/-2)$ old and had 0–3 years of professional experience. The participants were familiar with the specification styles.

The results from this first run showed no difference between the *specification styles* with respect to the number of correctly answered questions. Even when taking in addition the *type of question* or *phase* into account we could not observe a significant difference.

We repeated our analysis for the subset of answers in which the participants were sure about their answers (i.e., confidence ≥ 4). Still no significant differences between the styles were found. We found larger differences between the domains used in the experiment (Library System, Vacation Tracker) in relation to the phase (immediate recall, recall after 2 days, recall after 4 days), although they are still not significant. We asked the participants in the week after to comment on the results. Actually the participants perceived differences between the specification styles and the participants preferred one or the other. The participants made a separation between "*ease of reading*" and "*ease of recalling*" and stated that both are *not* correlated. Instead, a specification style was perceived as not so easy to read, but easier to recall afterwards. Moreover, it seems that the vacation tracker domain was more easily accessible that the library, as the former is used in a quite similar way in the company. Finally, the participants disliked a question type severely.

The results do not imply that there are no differences between specification styles at all. We identified a couple of reasons for the lack of significance: (1) we had a low number of participants in the groups (5–7 per group). (2) The participants executed the experiment after their daily obligations in the company. That is, a maturation effect may have happened and a few participants confirmed this in the interview. (3) Possibly, the specifications are too short, so the facts are easy to remember independently of the specification style. (4) The operationalization of memory performance by counting correct answers to a given set of questions - we developed different types of questions yet we cannot be sure that we have identified all important types. (5) The presented experimental design was developed with a broad approach in mind, i.e., different types of questions (open vs. closed and positive vs. negative, see Sect. 4). This approach appeared to be too broad to capture the concept of memory performance in requirements engineering. Our underlying assumption that memory performance in requirements engineering can be treated as a simple variable may be false.

6   Conclusion and Future Research

The results of the experiment indicate no clear superiority of one specification style over the other. Instead it raises a couple of interesting questions for further empirical research.

What is an adequate model to operationalize memory performance in requirements engineering? As stated above, memory performance appears to be more than a simple variable. A possible direction for future research could be the development of a more elaborate model for memory performance in requirements engineering.

Are there different personality types with respect to specification types? The interview of our participants revealed that some participants prefer a certain specification type. The origin of this preference is unclear. The preference may originate from the education or from other factors that are related to cognitive factors. Searching for such personality types is a possible direction for future research.

What is a practical perspective on memory performance in requirements engineering? Our experiment created an artificial situation to measure memory performance. A complementing research activity could be an industrial study (e.g. a series of qualitative interviews) to gain a broader understanding of the importance of human memory in requirements engineering work. We plan to repeat various smaller versions of the experiment with students to examine these questions in more detail.

References

1. IEEE guide for developing system requirements specifications. IEEE Std 1233, 1998 Edition, pp. 1–36, December 1998
2. Baddeley, A., Hitch, G.: Working memory. Psychol. Learn. Motiv.: Adv. Res. Theory **8**, 47–89 (1974)
3. Cockburn, A.: Writing effective use cases, the crystal collection for software professionals. Addison-Wesley Professional Reading, Boston (2000)
4. Durán, A., Bernárdez, B., Toro, M., Corchuelo, R., Ruiz, A., Pérez, J.: Expressing customer requirements using natural language requirements templates and patterns. In: Proceedings of the IMACS/IEEE CSCC 1999 (1999)
5. Engle, R.W.: Working memory capacity as executive attention. Curr. Dir. psychol. Sci. **11**(1), 19–23 (2002)
6. Heitmeyer, C., Labaw, B., Kiskis, D.: Consistency checking of SCR-style requirements specifications. In: Proceedings of the Second IEEE International Symposium on Requirements Engineering, pp. 56–63. IEEE (1995)
7. Lauenroth, K., Kamsties, E.: People's capabilities are a blind spot in RE research and practice. In: Daneva, M., Pastor, O. (eds.) REFSQ 2016. LNCS, vol. 9619, pp. 243–248. Springer, Heidelberg (2016). doi:10.1007/978-3-319-30282-9_17
8. Lenberg, P., Feldt, R., Wallgren, L.: Behavioral software engineering: a definition and systematic literature review. J. Syst. Softw. **107**, 15–37 (2015)
9. Miller, G.A.: The magical number seven, plus or minus two: some limits on our capacity for processing information. Psychol. Rev. **63**(2), 81 (1956)
10. Moody, D.L.: The physics of notations: toward a scientific basis for constructing visual notations in software engineering. IEEE Trans. Softw. Eng. **35**(6), 756–779 (2009)
11. Parnin, C.: A cognitive neuroscience perspective on memory for programming tasks. In: Programming Interest Group, p. 27 (2010)
12. Pohl, K.: Requirements Engineering: Fundamentals, Principles, and Techniques, 1st edn. Springer Publishing Company, Incorporated, Heidelberg (2010)
13. Tulving, E., Craik, F.I.M.: The Oxford Handbook of Memory. Oxford University Press, Oxford (2000)

Goal-Orientation in Requirements Engineering

How Can You Improve Your As-Is Models? Requirements Analysis Methods Meet GQM

Shoichiro Ito, Shinpei Hayashi[(✉)], and Motoshi Saeki

Department of Computer Science, Tokyo Institute of Technology,
Ookayama 2–12–1–W8–83, Meguro-ku, Tokyo 152–8552, Japan
{ito,hayashi,saeki}@se.cs.titech.ac.jp

Abstract. *Context & motivation*: To develop information systems providing high business value, we should clarify As-is business processes and information systems supporting them, identify the problems hidden in them, and develop To-be information systems so that the identified problems can be solved. *Question/problem*: In this development, we need a technique to support the identification of the problems, which can be seamlessly connected to the modeling techniques. *Principal ideas/results*: In this paper, to define metrics to extract problems of the As-is system, following the domains specific to it, we propose the combination of Goal-Question-Metric (GQM) with existing requirements analysis techniques. Furthermore, we integrate goal-oriented requirements analysis (GORA) with problem frames approach and use case modeling to define the metrics of measuring the problematic efforts of human actors in the As-is models. This paper includes a case study of a reporting operation process at a brokerage office to check the feasibility of our approach. *Contribution*: Our contribution is the proposal of using of GQM to identify the problems of an As-is model specified with the combination of GORA, use case modeling, and problem frames.

Keywords: Goal-Question-Metric paradigm · Goal-oriented requirements analysis · Use case modeling · Problem frames

1 Introduction

An information system should enhance business value in enterprise or organization. To develop information systems providing high business value, we should clarify the current situations of business processes and information systems supporting them, identify the problems hidden in the current situations of business value, and develop a newer version of the information systems so that the identified problems can be solved. The current situations are so-called As-is, while the newer situations are To-be. In requirements analysis phase of developing an information system, we construct an As-is model, identify problems from the As-is model, and then develop a To-be model where the problems can be solved. Although we have many modeling techniques that can be used in requirements analysis phase, there are few techniques to support the identification of

© Springer International Publishing AG 2017
P. Grünbacher and A. Perini (Eds.): REFSQ 2017, LNCS 10153, pp. 95–111, 2017.
DOI: 10.1007/978-3-319-54045-0_8

the problems, which can be seamlessly connected to the modeling techniques. Activity-based costing (ABC), which is one of the most popular but too general techniques to identify problems only from cost effectiveness [10], uses the metrics to estimate costs necessary to enact business processes. It focuses on costs only, and we need some effective metrics specific to domains where the As-is system operates. That is to say, we need a technique to define metrics to extract problems of the As-is system, following the domains specific to it, and the technique should be combined with modeling methods of As-is and To-be systems. Goal-Question-Metric (GQM) is one of the approaches to develop metrics based on for what we like to measure [1] and we use it in this paper.

Goal-oriented requirements analysis (GORA) is one of the popular techniques to elicit requirements to business processes, information systems, and software (simply, systems hereinafter) and is being made into practice [11,17]. It is useful to identify hierarchical structures and relationships on elicited requirements, in particular, their rationales why the elicited requirements could be led up to. We use GORA to construct As-is and To-be models. However, some of their weak points are clarified; for example, it is difficult to represent the behavior of systems explicitly. The metrics to measure behavioral properties of As-is and To-be models are necessary for our objective, and they are difficult to be defined on GORA. So, we combine GORA with some modeling techniques that can specify behavioral aspects of models. We adopt two modeling techniques, problem frames (PFs) [7] and use case modeling, and integrate GORA with them.

In the technique we propose in this paper, we model an As-is with the integrated technique: GORA, PFs and use case modeling, define metrics to identify problems of the As-is using GQM on the integrated technique, and derive a To-be model to solve the identified problems based on the values of the metrics. In addition, when deriving solutions, we should take care of the rationales of the requirements originated in the As-is model and avoid the conflicts to them of the requirements newly added as a solution. GORA is useful to explore rationales of the requirements.

The rest of the paper is organized as follows. In the next section, we have brief introductions of GORA, PFs, and use case modeling. Section 3 presents our integrated method and illustrates how to get a To-be model. In Sect. 4, we develop our metrics to identify problems to be solved in an As-is model using the GQM approach. A case study is presented in Sect. 5. On account of space, we pick up the case study of a reporting operation process at a brokerage office, where brokerage analysts create reports of stocks and distribute them to their customers. Sections 6 and 7 are for related work and concluding remarks, respectively.

2   Preliminaries

2.1   Goal-Oriented Requirements Analysis

In goal-oriented requirements analysis (GORA), customers' needs are modeled as goals to be achieved finally by software-intensive systems that will be developed,

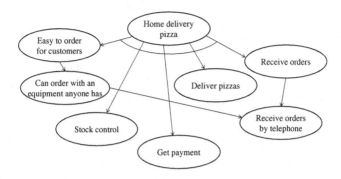

Fig. 1. Example of a goal graph.

and the goals are decomposed and refined into a set of more concrete sub-goals. After finishing goal-oriented analysis, the analyst obtains an acyclic (cycle-free) directed graph called *goal graph*. Its nodes express goals to be achieved by the system that will be developed, and its edges represent logical dependency relationships between the connected goals. More concretely, a goal can be decomposed into sub-goals, and the achievement of the sub-goals contributes to its achievement. We have two types of goal decomposition; one is AND decomposition, and the other is OR. In AND decomposition, if all of the sub-goals are achieved, their parent goal can be achieved or satisfied. On the other hand, in OR decomposition, the achievement of at least one sub-goal leads to the achievement of its parent goal. Figure 1 illustrates a part of the goal graph which has been obtained from requirements analysis of a home delivery service of pizzas. Ovals (nodes) and arrows (directed edges) express goals and decomposition relationships among the goals. The edges attached with an arc outgoing from a parent node show an AND decomposition, and for example, five goals "Easy to order for customers", "Stock control (of ingredients and seasonings such as cheese and onion)", "Get payment (when delivering ordered pizzas)", "Deliver pizzas (to customers)", and "Receive orders (of pizzas from customers)" should be achieved in order to achieve their parent goal "Home delivery pizzas" in the figure, and this decomposition is AND one. The usage of this type of graph, so called AND-OR graph, is a common feature in a family of goal-oriented analysis.

2.2 Problem Frames and Use Case Modeling

Problem frames approach (PF) has been proposed by Jackson [7], and it contains the separated concepts of domains, requirements, and machines. Domains are elements of the real world and interact with each other via shared events, and the idea of these interactions is Hoare's CSP. Requirements are descriptions that constrain the behavior of the shared events. Furthermore, PF approach defines two types of diagrams: context diagram and problem diagram. The former specifies domains, machines, and their shared interactions only, and the latter has requirements. Furthermore, Jackson abstracted and cataloged various problem diagrams to patterns, so-called *problem frames*.

A use case model describes the functions of the system from a behavioral view and the model consists of two parts: use case diagrams and use case descriptions. A use case diagram presents the relationships among use cases and between actors and use cases in a diagrammatic form while a use case description is written in (structured) natural language to specify the flow of actions in the use case, i.e., the behavior of the use case, as scenarios. In our approach, although the original version of PF does not specify how to define the inner behavior of a domain or a machine, we consider that a domain and a machine includes use cases and therefore its inner behavior of a domain or a machine can be specified with use cases and their descriptions. The details of integrating GORA, PFs, and use case modeling will be mentioned in the next section using a simple illustration.

3   Our Approach

3.1   Integrating GORA, PFs, and Use Cases

Figure 2 shows an example of a part of home delivery service of pizzas, and it is a combined version of a context diagram of PFs and use case descriptions. Rectangle boxes stand for domains of PFs, and this example has three domains: Staff, Customer, and Invoice. A customer calls a telephone to a pizza delivery shop to order pizzas, and it is specified with the shared event "C! Telephone ringing" on the dashed line between Customer and Staff. The meaning of this event is that Customer (C) generates "telephone ringing" to trigger Staff. The behavior of Staff, when "telephone ringing" is generated, is specified with a use case description of the use case "Receive orders by telephone". For brevity, to avoid a complicated diagram, we omit from the figure the several elements irrelevant to "Receive orders by telephone".

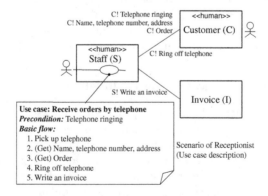

Fig. 2. Context diagram and use case.

Goal graphs, context diagrams of PF, and use case models have shared components. Operational goals in a goal graph correspond to the use cases that achieve them, and the steps in a use case description may appear as shared events in a context diagram. The goal "Receive orders by telephone" corresponds to the use case having the same name in Fig. 2, and the shared events in the context diagram such as "Telephone ringing", "Name, telephone number, address", and "Write an invoice" appear in the use case description of "Receive orders by telephone" which is executed by the domain Staff. Figures 1 and 2 show an As-is model of home delivery service of pizzas in our integrated method.

3.2   From As-Is Models to To-Be Models

In this subsection, we illustrate how to derive a To-be model from an As-is model which is represented with our integrated model by using the example of home delivery service of pizzas. Our procedure consists of four steps. First of all, we represent an As-is model with our integrated approach, i.e., goal graphs, context diagrams of PFs, and use cases (Step 1). Second, we identify the problems from the As-is model by applying predefined metrics, and the results of measurements suggest us what problems are included and where they are (Step 3). We pick up the goal graph of the As-is model and add some goals to solve the problems. We refine them to sub goals until we obtain operational goals that achieve them. During refining the goal graph, we can know the rationales of the existing goals in the As-is model and pay attentions to avoiding conflicts of the newly created goals to the existing ones. That is to say, the goal model plays a role of navigating goal refinement. The resulting goal graph is an element of a To-be model. In the last step (Step 4), we construct use cases and a context diagram of the To-be model from the goal graph obtained in Step 3. Figure 3 illustrates the flow of the above steps.

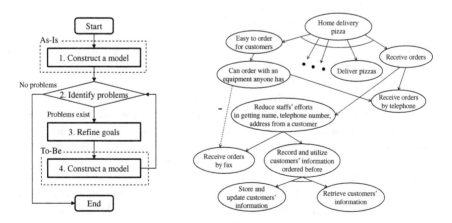

Fig. 3. Steps to derive a To-be model. **Fig. 4.** Goal graph to derive a To-be model.

Step 1: Construct an As-Is Model. We construct an integrated model to capture the current situation of a system to be developed. In our example, we have the As-is model shown in Figs. 1 and 2. Generally speaking, in the situation where we do not have any models yet, we begin with the construction of a goal graph, and for each operational and leaf goal, we specify its scenario to achieve it as a use case description. We extract actors and steps from the use case descriptions. To construct a context diagram, we make the extracted actors correspond to domains or machines in the diagram and use the steps to identify shared events on the domains.

Step 2: Identify Problems. The As-is model is analyzed to identify problems in it from a view of human efforts. In Fig. 2, there are many shared events between Staff and Customer in the PF and actions in the use case descriptions, all of them should be executed by these human entities. The number of shared events and steps that should be executed by human actors can be formally calculated as a metric, and it will be mentioned in the next section, and a set of our metrics is derived by GQM [1] so that we can identify which domains and use cases have problems to be solved. In our example, we consider that the domain Staff and use case "Receive orders" have a problem that Staff has more efforts to achieve "Receive orders".

Step 3: Refine Goals. To solve the identified problems, we explore their solutions by refining the goal graph of the As-is model. In the previous step, we identified the use cases that had problems. We pick up the goals corresponding to the identified use cases and set up their sub goals for solving the identified problems. We refine these sub goals considering rationales of and conflicts to the existing goals, and finally, we obtain a goal graph of a To-be model. In our example, we identified the problems of more efforts in "Receive orders by telephone". In particular, we will reduce the Staff's efforts to get customers' name, their telephone numbers, and their addresses by telephone. Thus, we set up a new goal "Reduce staffs' efforts in getting name, telephone number, and address from a customer" as a sub goal of "Receive orders", as shown in Fig. 4. At first, we get the sub goal "Receive orders by fax" to solve the problem because a fax sheet includes all of the customer's information that the staff needs, and the staff can get it from the fax sheet without spending time in talking with the customers. However, every person can have a fax machine in any situation, so the goal "Receive orders by fax" prevents the achievement of the goal "Can order with an equipment anyone has". In the figure, we put the mark "−" on the dotted arrow between these two goals to show they have a conflict. Next, we consider the usage of a customers' database and put an alternative goal "Record and utilize customers' information ordered before" as a sub goal. Since we can resolve the conflict by adopting this goal, we continue its refinement. As a result, we obtain two operational sub goals "Store and update customers' information" and "Retrieve customers' information". The usage of a goal graph of an As-is model allows us to refine goals considering the rationales of and conflicts to the existing goals, and to avoid unreasonable refinement.

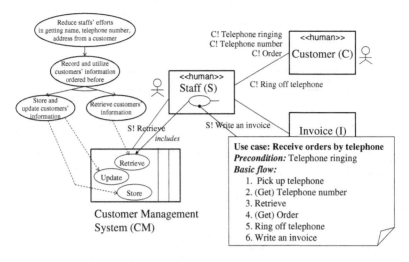

Fig. 5. To-be model of home delivery service of pizzas.

Step 4: Construct a To-Be Model. Until the previous step, we get some operational goals to be achieved, and next, we realize them by specifying their use case descriptions. This step is the same as Step 1. From the use case descriptions, the actors and the steps are extracted to add them as new domains, machines, and shared events. After getting a To-be model, we re-calculate the metrics that took values of lower quality and which caused the improvement to the To-be model and check if their values are improved.

Figure 5 shows a part of our final result in the example. We newly add three use cases "Retrieve", "Store", and "Update" and a machine "Customer Management System (CM)" having these use cases as functions. The existing use case "Receive orders by telephone" is changed and it has an action "Retrieve" to call the corresponding use case. As a result, the shared events that should be executed by Staff are reduced.

4   Evaluating Models via Metrics

For evaluating the As-is and To-be models, we build a GQM model [1] by making the following a top goal **G**: Specifying the possible locations of automation and/or effort reduction (i.e., finding problems of an As-is model). The built GQM graph is shown in Fig. 6. Based on the derived questions from the goals, we defined the following five metrics; NE and CE are calculated on a context diagram, and ACC and ANOS are for a use case.

CE: This metric is the number of distinct events related to each human domain. It is specified with an attached stereotype "≪human≫" which domains are human in the context diagram. The more distinct events a human domain has, the more various kind of work corresponding human should work, and she/he should have

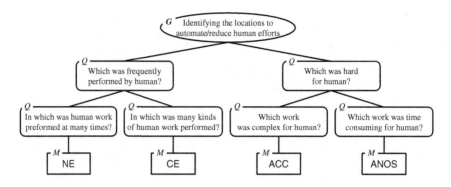

Fig. 6. GQM graph.

more effort in performing many different kinds of work. In the example of Fig. 2, Staff is a human domain, and we have five distinct events related to it, and so CE is 5 for Staff.

NE: This metric is the number of the event occurrences on each human domain in a context diagram. The more event occurrences related to a human, the more events she/he should receive, send and/or deal with, and as the result, she/he should perform work at more times. In the example of Fig. 2, we have five event occurrences related to Staff, and its NE is 5. Note that on calculating this metric, we should explore how many times events occur in the corresponding use cases because the same event may occur at multiple times in the corresponding use cases, and we should take into account these multiple occurrences. The details will be mentioned later.

ACC: This metric is calculated for each use case and is the number of its flows which include the steps related to human actors, i.e., the actors corresponding to human domains of a context diagram. If a use case includes a basic flow only, none of alternative flows, it has one flow. A use case can include more than one flow by branching to alternative flows, and the more branched flows related to a human, the more complex work she/he may perform. The number of flows is the number of alternative flows plus 1. This metric is similar to Cyclomatic complexity number of use cases [3]. The use case "Receive orders by telephone" of Fig. 2 has only one flow, which includes the steps performed by Staff, so ACC for this use case is 1.

ANOS: This metric is calculated for each use case and is the number of human-related steps included in its basic flow and alternative flows. If the flow includes calling other use cases, the values of their ANOS are added. For example, if a use case has 10 steps related to a human in a basic flow and two alternative flows both of which has three human-related steps, ANOS for the use case is 16 (= 10 + 3 + 3). The more steps related to a human are included in a use case, the longer time she/he should work for the use case, because she/he consumes a certain time in performing each step. The use case "Receive orders by telephone" of Fig. 2 has five steps, and all of them are related to human actors Staff and Customer, so its ANOS is 5.

Although these metrics are for identifying where the problems to be improved are in an As-is model, from the viewpoints of human efforts, we can use them to check if a To-be model can solve them or not. We observe how the values of the defined metric are changed from the As-is model to the To-be models, i.e., we confirm whether the metric values actually decrease or not.

5   Case Study

The case is the reporting operation of a brokerage office. The reporting operations are done in the terminal of each brokerage analyst. Analysts upload their report files to the distribution server as soon as they completed them. For improving the efficiency in writing a report, the information that analysts were used in writing a report are stored in the history server so that other analysts can refer the stored information when writing another report. The history server can be accessed only via a dedicated terminal. Analysts are required to download their past materials to a USB memory from the dedicated terminal and to complete their report in their own personal terminal. For distributing the completed reports, analysts convert their report to a PDF file and upload it to the distribution server.

On account of space, we start with Step 2, i.e., we have already got the As-is model. However, clarifying this case study, in the next subsection we explain the As-is model itself not presenting how to construct it.

5.1   As-Is Model

The use cases for the business process are UC1: Collect data, UC2: Write a report, UC3: Fetch a report, UC4: Store a report to the distribution server, UC5: Store a report to the history server, UC6: Fix a report in the history server, and UC7: Fix a report in the distribution server. For example, UC3, UC4, UC5, and UC6 are shown in Figs. 7, 8, and 9. These use cases contribute the achievement of "Reporting operation of a brokerage office".

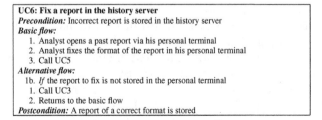

Fig. 7. Use case description of UC6 (As-is).

UC3: Fetch a report
Precondition: Past reports are not stored in the actor's personal terminal
Basic flow:
1. Analyst accesses the dedicated terminal
2. Dedicated terminal accesses the history server
3. Dedicated terminal receives past reports from the history server
4. Analyst receives past reports from the dedicated terminal via a USB memory
5. Analyst stores past reports to his personal terminal
Postcondition: Past reports are stored in the personal terminal

UC3′: Fetch a report
Precondition: Past reports are not stored in the actor's personal terminal
Basic flow:
1. Analyst accesses his personal terminal
2. Analyst's personal terminal accesses the report management system
3. Report management system accesses the history server
4. Report management system receives past reports from the history server
5. Report management system sends past reports to the dedicated terminal
Postcondition: Past reports are stored in the personal terminal

Fig. 8. Use case descriptions of UC3 (As-is) and UC3′ (To-be).

UC4: Store a report to the distribution server
Precondition: A report is created
Basic flow:
1. Analyst converts the report in his personal terminal to PDF file
2. Analyst uploads the PDF file from the personal terminal
3. Personal terminal sends the PDF file to the distribution server
Postcondition: The report is distributed

UC5: Store a report to the history server
Precondition: A report is created
Basic flow:
1. Analyst copies a report to the USB memory from his personal terminal
2. Analyst moves the report to the dedicated terminal via the USB memory
3. Dedicated terminal uploads the report to the history server
Postcondition: The report is stored

UC4–5: Store a report
Precondition: A report is created
Basic flow:
1. Analyst accesses his personal terminal
2. Personal terminal sends the report to the report management system
3. Report management system sends the report to the history server
4. Report management system converts the report to PDF file
5. Report management system sends the PDF to the distribution server
Postcondition:
• The report is distributed
• The report is stored

Fig. 9. Use case descriptions of UC4, UC5 (As-is), and UC4–5 (To-be).

The goal model is shown in Fig. 10. Leaf goals of the model correspond to the above seven use cases. The top goal "Reporting operation of a brokerage office" is refined into two sub goals with AND decomposition; one is "Manage reports", and the other is "Create a report". The goal "Manage reports" has three sub goals "Fetch a report", "Fix a report", and "Store a report". These goals also have their children; the goal "Store a report" has the goals of UC4 and UC5, and the goal "Fix a report" has the goals of UC6 and UC7.

An As-is context diagram was built from the use case descriptions and goal model. The extracted actors and steps in the use case descriptions were used for the domains and events in the context diagram, respectively. The built context diagram is shown in Fig. 11. The ID $(U.s)$ in the figure stands for a specific step

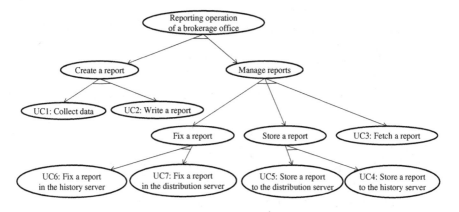

Fig. 10. As-is goal graph.

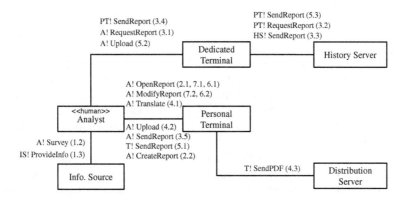

Fig. 11. As-is context diagram.

in a use case description; a use case ID and its step number are denoted by U and s, respectively. In a context diagram, the ID ($U.s$) specifies which use case step corresponds to the target event. For example, the event A! OpenReport is executed by Step 1 of UC2, UC6, and UC7.

5.2   Step 2: Identifying Problems

The metric values were measured for the As-is models of three types (use case descriptions, goal model, and context diagram) to find problems in the As-is models. In this approach, the metrics derived from the goal G mentioned in Sect. 4 were applied, and we focused on the higher values of them. We measured CE, NE, ANOS, and ACC. Because this case study has only one human domain Analyst, NE was calculated for Analyst only.

The measured metric values on the As-is model are shown in Table 1. For calculating the value of NE, we counted the occurrences of each event in use cases. For example, as shown in Fig. 11, A! OpenReport occurs in UC2, UC7, and

Table 1. As-is metric values.

Events on Analyst	#		Use cases	ANOS	ACC
A! RequestReport	1		UC1	5	1
A! Upload	2		UC2	2	1
A! SendReport	2		UC3	3	1
A! Translate	1		UC4	2	1
A! OpenReport	3		UC5	2	1
A! ModifyReport	2	CE	UC6	7	2
A! CreateReport	1	= 12	UC7	7	2
A! Survey	1				
PT! SendReport	1				
IS! ProvideInfo	1				
Total (NE)	15				

UC6, and all of its occurrences are in Step 1. Thus, we counted the occurrences of A! OpenReport as 3. Note that A! OpenReport occurred most frequently in all of the events related to Analyst. After counting the occurrences of each event, we obtained the value 15 as NE by calculating its total sum. For CE, we counted the distinct events related to the only one human domain Analyst and obtained the value 12.

The values of ANOS and ACC were calculated for each use case. For ANOS, we should include the steps in alternative flows and the steps of called use cases. In the case of UC6, it has two steps related to a human actor (Analyst) in its basic flow, and two calls for the other use cases: UC5 from the basic flow and UC3 from the alternative flow. Since the ANOS values of UC5 and UC3 were 2 and 3 (see Table 1), we have $2 + 2 + 3 = 7$ as ANOS value of UC6. Note that UC6 (Fig. 7) and UC7 have the highest value in ANOS (=7) over the other use cases. Also for ACC, UC6 and UC7 were measured as the highest (=2). ACC can be calculated by counting the basic and the alternative flows that have human-related steps in a use case. In UC6, it has the human related steps in its basic flow, e.g., Step 1 (Analyst opens a past report via his personal terminal) having a human actor as a subject. Although its alternative flow calls UC3 only, UC3 has human-related steps, e.g., Step 1 in UC3. To sum up, we found that UC6 has two flows (one basic and one alternative one), and both of them include human-related steps. Thus, we can obtain ACC value 2. Note that UC6 and UC7 have the highest ACC value.

As a result, UC6 and UC7 were regarded as having problems because they execute A! OpenReport and have the highest value of ANOS and ACC. Since both UC6 and UC7 include UC3 (Fig. 8), it was also regarded as a problematic one for the analyst.

5.3 Step 3: Goal Refinement (Building Solutions)

The To-be goal graph was constructed by applying some solutions against the problems detected in the analysis of the As-is model. More specifically, solutions are provided by defining alternatives for the problematic leaf goals or their parent goals by applying goal decomposition. In this case study, in the As-is goal graph shown in Fig. 10, the leaf goals corresponding UC6 and UC7 were detected as problematic. Against them, we focused on their parent goal "Manage reports" and defined its alternative "Report management system", which automates the tasks for the original goal as OR-decomposition.

The goal decompositions to achieve the defined alternative goal was done by referring the original As-is goal graph. Based on the connectivity of goals in the As-is goal graph, we can deduce that "Report management system" should consist of "Fetch a report", "Store a report", and "Fix a report". Also, "Store a report" and "Fix a report" should achieve the use cases defined in the As-is model. The defined To-be goal graph is shown in Fig. 12. Note that the dotted ovals in the figure are not goals of the To-be model, but of the As-is model. These are for clarifying which use cases of the As-is model were resolved by the new goals of the To-be model. As will be mentioned later, UC4 and UC5 were replaced with UC4–5 on account of the improvement of UC3 (As-is model) to UC3′.

5.4 Step 4: Constructing a To-Be Model

Next, use case descriptions and a context diagram were constructed for achieving the goals in the To-be goal graph built in the previous step. Based on the To-be graph, the use case to be modified was UC3, and the use cases to be added were "Fix a report" and "Store a report". These two use cases are expected to contribute "Fix a report in the history server" and "Fix a report in the distribution server", and "Store a report to the history server" and "Store a

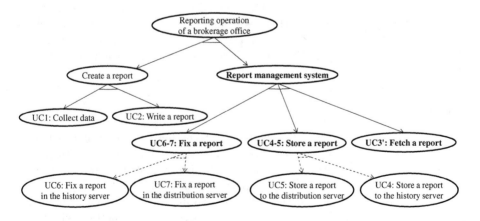

Fig. 12. To-be goal graph.

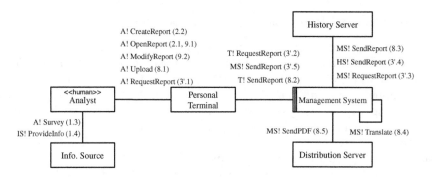

Fig. 13. To-be context diagram.

report to the distribution server" in the As-is goal graph, respectively. Then, the use case descriptions of "Report management system" were newly defined as shown in Figs. 8 and 9. For example, newly defined UC4–5 in the To-be model shown in Fig. 9 has special automated steps (3–5) that make the report to be uploaded to servers for satisfying the postconditions of UC4 and UC5 in the As-is model. Also, UC3 shown in Fig. 8 substitutes the manual data transfer via USB memory stick (Steps 1, 4, and 5), which contributed the increase of ANOS value, with To-be system (UC3′, Steps 3, 4, and 5).

To-be context diagram was defined as shown in Fig. 13 based on the updated use case descriptions. The steps in newly defined use case descriptions were added as the events in the context diagram.

To confirm the effectiveness of the defined To-be model, we calculated the differences of the values of the metrics between the As-is model and the To-be one. The deltas (the differences) were calculated as: $\Delta = To\text{-}be - As\text{-}Is$. If the difference of a metric is a negative number, we can recognize the improvement in the To-be model from the viewpoint of the metric. In Fig. 13, the values of CE and NE are 12 and 15, respectively. Thus, changes made provided the deltas of metric values $\Delta CE = 7 - 12 = -5$, $\Delta NE = 8 - 15 = -7$, which indicate that the human work was reduced. The changes from UC3 to UC3′ provided the deltas of metric values $\Delta ACC(UC3) = 0$ and $\Delta ANOS(UC3) = -2$, which indicate the reduction of hard work. We conclude that our approach could identify the effectiveness of To-be model.

5.5   Discussion

The result of this case study indicates that our technique can find problems in the As-is model and can also show the effectiveness of model updates from the As-is to the To-be using the defined set of metrics. It also suggests the possibility that our technique enables us to find problematic use cases and build appropriate To-be model. In our case study, we used the general metrics, i.e., related to human efforts. There are some rooms to consider the other various metrics related to human efforts, for example, the skills or health conditions of a human actor.

Some of them cannot be specified in the adopted modeling technique. Although it was not so difficult to find the metrics used in the case study, to investigate the difficulties in developing metrics specific to problem domains, we should have wide varieties of case studies. Generally speaking, there seem to be some difficulties in finding metrics even using GQM. So guidelines in finding metrics and/or reusable metrics catalogs may be necessary to make our approach more practical.

6 Related Work

The techniques of metrics to detect problems included in As-is systems have been proposed, and Activity-based costing (ABC) is one of the most popular one [10]. In ABC, a total cost consumed in an organization is allocated into activities that were performed in the organization, and each activity is assessed by using the allocated cost and its spent time. As a result, we can identify the activities whose efficiency should be improved. The measures of ABC are cost and time while in our approach we can define wide varieties of measures using GQM. In addition, although ABC can find problematic activities, it does not have a methodology to get a To-be model and in our approach, we use GORA to do. Kaiya *et al.* defined some metrics on strategic dependency (SD) diagrams of i^* to measure efforts on dependency relationships between actors and goals, and applied graph transformation to the generation of the SD diagram of a To-be model [9]. Their metrics are subjective and ad-hoc weighted factors attached to dependency relationships while ours are systematically derived with GQM and includes behavioral aspects of As-is models. Although the support to generate a To-be model with graph transformation is useful, their approach does not take into account the rationales of and the conflicts to the existing goals of the As-is model.

The idea of integrating GORA and PFs is not new, and we can find some work. Jin *et al.* proposed a modeling technique where i^* and PFs are combined and applied it to a meeting scheduler system [8]. Furthermore, Yang *et al.* identified recurring requirements knowledge from literature and represented it with their integrated approach as requirements patterns [16]. In their integration, dependency relationships in a SD model are made to correspond to shared events appearing a problem diagram, and they did not provide a technique to specify the behavior of tasks in the SD model or the inner behavior of domains and machines. In our approach, we adopted use case modeling to bridge GORA to PFs and to specify detailed behavior, and it allows us to define metrics for detecting problems included in an As-is model. Mohammadi *et al.* proposed a technique to combine KAOS with PFs [12]. In their technique, they make goals in a KAOS model correspond to requirements in a problem diagram of PFs. The behavior of domains and machines are illustrated with message sequence charts (MSCs), and both of the problem diagram and the MSCs are used to refine the goals. Although their approach contains MSCs, the way how to integrate GORA and PFs in their approach is different from ours. In their approach, a goal corresponds to requirements appearing in a problem diagram, while in our approach it corresponds to a use case. The approach proposed by Beckers *et al.* adopted not KAOS but SI* as GORA to elicit security requirements [2]. The correspondence of elements of SI* to PFs is similar to the approach of Jin *et al.* [8] because SI* is a variant of *i** specific to security requirements elicitation such as trust relationship between actors, while a goal of SI* corresponds to requirements of PFs. Supakkul *et al.* made soft goals of NFR framework correspond to requirements of a problem diagram as stakeholders' problems [14]. Goal refinement of soft goals allows us to clarify interdependency relationships among the requirements. These approaches do not have a technique to represent behavioral specification in the same as Jin *et al.* [8]. There are some work to establish mapping of GORA to business process description languages which can specify the behavior of activities in the processes [4,6]. In addition, we can find the studies to integrate use case modeling or scenarios to GORA [5,13,15]. All of them did not include the integration of PFs. One of the benefits to use PFs is the clear differentiation of human domains from machines and the identification of activities related to the humans. It is very helpful to estimate the complexity and size of human activities. In fact, some of the metrics that we proposed are on context diagrams of PFs, and in Sect. 5, CE and NE were very useful to detect the problems hiding in the As-is model. In our modeling technique, domains of PFs include several use cases specifying their behavior, and they can be similar to the concept of system boundary of use case diagrams. In this sense, adopting PFs allows us to get a bird's eye view of a business process where humans' interactions are complicated. Although there are similar work to ours, any of the above approaches do not include the technique of metrics to find problems in an As-is model.

7   Concluding Remarks

In this paper, we proposed a technique for modeling As-is and deriving To-be by combining goal-oriented requirements analysis, problem frames, and use case modeling. In our technique, the metrics derived using GQM paradigm enables us to find problematic elements in As-is model automatically. The conducted case study of a reporting operation of a brokerage office indicated the effectiveness of our technique.

Possible future work can be listed up as follows:

1. defining more metrics to extract more problems and making guidelines how to construct GQM trees, furthermore making catalogs of metrics, and
2. automated transformation from As-is to To-be models by defining evolution patterns as model transformations formally.

Acknowledgements. This work was partly supported by JSPS Grants-in-Aid for Scientific Research Number 15K00088.

References

1. Basili, V., Caldiera, C., Rombach, D.: Goal, question, metric paradigm. Encycl. Softw. Eng. **1**, 528–532 (1994)
2. Beckers, K., Faßbender, S., Heisel, M., Paci, F.: Combining goal-oriented and problem-oriented requirements engineering methods. In: Cuzzocrea, A., Kittl, C., Simos, D.E., Weippl, E., Xu, L. (eds.) CD-ARES 2013. LNCS, vol. 8127, pp. 178–194. Springer, Heidelberg (2013). doi:10.1007/978-3-642-40511-2_13
3. Bernárdez, B., Durán, A., Genero, M.: Empirical evaluation and review of a metrics based approach for use case verification. J. Res. Pract. Inf. Technol. **36**(4), 247–258 (2004)
4. Bresciani, P., Perini, A., Giorgini, P., Giunchiglia, F., Mylopoulos, J.: Tropos: an agent-oriented software development methodology. Auton. Agent. Multi-Agent Syst. **8**(3), 203–236 (2004)
5. Cockburn, A.: Structuring use cases with goals. http://alistair.cockburn.us/Structuring+use+cases+with+goals
6. Guizzardi, R., Reis, A.N.: A method to align goals and business processes. In: Johannesson, P., Lee, M.L., Liddle, S.W., Opdahl, A.L., López, Ó.P. (eds.) ER 2015. LNCS, vol. 9381, pp. 79–93. Springer, Heidelberg (2015). doi:10.1007/978-3-319-25264-3_6
7. Jackson, M.: Problem Frames. Addison-Wesley, Boston (2001)
8. Jin, Z., Liu, L.: Requirements analyses integrating goals and problem analysis techniques. Tsinghua Sci. Technol. **12**(6), 729–740 (2007)
9. Kaiya, H., Morita, S., Ogata, S., Kaijiri, K., Hayashi, S., Saeki, M.: Model transformation patterns for introducing suitable information systems. In: Proceedings of the 19th Asia-Pacific Software Engineering Conference, pp. 434–439 (2012)
10. Kaplan, R.S., Bruns, W.: Accounting and Management: A Field Study Perspective. Harvard Business School Press, Brighton (1987)
11. van Lamsweerde, A.: Requirements Engineering: From System Goals to UML Models to Software Specifications. Wiley, Hoboken (2009)
12. Mohammadi, N.G., Alebrahim, A., Weyer, T., Heisel, M., Pohl, K.: A framework for combining problem frames and goal models to support context analysis during requirements engineering. In: Cuzzocrea, A., Kittl, C., Simos, D.E., Weippl, E., Xu, L. (eds.) CD-ARES 2013. LNCS, vol. 8127, pp. 272–288. Springer, Heidelberg (2013). doi:10.1007/978-3-642-40511-2_19
13. Rolland, C., Achour, C.B.: Guiding the construction of textual use case specifications. Data Knowl. Eng. **25**(1–2), 125–160 (1998)
14. Supakkul, S., Chung, L.: Extending problem frames to deal with stakeholder problems. In: Proceedings of the ACM Symposium on Applied Computing, pp. 389–394 (2009)
15. Watahiki, K., Saeki, M.: Combining goal-oriented analysis and use case analysis. IEICE Trans. **87-D**(4), 822–830 (2004)
16. Yang, J., Liu, L.: Modelling requirements patterns with a goal and PF integrated analysis approach. In: Proceedings of the 32nd Annual IEEE International Computer Software and Applications Conference, pp. 239–246 (2008)
17. Yu, E.S.: Social modeling and i^*. In: Borgida, A.T., Chaudhri, V.K., Giorgini, P., Yu, E.S. (eds.) Conceptual Modeling: Foundations and Applications. LNCS, vol. 5600, pp. 99–121. Springer, Heidelberg (2009). doi:10.1007/978-3-642-02463-4_7

Integrating Goal Model Analysis with Iterative Design

Claudio Menghi[1(✉)], Paola Spoletini[2], and Carlo Ghezzi[1]

[1] Politecnico di Milano, Milan, Italy
{claudio.menghi,carlo.ghezzi}@polimi.it
[2] Kennesaw State University, Marietta, Georgia
pspoleti@kennesaw.edu

Abstract. *Context and Motivation*: *Goal-oriented* methods can be used by analysts to produce a set of system requirements that reflect the customer needs and are used as guidelines in the subsequent system design, in which a model of the system is produced. The design model is used to analyze the coherence of the system behavior with the requirements. *Question/problem*: Design is an exploratory activity. Before the final model is developed, different alternatives are explored and models evolve back and forth from partial to complete. Partial models embed portions that are currently left unspecified and will later be refined. Recent formal verification techniques allow the designers to verify the satisfaction of requirements even for partial models. However, there is still no way to interpret the results of the verification over the original goal model. *Principal idea/results*: The ability to reflect the results of verification back to the goal model would improve the design process by making the developer aware of the consequences of design choices on goal satisfaction. It would also support early detection of design errors and improve requirements negotiation between designers and requirements analysts. *Contribution*: This paper proposes COVER, a unified framework to support goal model analysis during software design. COVER allows the goal model produced by the requirements analysts to be kept alive and updated while the system is designed. At each development round, the model is verified against the requirements of interest and the verification results can be used to update either the design model or the goal model.

Keywords: Iterative design · Goal model analysis · Partial models

1 Introduction

Goal models (e.g., KAOS [7], TROPOS [4] and i^* [31]) are formalisms supporting the requirements analyst in capturing system goals and high-level requirements by showing how functional and non-functional goals relate to each other and eventually how they relate to software requirements and environment assumptions [29]. Goal model analysis techniques allow the requirements analyst to better understand the relation between the satisfaction of different goals. Some

© Springer International Publishing AG 2017
P. Grünbacher and A. Perini (Eds.): REFSQ 2017, LNCS 10153, pp. 112–128, 2017.
DOI: 10.1007/978-3-319-54045-0_9

of the existing analysis techniques, such as [16], verify whether a specific goal is satisfiable. Others, such as [12], analyze the consequences of some goals satisfaction over the other goals of the model. Despite the increasing number of techniques and tools proposed in literature to analyze goal models, this reasoning activity is in the requirements analyst's hands and not in the developer's. The goal of most existing work has been to guide in precisely formulating requirements, ensuring that the subsequent design process is only initiated after successful completion of the requirements phase. This, however, hardly corresponds to modern development processes, which are highly iterative and incremental.

Differently from the traditional waterfall process in which each activity has to be terminated before the next one can start, modern development lifecycles promote adaptive planning, evolutionary development, early delivery, continuous improvement, and encourage rapid and flexible response to changes. From the analysis perspective, agile methodologies intrinsically call for techniques satisfying the "verify-while-develop" principle [8]. Verification techniques allow reasoning on the behavior of the system by checking whether the system possesses specific properties. In this incremental development setting, it is often the case that the designer, rather than having the fully specified design of the system, only owns at a given time an incomplete and partially specified design. However, the designer would still like to check the system's properties when design decisions are taken, e.g., when incomplete parts are refined. This is a primary goal in particular when a top-down development strategy is adopted. Several techniques have been proposed to verify requirements satisfaction over incomplete [23] or uncertain [18,19] models. It would be quite useful to interpret the results of verification over the original goal model. This would allow the designer to better understand the consequence of certain design choices and may possibly lead the requirements analyst in revising goals and requirements.

We believe the lack of integration between requirements and design is a major issue in the current approaches, most notably in the context of modern adaptive systems, as recognized in [26]. Although there has been a lot of work that attempts to link goal models to design [14], most of this work links requirements to running systems or just does a straight transformation to design, not explicitly supporting the co-evolution of design and requirements. To mitigate the problem, we propose COVER (Change-based gOal VErifier and Reasoner), a unified framework that enables goal model analysis during software design. In COVER requirements and design evolve together. The goal model produced to represent the elicited requirements is kept alive and updated during the iterative design of the system. At each development round, i.e., whenever the designer produces a new increment or changes something in the model, the new (incomplete) design of the system is verified. Since the model is incomplete, the verification procedure may return three different values: $\top$ if the property is satisfied by the current design, no matter how the undefined parts of the system will be later refined; $\bot$ if the property is not satisfied; ? whether its satisfaction depends on the parts which still have to be refined. Verification results are used to trigger goal model analysis to examine the consequences of requirement satisfaction over the goals of the goal model. This technique offers two major benefits. First, it makes designers aware of the consequences of their design choices. Whenever a new increment is proposed, designers may analyze the consequences of their changes over the entire goal model. This allows early detection of design errors. For example, the designer may realize that the increment she/he has proposed unexpectedly impacts on the satisfaction of some goals. Second, the requirements analyst may perceive that some of the requirements must be strengthened or relaxed, or that the relation between certain goals of the goal model must be changed. These benefits result in an earlier requirements negotiation between the developer and the requirements analyst.

To make the contribution concrete, we show an instantiation of COVER where the variation of the TROPOS modeling language presented in [21], Modal Transition Systems (MTS) [19], and Fluent Linear Temporal Logic (FLTL) [11] are chosen as a goal model framework, model for the design of the system, and specification language for functional requirements, respectively. We use TRO-POS since it comes with a nicely formalized and implemented label propagation algorithm that allows the analysis of the goal model [12]. We select MTSs since they are a standard way to incrementally design the system and FLTL since it is a logic commonly used to specify properties of MTSs. However, the COVER framework is independent of the chosen modeling and specification formalism and can be instantiated also in different ways. The use of this specific instance of COVER is recommended in case mathematical guarantees on the correctness of a system design are required and assumes that analysts and designers are familiar with formal tools, namely TROPOS, MTSs and FLTL. We show the benefits of the approach on the book seller example, previously used in [21,22] to assess an algorithm that identifies design alternatives given a set of preference specifications over the goals of the goal model. In this paper, it will be used to present the mock-up design process, where we propose three (simple) models that represent three different refinement rounds performed by the designer.

The paper is organized as follows. Section 2 provides the background over the formalisms used in the instantiation of COVER presented in this work. Section 3 describes COVER. Section 4 describes our tool support and evaluates the approach. Section 5 compares our approach with related work. Finally, Sect. 6 concludes the paper.

2   Background

In order to show how COVER works in practice, we instantiated it using the variation of the TROPOS goal modeling language presented in [21] as goal modeling formalism, Fluent Linear Time Temporal Logic [25] to formally specify requirements, and Modal Transition Systems [19] to model the system design. This section presents an overview of these formalisms helpful to understand the rest of the paper. We will use the book seller as an illustrative example. The full formalization of the example can be found at https://github.com/claudiomenghi/COVER.

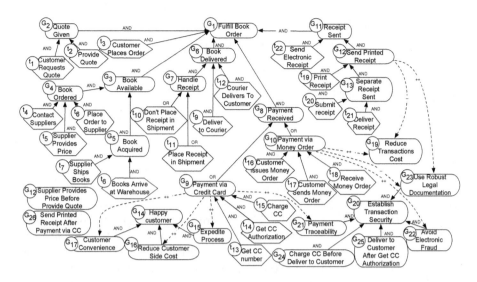

Fig. 1. Goal model for the wholesale book seller example.

TROPOS. The main entities of TROPOS [21] are goals. Goals are related to each other and decomposed into sub-goals by means of AND- or OR-decomposition. When a goal is AND-decomposed, it is necessary to satisfy all sub-goals for its achievement. For example, consider the goal model of the book seller example [21], presented in Fig. 1. The *Book Available* goal is AND-decomposed into the goals *Book Ordered* and *Book Acquired*, meaning that, to be available in the warehouse (WH), a book must be ordered and received by the WH. Conversely, when a goal is OR-decomposed it is sufficient to fulfill one of its sub-goals for its achievement. Goal decomposition allows the definition of both functional and non-functional requirements. A requirement is a terminal goal. The AND- and OR-decomposition is also used to decompose requirements into the tasks that imply their satisfaction. Tasks are specified in Fig. 1 with hexagonal boxes. For example, the goal *Handle Receipt* is OR-decomposed into the tasks *Don't Place Receipt in Shipment* and *Place Receipt in Shipment*. When a goal g is OR (AND)-decomposed into goals and tasks, the satisfaction of one of (all) the goals or (and) tasks is necessary for the satisfaction of g. In addition to AND- and OR-decomposition goals and tasks are connected via *break* ($\xrightarrow{--}$) and *make* links ($\xrightarrow{++}$). Break links indicate that the satisfaction of the origin causes the denial of the destination. Make links specify that if the origin is satisfied then the destination is satisfied. For example, the goal *Payment via credit card* is connected to the goals *Customer Convenience, Reduce Customer Side Cost, Expedite Process* and *Payment Traceability* through make links.

Fluent Linear Time Temporal Logic (FLTL). FLTL [11] is the formal language we adopted to specify the properties of interest. A *fluent* is a property of the world that holds after it is initiated by an event and ceases when it is

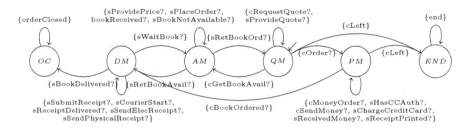

Fig. 2. A Modal Transition System.

terminated by another event. Given the set *Act*, which contains the events of the system, a *fluent Fl* is a pair $\langle I_{Fl}, T_{Fl}\rangle$, where $I_{Fl} \subset Act$ is the set of initiating events, $T_{Fl} \subset Act$ is the set of terminal events and $I_{Fl} \cap T_{Fl} = \emptyset$. A fluent may be *true* or *false*. A fluent is *true* if it has been initialized by an event $i \in I_{Fl}$ at an earlier time point and has not yet been terminated by another event $t \in T_{Fl}$; otherwise, it is *false*. The initial value of the fluent is specified using the attribute $Initially_{Fl}$ [24].

Given a set of fluents Φ and an infinite trace $\pi = l_0, l_1, \dots$ over the set *Act*, an FLTL *interpretation* of π is an infinite trace $f_0, f_1, \dots$ over 2^Φ which assigns to each index i of π the set of fluents that hold in position i. For example, consider the fluent $F\_PendingQuoteRequest = \langle\{cRequestQuote\}, \{sProvideQuote\}\rangle$, which is initially *false*. $F\_PendingQuoteRequest$ holds in a trace from the moment at which the client requests a quote (the *cRequestQuote* event occurs) and until the system provides the quote (the *sProvideQuote* event occurs).

An FLTL formula is obtained by composing fluents with LTL operators: $\bigcirc$ (next), $\Diamond$ (eventually), $\square$ (always), $\mathcal{U}$ (until) and $\mathcal{W}$ (weak until).

Modal Transition Systems. Modal Transition Systems (MTSs) [19] extend Labelled Transition System (LTSs) to allow explicit modeling of unknown behaviors. Extensions support specification of a set of *possible transitions*, i.e., transitions that may exist or not in the final model. Formally, an MTS $\mathcal{M}$ is a structure $\langle S, Act, \Delta_r, \Delta_p, s_0\rangle$, such that $\Delta_r \subseteq \Delta_p$. S is the set of the states of the MTS; *Act* is the set of the events; $\Delta_r \subseteq (S \times Act \times S)$ is the set of the required transitions; $\Delta_p \subseteq (S \times Act \times S)$ is the set of the possible transitions. We refer to transitions in the set $\Delta_p \setminus \Delta_r$ as *maybe transitions*. Graphically, the initial state of the MTS is marked with an incoming arrow. The events that label maybe transitions are suffixed with the character ?. An example of MTS is presented in Fig. 2. The self-loop over the state QM is a maybe transition, while the transition between state PM and END is required.

An MTS can be iteratively refined into a more precise description as new knowledge about maybe transitions becomes available. A refinement is obtained by converting maybe transitions into required transitions or removing them. A formal definition of refinement is presented in [27]. In this paper we refer to it informally, with the aid of an example. Figure 3 presents a refinement of the

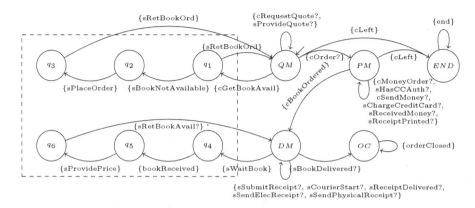

Fig. 3. A refinement of the Modal Transition System presented in Fig. 2

MTS of Fig. 2. Intuitively, the MTS of Fig. 3 refines the behaviors described by the MTS of Fig. 2 by restricting the sequences of events that can occur in state AM as shown by the fragment enclosed in a dotted box in Fig. 3. This refinement removes all uncertainties that were originally represented in Fig. 2 through the maybe self-loop transitions in state AM and its incoming and outgoing maybe transitions. Notice that the behaviors originally specified by the MTS in Fig. 2 while in state AM are different in the refinement when the state is entered from QM or from DM. Specifically, whenever the state is entered from QM, the refinement allows execution of the transitions labeled *sBookNotAvailable* and *sPlaceOrder*, and returns to state QM through the transitions labeled *sRetBookOrd*. If it is entered from DM, it allows execution of the transition labeled *bookReceived* and *sProvidePrice*, and returns to state DM through the transition labeled with the event *sRetBookAvail*.

Verification of MTSs. The verification of an MTS against FLTL properties can be done using standard procedures (see for example [28]). The verification framework chosen in this work is based on the three-valued semantic of LTL formulae. This semantic is used by MTSA [9], the tool we assume the designer is using to design the system.

Tropos Goal Model Analysis. We consider the label propagation algorithm presented in [12]. This algorithm has been proposed to propagate partial evidence about the satisfiability and deniability of goals. The algorithm introduces the predicates $FS(g)$ and $PS(g)$ over the goals of the graph, meaning that there exist a *full* or *partial evidence* that the goal g is satisfied, respectively. An additional proposition $\perp$ is used to represent the (trivially true) statement that there is at least null evidence that the goal is satisfied. The predicates $FD(g)$ and $PD(g)$ specify that there exists full and partial evidence that goal g is denied. Note that if there exist full evidence for a goal to be satisfied (denied) there is also partial evidence.

To check whether there exist full/partial evidence for a goal to be satisfied (denied), each goal of the graph is associated with a variable $Sat(g)$, which is initialized with a value defined over the domain $\{F, P, N\}$. The values F, P, N, such that $F > P > N$, specify that there is a full, partial and no evidence for g to be satisfied (denied). The goal model is used to iteratively propagate these values until a fixed point is reached. The final assignments are used to detect whether there is a full/partial o null evidence for a goal to be satisfied. For example, if $Sat(g) \geq P$ there is at least partial evidence for g to be satisfied.

3   The COVER Framework

COVER is a framework that supports the interplay between requirements analysis and design. It allows the continuous verification of the requirements of the system throughout design iterations, and enables the analysis of the verification results over the goal model produced during the requirements analysis. COVER does not take neither the goal model nor the design model as static oracles, but rather supports their co-evolution to improve each side iteratively. An overview of COVER is presented in Fig. 4. Hereafter we illustrate how the components of COVER shown in Fig. 4 enable the interplay between requirements and design.

Goal Model Design. The requirements analyst develops a goal model for the system. The goal model specifies goals, requirements, tasks, and the relations between them. Goals describe what the stakeholders want to achieve, i.e., strategic concerns that have clear-cut definition and clear-cut criteria to judge if they are satisfied. Goals are refined until requirements are identified. Requirements are goals that can be defined in terms of variables that can be monitored and controlled. Once identified, requirements are then decomposed into tasks, i.e., executable processes that represents functionalities that operationalize requirements. We assume here that the requirements analyst uses TROPOS to analyze the goals of the system and identify its requirements. For example, the goal model for the book seller example is presented in Fig. 1.

During goal model development, the requirements analyst may use some analysis tool to analyze the consequences of requirements/goals satisfaction.

Binding Tasks to System Events. Tasks represent the functionalities the system has to provide. By binding the tasks to system events, a bridge is established between the requirements analyst's and the designer's concerns. The completion of a task is indicated by the designer with an event: the system generates the event if and only if the task of interest has been accomplished. For example, assume that the requirements analyst identifies the *log in* task. This task is bound to the event *userLoggedIn*, which is used by the designer to specify that the task *log in* has ended.

Requirements Specification. In the requirements specification phase, the analyst uses the previously identified events to provide a formal description of some of the goals of the system. The analyst chooses the set of requirements to be formally specified and the formalism used in the formalization. The selected

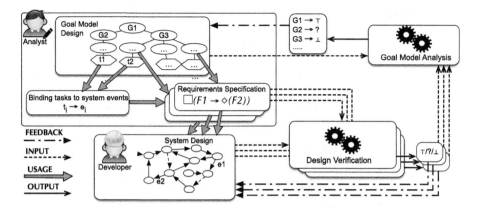

Fig. 4. An overview of the COVER framework.

formalism should be sufficiently expressive to describe the properties of interest. For example, depending on whether functional or non-functional properties must be specified, the analyst may choose a different formalism.

As in [20], we allow the specification of system goals (requirements) with a textual description for the communication with stakeholders and an FLTL formula which enables formal reasoning. Consider the previously introduced wholesale book seller example. The goal *Book Delivered* may be specified as follows:

Goal. (*G6*) *Book Delivered.*
Definition. *Before closing an order, the book is delivered to the customer.*
FormalDef. $(\neg F\_oc)\mathcal{W}(F\_sBookDelivered \wedge \neg F\_oc)$

where the fluents F_oc and $F\_sBookDelivered$ are defined as $\langle\{orderClosed\}, Act \setminus \{orderClosed\}\rangle$ and $\langle\{sBookDelivered\}, Act \setminus \{sBookDelivered\}\rangle$, respectively, and hold whenever the events *orderClosed* and *sBookDelivered* occur. The FLTL formula specifies that the fluent $F\_sBookDelivered$ must hold before F_oc. FLTL formulae can be specified starting from well known specification patters [10] or from subsets of natural languages [2].

Table 1 contains the definitions of the goals of the book seller example, each formalized by means of an FLTL formula reported in Table 2. In the formulae, we used the notation F_e to identify a fluent that is true when event e occurs. Formally, F_e is specified as $\langle\{e\}, Act \setminus \{e\}\rangle$. This formalization does not exploit all the capabilities of FLTL, but is sufficient to describe the properties of interest. For conciseness, in Table 1, we used F_oc, $F\_sProvPrice$, $F\_sRcptDel$ and $F\_rcvMoney$ to indicate fluents $F\_orderClosed$, $F\_sProvidePrice$, $F\_sReceiptDelivered$ and $F\_sReceivedMoney$, respectively. Note that, not all goals need to be formalized. The choice is left to the requirements analyst. For example, in Table 2 the goals G_{14}-G_{17} and G_{19}-G_{23} are not formally specified.

System Design. The requirements of the system are used by the designer as guidance for the system design. The designer usually starts by producing a high-

Table 1. Definitions of the goals of the wholesale book seller example of Fig. 1 that are formalized through FLTL formulae.

G	Name	Definition
G_2	Quote Given	If the client requests the quote, the system provides the price
G_3	Book Available	A book is finally available in the WH
G_4	Book Ordered	If a book is not available in the WH, it is ordered
G_5	Book Acquired	When the WH waits a book, the book is finally received
G_6	Book Delivered	Before closing an order, the book is delivered to the customer
G_7	Handle Receipt	If the WH submits a receipt, it is finally received by the client
G_8	Payment Rec	A succeeding order requires the payment from the user
G_9	Payment via CC	A succeeding order requires the money to be charged on the CC
G_{10}	Mon. Payment	A succeeding order relies on a bank transfer
G_{11}	Receipt Sent	A physical or electronic receipt is sent
G_{12}	Send Print Rec	The physical receipt is finally delivered
G_{13}	Separate Rec	The receipt is finally received
G_{18}	Price than quote	The supplier provides prices before quotes
G_{24}	CC before cust	The charge on CC can only occur before delivering to customer
G_{25}	Courier after CC	Charging CC can only be performed before the courier starts
G_{26}	Receipt after pay	The receipt is received by the user after the payment

level model of the system to be. Then, she/he iteratively decomposes the system until the behaviors of all of its components are defined. The system design is not a straightforward activity; it is an incremental process in which the high-level model of the system is iteratively detailed. For this reason, at a particular development step, the model can be incomplete and some of its parts may be detailed in a subsequent refinement round.

We assume that the designer uses MTSs to describe the behavior of the system. The set of events of the MTS includes the events that are bound to the tasks and are used by the developer to indicate that specific tasks ended. For example, the designer may propose the MTS shown in Fig. 2 as an initial model for the book seller example. The MTS has five states, each representing a functional component of the system: Quote Manager (QM), which is responsible for showing the quotes to the user, Book Availability Manager (AM), which is responsible for checking the book availability, Payment Manager (PM), which is responsible for managing the payment system, book Delivery Manager (DM), in charge of supervising book delivery. In addition, state Order Closed (OC) specifies that the order is closed and End (END) specifies that the user left the system. The transitions specify how the state of the system changes. Figures 3 and 5 present two MTSs that refine the MTS of Fig. 2 and we assume that they have been produced by the designer in subsequent refinement rounds.

Design Verification. After the designer has produced a model of the system, she/he may want to verify whether the requirements of interest are satisfied by the current design. The verification framework discussed in Sect. 2 is used to

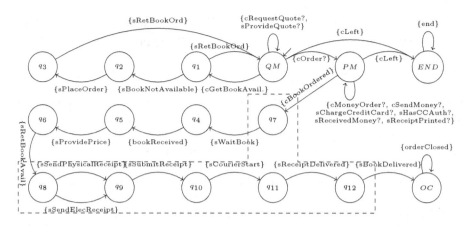

Fig. 5. A refinement of the Modal Transition System presented in Fig. 3

check whether the MTS that describes the system satisfies the FLTL properties of interest. For each requirement ϕ, the verification procedure returns "yes" ($\top$), "maybe" (?), or "no" ($\bot$), depending on the satisfaction of ϕ in the current model. The value $\top$ is returned if the property holds, independently of how currently unknown parts will be designed. The value $\bot$ is returned if the property is violated, no matter how currently unknown parts will be designed. In all the other cases, the analyzer returns ?, which specifies that the unknown parts affect the satisfaction of the property. For example, it can be proved that the design of Fig. 2 only possibly satisfies goal $G5$ since there is no assurance that a $sWaitBook$ event is followed by a $bookReceived$. Instead, since the $sWaitBook$ event is followed by a $bookReceived$, the designs of Figs. 3 and 5 satisfy $G5$. The results of the verification are used by the designer to check whether the current design must be revisited to satisfy its requirements.

Goal Model Analysis. Goal model analysis enables the interaction between the designer and the requirements analyst. The values obtained from the verification of the system design are used to trigger the analysis of the goal model. Each goal of the goal model is associated with an initial value, which specifies whether it is satisfied, possibly satisfied, or not satisfied by the current design. The goals that have not been formalized are considered as not satisfied. A label propagation algorithm is then used to propagate the initial values.

The label propagation algorithm defined in TROPOS and recalled in Sect. 2 is used by COVER to analyze goals' satisfaction. In our context, predicates $FS(g)$, $PS(g)$ are used to indicate that a goal g is satisfied and possibly satisfied, respectively, instead of indicating the existence of full and partial evidences. Proposition $\bot$ indicates that the goal is not satisfied instead of indicating that there is null evidence for the goal to be satisfied. Predicates $FD(g)$ and $PD(g)$ are not used by the label propagation algorithm since the algorithm is not used for identifying contradictory situations on the goal satisfaction. Finally, $Sat(g)$ is associated with values $\{\top, ?, \bot\}$ (instead of $\{F, P, N\}$) meaning that g is satisfied, possibly satisfied or not satisfied, respectively. This mapping imposes the total ordering $\top >? > \bot$, which is commonly used when three-valued logics are considered (see for example [6]). The choices previously described assume that the developer agrees on the total ordering relation $\top >? > \bot$ and with the rules used by the label propagation algorithm. For example, the label propagation algorithm associates the value $\bot$ with the goals that are destinations of break links. However, other truth orderings and propagation algorithms can be used.

The obtained results are used by the designer to reason about the impact of her/his design choices over the goals satisfaction. For example, if the designer defines a component that aims at satisfying a goal g, and g is not satisfied after the execution of the label propagation algorithm the current design must probably be revisited. The execution of the label propagation algorithm allows the designer to deduce that, for example, g is satisfied if it is AND- decomposed and all of its sub-goals are satisfied. From the requirements analyst perspective, the results obtained by running the label-propagation algorithm can be used to check for errors and improve the goal model. For example, consider a goal g that is specified through an FLTL formula that is possibly satisfied by the current design. If g is satisfied after the label propagation, g could be not specified correctly, or the satisfaction of g can be a consequence of the satisfaction of a sub-goal of g that has not been identified during the goal model design. Let us consider the bookshop goal model of Fig. 1 and the goals *Payment via Credit Card* (G_9) and *Payment Received* (G_8). If G_9 is satisfied and G_8 is not, the values of $Sat(G_9)$ and $Sat(G_8)$ are initialized to $\top$ and $\bot$, respectively. By propagating the values, we can deduce that the goal *Payment Received* is also satisfied.

4   Implementation and an Illustrative Example

We evaluated the proposed approach over the wholesale book seller example. We used the example to answer the following research questions: **RQ1**: how can COVER improve the detection of design errors? **RQ2**: how can COVER improve the detection of errors in the goal model?

To answer these questions we used COVER to analyze the consequences of the design alternatives described in Figs. 2, 3, 5 over the satisfaction of the goals of the goal model in Fig. 1. For RQ1 we checked how COVER guides the designer in the development of the model of the system. For RQ2 we verified how COVER supports the requirements analyst in the improvement of the goal model.

Implementation. We implemented the approach in the COVER framework[1]. The COVER framework is a Java 8 application that uses *(a)* the Goal Reasoning Tool (Gr-tool) [13] as a design framework of goal models and for the label propagation; *(b)* the Modal Transition System Analyzer (MTSA) [9] for supporting the designer in the development of the system design.

---

[1] The tool is available at https://github.com/claudiomenghi/COVER.

Results. Table 2 shows the results obtained by COVER when the designs $D1$, $D2$ and $D3$ presented in Figs. 2, 3, 5 are considered. The columns I and F show the *initial* values associated with the goals, i.e., the ones returned by the model checker, and the *final* values, i.e., the ones obtained after the execution of the goal model analysis, respectively. As previously discussed, the value $\bot$ is automatically assigned to the goals that are not associated with an FLTL formula. These goals are marked with a − symbol in the FormalDef column.

Table 2. Goal model analysis results for the designs D1, D2 and D3.

G	FormalDef.	D1		D2		D3	
		I	F	I	F	I	F
G_1	−	$\bot$	?	$\bot$	?	$\bot$	?
G_2	$\Box(F\_cRequestQuote \rightarrow \Diamond F\_sProvideQuote)$	?	?	?	?	?	?
G_3	$(\neg F\_orderClosed)\mathcal{W}(F\_bookReceived \wedge \neg F\_orderClosed)$	?	?	?	⊤	⊤	⊤
G_4	$\Box(F\_sBookNotAvailable \rightarrow \Diamond F\_sPlaceOrder)$	?	?	⊤	⊤	⊤	⊤
G_5	$\Box(F\_sWaitBook \rightarrow \Diamond F\_bookReceived)$	?	?	⊤	⊤	⊤	⊤
G_6	$(\neg F\_oc)\mathcal{W}(F\_sBookDelivered \wedge \neg F\_oc)$	⊤	⊤	⊤	⊤	⊤	⊤
G_7	$\Box(F\_sSubmitReceipt \rightarrow (\Diamond F\_sRcptDel))$	?	?	?	?	⊤	⊤
G_8	$(\neg F\_oc)\mathcal{W}(F\_rcvMoney \wedge \neg F\_oc)$	?	?	?	?	?	?
G_9	$(\neg F\_oc)\mathcal{W}(F\_sChargeCreditCard \wedge \neg F\_oc)$	?	?	?	?	?	?
G_{10}	$(\neg F\_oc)\mathcal{W}(F\_cSendMoney \wedge \neg F\_oc)$	?	?	?	?	?	?
G_{11}	$(\neg F\_oc)\mathcal{W}(F\_sSubmitReceipt \wedge \neg F\_oc)$	?	?	?	?	⊤	⊤
G_{12}	$\Box((F\_sSendPhysicalReceipt) \rightarrow (\neg F\_oc\mathcal{W}(F\_sRcptDel)))$	?	?	?	?	⊤	⊤
G_{13}	$(\neg F\_oc)\mathcal{W}(F\_sRcptDel \wedge \neg F\_oc)$	?	?	?	?	⊤	⊤
G_{14}	−	$\bot$	?	$\bot$	?	$\bot$	?
G_{15}	−	$\bot$	?	$\bot$	?	$\bot$	?
G_{16}	−	$\bot$	?	$\bot$	?	$\bot$	?
G_{17}	−	$\bot$	?	$\bot$	?	$\bot$	?
G_{18}	$(\neg F\_sProvPrice)\mathcal{W}(F\_sProvideQuote \wedge \neg F\_sProvPrice)$	?	?	?	?	?	?
G_{19}	−	$\bot$	?	$\bot$	?	$\bot$	⊤
G_{20}	−	$\bot$	?	$\bot$	?	$\bot$	?
G_{21}	−	$\bot$	?	$\bot$	?	$\bot$	?
G_{22}	−	$\bot$	?	$\bot$	?	$\bot$	?
G_{23}	−	$\bot$	?	$\bot$	?	$\bot$	⊤
G_{24}	$\Box(F\_sBookDelivered \rightarrow \Box(\neg F\_sChargeCreditCard))$	⊤	⊤	⊤	⊤	⊤	⊤
G_{25}	$\Box(F\_sCourierStart \rightarrow \Box(\neg F\_sChargeCreditCard))$	?	?	⊤	⊤	⊤	⊤
G_{26}	$\Box((\neg F\_rcvMoney) \vee \Diamond(F\_rcvMoney \wedge \Diamond F\_sRcptDel))$	?	?	?	?	?	?

Design D1. *RQ1*: the *initial* values inform the designer about the satisfaction of the FLTL properties over the current design. All the goals associated with

FLTL properties are satisfied or possibly satisfied. Surprisingly, goals G_{24} and G_6 are already satisfied (despite the unknown parts). Indeed, in the case of G_{24}, the credit card (CC) is charged before the book is delivered to the customer, i.e., the event *sChargeCreditCard* can occur only before *sBookDelivered*.

RQ2: the *final* values describe the consequences of the design choices over the goal satisfaction. The requirements analyst may manually inspect the results of the goal model analysis to improve his/her goal model. Thus, the results of Table 2 are considered w.r.t. the goal model of Fig. 1. Even if the goal *Book Delivered* is satisfied, the goal *Happy Customer*, whose satisfaction is intuitively related with the delivering of the book, is "only" possibly satisfied after the goal model analysis. Indeed, the goals *Book Delivered* and *Happy Customer* are not connected with a make link' in the current goal model.

Design D2. *RQ1*: the *initial* values inform the designer that no properties are violated by the current design. Goal G_4 is satisfied since the design ensures that, if a book is not available in the WH, it is ordered. Goal G_5 is satisfied since, if the WH waits for a book, the book is finally received. Goal G_3 is only possibly satisfied since the design $D2$ does not provide any assurance that a book is finally available. Is this a design error? Should this goal be satisfied?

RQ2: the *final* values specify that no goals are violated by the current initial values. Since both G_4 and G_5 are satisfied, the label propagation algorithm states that G_3, which was initially possibly satisfied, is also satisfied. The analyst may wonder why. Specifically, a deep analysis of the goal model raises the following question: whenever the customer orders a book, is goal *Book Available* satisfied if the book is already in the WH? Indeed, in $D2$, to make the book available, the transition labeled with *sWaitBook* must be fired. Should the requirements analyst add the goal *Manage Local WH* associated with a task *Check Book Presence in the WH* as sub-goal of *Book Available*?

Design D3. *RQ1*: differently from $D2$ the *initial* values specify that also G_{11}, G_{12}, G_{13} and G_7 are satisfied. The first three goals are the goal *Receipt Sent* and its (sub-)goals, the last is the goal *Courier Deliver To Customer*. This gives the developer more confidence on the correctness of his design, since the only goals that remain to be satisfied are the ones related with the payment procedure and the quoting of the books which still have to be refined.

RQ2: the initial values show that G_{11}, G_{12}, G_{13} are satisfied together with G_7. This raises the following question: *is there any relation between these goals?* In particular, is the sub-goal *Handle Receipt* of *Books Delivered* not related with *Receipt Sent*? Should these two goals be related? Could *Receipt Sent* be a sub-goal of *Handle Receipt*?

Discussion. The book seller example showed the potential advantages of using COVER during the development process. COVER proved to be an extremely useful instrument for the designer perspective to answer the following questions: *is my design correct? does it satisfy its requirements? given the current design, which goals are satisfied?*, while for the requirements analyst perspective it helps in answering the following questions: *given a design, which requirements/goals* *are satisfied? Should also other requirements/goals be (possibly) satisfied? Is it necessary to modify the goal model?* The potential advantages of using COVER are witnessed by designs $D2$ and $D3$, which showed how COVER can improve the interaction between the requirements analyst and the designer. For example, the possible satisfaction of G_3 may uncover a design error or may require a change in the goal model. One problem with TROPOS-style analysis is that it tends to converge to many conflicting values, thus not really providing helpful analysis results for the users [30]. A similar problem occurs for propagation of uncertainty. We can see evidence of this problem in Table 2 for the initial design rounds. When the design is somewhat uncertain, the goal model analysis results are very uncertain (and not very useful). This does get better as the design becomes more certain.

Threats to Validity. The main threat to validity concerns the designs proposed for the book seller case study. In absence of a real case study in which both the goal model and the system design are provided, we proposed the models in Figs. 2, 3 and 5 for the book seller case study.

Scalability. Checking satisfaction of all the requirements took around 1s, for designs $D1$, $D2$ and $D3$. Instead, the goal model analysis required around 3ms. The label propagation algorithm used in the goal model analysis has been proved to be correct and complete and to terminate in at most $6 \times |G| + 1$ iterations. As discussed in [12], this technique can be applied in real life applications where goal models can count more than hundred goals. The verification of FLTL formulae over MTS reduces to two classical FLTL model-checking over LTS and has been used to evaluate realistic case studies, see for example [28]. Hence, the overall approach seems to be applicable also to realistic case studies.

5   Related Work

The related work includes 1. how to analyze goal models in presence of uncertainty; 2. how to verify incomplete/uncertain system designs; 3. work that relates the goal model analysis with the verification of the system design.

Uncertainty in the goal model. Several techniques have been proposed in literature to analyze goal models. An extensive survey can be found in [17]. Some of these techniques can also be applied in the context of uncertainty, such as [12,15]. However, these techniques do not use the results obtained by the verification of the system design to trigger the analysis of the goal model.

Uncertainty in the system design. Several techniques have been proposed to analyze requirements over incomplete and partially specified designs, such as [5, 19,23]. An extensive description of some of these techniques can be found in [27]. However, the impact of the verification results over the original goal model is usually not considered.

Relating goal modeling and system design. Several techniques have been proposed to derive a model of the system from its goal, e.g., [20], and properties, e.g., [28]. However, these works do not analyze how changes on the generated design influence the goal satisfaction. Vice versa, some approaches trigger reasoning techniques when the environment in which the application is running changes [1,3]. However, they usually do not consider goal models as an instrument to enable the verification of the system design. The lack of integration between requirements analysis and the verification of the system design has also been evidenced as a major issue in [26]. COVER has been developed exactly to solve this problem and provides a unified framework which supports the evolution of the goal model together with the design of the system.

6   Conclusion and Future Work

We presented COVER, a unified framework that enables goal model analysis during the software development. The goal model produced by the requirements analyst is kept alive during the design of the system. At each refinement round, i.e., whenever the designer produces a new increment or changes something in the model, the new (incomplete) design of the system is verified. The verification results are used to analyze the set of goals of the goal model that are currently satisfied, possibly satisfied and not satisfied. We implemented COVER as a Java 8 stand alone application and we evaluated its benefits over the wholesale book seller example [21]. COVER proved to be useful in supporting the detection of design errors, as well as to evidence weaknesses of the goal model as the development proceeds.

As future work, we aim to evaluate the approach over a realistic case study, which would allow us to establish the effectiveness of the approach in a real setting. Moreover, we plan to analyze the applicability of COVER with other modeling formalisms, such as KAOS as a goal model and UML as a design formalism. Furthermore, we plan to extend COVER by developing algorithms that helps the requirements analyst and the developer in interpreting the results of the label propagation algorithm. These algorithms may search for results that are likely consequences of design errors or require changes in the goal model. Finally, we would like to consider quantitative reasoning. This might enable the analysis of contradictory situations where, for example, there is a partial evidence for a goal to be satisfied and denied.

References

1. Ali, R., Dalpiaz, F., Giorgini, P.: A goal-based framework for contextual requirements modeling and analysis. Requir. Eng. 15(4), 439–458 (2010)
2. Autili, M., Grunske, L., Lumpe, M., Pelliccione, P., Tang, A.: Aligning qualitative, real-time, and probabilistic property specification patterns using a structured english grammar. Trans. Softw. Eng. 41(7), 620–638 (2015)
3. Baresi, L., Pasquale, L., Spoletini, P.: Fuzzy goals for requirements-driven adaptation. In: Requirements Engineering Conference, pp. 125–134. IEEE (2010)

4. Bresciani, P., Perini, A., Giorgini, P., Giunchiglia, F., Mylopoulos, J.: Tropos: an agent-oriented software development methodology. Auton. Agents Multi-Agent Syst. **8**(3), 203–236 (2004)
5. Bruns, G., Godefroid, P.: Model checking partial state spaces with 3-valued temporal logics. In: Halbwachs, N., Peled, D. (eds.) CAV 1999. LNCS, vol. 1633, pp. 274–287. Springer, Heidelberg (1999). doi:10.1007/3-540-48683-6_25
6. Chechik, M., Devereux, B., Easterbrook, S., Gurfinkel, A.: Multi-valued symbolic model-checking. Trans. Softw. Eng. Methodol. **12**(4), 371–408 (2003)
7. Dardenne, A., Van Lamsweerde, A., Fickas, S.: Goal-directed requirements acquisition. Sci. Comput. Program. **20**(1), 3–50 (1993)
8. De Roever, W.-P.: Concurrency Verification: Introduction to Compositional and Non-compositional Methods, vol. 54. Cambridge University Press, Cambridge (2001)
9. D'Ippolito, N., Fischbein, D., Chechik, M., Uchitel, S.: MTSA: the modal transition system analyser. In: International Conference on Automated Software Engineering, pp. 475–476. IEEE (2008)
10. Dwyer, M.B., Avrunin, G.S., Corbett, J.C.: Patterns in property specifications for finite-state verification. In: International Conference on Software Engineering, pp. 411–420. IEEE (1999)
11. Giannakopoulou, D., Magee, J.: Fluent model checking for event-based systems. In: Symposium on Foundations of Software Engineering, pp. 257–266 (2003)
12. Giorgini, P., Mylopoulos, J., Nicchiarelli, E., Sebastiani, R.: Formal reasoning techniques for goal models. In: Spaccapietra, S., March, S., Aberer, K. (eds.) Journal on Data Semantics I. LNCS, vol. 2800, pp. 1–20. Springer, Heidelberg (2003). doi:10.1007/978-3-540-39733-5_1
13. Giorgini, P., Mylopoulos, J., Sebastiani, R.: Goal-oriented requirements analysis and reasoning in the tropos methodology. Eng. Appl. Artif. Intell. **18**(2), 159–171 (2005)
14. Horkoff, J., Li, T., Li, F., Salnitri, M., Cardoso, E., Giorgini, P., Mylopoulos, J.: Using goal models downstream: a systematic roadmap and literature review. Int. J. Sci. Manag. Dev. **6**(2), 1–42 (2015)
15. Horkoff, J., Salay, R., Chechik, M., Di Sandro, A.: Supporting early decision-making in the presence of uncertainty. In: Requirements Engineering Conference, pp. 33–42. IEEE (2014)
16. Horkoff, J., Yu, E.: Finding solutions in goal models: an interactive backward reasoning approach. In: Parsons, J., Saeki, M., Shoval, P., Woo, C., Wand, Y. (eds.) ER 2010. LNCS, vol. 6412, pp. 59–75. Springer, Heidelberg (2010). doi:10.1007/978-3-642-16373-9_5
17. Horkoff, J., Yu, E.: Analyzing goal models: different approaches and how to choose among them. In Symposium on Applied Computing, pp. 675–682 (2011)
18. Huth, M., Jagadeesan, R., Schmidt, D.: Modal transition systems: a foundation for three-valued program analysis. In: Sands, D. (ed.) ESOP 2001. LNCS, vol. 2028, pp. 155–169. Springer, Heidelberg (2001). doi:10.1007/3-540-45309-1_11
19. Larsen, K.G., Thomsen, B.: A modal process logic. In: Logic in Computer Science, pp. 203–210. IEEE (1988)
20. Letier, E., Kramer, J., Magee, J., Uchitel, S.: Deriving event-based transition systems from goal-oriented requirements models. Autom. Softw. Eng. **15**(2), 175–206 (2008)
21. Liaskos, S., McIlraith, S.A., Sohrabi, S., Mylopoulos, J.: Integrating preferences into goal models for requirements engineering. In: Requirements Engineering Conference, pp. 135–144. IEEE (2010)

22. Liaskos, S., McIlraith, S.A., Sohrabi, S., Mylopoulos, J.: Representing and reasoning about preferences in requirements engineering. Requir. Eng. **16**(3), 227–249 (2011)
23. Menghi, C., Spoletini, P., Ghezzi, C.: Dealing with incompleteness in automata-based model checking. In: Fitzgerald, J., Heitmeyer, C., Gnesi, S., Philippou, A. (eds.) FM 2016. LNCS, vol. 9995, pp. 531–550. Springer, Heidelberg (2016). doi:10.1007/978-3-319-48989-6_32
24. Miller, R., Shanahan, M.: The event calculus in classical logic - alternative axiomatizations. Electron. Trans. Artif. Intell. **3**(A), 77–105 (1999)
25. Sandewall, E.: Features and Fluents: The Representation of Knowledge about Dynamical Systems, vol. 1. Oxford University Press, Inc., Oxford (1995)
26. Sawyer, P., Bencomo, N., Whittle, J., Letier, E., Finkelstein, A.: Requirements-aware systems: a research agenda for re for self-adaptive systems. In: Requirements Engineering Conference, pp. 95–103. IEEE (2010)
27. Uchitel, S., Alrajeh, D., Ben-David, S., Braberman, V., Chechik, M., De Caso, G., DIppolito, N., Fischbein, D., Garbervetsky, D., Kramer, J., et al.: Supporting incremental behaviour model elaboration. Comput. Sci.-Res. Dev. **28**(4), 279–293 (2013)
28. Uchitel, S., Brunet, G., Chechik, M.: Synthesis of partial behavior models from properties and scenarios. Trans. Softw. Eng. **35**(3), 384–406 (2009)
29. Van Lamsweerde, A.: Goal-oriented requirements engineering: a guided tour. In: Requirements Engineering Conference, pp. 249–262. IEEE (2001)
30. Lamsweerde, A.: Reasoning about alternative requirements options. In: Borgida, A.T., Chaudhri, V.K., Giorgini, P., Yu, E.S. (eds.) Conceptual Modeling: Foundations and Applications. LNCS, vol. 5600, pp. 380–397. Springer, Heidelberg (2009). doi:10.1007/978-3-642-02463-4_20
31. Yu, E.S.: Towards modelling and reasoning support for early-phase requirements engineering. In: Requirements Engineering Conference, pp. 226–235. IEEE (1997)

Communication and Collaboration

Patterns of Collaboration Driven by Requirements in Agile Software Development Teams

Findings from a Multiple Case Study

Irum Inayat[1]([⊠]), Sabrina Marczak[2], Siti Salwah Salim[3],
and Daniela Damian[4]

[1] Department of Computer Science, FAST National University of Computer
and Emerging Sciences, Islamabad, Pakistan
irum.inayat@nu.edu.pk
[2] Computer Science School, PUCRS, Porto Alegre, Brazil
sabrina.marczak@pucrs.br
[3] Faculty of Computer Science and Information Technology,
University of Malaya, Kuala Lumpur, Malaysia
salwa@um.edu.my
[4] Computer Science Department, University of Victoria, Victoria, Canada
danielad@cs.uvic.ca

Abstract. *Context and motivation*: Due to their emphasis on communication, agile methods and requirements engineering activities seem to mutually support each other in software development. *Question/Problem*: But how do agile teams manage the collaboration required to perform requirements related activities, especially when their members work from geographically distributed locations? *Principle Ideas/Results*: In this paper we investigated the requirements-driven collaboration translated as communication and awareness among agile teams from four distributed projects. We identified some collaboration patterns that are similar to those reported in the literature for the traditional, non-agile teams, but also some more specific to agile teams. For instance, we found that the number of team members involved in actual collaboration is different than the number of assigned members, that little communication exists with members outside the team, and that project managers are still key players in knowledge sharing patterns. We also found that distance does not matter for knowledge management, that familiarity from past projects facilitates awareness, and communication is still an important source of awareness. *Contributions*: Our results suggest an exploration on the role of project managers as the key players in agile teams. Also, the correlation of distance and communication needs to be investigated in largely distributed agile teams.

Keywords: Requirements-driven collaboration · Agile development · Social network analysis · Empirical research · Case study

P. Grünbacher and A. Perini (Eds.): REFSQ 2017, LNCS 10153, pp. 131–147, 2017.
DOI: 10.1007/978-3-319-54045-0_10

1 Introduction

Agile methods are collaborative in nature and entail an organic management of requirements, unlike traditional software development methods [1]. In such a dynamic process, requirements are highly volatile and constant collaboration is essential to cope with ever changing requirements for risk mitigation due to dependencies [2]. Developer collaboration is dependent on the communication of changes of new tasks, as well as on the awareness of what others are doing and whether they are available to help [3].

Empirical evidence of collaboration patterns of requirements engineering activities exists in the literature. Studies such as Damian et al. [5], for example, studied traditional (i.e., waterfall model) distributed projects of a large multinational company and identified that such collaboration, referred to as requirements-driven collaboration (RDC) [4], was highly dynamic and included important cross-site interactions. More people collaborated during the development of each requirement than was originally planned, and over one-third of interactions in the team were with people that have not being assigned to work in the project, named emergent members. Although they found that team members had general awareness of others working on the same requirements, regardless of geographical location, more communication was correlated with high awareness in the project. Distance did affect the frequency as well as ease of communication with remote members. However, very little is still known about the "agile way" of dealing with requirements and how RDC in such teams takes place.

Unlike traditional teams, agile teams are closely knit, cross-functional, and highly interactive with constant communication free of imposed organizational barriers. Team members are self-manageable and empowered to make decisions on their own in contrast to the traditionally centralized structures dependent on project managers. Therefore, interesting questions about RDC relate to this new team structure: (RQ1) Which roles collaborate with each other?, (RQ2) Which members presence emerge throughout the project?, (RQ3) What kind of communication patterns exist within- and cross-roles?, (RQ4) What kind of communication and awareness patterns exists within- and cross sites?, (RQ5) What role distance plays in the communication and awareness patterns?, and (RQ6) What role communication plays in disseminating awareness to team members?

Drawing on Damian et al.' work, we sought to investigate these research questions and more broadly to identify overall collaboration patterns of agile teams. We report from a multiple case study of four projects following the agile methodology, in which we used a combination of on-site observations, interviews and a questionnaire to obtain detailed information about their collaboration around requirements development. We also discuss the findings in light of current literature and briefly present implications for research and practice.

This paper is organized in following sections. Section 1 explains introduction on the topic. Section 2 describes the background of our work. Section 3 presents the research methods used to conduct this research study. Section 4 demonstrates the findings. Section 5 discusses the findings. Section 6 explains the limitations and Sect. 7 drives the implications of our work. Section 8 concludes this research study.

2   Background and Related Work

The importance of agile methods is undeniable in today's software development practice. However, only a small number of studies have explored collaboration patterns among agile teams so far (e.g. [5, 6]). Cataldo and Ehrlich investigated the impact of the role of hierarchy and small-world communication structures (i.e. when two nodes are connected to each other through the smallest path [7]) on iteration performance and quality in a large distributed agile team. Results showed a strong positive effect for hierarchy but a marginal negative effect for small-worlds on team performance, and a negative effect for hierarchy but a very strong positive effect for small-worlds on quality. Given that requirements drive the development cycle, we decided to take their lens to collect a more detailed and broader view of how team members collaborate.

Requirements communication has been discussed in literature in terms of investigating what role distance plays in it [8], and how interaction among roles for requirements communication shape their communication structures [9], among others. We draw on the work of Damian et al., which examined RDC in traditional teams. We use the concept of a Requirements-Centric Agile Team based on the Requirement-Centric Team concept from Damian et al. [4]. The Requirements-Centric Team refers to the team of people collaborating around a certain requirement, while a Requirements-Centric Social Network refers to the social network that represents the collaboration that takes place within that team. Therefore, in our work, a Requirements-Centric Agile Team is a group of cross-functional and self-organizing members working on a certain set of interdependent requirements [10]. It includes the team members that are assigned to work on the project only. However, those members whose participation 'emerges' throughout the life cycle for some reason (e.g. to resolve some issue or to get clarification on some matter) are also considered a part of the Requirements-Centric Agile Team. We name these as *emergent members*. For instance, if a team members want to clarify certain issues from Management or Technical Support Team members, they will be considered as emergent members since they were not a part of assigned team. Similarly, a Requirements-Centric Social Network [4] for an Requirements-Centric Agile Team (RCAT) represents agile team members as actors and their established relationships (communication or aware of) as ties between pairs of actors. We name these *Requirements-Centric Agile Social Network* (RCASN) [10].

3   Research Method

We have conducted a multiple-case study of four large distributed IT organizations. In this section we briefly present each of the projects and describe the procedures for data collection and analysis.

3.1   Projects' Background

Overall, the four projects follow Scrum to develop their products. The projects were mid-sized ranging from 3 to 5-months life span each, organized in 2 to 3 iterations according to the project size. More specifically, project *Case 1* is from an organization that develops in-house internet security software and focused on developing a Mobile Internet Security software. The team was composed of 10 members distributed in Malaysia (MAL) and in Finland (FIN) as presented in Table 1. Atlassian JIRA was used for requirements management. Project *Case 2* is from a company that develops Graphical System Design Platforms for diverse industries and aimed to track and monitor the shortfall in supply of components. The team had 5 members distributed in Malaysia (MAL) and in the United States (USA) as indicated in Table 1. The team uses Xplanner and JIRA for requirements management. As per project *Case 3*, it is from a company that provides extensive solutions and information management consulting. The project goal was to develop a Web-based physical and electronic data indexing and cataloging solution for storing, managing, and categorizing core rock samples and seismic map data stored at variable geographical locations. The team was comprised of 7 members distributed in Pakistan (PK) and in United Kingdom (GB), as per Table 1. JIRA was used for project management. And project *Case 4* belongs to an organization that produces customized solutions and product suites for business processes. The project studied was a healthcare revenue cycle management system. The team had 9 members distributed in Pakistan (PK) and in the Republic of Philippines (RP) as Table 1. IBM Rational Team Concert (RTC) tool was adopted to support the entire project development life cycle.

Table 1. Project members details

Project	Case 1	Case 2	Case 3	Case 4
Project Manager (PM)	1 FIN	1 USA	1 PK	1 PK
Product Owner (PO)	1 FIN			
Developer (Dev)	4 MAL, 1 FIN	2 MAL, 1 USA	1 PK, 2 GB	3 PK, 1 RP
Tester (Test)	1 MAL		1 PK	1 PK, 1 RP
User Exp. Designer (UX)	1 FIN			
Software Architect (Arch)		1 USA	2 PK	2 RP
Number of members	10	5	7	9

3.2 Data Collection Methods

We collected data through observations, interviews, and a questionnaire. We gathered data for two iterations in each project after spending about a month in each organization. We observed team members present in PK and MAL only, those from the other locations attended team meetings on Skype calls, to see how team members collaborate on a daily basis, how they use the tools, and how they execute the agile practices adopted by the companies.

Information about the company and the software products were collected from the observation sessions and through interviews. The first author spent about 4 weeks with each team on site attending daily sprints, scrum meetings, and daily activities of the development teams. The interviews mostly served the purposed of identifying on which requirements (or user stories) each team was working on and which team members has been assigned to work on each iteration. During the interviews, the first author also learned that in all projects team members self-assigned themselves to work on a certain user story. Information gathered about the requirements and team members was used later to design the questionnaire. A total of 9 interviews were conducted with project managers and senior developers, resulting in 5.25 h of voice recorded data and 38 pages of transcribed text.

The questionnaires asked with whom, about what and with what frequency the respondent communicated in the team. A list of all team members assigned to the iteration was provided. It also asked whom the respondent was aware of and how aware she was of others. In addition, we asked the respondent to point out whether she had communicated (or was aware of) with team members that have not been listed. All team members responded to the questionnaire. We built the social networks from this data.

The communication RCASN is the social network formed on the basis of communication that happened between team members for variable reasons including: discussion of bugs, communication of changes, code issues, code refactoring, code reviews, code synchronization, coordination, management issues, quality issues, sprint planning, support, user story clarification, and user story negotiation. Similarly, awareness RCASN is formed on the basis of the perception of awareness. We collected information on whether project members were aware of each other's presence, professional background, work status, and current tasks. We named these four kinds of awareness as: (i) availability, how easy is for one to reach a person when one needs help about the project [11]; (ii) general awareness, how aware one is of a person's professional background [11]; (iii) current awareness, how aware one is of the current set of tasks that a certain person is working on [11]; and (iv) work status awareness, how aware one is of a colleague's current progress of work that is related to the project. This fourth type of awareness has been defined by us given the relevance of constant progress report in agile teams. The questionnaire was deployed twice, once for each iteration.

3.3   Data Analysis

We used observations and interviews to develop an initial understanding about the projects, i.e., goal, team structure (roles and responsibilities), means of communication (media use and frequency), role of tool support, etc. We manually inspected the transcription of the interviews and used the developed knowledge to fill in the members' list options in the designed questionnaire to later build the RCASN from it.

As previously explained, in the questionnaire, each respondent had to indicate with whom from the provided team members' list did she communicate and what was the conversation about. Also, who from the same provided team members' list one was aware of. For instance, if team member A indicated she communicated about changes with member B a directed tie from A to B was created in the communication of changes

RCASN. Also, if A reported that she communicated about changes with a member Y that has not been assigned to the project, then we created a directed tie from A to Y and marked this tie as *emergent* in order to represent that the relationship between A–Y indicates a situation that has not been initially foreseen to take place in the project. Note that communication and awareness were considered directional, i.e. if a pair 'source-target' (A and B) reported communication and this same pair 'target-source' (B and A) also reported communication, we considered that two instances of communication had taken place.

The data from questionnaires helped us to see who communicated with whom and for what reason, and also who was aware of whom. This data were then used to build the respective communication and awareness networks called RCASNs. The RCASNs were then visualized to collect some initial insights of the collaboration behavior of the teams (e.g., no emergent participation was detected, member A was the most sought member to discuss changes, etc.).

The self-reported data from questionnaires were then imported to an Excel spreadsheet for a descriptive analysis of the communication and awareness reported relationships. The data were recorded in the Excel sheets in a matrix format such that all the team members who were identified communicating for a certain reason (or were aware of each other) were listed on X and Y axis. Then for each existing tie (i.e. existing communication and awareness) among member A and B we placed a '1' and '0' for otherwise. Likewise, we calculated the number of communication and awareness ties within and cross roles. For examples for cross roles communication we calculated 29 ties between PM-Dev and for within roles communication 58 ties among Devs. We call this analysis the "ties statistics".

Following the aforementioned method, we coded within and cross site communication and awareness ties as well. Yet another Excel spreadsheet in a matrix format (with team members on X and Y axis) was built for each communication reason and awareness type; this time indicating '1' for a communication or awareness tie between people located in different countries and '0' otherwise. For instance, in Case 1 a communication tie recorded for bugs discussion between a team member A and a member B both located in MAL was considered a 'within-site' tie (coded as 0) and for a communication tie between member A located in MAL and a member C located in the USA, we coded it as a cross-site tie (coded as 1). In addition, we created a distance matrix (see Sect. 5) to see the effect of distance on team members' communication frequency and awareness types. Then correlation is calculated between communication ties, awareness ties, and distance matrix to find out their effect on each other. The correlation analysis was performed in UCINet (http://www.analytictech.com/). Results of these and the other referred analysis are presented next.

4 Findings

In this section we report the patterns we identified across the RCASNs.

4.1 Characterization of the Requirements-Centric Agile Social Networks (RCASNs)

Communication Within the Actual RCASNs

(a) (RQ1) how many team members actually communicated? For each user story identified, we generated a RCASN. Table 2 indicates number of team members who communicated in total for all actual RCASNs for each communication reason. For instance, the first entries of the table (column 1–2 and row 1 after header) describe that 5 team members from MAL (4 Dev and 1 Test) and 6 from FIN (1 PM, 1 PO, 1 Dev, 1 UX, and 1 emergent member) talked to each other for bugs discussion in Case 1 iteration 1. However, it can be seen that 5 team members were in FIN which shows the presence of an emergent member in this communication network. The majority of the teams involved in the actual communication networks are slightly smaller than the teams assigned, except for the team in the UK for Case 3 and the team in Malaysia for Case 2 (Iteration 1 only).

Table 2. Number of members per actual communication RCASN Iteration 1 and 2

Com. type	Case 1		Case 2		Case 3		Case 4		Case 1		Case 2		Case 3		Case 4	
	MAL	FIN	MAL	USA	PK	GB	PK	RP	MAL	FIN	MAL	USA	PK	GB	PK	RP
Total Members	5	5	2	3	5	2	5	4	5	5	2	3	5	2	5	4
Bugs	5	6	2	3	5	2	4	4	6	5	2	3	5	2	4	4
Changes	6	4	2	5	5	2	5	4	6	4	2	3	5	2	5	4
Issues	5	2	2	1	4	2	4	2	6	2	2	1	4	2	5	4
Refactoring	4	2	2	1	4	2	4	2	4	2	2	1	3	2	3	2
Review	6	3	2	1	1	2	4	2	6	2	2	1	1	2	4	2
Synchronization	4	3	2	1	4	2	4	2	3	1	2	1	3	2	4	3
Coordination	6	4	2	2	5	2	5	4	6	4	2	3	5	2	5	4
Management	6	4	2	3	6	3	5	2	5	5	2	4	6	3	4	3
Quality	6	2	2	3	5	2	5	2	6	4	2	3	5	2	4	3
Sprint Planning	4	3	2	1	4	2	5	3	6	4	1	2	5	2	4	3
Support	6	5	2	3	4	2	6	3	6	5	1	3	5	2	3	4
Clarification	6	5	2	3	3	3	6	4	5	5	2	4	5	2	6	4
Negotiation	6	5	2	4	4	3	6	4	5	5	2	4	5	2	6	4

(b) *(RQ2) Emergent members in the actual communication RCASNs.* Analyzing the actual communication RCASNs, we found that a small number of emergent members (members who are not a part of assigned project team, yet their participation is required by the team members due to any reason) were also involved in the project communication. Table 2 highlights the presence of emergent members in grey. These emergent members are non-unique, i.e. there are duplicates across the RCASNs. When present, only one or two members were emergent per network. Some were contacted more than once. Overall, 4.4% of the total interaction happened with emergent members for Iteration 1 and 2.4% for Iteration 2. It indicates that communication with emergent members was very low. Most of the communication ties with emergent members exist between Project Manager, Support team, Customer, and Executives (Case 2 and 3), Management Team (Case 3 and 4), and Area Experts (Case 2).

(c) *(RQ3) Roles involved in the actual communication RCASNs.* Tables 3 and 4 present the number of communication ties between members playing the same and distinct roles, respectively. Cells indicated no communication as 'NA' since there is only one member playing the respective role. Blank cells indicate a role not assigned to the project. Given the low instances of emergent communication, we do not show emergent communication in these tables.

Table 3. Communication within-roles

(It1-2) Role	Case 1	Case 2	Case 3	Case 4	Total	Case 1	Case 2	Case 3	Case 4	Total
PM	NA	NA	NA	NA	0	NA	NA	NA	NA	0
Dev	53	44	46	92	235	75	46	49	86	256
Test	5		NA	3	8	5		NA	3	8
Arch		NA	12	4	16		NA	12	4	16
UX	NA				0	NA				0
PO	NA				0	NA				0
Total	58	44	58	99	259	80	46	61	93	280

Table 4. Communication cross-roles

It 1-2 Roles	Case 1	Case 2	Case 3	Case 4	Total	Case 1	Case 2	Case 3	Case 4	Total
PM-Dev	46	29	29	38	142	41	32	28	32	133
PM-UX	5				5	3				3
PM-PO	8				8	9				9
PM-Arch		14	17	15	46		16	17	13	46
PM-Tester	20		9	19	48	16		8	14	38
Dev-UX	13				13	8				8
Dev-PO	25				25	18				18
Dev-Arch		22	20	15	57		24	20	19	63
Dev-Tester	35		17	23	75	35		19	24	78
Tester-UX	4				4	1				1
Tester-PO	5				5	4				4
Tester-Arch			12	2	14			7	3	10
UX-PO	2				2	2				2
Total	163	65	104	112	444	137	72	99	105	413

Most of the interactions took place cross-roles (n = 444 for Iteration 1 and n = 413 for Iteration 2). A closer look on within-roles data (Table 2) reveals that most of this communication is between pairs of developers and that their communication has increased by 9% in Iteration 2 (n = 256) in comparison to Iteration 1 (n = 235).

Least communication among same roles is between Testers for both iterations. Technical Architects (Arch) also communicated among themselves.

The communication ties cross-roles (Table 3) decreased in Iteration 2 (= 413) by 7% as compared to Iteration 1 (n = 444). For Iteration 1, Dev is the role who interacted the most with others (n = 312) and UX is the role who less interacted with teammates (n = 24) across the four projects. Interestingly, the number of communication ties with PM is very high (n = 249/444, 56%) if we take into account that each project had only one PM. For Iteration 2, although with smaller numbers, the patterns repeat themselves. Dev is the role who most interacted with others (n = 300) and UX is the role who less interacted with teammates (n = 14) across the four projects. The number of communication with PM(s) is still quite high (n = 229/413, 55%).

(d) *(RQ4) Characterization of interactions and information exchange within the actual communication RCASNs.* We further our analysis by identifying which communication took place cross-sites and within-sites, i.e. between two members at different locations and between two members at the same location. Out of the total of 735 ties of communication reported for Iteration 1, 341 of them (46%) are cross-sites and 394 (54%) are within-sites. For Iteration 2, out of the 710 ties reported, 316 are cross-sites (44%) and again 394 (56%) are within-sites.

For the cross-sites communication in Iteration 1, we found that bugs and communication of changes are the two most-often reported interactions for three of the projects. Similarly, for Iteration 2, bugs and communication of changes are the two most-often reported interactions for three projects.

For the within-sites communication in Iteration 1, bugs and user story clarifications are the two most-often discussed topics for two of the projects. A similar trend is identified for Iteration 2. Communication of changes is the next most discussed topic for three projects.

Awareness Within the RCASNs

(a) *(RQ1) Team members involved in the actual awareness RCASNs.* Table 5 indicates how many members were assigned to work in each iteration as well as reported as being aware of others in total for all actual RCASNs of each awareness type.

Table 5. Number of members per actual awareness RCASN

It 1-2	Case1		Case2		Case3		Case4		Case1		Case2		Case3		Case4	
Awar. type	MAL	FIN	MAL	USA	PK	GB	PK	RP	MAL	FIN	MAL	USA	PK	GB	PK	RP
Assigned	6	4	2	3	5	2	5	4	6	4	2	3	5	2	5	4
Availability	6	5	2	7	7	4	8	4	6	6	2	7	7	2	8	4
General	6	5	2	7	7	4	8	4	6	6	2	7	7	4	8	4
Current	6	4	2	3	5	2	5	4	6	4	2	3	5	2	5	4
Work status	6	3	2	3	5	2	5	4	6	4	2	3	5	2	5	4

Most of the teams in the actual awareness networks have more members than the ones assigned to work per iteration, except for the team located in Malaysia for Case 1 and for Case 2, and for the team located in the Philippines for Case 4 that are about the same size (Iteration 1 and Iteration 2).

(b) *(RQ2) Emergent members in the actual awareness RCASNs.* Analyzing the actual awareness RCASNs, we found a small number of emergent members. Table 5 highlights in grey the RCASNs in which emergent members are present. These are also non-unique members. When present, from 1 to 4 members were emergent per network. Overall, 8% of the total reported awareness ties involve emergent members for Iteration 1 and 6% for Iteration 2. These numbers indicate that awareness of emergent members collaborating with the project is low. Most of the awareness ties with emergent members were reported by the Project Managers (for all cases). These emergent members are the Support team and Customer (for all Cases), Executives (Case 2 and Case 3), the Management Team (Case 3 and Case 4), and Area Experts (Case 2).

(c) (RQ3) Roles involved in the actual awareness RCASNs. Tables 6 and 7 present the number of awareness ties within- and cross-roles, respectively. The majority of the awareness ties reported are cross-roles (n = 307 for Iteration 1 and n = 326 for Iteration 2). A closer look in the awareness within-roles (Table 6) reveals that developers are the ones who most-often reported being aware of peers (n = 113 for Iteration 1 and n = 148). The amount of awareness ties reported increased in 31% from Iteration 1 (n = 127) to Iteration 2 (n = 168).

Table 6. Awareness within-roles

Within-Roles It 1-2	Case1	Case2	Case3	Case4	Total	Case1	Case2	Case3	Case4	Total
PM	NA	NA	NA	NA	0	NA	NA	NA	NA	0
Dev	45	22	24	22	113	63	23	24	38	148
Test	4		NA		4	5		NA	5	10
Arch		NA	8	2	10		NA	8	2	10
UX	NA				0	NA				0
PO	NA				0	NA				0
Total	49	22	32	24	127	68	23	32	45	168

Table 7. Awareness cross-roles

Roles It 1-2	Case1	Case2	Case3	Case4	Total	Case1	Case2	Case3	Case4	Total
PM-Dev	29	17	18	22	86	29	13	18	22	82
PM-UX	3				3	5				5
PM-PO	4				4	4				4
PM-Arch		6	12	8	26		5	12	8	25
PM-Test	9		6	8	23	8		6	8	22
Dev-UX	5				5	6				6
Dev-PO	25				25	24				24
Dev-Arch		20	24	10	54		22	29	15	66
Dev-Test	30		10	5	45	30		14	13	57
Test-UX	3				3	3				3
Test-PO	8				8	7				7
Test-Arch			14	7	21			15	6	21
UX-PO	4				4	5				4
Total	120	43	84	60	307	121	40	94	72	327

Similarly, Table 6 shows that the amount of ties reported cross-roles has also increased from Iteration 1 (n = 307) to Iteration 2 (n = 326). The increase is of 6.2%. We also found that Developer is the role more present in the reported awareness ties (n = 215/307 for Iteration 1 and n = 235/326 for Iteration 2) while User Experience Designer is the less present (n = 15 for Iteration 1 and n = 18 for Iteration 2). It is also important to highlight that project managers are present in a significant number of cross-roles ties (n = 142/307 for Iteration 1, 46%; and n = 138/326 for Iteration 2, 42%).

(d) *(RQ4) Characterization of awareness found in the RCASNs.* We further the characterization of the awareness by identifying awareness of others located in the remote site (cross-sites) and of others located in the same site (within-sites). Out of the total of 471 ties of awareness reported for Iteration 1, 189 (39%) of them are cross-sites and 282 (61%) are within-sites. For Iteration 2, out of the 533 ties reported, 230 (43%) are cross-sites and 303 (57%) are within-sites.

Awareness ties have increased 13% in iteration 2. For the cross-sites awareness, we found that Availability and General awareness are the two most-often reported awareness types for Case 1 to Case 3 in iteration 1. No type of awareness stands out in Case 4. However, for Case 4 Work status awareness is the most cited by the participants. For the within-sites awareness for Iteration 1, Availability and General awareness are also the two most-often reported awareness types for Case 2 and Case 4.

4.2 The Interplay Between Distance, Communication, and Awareness

(RQ5) Relationship between distance, communication, and awareness. We performed multiple correlation tests between distance and the factors of communication frequency and types of awareness, namely Availability, General awareness, Current awareness, and Work status awareness. For the factor distance, we coded pairs of people as 'collocated' if they were both working in the same country, and as 'remote' if they were working in different countries. The correlation is calculated using QAP (quadratic assignment procedure). Because network data is not independently measured, traditional parametric correlation methods cannot be used. Table 8 provides the results of the QAP correlation tests for each project and per iteration. We can observe that there is

Table 8. Relationship between distance, communication frequency, and types of awareness

	Iteration 1				Iteration 2			
Variable	Case1	Case2	Case3	Case4	Case1	Case2	Case3	Case4
	Beta	Beta	Beta	Beta	Beta	Beta	Beta	Beta
Comm. frequency	0.137	0.312	0.432*	0.315*	0.254*	0.429	0.573*	0.164
Availability	-0.136		0.083*	0.222	-0.136		0.164	0.289*
General	0		0.613*	0.336*	0		0.613*	0.183
Current	0.223*	-0.031	0.476*	0.111	0.223*	0.023	0.384*	0.056
Work status	0.021	0.089	0.476*	0.138	0.021	-0.048	0.384*	-0.118
P<0.01**	p<!n= 10		n=5	n=7	n=9			

no pattern across all four projects; however, Case 3 indicates an influence of distance in communication and all types of awareness, except Availability.

For Iteration 1, for Case 3 and Case 4, we found a significant decline of Communication frequency over distance ($r = 0.432$, $r = 0.315$ and $p < 0.05$) and General awareness over distance ($r = 0.613$, $r = 0.336$ and $p < 0.05$), meaning that the communication with the remote colleagues was less frequent then with the local ones, and those team members are less familiar with the professional background of their remote colleagues than with the local ones respectively. There is also a significant decline of Current awareness for Case 1 and Case 3 ($r = 0.233$, $r = 0.476$ and $p < 0.05$) over distance, indicating that team members are less aware of the set of tasks the remote colleagues are working on than the ones the local colleagues are assigned to. Work status awareness has a significant decline over distance ($r = 0.476$, $p < 0.05$) for Case 3 only. This indicates that, for this case, team members were less aware of the current work progress of remote members than of the local ones.

Table 8 shows a similar trend for Iteration 2, except that Communication frequency declines over distance for Case 1 and Case 3, and General awareness declines for Case 3 only. In addition, Availability has a significant decline over distance for Case 4 ($r = 0.289$, $p < 0.05$), meaning that remote team members are more difficult to reach than the local ones.

(2) (RQ6) Relationship between communication and awareness. Table 9 shows the QAP correlation between the communication frequency factor and awareness. For Iteration 1, we found a significant decline of Availability ($r = 0.235$, $r = 0.444$ and $p < 0.05$), Current awareness ($r = 0.420$, 0.377 and $p < 0.05$), and Work status awareness ($r = 0.330$, $r = 0.241$ and $p < 0.05$) for Case 1 and Case 4 when frequency of communication was lower. This indicates that people were more likely to communicate with someone who they were aware of. We also found a significant decline of General awareness when communication frequency was lower for Case 1, Case 3, and Case 4 ($r = 0.308$, $r = 0.363$, $r = 0.377$ and $p < 0.05$), indicating that people were more likely to communicate with those who they know can help in the work. Iteration 2 yields similar results. However, General awareness declines for Case 3 and 4 only, and Work status for Case 1 and Case 3.

Table 9. Relationship between communication frequency and types of awareness

Variable /Beta	Iteration 1				Iteration 2			
	Case1	Case2	Case3	Case4	Case1	Case2	Case3	Case4
Availability	0.235**		0.026	0.444*	0.224**		0.11	0.368*
General	0.308**		0.323**	0.377*	0.196		0.533*	0.281*
Current	0.420*	-0.057	0.203	0.377**	0.444*	-0.023	0.316	0.458*
Work status	0.330**	-0.042	0.203	0.241*	0.401*	0.048	0.316*	0 231
P<0.01**		p<!n= 10		n=5		n=7	n=9	

5   Discussion

Our findings yielded seven main patterns in RDC. We discuss them here.

5.1   Team Members Involvement Was Different Than Assigned

We found that team size for the communication networks were slightly smaller than the size of the assigned teams in Iteration 1 and Iteration 2. Considering the fact that agile teams are self-organizing and have the ability and authority to take decisions and readily adapt to changing demands through constant feedback in short cycles, we found that people get involved with a user story when they feel they have the expertise to help. Our finding show that mostly self-assigned team members collaborated on a user story. This is in contrast to Damian et al. [12]'s finding that the communication requirements-centric social networks are larger than planned, having about one-third emergent members. The difference of nature between self-organizing agile teams and traditional software development teams in which members strictly play allocated roles is the reason behind this. The on-demand involvement of emergent members in the team helps the team to get through the hurdles smoothly rather than getting stuck on a certain point leading to delays and failures.

On the other hand, we found that awareness networks were slightly bigger than assigned in both iterations. This is justified by the fact that assigned members reported to be aware of how easy emergent members were to be reached (Availability) and how their skills could help with the project (General awareness). The fact that they did not report to be aware of what emergent members were doing (Current awareness) and their current work status (Work status awareness) suggests that they only contacted these members to seek for help and not to get them involved in the work to be done.

5.2   Agile Teams are Self-contained

On the basis of the small number of emergent interactions encountered in the communication networks (4.4% of the total interactions in Iteration 1 and 2.4% in Iteration 2), we can say that agile teams are self-contained and no knowledge needs to be sought from outside the team. It can be considered that the communication with emergent members decreased to about half in Iteration 2. This finding suggests that gathering information from outsider members, when applicable, is more necessary at the start of the project. This is supported by the emergent members roles contacted, namely: the Support team, the Management team, Customers Area Experts, and Executives.

This finding contrasts the organic patterns of traditional teams found by Damian et al. [12]. Our current investigation suggests that the collaborative way of agile teams promotes knowledge to be more easily transferred among team members and reduces the need for collaboration with former members. We also found that the amount of awareness ties reported with emergent members was small (8% of the ties in Iteration 1 and 6% in Iteration 2), suggesting that the assigned team members were not aware of the emergent members, contrary to Damian et al.'s findings [12].

5.3   Project Managers are Key Players in Communication

Although we found that developers communicated the most with other roles for all projects in both iterations, the high number of cross-roles ties reported involving PM(s) (56% in Iteration 1 and 55% in Iteration 2) was surprising. In the awareness networks, the number of ties involving this role represents 46% and 42% of the total cross-roles ties. In Scrum, Scrum Master and the Coach roles are the replacement of traditional PM. These roles aim to mentor the team in how to adopt agile practices and how to solve overall issues related to the project. Although called 'project managers', they acted as mentors for their teams. Therefore, one would expect they do not get as involved in the project as a 'traditional' PM. Our findings suggest that PM(s) are still key players distributing information to others and being aware of others, and are essential to the development of the project requirements. Our findings corroborate the results of Ehrlich and Cataldo [13] that state the central role of technical leaders in agile teams communication networks confirming the fact that some roles can be central even in self-organizing and cross functional agile teams.

5.4   Distance Does not (Seem to) Matter

We found that over 40% of the total communication ties reported for both iterations (46% in Iteration 1 and 44% in Iteration 2) are between cross-sites. Similarly, about 40% of awareness ties (39% in Iteration 1 and 43% in Iteration 2) are also cross-sites. These findings suggest that distance seem to not matter for agile distributed teams, corroborating recent literature on the topic (e.g., [14]). This high presence of interactions with and awareness of remote members might be explained by the teams' daily routines. All teams had daily stand up meetings to synchronize information and progress. Case 2 was an exception due to the large time difference (11 h) as compared to the others. Therefore, they used to send e-mails at the end of the working day and once a week meet after hours through Skype. Other team members interacted through Skype whenever it was necessary simulating collocation. Although not conclusive, our correlation test of the distance factor over communication and awareness supports this finding to a certain extent. About 40% of the networks showed a significant influence of distance, replicating Damian et al. [4] finding that distance is not an issue for development teams despite the approach they are following contrary to Bjarnason and Sharp's [8] findings which state that distance impacts requirements communication and project coordination.

5.5   Bugs Discussion, Communication of Changes, and User Story Clarification as the Most Discussed Topics

These are the most-often discussed topics among the team members, cross- and within-sites. Two important characteristics of agile methods are the proximity with the customer, who allows for detailed clarifications of what needs to be implemented and delivered; and constant changes, that allows for on-the-fly adjustments of what the customer considers relevant for the product. Our findings support such characteristics.

As any agile team, the dynamics of the observed teams consisted of defining a product backlog for certain iteration and then starting the detailed user story clarification process. Clarifications were requested as the code evolved and verification of the specifications was done through integrated tests. Bugs identified in these tests were immediately discussed and fixed as opposed to the traditional development life cycle. Changes resulting from clarification requests or directly from the customer were constantly observed, thus justifying this as the most-discussed topic. The clarifying-changing-fixing cycle imposed by agile methods was indeed in place ensuring the quality of the product to be delivered. Interestingly, Damian et al. [4] also found that communication of changes was the most discussed topic. This reinforces anecdotal knowledge that requirements are by nature volatile. Agile methods better tackle their constant changes.

5.6   Familiarity from Past Projects Facilitates Awareness

Most of the team members have worked together in previous releases of the product, being familiar with each other. Such familiarity suggests influencing how easy team members perceive others to be reachable and how much they believe their colleagues skills can help with the project. Availability and general awareness are the two type of awareness that are important to support expertise seeking and task completion [11]. This finding highlights the importance of familiarity to information seeking and corroborates previous literature findings [12].

5.7   Communication is Still an Important Source of Awareness

Our QAP results for the correlation of communication frequency and awareness show a trend of influence of one over another, corroborating previous findings that communication is still an important source of awareness [4, 11] despite recent advances in project management tool support. Collocated agile teams use face to face communication and daily status meetings to constantly share what is going on in the project. Our findings show that distributed agile teams also follow these practices despite the physical distance and potential communication barriers it imposes. Moreover, our finding also suggests that team members communicate more with those they are more aware of, partially supporting the earlier finding that team members communicate more with those they knew who could help [12].

6   Limitations of the Study

We are sensitive to the fact that the data to build the RCASNs, was self-reported. However, we took actions to minimize the impact of self-reported data. First, we deployed the questionnaire at the end of each iteration. We also followed-up on missing questions as the questionnaires were filled out reducing the effort the participant had to make to provide clarifications. Second, we triangulated data through interviews in order to learn how participants perceived their collaboration with others in the team.

Interviews were transcribed and further analyzed in comparison to the questionnaire responses.

Social networks are dynamic. Therefore, we designed a longitudinal study with two distinct data collection points to construct the RCASNs and observe their behavior over time that indicates the stability of our findings. However, by contrasting two iterations we have valuable indications of changes on collaboration patterns and have overcome one of the main limitations of Damian et al.'s previous work.

Generalizability of findings is another concern of software engineering empirical studies. Our multiple case study increased the likelihood of having results that represent a large sample of the population. This fact in conjunction with the longitudinal study contributes to a broader contribution than typically seen in software engineering empirical studies. However, interpretations of the findings could have been supported by rich details used to support the arguments made in terms of numbers.

7 Implications for Research and Practice

Managers can invest in having well defined infrastructure in place to allow team members to contact their remote colleagues and practices to allow everyone to know how to work to achieve similar situations.

Our findings also suggest topics for future academic investigation. Our current study indicates that distance does not seem to matter, despite the apparent contradiction between communication frequency and distance. However, the correlation results between distance, communication, and awareness factors are inconclusive when looking across the four projects. It would be interesting to investigate other projects with similar or larger distribution configurations to learn whether our findings hold.

We also found that project managers are still key players in agile teams. Although the members playing this role acted as mentors, it would be interesting to expand investigation of this role ideally by collecting self-reported data on how team perceives the mentors (e.g., Scrum Masters, Coaches) to develop and manage user stories.

8 Final Considerations

Requirements management is a complex activity involving collaboration. Requirements documentation or structured processes in the more traditional, non-agile development teams facilitate further requirements knowledge management. In contrast, agile teams rely on ad hoc communication and dynamic patterns of knowledge sharing. In this paper we identified some collaboration patterns of requirements-centric agile teams in four multinational companies located in distinct parts of the world. Our seven major patterns of collaboration refer to which roles communicate, as well as which topics predominate in the requirements-centered discussions, and which factors contribute to awareness in the distributed teams. Some of our findings corroborate patterns of traditional teams as found in previous related work or are more specific of agile teams.

Our empirical investigation also yields future research work and implications for practice. Although this is a multiple case study, generalization of our findings has to be considered with caution especially while considering other configurations such as larger team members' distribution and larger number of user stories per iteration.

References

1. Cao, L.C.L., Ramesh, B.: Agile requirements engineering practices: an empirical study. IEEE Softw. **25**(1), 60–67 (2008)
2. Martakis, A., Daneva, M.: Handling requirements dependencies in agile projects: a focus group with agile software development practitioners. In: International Conference on Research Challenges in Information Science, Paris, France, pp. 1–11. IEEE (2013)
3. Damian, D., Izquierdo, L., Singer, J.: Awareness in the wild: why communication breakdowns occur. In: International Conference on Global Software Engineering, New Delhi, India, pp. 81–90 (2007)
4. Damian, D., Kwan, I., Marczak, S.: Requirements-driven collaboration: leveraging the invisible relationships between requirements and people. In: Mistrík, I., Grundy, J., Hoek, A., Whitehead, J. (eds.) Collaborative Software Engineering, pp. 57–76. Springer, Heidelberg (2010)
5. Damian, D., Marczak, S., Kwan, I.: Collaboration patterns and the impact of distance on awareness in requirements-centred social networks. In: International Requirements Engineering Conference, New Delhi, India, pp. 59–68. IEEE (2007)
6. Pikkarainen, M., Haikara, J., Salo, O., Abrahamsson, P., Still, J.: The impact of agile practices on communication in software development. Empirical Softw. Eng. **13**(3), 303–337 (2008)
7. Cataldo, M., Ehrlich, K.: The Impact of the Structure of Communication Patterns in Global Software Development: An Empirical Analysis of a Project Using Agile Methods, pp. 1–17. IRS, Carnegie Mellon University, Pittsburgh (2011)
8. Bjarnason, E., Sharp, H.: The role of distances in requirements communication: a case study. Requirements Eng. (2015)
9. Marczak, S., Damian, D.: How interaction between roles shapes the communication structure in RDC. In: 19th International Conference on Requirements Engineering, Trento, Itlay, pp. 47–56. IEEE (2011)
10. Watts, D.J., Strogatz, S.H.: Collective dynamics of 'small-world' networks. Nature **393**(6), 440–442 (1998)
11. Inayat, I., Marczak, S., Salim, S.S.: Studying relevant socio-technical aspects of requirements-driven collaboration in agile teams. In: International Workshop on Empirical Requirements Engineering, in Conjunction with International Requirements Engineering Conference, Rio de Janeiro, Brazil. IEEE (2013)
12. Ehrlich, K., Chang, K.: Leveraging expertise in global software teams: going outside boundaries. In: International Conference on Global Software Engineering, Florianópolis, Brazil, pp. 149–158. IEEE (2006)
13. Ehrlich, K., Cataldo, M.: The communication patterns of technical leaders: impact on product development team performance. In: International Conference on Computer Supported Cooperative Work, Baltimore, USA, pp. 733–744 (2014)
14. Holmstrom, H., Fitzgerald, B., Agerfalk, P.J., Conchuir, E.O.: Agile practices reduce distance in global software development. Inf. Syst. Manag. **23**(3), 7–18 (2006)

Common Mistakes of Student Analysts in Requirements Elicitation Interviews

Beatrice Donati[1], Alessio Ferrari[2(✉)], Paola Spoletini[3], and Stefania Gnesi[2]

[1] University of Florence, DILEF, Florence, Italy
beatrice.donati@unifi.it
[2] CNR-ISTI, Pisa, Italy
{alessio.ferrari,stefania.gnesi}@isti.cnr.it
[3] Kennesaw State University, Marietta, GA, USA
pspoleti@kennesaw.edu

Abstract. *Context and Motivation*: Customer-analyst interviews are among the most common techniques for eliciting requirements. However, students of computer science-related disciplines have little material and time for learning how to perform an effective interview. As a result, once out of the class, the effectiveness of analysts in interviewing highly depends on their *experience*. *Question/problem*: Since learning from failures is recognised as a wise strategy for professional improvement, this work aims at identifying *communication mistakes* of student requirements analysts. *Principal idea/results*: We conducted a case study involving 36 students to which we gave a typical introduction to requirements elicitation interviews. Then, we arranged and recorded 18 elicitation interviews involving the students. The interview recordings were analysed by interview experts. The experts produced a list of 9 main communication mistakes, which we report in this paper. *Contribution*: This is the first work that provides a concise list of mistakes of student analysts, with corrective recommendations and examples. It can be useful for instructors of software engineering courses, as well as for practitioners, who may commit the same mistakes of the students without being aware of it.

Keywords: Requirements elicitation · Interviews · Student analysts · Requirements engineering education · Communication mistakes · Role playing

1 Introduction

Real-world software development projects often start with an interview between a customer and a requirements analyst [1,14]. Interviews are indeed recognised as one of the most effective means to capture requirements, and to transfer system-relevant knowledge between customer and analyst [8,9,15,29]. Most of the works on requirements elicitation have studied the effect of specific variables on the success of interviews and similar techniques (e.g., focus groups,

© Springer International Publishing AG 2017
P. Grünbacher and A. Perini (Eds.): REFSQ 2017, LNCS 10153, pp. 148–164, 2017.
DOI: 10.1007/978-3-319-54045-0_11

workshops [33]). In particular, the influence of domain knowledge [3, 14, 17], and cognitive strategies [21] were evaluated, as well as the combination of other individual factors, such as the expressive ability of the customer, and the absorptive capacity of the analyst [10]. Overall, analyst's communication talent and skills are considered among the major factors influencing the success of an interview [14, 33].

While talent cannot be taught, skills can be acquired, and learning how to perform an effective interview is one of the primary objectives of requirements engineering courses [34]. When teaching requirements elicitation interviews to students that, one day, may become professional analysts, it is important to provide guidelines on how to conduct an interview [22, 23], but it is also advisable to allow them to learn from their mistakes [4]. By doing so, students can build their skills on the solid ground of their personal failures. In this sense, existing research in the field of Requirements Engineering Education (REE) [19] have shown that *role playing* is an effective pedagogical approach to enable students to learn from experience [24, 30, 34]. With role playing, students are required to play the role of analysts – and of customers, in case *role reversal* is applied [34] – in a simulated interview. However, understanding personal errors in a fictional setting is not easy, since the consequences of mistakes are less tangible than in the real world. For example, Zowghi and Paryani [34] employed tutors to monitor requirements elicitation activities and provide corrective advice to students, but this is not always possible due to limitations of resources [12]. Hence, having a list of communication mistakes committed by other students might allow budding analysts to monitor themselves, leveraging other people's failures.

This paper aims to contribute to the field of REE with a list of communication mistakes of student analysts. Since this is the first work that addresses this goal, we considered suitable to perform an exploratory case study, in which expert opinion was used to identify the mistakes. A set of 18 customer-analyst unstructured interviews were performed at Kennesaw State University (KSU) involving undergraduate students of the User Centered Design course. Analysts and customers were both played by students. To identify the mistakes of student analysts, interviews were tape recorded, and three experts independently reviewed them and produced a list of mistakes, together with representative examples. This paper presents the list of mistakes produced, and some recommendations to avoid them. Although coming from a case study conducted on a specific university course, with the limitations entailed by this restricted context, we believe that our experience can provide a useful baseline for future research, as well as a handy reference for practitioners and teachers.

Related Work. As noted by Aranda *et al.* [3], although interviews are widely used for requirements elicitation, little empirical research has been performed on the topic. Besides the mentioned studies that focus on the impact of specific variables on the success of interviews [3, 10, 14, 17, 21], some works exist that are specifically oriented to improve communication in interviews. For example, Pitts and Browne [22] show that using procedural prompts that stimulate cognition, instead of interrogatories ones, lead to more successful interviews. Shuraida and Barki [28] show that analysts that encourage the use of concrete examples are more likely to produce satisfactory requirements. From a practitioner's perspective, Portugal [23] provides a textbook with general guidelines on how to conduct interviews. Concerning related studies in REE, existing works (e.g., [24,30,34]) are mainly oriented to analyse the pedagogical effectiveness of role playing strategies. To our knowledge, none of the studies focuses on identifying communication mistakes of student analysts during role playing.

The remainder of the paper is structured as follows. Section 2 summarises the methodology followed. Section 3 lists the mistakes. Section 4 discusses the limitations of our work. Section 5 outlines conclusions and future work.

2   Methodology

A set of 38 students was recruited from Kennesaw State University (KSU). The recruited sample belonged to the User Centered Design course, composed of undergraduate students of the third and fourth year. The students were divided into 2 groups, namely analysts and customers. The customers were required to think about a novel computer intensive system that they would like to be developed, and were given a week to think about the product. The analysts were first asked their degree of experience in conducting interviews (on a 5-points Likert scale, 33.3% declared to have no or low experience, 22.2% moderately low experience, 33.3% average, 11.2% moderately high, 0% high). Then, the analysts were provided with a two hour lecture on requirements elicitation interviews delivered by the third author, in which they received an introduction on different types of interviews and general guidelines on how to conduct each of the main types. The class uses a reference book [27] and additional lecture notes. The interviews took place simultaneously at KSU, and the time slot allocated for the interviews was 20 min. The students conducted unstructured interviews. Indeed, to the best of our knowledge, structured and semi-structured interviews were not appropriate in this context, where the analyst is exploring for the first time the idea for new products for which he/she has no previous background information.

The analysts were required to record the audio of their interviews, but not the video. This choice is motivated by the assumption that most of the requirements-related information is conveyed through speech. Inspection of behavioural and gesture aspects would have required a more complex analysis, which would have been overwhelming at this stage of the work. The output of the interviews was a set of 19 interview recordings, one of which resulted corrupted. Hence, 18 recordings were available for review. Brief summaries of the products discussed along the interviews, together with their duration, are reported in Table 1 (interviews will be referred in the rest of the paper as I-<ID>).

The recordings were independently reviewed by the first three authors – one professional analyst (1st author), one researcher in requirements elicitation (2nd author), and the students' instructor (3rd author) –, which are here referred as *experts*, who had two weeks to listen to the recordings. Each expert was required

Table 1. List of Interviews

ID	Title	Summary	Time
1	Ubiquitous multi-player video game	Multi-player video game with associated mobile application to monitor the status of the characters	00:21:04
2	3D file manager	3D holographic visualisation and navigation mechanism to explore files	00:23:30
3	Timed SMS sender	Mobile application to send SMS at a specific date and time	00:12:57
4	Topic aggregator for University newsletter	Mobile application to aggregate by topic the information received from the university newsletter	00:14:22
5	Personal Video aggregator	Mobile application to aggregate the videos watched by the user in different websites	00:09:58
6	Soccer gambling recommender	Mobile application that provides information about soccer players to support gambling	00:20:55
7	Expriration dates tracker	Mobile application to keep track of the expiration dates of the grocery products purchased by the user	00:13:00
8	Multi-ball puzzle game	Mobile game with multi-color balls that should go into holes of their color based on obstacles set by the user	00:13:50
9	Live translator	Device with associated mobile application to translate conversations between two speakers of different languages	00:17:34
10	Diet tracker	Mobile application that keeps track of the user's diet considering the nutrition facts of the food	00:10:08
11	School-branded tablet	Tablet device with educational ebooks specific for a certain school	00:07:36
12	Travellers' network	Social network specific for travellers	00:17:20
13	Campus navigator	Mobile application embedding a GPS navigator specialised for navigating on a University campus	00:18:14
14	Survival video game	Survival video game with focus on crafting	00:13:47
15	Smart pen	Pen with different inks and a LCD screen to monitor the status of inks and battery	00:10:50
16	Date counter	Mobile application that given a date D1 and a number of days N computes the date D2 which is N days after D1.	00:16:44
17	Student's club app	Mobile application to estimate the participation of students to the activities of a student's club.	00:11:24
18	Digital shopping list	Mobile application to share a shopping list between people living in the same house.	00:07:29
Total			04:20:42
Average			00:14:29

to provide a list of relevant mistakes of the analysts. For each mistake, the experts were required to provide representative examples, and possible recommendations to the students. The experts were not provided with a predefined explicit model of a good interview, but they used as model their personal, yet *diverse*, experience. After this phase, the experts discussed in a three hours workshop the identified mistakes, and came out with an homogeneous list. An experienced professor (4th author) reviewed the mistakes, to check that the judgment of the experts was reasonably tolerant, considering the context of the interviews.

3   Mistakes

This section discusses the mistakes identified by the experts, referring examples from the interviews. Part of the mistakes are errors of *commission*, for which we can present speech fragments that show the incorrect behaviour, while others are errors of *omission*. In these second cases, we present virtuous examples on how some of our analysts were able to overcome the difficulties of their colleagues. In the following, speech fragments marked with *(A)* are uttered by analysts, and those marked with *(C)* belong to customers.

3.1   Wrong Opening

In the entire set of our recordings, analysts start the interview with the sentence *Tell me about your idea*, or other expressions with analogous meaning, without giving any guideline for the customer for structuring his/her discourse. As a consequence, except in those cases in which the customer is sensitive enough to start by providing some *context* for his/her idea, the first sentences of the customer describes the product that he/she has in mind, normally at a quite general level. Without a context, these abstract descriptions appear confusing, or apparently obvious, until the conversation reaches a point in which they start to make sense.

Example 3.1. One interesting example is the first sentence of the customer in I-16: *(C) My idea is a simple day counter, counts the days between, I don't know, one day and a future date.* The analyst rephrased: *(A) So you input a date in the software, and then it counts the days from today?* At this point, understanding that his idea was unclear, the customer started to provide some motivation: *(C) I come from background of UPS sales, and in the sales department of UPS, insurance is done in 45 day increments, and currently this requires UPS sales persons to pretty much know what is 45 days from any day, and involves a lot of back-of-the-hand calculations [...], we would like to automate that process.* The analyst asked further clarifications about the insurance process, and the customer said: *(C) UPS is the United Parcel Service, and there are two sites of that, there is delivering packages, and there is insuring a package against any damages [...], every bit of the insurance is done out in 45 days increments, [...] currently an insurance person has to pull out their calendar and count ahead 45 days* [to schedule insurance subscriptions]. In this example, the customer started from the *requirements* of the system (i.e., counting days), then explained the *goal* (i.e., automate the process), and finally described the *context* (i.e., how the UPS package insurance system currently works). Only after these further descriptions, it was clear that the requirement that the customer had in mind actually was: *Given a date D1 and a number of days N, the system shall compute the date D2 that is N days after D1.* It is worth noticing that this requirement did not match with the initial requirement understood by the analyst.

To prevent situations like the one exemplified, in which the idea of the customer remains unclear for large part of the interview, the customer should have structured his discourse starting from a description of the context and an explanation of the goal, before stating the requirement. In general, to trigger such abstract-to-detailed explanations, the analyst should start by saying: *First tell me how are the things now, without the system that you have in mind, and then explain me how things would change with your system.* This *incipit* is in line with the recommendations of Pitts and Browne [22] for prompting customer's reasoning, and can help the analyst in understanding the system-as-is, and the domain aspects connected to it, before starting to speak about the system-to-be.

3.2 Ambiguity Not Leveraged

As highlighted in our previous work [11], the detection of ambiguity in the customer's words can be a powerful tool to identify *tacit knowledge*, i.e., system-relevant information that is known to the customer and unknown to the analyst [13]. Indeed, the occurrence of an ambiguity might reveal the presence of unexpressed, system-relevant knowledge that needs to be elicited. Ambiguity can be perceived by the analyst in various forms, and the most frequent in interviews are *interpretation unclarity*, i.e., when the analyst cannot give any interpretation to the words of the customer, and *acceptance unclarity*, i.e., when the analyst can give an interpretation to what s/he hears, but such interpretation appears inconsistent or insufficient with respect to his/her view of the problem [11]. In our interviews, student analysts appear too *passive* and often accept what the customer says without asking clarifications, even though the words of the customer are evidently unclear or contradictory. In other terms, they do not leverage ambiguity to disclose tacit knowledge. This general weakness can be detected in almost all the interviews. Here we provide two examples.

Example 3.2. In I-5, the customer wishes to develop a video aggregator for *anime* series. The typical anime series spectator follows several series at the same time. Multiple Websites are available that provide these series, and it is complex for the spectator to keep track of the number of episode of each series that he/she is watching. The software required by the customer is expected to keep track of watched and not watched episodes of each series that a user is following. In addition, the software should aggregate in the same user interface the videos of the episodes coming from different Websites. The analyst tries to propose a main page for the application: *(A) So it records exactly each site you are watching each one on, and it bring you a link to go to the Website.* The customer replies: *(C) No it is more on the line of...where you just put down like what anime like...it could do that, but I was more thinking on the line of putting what anime you are watching from each website kind like under-tabs.* This answer is very confusing – as listeners, we perceived an *interpretation unclarity* – and does not clarify the customer's idea. It excludes the possibility of having a link to an external Website, but it does not specify how to reach the anime episodes. However, the analyst does not ask any further question to clarify this point.

Example 3.3. In I-9, the customer wants a mobile application with associated hear device to translate conversations between two speakers in face-to-face conversations. She is explaining that the system allows her to write a sentence on a mobile application, and this application translates the sentence in a desired language. She says: *(C) It* [the application] *will send it* [the translated sentence] *back to the hear device, and it* [the hear device] *will tell in French, slowly, and so you can like...communicate.* If the analyst did not have a passive attitude, he probably would have perceived and revealed an *acceptance unclarity,* and would have asked why the application should repeat the sentence to the user, instead of repeating it directly to the interlocutor. Probably this hides the goal of *learning* a new language through the application (implicit goals are discussed in Sect. 3.3), but this goal was never explicitly mentioned.

Even when our analysts ask specific questions to discuss some unclear points, the customer sometimes misunderstands their questions. In these cases, the passive attitude of our analysts emerges again, since they do not try to rephrase their questions, as in the following example.

Example 3.4. In I-12, the customer wants to create a social network dedicated to those travelers interested in nature and wilderness, and, among other features, he requires users to register to his platform. The analyst is not convinced of the necessity of a login mechanism. The fact that the analyst is reluctant to accept this feature is probably a sign of some sort of misunderstanding. The analyst asks: *(A) You want to make it exclusive, only to users who login. Can you explain more about the reasons why people need to login? (C) Look, I'm a traveller, a tourist or a naturalistic enthusiast who want to see animals in the wild. [...] If I want to see a polar bear I have to know that polar bears are not something that you can find everywhere in the word, you can find it only in the southern part of the globe [...] and it is the kind of information you find in the system.* The customer clearly misunderstood the question. Instead of solving the misunderstanding, the analyst decides to let the customer talk. This might be motivated by the fact that the customer explanation allowed him to partially answer to his doubt. However, making the reason for logging in more explicit would have guaranteed that no actual misunderstanding was tacitly occurring.

Overall, our analysts might have thought that interrupting the customer while s/he is talking could be perceived as a disrespectful behavior. Although we encourage analysts' courtesy, it is also important for them to *take note* of ambiguities, let the customer finish his/her discourse, and then resolve these miscommunication events.

3.3   Implicit Goals

In early interviews, identifying *goals,* i.e., high-level objectives to be satisfied with the development of the system, is crucial [18]. Our analysts appeared to find difficult the process of supporting customers in articulating their goals, and, in several cases, goals remained implicit, as in the following example.

Example 3.5. The first sentence expressed by the customer in I-11 was: *(C) The product I would like to discuss is a sort of a combination, I would say, between hardware and software, a kind of electronic book, instead of paper book,* *that high schools could use for students.* The analyst asked: *(A) Like a Kindle?* The customer started explaining that the product was more similar to a tablet, with editing capabilities, but after five minutes of interview (the interview lasted about seven minutes), the analyst asked again: *(A) What makes this product different from Kindle?* After some discussion, the customer said that he wanted to develop a new paradigm for educational textbooks, in which a school rents a set of tablets for its students. These tablets have restricted features oriented solely to download the educational textbooks selected by the school. Even after these explanations, the actual *goal* of the product remained unclear. As listeners, we could think that the goal could be (a) to reduce the expenses for students, since the school could purchase e-books on behalf of the students at a more convenient price; or (b) to facilitate reuse of e-books across different years. However, none of these goals was explicitly stated.

Situations in which goals are not explicitly stated can be prevented by asking questions such as the one recommended in Sect. 3.1, in which the customer is guided to describe the system-as-is and its problems, whose solutions can be regarded as goals for the system. However, as also noticed by Bubenko *et al.* [5] and by Anton [2], customers are not necessarily acquainted with goal-oriented reasoning, and it is preferable for the analyst to explicitly suggest clear goals, and ask confirmation to the customer. In the example above, the analyst should have asked, e.g.: *So, the objective of your system would be to reduce students expenses or to facilitate reuse of books across the years?*

The next example is also interesting in terms of goals that remained implicit, since the analyst appeared to take an effort to understand the goal, but – from our point of view – without success.

Example 3.6. In I-3, the customer starts as follows: *(C) The name of the app is gonna be Text Later, and basically what it's gonna do is, I'm gonna put a text into a field, I'm gonna set a time, I'm gonna set the recipient, and it's gonna text that person at that time (A) That's interesting, do you have a particular user group in mind? (C) Anyone who wants to...basically the problem happens when you want to text someone at a certain time, but then you do not remember to text them at that time, so basically it's just a timer that goes off, and the text automatically goes from my phone (A) Can you think of a particular use case for this? (C) Ok, I sleep late at night at 1 a.m., but I want to text someone at 6 a.m., I will not wake up at 6, I just put that text in, set a timer, and it's good to go (A) Ok.* The analyst appears to ask for a particular use case, since the application does not seem to have a reasonable goal. The use case does not sound realistic: why should one need to text someone at a specific time? In this example, we do not know whether the analyst has actually understood the goal, or if he said *Ok* just to close this argument and start discussing other aspects.

In cases like the one exemplified, in which the analyst has no clue of the goal, he should have clarified that he had a doubt, and should have asked more concrete details: *The use case is not totally clear to me. Can you specify, for example, what would you write in the text?* Although arguing on customer's goals when requirements are clear is not in the best interest of an analyst – the application will be payed anyway – developing something without having understood its *motivation* is not recommended [32], since it could lead to future misunderstandings with the customer at subsequent development stages.

3.4   Implicit Stakeholders

Our student analysts belong to a User Centered Design course, and appear particularly active in identifying system users, asking questions such as *Which is your user base?*, and *Who is going to use this system?* However, in all the cases, they appear to forget to consider one question: *does the project depend on the contribution of some other entity apart from me, the customer, and the users?* In other terms, they do not take into account, or leave implicit, the other *stakeholders* (e.g., regulators, technical experts, consultants, see [25] for an educational reference) that should take part to the project.

Example 3.7. A representative example is I-11, already introduced in Example 3.5. The customer wants to design a tablet that high schools can provide to their students. What a student can do with it is strictly controlled, and the device contains only educational material and school-related utilities. As noted in Example 3.5, the analyst is not totally convinced of the idea, and asks: *(A) Who should pay for this?* The customer hesitates, and then answers: *(C) The school would have to pay for this.* Hence, in this case, the analyst was able to highlight a key stakeholder to involve (i.e., the school representatives). However, another relevant set of stakeholders, i.e., the companies providing educational materials, was never mentioned, although publishing companies clearly have a part in the feasibility of the project. In addition, hardware providers were also never considered as part of the stakehoders.

A precise identification of all the stakeholders involved in the project is normally part of a later phase that follows the project *blastoff* [25]. This is an initial meeting that gather *key* stakeholders, and in which other stakeholders are possibly identified. Furthermore, several methods exists to identify stakeholders [20]. In a first interview, especially in a *role playing* setting, it is important for the students to at least consider that other parties might have a voice in the project, and this voice might affect its feasibility. To identify these stakeholders during the interview, we suggest analysts to ask the customer: *If this interview was a group meeting to discuss the project, who, besides us, do you think should participate to the meeting?*

In some cases, relevant stakeholders do not necessarily need to participate to the imaginary workshop, for example when they are providers of services, software, or hardware. However, in our interviews, analysts seem to neglect the possibility of introducing third-party providers in the development of the product. A representative example in this sense is I-13, in which requirements for a campus navigator are elicited. The core of the project requires a navigable map of the campus. This is usually something that a generic software developer company does not implement autonomously, but can be easily bought from specific providers. This aspect doesn't seem to be taken into account by our analyst.

3.5   Limitations in Terms of Resources Not Considered

In the first interview with the customer, the analyst should understand the constraints of the customer in terms of budget and time. Our analysts rarely discussed cost-related issues, and did not challenge the customer even when s/he was proposing a software that was clearly beyond the monetary capabilities of his/her customer profile. Self-explanatory examples in this sense are the computer games required in I-1 and I-14, both high-budget projects for which no question was raised about the cost. Although it is normally recommended to stay at the goal/needs level during early interviews, we argue that having an idea of the customer's budget can help the analyst in providing a better guidance during the interview, evaluating the feasibility of what is required in light of the budget. In addition, a customer is not required to know how much the implementation of a certain feature affects the total development effort; discussing the cost and the opportunity of what s/he proposes forces her/him to express more precisely if and why s/he needs a particular feature. Our analysts, however, appeared not to be aware of the consequences in terms of cost of adding *specific* features to the product. Examples in this sense are reported below.

Example 3.8. In I-18, the customer wishes to develop an electronic shopping list to be shared between people living in the same apartment. *Push notifications* (i.e., delivery of information from a server to a client, without a request from the client) are mentioned by the customer, who says: *(C) The shopping list has to be updated each time someone adds some new item, and push notifications would be nice.* The analyst does not provide any comment to this requirement. We know that including push notifications and shared information in a mobile app implies at least a dedicated server, and someone to take care of it. This means a back-end developer and some maintenance strategy. The budget, the resources involved and the delivery date will be certainly be affected by this choice but the analyst does not investigate further.

Example 3.9. In I-6 the customer asks for a mobile app to help him in gambling in soccer matches. He clarifies immediately that the app is developed only for private use on his private devices; this excludes the need of a user registration system, and simplifies the security strategy since personal devices already have controlled access. This aspect seems to be ignored by the analyst when he asks: *(A) Would you like to have your personal account to login?* Even if the strategy of the analyst *might* be to increase the complexity of the project in order to rise more money, he should have clarified to the customer that an account registration mechanism will affect the total amount of work. Especially since the answer of the customer reveals, in fact, that he doesn't strongly need it: *(C) it is not a big deal to me, but yes, it would be nice to have it.*

One last comment about money estimate: the cost of the development and the delivery deadlines have to be discussed in a second phase. The aim of the first interview is indeed to collect all the information necessary in order to produce a cost estimate and a delivery calendar. Those are products of a feasibility evaluation phase based on the information collected in the interview. This is why discussing resources with the customer does not mean that the analyst has to agree on the actual cost during the interview. There is actually only one interview in which money is explicitly mentioned and it is a very good example of what an analyst should *not* do.

Example 3.10. In I-13 the customer asks the analyst: *(C) How much the application is going to cost?* Notice that this happens at the very beginning of the interview – minute 2:00 on an 18 min interview. What happens next is quite instructive. The analyst provides a putative sum of *8 to 10 thousand dollars*, before terminating the requirements elicitation interview and with no idea of the customer's resources. The customer replies: *(C) Oh that's it? Very cheap application! You don't pay your developers very much at all!* In this case, the analyst should have stopped the customer after his first question, and reformulate the question in the opposite direction: *I can't give you estimates at the moment. Can you give me an idea of your maximum budget?*

3.6   Non-functional Requirements Not Elicited

Non-functional requirements are qualities to be exhibited by the system, such as usability, availability, maintainability, compatibility, security, cost, *etc.* [6]. As noticed, e.g., by Chung and Prado Leite [7], real-world issues are more non-functionally oriented rather than functionally oriented. In practice, it is more likely for a customer to complain for the cost of a product or its poor performance, rather than about a missing functionality. Although some non-functional requirements can be decided and evaluated only at later stages of development (e.g., design decisions, degree of usability), many of them (e.g., OS or hardware to be used, development time) may have an impact on early decisions, and, as noticed, e.g., by Mylopoulos *et al.* [16], dealing with ignored non-functional requirements once a system is developed is among the most expensive and difficult activities in a software project.

In our interviews, with the exception of user interface requirements and security requirements, which were often discussed, only one of the analysts appeared to have a clear view of the relevance of non-functional requirements at the early stages of development, and defined appropriate questions to elicit them. The questions are not presented in the clearest manner possible – discussion on this aspect are reported in Sect. 3.8 – but the dialogue with the customer can give an idea of what are the major concerns to be discussed for a mobile application from a non-functional perspective.

Example 3.11. In I-13, the customer wants the analyst to develop a mobile application that works as a GPS navigator for the KSU campus. After one minute of interview, the analyst started to ask about non-functional aspects: *(A) First let's start talking about **development time** (C) [...] About three months [...]; (A) What do you envision your **user base** to entail? (C) [...] We are targeting students on campus, mainly first year students [...]; (A) Who do you believe will* *have access to add, or keep up* **maintenance** *with this application (C) Once it is developed [...], I assume our team of programmers to handle updating the system if it needs updates [...]; (A) What kind of* **availability** *we're talking about here, 24-7? (C) The application should be available anytime, all the time, unless we have clearly defined maintenance hours, like from 12 a.m. to 3 a.m. on Sunday, [...] every week; (A) Now, we're talking about Android and i-OS development, what kind of* **versioning** *kernels are we talking here, how far back? Are we talking a couple of years back? Are we talking about a ten years of range (C) [...] I'd like to support at least [...] six years; (A) What kind of* **security** *measures are we talking about, [...] obviously the most straightforward way would be: all the students have their own login [...], or would it be totally open? (C) [...] I don't think we need a login system for this application; (A) What time is a decent* **loading speed**? *(C) I don't need to be instant but I would like the application to load the map in 15 seconds.*

3.7   Interrogatory-Like Interviews

One of the main benefit of unstructured interviews is that the questions that the analyst asks can be based on the previous answers of the customer. To exploit this benefit, analysts shall be able to listen to the customer, on-the-fly analyze his/her response, and react accordingly with follow-up/clarifying questions, if needed. Notice that it is not only important to analyze and react to a response, but it is needed to do it on the spot, because going back and forth among topics can be very confusing for the customer who is not guided in presenting his/her thoughts, but is *interrogated* with direct questions on different topics. Our analysts appear to find this task of making the interview a free-form, yet logical, *flow* of questions and answers particularly difficult.

Example 3.12. In I-6, the customer asks for a mobile application that provides information about soccer players and teams to support gambling. After an initial conversation on system features, the analyst started asking: [**10:31**] *(A) How would you like to see the search, would you like to see more like a Facebook, where it suggests the names of the players, or you would like to see more a database called by a team...? (C) I would like to see a database, per team... nonono, I think a little bit of both [...] (A) So have statistics on the league too? (C) Yeah, yeah, absolutely* [**11.17 − 11.45**] *(A) What about new recruited members, the same? You would like to see them? (C) If there's no statistics, I would like for them to be included [...]* [**12.04 − 12:37**] *(A) How about the attendance of the stadium [...], the audience can have an influence on how the players play, so would you like to see [...] how many people from that particular team are going to attend the stadium? (C) Yeah, more information is useful.*

In this example, features appear as a scattered list of items, while in a first interview it is also important to have a cohesive, procedural, view of the different features [22]. Overall, triggering the customer to use the communication tactics called *imagining* by Urquhart [31], and *scenario building* by Pitts and

Browne [22], can provide some help. In example 3.12, the analyst should have asked: *Please, let me visualise the first page of your application, and tell me step-by-step how should I interact with the application to select the team that I should bet on.* It is important to notice that, as recommended by Portugal [23], the analysts should ask the customer to act as *teacher*, to reinforce the idea that s/he is the expert there.

Another aspect that we noticed with this style of interview, was that the analyst tended to *run out of questions.* The reader is encouraged to check the time intervals between one question and the other in the previous example, to convince him/herself of the effort of the analyst in inventing new questions. In the specific example, the analyst also exclaimed: *I think I asked a lot of questions!* In other cases, in which the fantasy of the analyst was less fruitful, interviews were closed much earlier than the 20 min that were allocated for the task. Triggering scenarios can also help in inventing questions, since, as observed, e.g., by Rolland and Salinesi [26], scenarios expressed in the form of narratives can disclose unexplored goals, and hence open other topics of discussion.

3.8 Problems in Phrasing Questions

An important aspect of interviews is how questions are formalized. In structured interviews, analysts prepare the questions in advance and they have time to create clear, short and unambiguous questions. In unstructured interviews, the questions are created on-the-spot, and this requires a prompt effort of clarity from analysts in phrasing their questions. This effort was rarely observed in our interviews. Often our analysts ask questions that are too *direct* and this makes them difficult to be interpreted by the customers. An amusing example comes from I-9 (Live Translator, see Example 3.3), in which the analyst suddenly asks: *(A) Does it* [the system] *have any attachment?*, and the customer, after a long silence, replies: *(C) Can you give me another question?* As analysts require a context to understand the requirements (see Sect. 3.1), so the customer needs some minimal background to understand analyst's questions. In the previous case, the analyst should have said: *I understand that you want a mobile application for translating communications. Does the mobile application require any external device?*

Sometimes our analysts also create too long or articulated questions in which they ask for different kinds of requirements.

Example 3.13. In I-12, concerning a social network for travellers (Example 3.4), the analyst says: *(A) Could you tell me more about the kind of interface and how would you like to distribute this kind of application, which platform? What kind of platform?* Platform and interface choices require at least two articulated answers, and asking them together overwhelms the customer, who ends up not describing all the required information: *(C) This app should be compatible with all different kinds of operating systems [...].* The question about the interface remains unanswered.

We have also observed that our student analysts often use a computer science-oriented terminology, which is a *jargon* that is not necessarily known by customers. However, we did not observe too many miscommunication events related to this issue, since our customers were all computer science students.

3.9 Wrong Closing

The end of interview is as important as its beginning. The majority of our analysts closed the interview by saying *I think I have a good understanding, thank you*. This *good understanding* needs to be assessed, and the earlier, the better. To this end, it is important for the analyst to perform a final summary of the interview to the customer. The role of this summary is twofold. First, it provides an early, oral contract with the customer. Secondly, in our experience [11], a summary can trigger novel clarifications from the customer's side. Although this did not happen in the few cases in which a summary was provided by our analysts, it happened when one of our analysts decided to rephrase one of the features required earlier in the interview.

Example 3.14. In I-5, the customer wishes to develop a video aggregator for anime series, discussed already in Example 3.2. At minute 1:20, the customer says: *(C) You put what anime you are watching from which site, [...], you would input yourself manually*. At minute 6:50, the analyst says: *(A) There's actually something I would like to recap on, you said that you input it manually, so [...] you type the anime you are watching, what episode you're on, and you go through everything*. The customer interrupts: *(C) Well, that would be an issue*. After identifying this issue through the summary, the discussion goes on and lasts for three additional minutes.

If a summary of the interview is not provided, at the end of interview the customer is not aware of the real understanding of the analyst. Hence, if the analyst asks a generic question such as *Do you have anything to add?*, the customer might find difficult to answer since he/she cannot be sure about the information already collected by the analyst.

4 Limitations

This paper reports the results of a case study conducted intentionally in the absence of a strong experimental scheme. At this stage, our goal was to observe role playing interviews in their real-world context, to identify an initial set of mistakes of student analysts, to be further consolidated with a more structured experiment. Given that, we acknowledge a set of limitations of our work. First of all, the limited sample, composed of students from a single course of a single university. This limitation, and the absence of profiling, does not allow us to evaluate the impact of aspects as culture, technical knowledge, and experience. Another limitation is the absence of a written output for the interviews. Indeed, the students were not required to produce a list of requirements, and hence some mistakes might have derived from them not being compelled in producing written material, as required in other works [3,22]. Without this requirements document, we could not check the results with the customer, a task that would have revealed other misunderstandings and mistakes. Finally, although the experience of our experts is diverse, they are all requirements engineers, and cognitive scientists/psychologists should be involved, to identify other types of mistakes.

5   Conclusion and Future Work

This paper presents a set of 9 mistakes of requirements analysts in requirements elicitation interviews, identified by a panel of inflexible teachers. The identified errors can be used by instructors to better focus their training courses, in which our examples can be used as a practical list of *don'ts* for the students. Our final aim is to provide guidance for conducting unstructured interviews, without losing the benefit of this method, which resides in the possibility of scoping customer's needs following the flow of the dialogue. Our primary objective for future works is to consolidate the findings of our case study with an appropriate experimental design, which will take into account the limitations of the current work, and will complete the current results with reliable quantitative data. Then, our goal will be to better structure and validate the recommendations provided for avoiding the mistakes. At this stage, the recommendations are partly taken from the literature, and partly come from the authors' experience. Hence, they require validation with students. Another interesting perspective is to empirically study how the students' mistakes found differ from those made by experts.

References

1. Agarwal, R., Tanniru, M.R.: Knowledge acquisition using structured interviewing: an empirical investigation. JMIS **7**(1), 123–140 (1990)
2. Anton, A.I.: Goal-based requirements analysis. In: RE 1996, pp. 136–144. IEEE (1996)
3. Aranda, A.M., Dieste, O., Juristo, N.: Effect of domain knowledge on elicitation effectiveness: an internally replicated controlled experiment. TSE **42**(5), 427–451 (2016)
4. Argyris, C., Schon, D.A.: Theory in Practice: Increasing Professional Effectiveness. Jossey-Bass, Hoboken (1974)
5. Bubenko, J., Rolland, C., Loucopoulos, P., DeAntonellis, V.: Facilitating fuzzy to formal requirements modelling. In: RE 1994, pp. 154–157. IEEE (1994)
6. Chung, L., Nixon, B.A., Yu, E., Mylopoulos, J.: Non-functional Requirements in Software Engineering. Springer Science & Business Media, Berlin (2012)
7. Chung, L., Prado Leite, J.C.S.: On non-functional requirements in software engineering. In: Borgida, A.T., Chaudhri, V.K., Giorgini, P., Yu, E.S. (eds.) Conceptual Modeling: Foundations and Applications. LNCS, vol. 5600, pp. 363–379. Springer, Heidelberg (2009). doi:10.1007/978-3-642-02463-4_19
8. Coughlan, J., Macredie, R.D.: Effective communication in requirements elicitation: a comparison of methodologies. REJ **7**(2), 47–60 (2002)

9. Davis, A., Dieste, O., Hickey, A., Juristo, N., Moreno, A.M.: Effectiveness of requirements elicitation techniques: empirical results derived from a systematic review. In: RE 2006, pp. 179–188. IEEE (2006)

10. Distanont, A., Haapasalo, H., Vaananen, M., Lehto, J.: The engagement between knowledge transfer and requirements engineering. IJKL **1**(2), 131–156 (2012)

11. Ferrari, A., Spoletini, P., Gnesi, S.: Ambiguity and tacit knowledge in requirements elicitation interviews. REJ **21**(3), 333–355 (2016)

12. Gabrysiak, G., Giese, H., Seibel, A., Neumann, S.: Teaching requirements engineering with virtual stakeholders without software engineering knowledge. In: REET 2010, pp. 36–45. IEEE (2010)

13. Gervasi, V., Gacitua, R., Rouncefield, M., Sawyer, P., Kof, L., Ma, L., Piwek, P., De Roeck, A., Willis, A., Yang, H., et al.: Unpacking tacit knowledge for requirements engineering. In: Maalej, W., Thurimella, A.K. (eds.) Managing Requirements Knowledge, pp. 23–47. Springer, Heidelberg (2013)

14. Hadar, I., Soffer, P., Kenzi, K.: The role of domain knowledge in requirements elicitation via interviews: an exploratory study. REJ **19**(2), 143–159 (2014)

15. Hickey, A.M., Davis, A.M.: A unified model of requirements elicitation. J. Manag. Inf. Syst. **20**(4), 65–84 (2004)

16. Mylopoulos, J., Chung, L., Nixon, B.: Representing and using nonfunctional requirements: a process-oriented approach. TSE **18**(6), 483–497 (1992)

17. Niknafs, A., Berry, D.M.: An industrial case study of the impact of domain ignorance on the effectiveness of requirements idea generation during requirements elicitation. In: RE 2013, pp. 279–283. IEEE (2013)

18. Nuseibeh, B., Easterbrook, S.: Requirements engineering: a roadmap. In: FOSE 2000, pp. 35–46. ACM (2000)

19. Ouhbi, S., Idri, A., Fernández-Alemán, J.L., Toval, A.: Requirements engineering education: a systematic mapping study. REJ **20**(2), 119–138 (2015)

20. Pacheco, C., Garcia, I.: A systematic literature review of stakeholder identification methods in requirements elicitation. JSS **85**(9), 2171–2181 (2012)

21. Pitts, M.G., Browne, G.J.: Stopping behavior of systems analysts during information requirements elicitation. J. Manag. Inf. Syst. **21**(1), 203–226 (2004)

22. Pitts, M.G., Browne, G.J.: Improving requirements elicitation: an empirical investigation of procedural prompts. Inf. Syst. J. **17**(1), 89–110 (2007)

23. Portugal, S.: Interviewing Users: How to Uncover Compelling Details. Rosenfeld Media, Brooklyn (2013)

24. Regev, G., Gause, D.C., Wegmann, A.: Experiential learning approach for requirements engineering education. REJ **14**(4), 269–287 (2009)

25. Robertson, S., Robertson, J.: Mastering the Requirements Process: Getting Requirements Right. Addison-Wesley, Boston (2012)

26. Rolland, C., Salinesi, C.: Supporting requirements elicitation through goal/scenario coupling. In: Borgida, A.T., Chaudhri, V.K., Giorgini, P., Yu, E.S. (eds.) Conceptual Modeling: Foundations and Applications. LNCS, vol. 5600, pp. 398–416. Springer, Heidelberg (2009). doi:10.1007/978-3-642-02463-4_21

27. Sharp, H., Rogers, Y., Preece, J.: Interaction Design: Beyond Human Computer Interaction, 4th edn. Wiley, Hoboken (2015)

28. Shuraida, S., Barki, H.: The influence of analyst communication in is projects. J. Assoc. Inf. Syst. **14**(9), 482 (2013)

29. Sutcliffe, A., Sawyer, P.: Requirements elicitation: towards the unknown unknowns. In: RE 2013, pp. 92–104. IEEE (2013)

30. Svensson, R.B., Regnell, B.: Is role playing in requirements engineering education increasing learning outcome? REJ, 1–15 (2016). http://link.springer.com/article/10.1007/s00766-016-0248-4
31. Urquhart, C.: Exploring analyst-client communication: using grounded theory techniques to investigate interaction in informal requirements gathering. In: Lee, A.S., Liebenau, J., DeGross, J.I. (eds.) Information Systems and Qualitative Research, pp. 149–181. Springer, Heidelberg (1997)
32. Yu, E., Giorgini, P., Maiden, N., Mylopoulos, J.: Social modeling for requirements engineering: an introduction. Social Modeling for Requirements Engineering, pp. 3–10 (2011)
33. Zowghi, D., Coulin, C.: Requirements elicitation: a survey of techniques, approaches, and tools. In: Aurum, A., Wohlin, C. (eds.) Engineering and Managing Software Requirements, pp. 19–46. Springer, Heidelberg (2005)
34. Zowghi, D., Paryani, S.: Teaching requirements engineering through role playing: lessons learnt. In: RE 2003, pp. 233–241. IEEE (2003)

Process and Tool Integration

How Can Quality Awareness Support Rapid Software Development? – A Research Preview

Liliana Guzmán[1(✉)], Marc Oriol[2], Pilar Rodríguez[3], Xavier Franch[2],
Andreas Jedlitschka[1], and Markku Oivo[3]

[1] Fraunhofer IESE, Kaiserslautern, Germany
{liliana.guzman,
andreas.jedlitschka}@iese.fraunhofer.de
[2] Universitat Politècnica de Catalunya, Barcelona, Spain
{moriol,franch}@essi.upc.edu
[3] University of Oulu, Oulu, Finland
{pilar.rodriguez,markku.oivo}@oulu.fi

Abstract. *Context and Motivation:* Rapid software development (RSD) refers to the organizational capability to develop, release, and learn from software in rapid cycles without compromising its quality. To achieve RSD, it is essential to understand and manage software quality along the software lifecycle. *Question/Problem:* Despite the numerous information sources related to product quality, there is a lack of mechanisms for supporting continuous quality management throughout the whole RSD process. *Principal ideas/Results:* We propose Q-Rapids, a data-driven, quality-aware RSD framework in which quality and functional requirements are managed together. Quality requirements are incrementally elicited and refined based on data gathered at both development time and runtime. Project, development, and runtime data is aggregated into quality-related indicators to support decision makers in steering future development cycles. *Contributions:* Q-Rapids aims to increase software quality through continuous data gathering and analysis, as well as continuous management of quality requirements.

Keywords: Software quality · Quality requirements · Rapid software development

1 Introduction

Agile software development (ASD) enables organizations to adapt to business dynamics by facilitating more flexible development through iterative methods that rely on extensive collaboration. ASD is prevalent in the software industry [1]. A recent evolutionary step from ASD is rapid and continuous software engineering, which refers to the organizational capability to develop, release, and learn from software in rapid cycles [2]. This capability is known as Rapid Software Development (RSD) [3]. RSD combines methods, practices and principles from ASD, lean software development, and continuous deployment to minimize time-to-market through reduced release cycles [4].

© Springer International Publishing AG 2017
P. Grünbacher and A. Perini (Eds.): REFSQ 2017, LNCS 10153, pp. 167–173, 2017.
DOI: 10.1007/978-3-319-54045-0_12

In RSD, faster and more frequent release cycles should not compromise software quality. Thus, understanding and managing software quality is essential to ensure that new releases will lead to progressive improvement. But despite the numerous sources of information related to product quality that RSD provides (e.g., usage data), there is a lack of methods to support continuous quality management throughout the whole RSD process [4]. Recent empirical studies found the deficient management of quality requirements (QRs) [5] to be the main reason for rework in RSD [1].

In this research preview, we summarize the state of the art and challenges related to continuously managing QRs along the RSD process (Sect. 2). We also introduce Q-Rapids as a data-driven, quality-aware RSD framework that jointly manages QRs and functional requirements (FRs) throughout the RSD process (Sect. 3). Then we outline the strategy selected to develop and evaluate Q-Rapids (Sect. 4). Finally, we summarize our contributions and discuss future research (Sect. 5).

2   Challenges in Managing Quality Requirements

Quality Requirements and Their Management. QRs are a subset of non-functional requirements that state conditions on "characteristics that make the product attractive, usable, fast or reliable" [6]. An example of a QR is: "The system should provide an availability of at least 98% for given time period". Thus, optimal management of software quality demands proper consideration of QRs in the software lifecycle. However, QRs have not received the same degree of attention as FRs [6]. Neglecting QRs is one of the top ten risks of requirements engineering [7], and errors in considering QRs are the most expensive and difficult to correct [8].

Another problem is the elicitation and specification of QRs. Modern approaches to elicit QRs rely on explicit user feedback [9]. However, explicit feedback may be incomplete, biased, or ambiguous. Implicit feedback (usage data) is a promising alternative to elicit QRs [10]. For example, QRs related to performance can be elicited by identifying how many users leave the system after waiting two seconds for a system response. So, QRs regarding response time can be specified by analyzing together the system and user behavior. Current approaches neither derive QRs automatically nor combine usage data with other data sources (e.g., software repositories). Furthermore, whereas FRs have clear-cut satisfaction criteria, QRs are initially elicited as "soft goals" [8] and need to be elaborated into measurable conditions. Finally, current tools for managing QRs do not manage them throughout the entire software lifecycle [11].

Thus, there is a need for (1) data-driven QR elicitation and specification; and (2) data-driven understanding of the strategic impact of QRs on management and business.

Quality Requirements in Rapid Software Development. Current RSD approaches are mostly driven by FRs. For example, in Scrum [12] requirements are specified as user stories stored in the product backlog. User stories are prioritized in each development cycle from a customer value perspective. Although QRs are usually included as acceptance criteria for user stories [13], mainly focusing on customer value when prioritizing requirements is problematic because other important factors (e.g. security, performance, and scalability) tend to be underestimated [1]. More recently, mechanisms such as automation, integration of R&D with operations and maintenance teams (also referred to as DevOps), and post-deployment customer-data monitoring [4] have been introduced to further ensure quality and quick delivery in RSD. However, using mechanisms such as post-deployment data is not free from challenges. The growing size of data is a challenge, and systematic approaches for collecting, analyzing, and integrating data into the product development process are missing [14]. Moreover, there is a lack of methods and tools for integrating, analyzing, and visualizing collected data to make QRs transparent and support real-time decision-making on QRs [15], and to jointly manage QRs and FRs along the RSD process [4].

We conclude that there is a need for (1) seamless integration of QRs and FRs; (2) methods and tools for real-time monitoring of QRs; and (3) flexible, iterative, and dynamic generation and management of QRs in RSD.

Data-Driven Quality Decision Making. As systems scale and their complexity increases, data generated and used during the software lifecycle is becoming increasingly important. Source code repositories, bug reports, and runtime logs contain a lot of hidden information about software quality. Applying analytics to extract this information can help decision makers to identify and monitor quality issues and to steer development activities in order to improve the overall quality in RSD.

However, integrating software analytics research results into tools established in practice is still challenging [17]. Regarding the analysis of historical data, Mining Software Repositories is an important research area to uncover information about software systems. An overview is given in [16]. Still, there are only a few reports (e.g., [23]) on the practical impact of data mining analytics on the development process. Regarding the analysis of runtime data, several approaches exist. For example, profiling and automated instrumentation techniques are usually used to study the runtime behavior of software systems [18]. Such techniques impose high overhead and slow down the execution. They also lead to a large volume of results that are impractical to interpret. Finally, analyzing heterogeneous and time-evolving streaming data can get very complex and lead to poor performance of analysis techniques. MapReduce [19], the Lambda Architecture [20], and modern analytics like Spark can help to address this problem.

We found there is a need for (1) in-time, scalable, and efficient QR-driven data analysis to support decision making; and (2) scalable and efficient gathering and monitoring of heterogeneous data at development time and runtime.

3   The Q-Rapids Framework

Based on the needs identified in Sect. 2, we conclude that the software industry needs methods and tools for handling software quality in the RSD context. To achieve this, we propose the Q-Rapids framework (cf. Fig. 1). Q-Rapids relies on a generic data-driven, quality-aware, rapid development process characterized by integrated management of QRs and FRs. Q-Rapids aims to: (1) improve the software products' quality with an effective and seamless data gathering and analysis; (2) increase the productivity of the software lifecycle with a seamless integration of QRs into the development process: and (3) reduce the time to market of software products by making optimal decisions based on

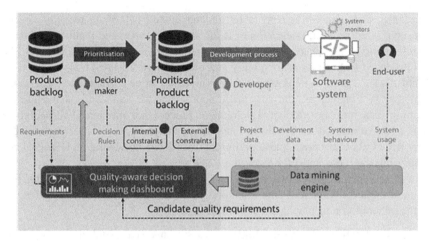

Fig. 1. The Q-Rapids framework

strong evidence and solid experience-based decision making models. Q-Rapids also aims to be a generic and suitable for managing different types of QRs in different application domains and project settings. To attain these goals, Q-Rapids will be developed in collaboration with four European companies in the domains of health, defense, crisis management, and telecommunication. These companies develop software products with different QRs and FRs in different project settings.

Effective and Seamless Data Gathering and Analysis Techniques. Q-Rapids will systematically and continuously track software quality based on quality-related indicators. It will combine different types of data sources to gather relevant indicators: project management tools, software repositories, and runtime data about quality of service and system usage by end users. This information will be selectively collected and pre-processed, and analyzed to support different decisions makers (e.g., product owners, developers, and testers). Q-Rapids will propose quality-critical indicators on the basis of a product-specific quality model based on the QUAMOCO approach [21]. Such approach will enable Q-Rapids to define a generic set of QRs as well as quality-related indicators that can be tailored according to the application domain, product characteristics, and project context. Examples of QRs that we plan to address in the Q-Rapids project include performance, reliability and usability.

Data gathering will be seamlessly integrated into the software lifecycle and later system usage. Q-Rapids will integrate different data collection instruments. For example, we plan to gather project data through a monitor of the project management, development data through a monitor of GIT, data on the system behavior through QoS monitors, and usage data through an event-tracking monitor. Deployment should be as easy as providing the URLs or directories for the software project repositories and a specification of the quality attributes that are of interest for the particular project in order to deploy only the needed monitors. Monitoring instruments will be deployed in different contexts considering the lifecycle phase in which they apply [22] and the architecture type (e.g., service-based architectures or cloud deployments).

Through the application of data analytics, elicited data will be analyzed, making it possible to support the comprehension of quality issues that will steer subsequent development activities, thus improving the overall software quality in a timely manner. An essential part of the analysis will be to find correlations. For instance, the correlation analysis between bug rate and QR types may help to understand which QR types are more error-prone and require more effort allocation when planning releases.

Quality-Aware Rapid Software Development Process. Q-Rapids will extend the RSD process with the comprehensive integration of QRs and FRs. Thus, we will focus on rapid practices such as product backlogs, release planning, and sprint planning but with seamless integration of both FRs and QRs. Our goal is to define a generic software development process based on the principles of RSD and, therefore, being lightweight, flexible, and adaptable to market fluctuations and customer changes, still properly considering the management of QRs in a way that rapid releases do not have negative repercussions on software quality. In particular, a quality-aware RSD process will be defined including existing practices, tools, and methods to be used in rapid development cycles and complex scenarios such as Scrum, Kanban and DevOps. The process will be based on key characteristics of agile methods and RSD, including the management of FRs and QRs using a holistic management of product backlogs, continuous integration, and short release cycles [1, 4, 13]. The quality-aware RSD process will provide the means needed to elicit, derive, and manage QRs in rapid cycles by addressing questions like "how should QRs be processed in RSD so that the result will be high-quality products?" Q-Rapids will focus on success factors for software companies and help managers to balance such issues as time to market and product quality. It will also consider business-related constraints and domain-specific requirements and regulations so that the framework can easily be tailored to different company's needs.

Q-Rapids will provide a novel rapid requirements engineering approach that will elicit QRs using a data-driven approach, followed by the implementation and assessment of QRs in rapid cycles. It will provide a generic quality-aware RSD process that can be customized based on the software company setting and their quality demands.

Quality-Aware Decision Making Dashboard. Q-Rapids will extend current tools for measuring and analyzing software quality (e.g., SonarQube™) by providing decisions makers with a highly informative dashboard to help them make data-driven strategic decisions related to QRs in rapid cycles. The Q-Rapids dashboard will aggregate the collected data into key strategic indicators related to, e.g., time to market, development costs, and overall quality. It will also comprise the product and iteration backlogs that contain the project requirements. Thus, the dashboard will help decision makers to analyze, e.g., the impact on time to market of selecting, leaving out, or discarding a QR. In addition, the dashboard will allow defining project-specific decision rules (e.g., how to handle conflicts between time and quality levels) as well as external and internal constraints. External constraints are conditions beyond the control of decision makers, e.g., a fixed budget. Internal constraints are development and organizational conditions influencing decision making, e.g., a maximum number of tasks per developer per week.

The Q-Rapids dashboard will provide models and advanced capabilities to (1) analyze and evaluate alternative solutions to current QR management decisions; (2) predict and analyze the impact of violations related to key strategic indicators; and

(3) suggest mitigation actions when violations are identified. The underlying rationale of previous analyses will be transparent to decision makers.

4   Development and Evaluation of the Q-Rapids Framework

Q-Rapids will be developed as part of the H2020 European project Q-Rapids following an iterative and incremental approach applying RSD principles. Its development will be driven by four use cases defined in collaboration with four European companies. The use cases were chosen to show the generalizability and suitability of Q-Rapids. They will serve as basis for understanding how QRs are managed as well as for evaluating Q-Rapids. The use cases cover managing QRs of single and multiple product lines in application domains such as health, defense, crisis management and telecommunication. The use cases also vary regarding the RSD approaches been used. The Q-Rapids development approach includes four phases: (1) requirements elicitation, (2) proof-of-concept, (3) consolidated approach, and (4) final solution.

To assess the impact of Q-Rapids, we plan a formative and summative evaluation. The outcomes of the proof-of-concept phase will be evaluated by themselves in small-scale, lab-like environments, with the goal of obtaining information on their general functionality (formative evaluation). Then, the (ready-to-integrate) intermediate components and the final framework will be evaluated in real context. Q-Rapids, as a whole, will be integrated into the industrial partners' development environments and evaluated regarding to predefined criteria (summative evaluation). Evaluation criteria will be derived from the Q-Rapids goals and selected use cases.

5   Summary

In this paper, we identified the challenges that need to be overcome to support decision makers in managing QRs throughout the whole RSD process. As a response to these challenges, we introduced the Q-Rapids framework, developed as part of the H2020 European project Q-Rapids. This project will follow an iterative and incremental approach applying RSD principles itself. A full 3-year validation plan has been designed, including a formative and summative evaluation involving four European companies, which will provide real projects that will allow scaling initial small-scale results produced in lab-like environments to ready-to-transfer solutions.

Acknowledgements. This work is a result of the Q-Rapids project, which has received funding from the European Union's Horizon 2020 research and innovation program under grant agreement N° 732253.

References

1. Inayat, I., Salim, S.S., Marczak, S., Daneva, M., Shamshirband, S.A.: Systematic literature review on agile requirements engineering practices and challenges. Comput. Hum. Behav. **51**(B), 915–929 (2014)
2. Fitzgerald, B., Stol, K.J.: Continuous software engineering: a roadmap and agenda. J. Syst. Softw. **123**, 176–189 (2017)

3. Mäntylä, M.V., Adams, B., Khomh, F., Engström, E., Petersen, K.: On rapid releases and software testing: a case study and a semi-systematic literature review. Empirical Softw. Eng. **25**(2), 1384–1425 (2015)
4. Rodríguez, P., Haghighatkhah, A., et al.: Continuous deployment of software intensive products and services: a systematic mapping study. J. Syst. Softw. **123**, 263–291 (2017)
5. Ramesh, B., Baskerville, R., Cao, L.: Agile requirements engineering practices and challenges: an empirical study. Inf. Syst. J. **20**(5), 449–480 (2010)
6. Wagner, S.: Software Product Quality Control. Springer, Berlin (2013)
7. Lawrence, B., Wiegers, K., Ebert, C.: The top ten risks of requirements engineering. IEEE Softw. **18**(6), 62–63 (2001)
8. Chung, L., Nixon, B.A., Yu, E., Mylopoulos, J.: Non-functional Requirements in Software Engineering, vol. 5. Springer Science & Business Media, Berlin (2000)
9. Dalpiaz, F., Korenko, M., Salay, R., Chechik, M.: Using the crowds to satisfy unbounded requirements. In: CrowdRE 2015, pp. 19–24 (2015)
10. Maalej, M., Nayebi, M., Johann, T., Ruhe, G.: Toward data-driven requirements engineering. IEEE Softw. **33**(1), 48–54 (2016)
11. Caracciolo, A., Lungu, L.F., Nierstrasz, O.: How do software architects specify and validate quality requirements? In: ECSA 2014, pp. 374–389 (2014)
12. Schwaber, K.: Agile Project Management with Scrum. Microsoft Press, Redmond (2004)
13. Leffingwell, D.: Agile Software Requirements: Lean Requirements Practices for Teams, Programs, and the Enterprise. Addison-Wesley Professional, Boston (2010)
14. Sauvola, T., Lwakatare, L.E., et al.: Towards customer-centric software development: a multiple-case study. In: Proceedings of Euromicro Conference on SEAA, pp. 9–17 (2015)
15. Yaman, S.G., Sauvola, T., Riungu-Kalliosaari, L., Hokkanen, L., Kuvaja, P., Oivo, M., Männistö, T.: Customer involvement in continuous deployment: a systematic literature review. In: Daneva, M., Pastor, O. (eds.) REFSQ 2016. LNCS, vol. 9619, pp. 249–265. Springer, Heidelberg (2016). doi:10.1007/978-3-319-30282-9_18
16. Kwan, I., Damian, D.: A survey of techniques in software repository mining. In: Technical report DCS-340-IR, University of Victoria (2011)
17. Zhang, D.: Software analytics in practice – approaches and experiences. Microsoft research. In: Keynote PROMISE (2015)
18. Thomas, S.W., Hassan, A.E., Blostein, D.: Mining unstructured software repositories. In: Mens, T., Serebrenik, A., Cleve, A. (eds.) Evolving Software Systems, pp. 139–162. Springer, Heidelberg (2014)
19. Dean, J., Ghemawat, S.: MapReduce: simplified data processing on large clusters. Commun. ACM **51**(1), 107–113 (2008)
20. Marz, N., Warren, J.: Big Data: Principles and Best Practices of Scalable Real Time Data Systems. Manning Publications Co., Greenwich (2015)
21. Wagner, S., Goeb, A., et al.: Operationalised product quality models and assessment: the Quamoco approach. Inf. Softw. Technol. **62**, 101–123 (2015)
22. Oriol, M., Franch, X., Marco, J.: Monitoring the service-based system lifecycle with SALMon. Expert Syst. Appl. **42**(19), 6507–6521 (2015)
23. Shihab, E., Hassan, A.E., Adams, B., Jiang, Z.M.: An industrial study on the risk of software changes. In: Proceedings of the Symposium on the FSE, Article 62 (2012)

Using Tags to Support Feature Management Across Issue Tracking Systems and Version Control Systems

A Research Preview

Marcus Seiler[✉] and Barbara Paech

Institute for Computer Science, Heidelberg University, Im Neuenheimer Feld 205, 69120 Heidelberg, Germany
{seiler,paech}@informatik.uni-heidelberg.de

Abstract. *Context & motivation*: Features are important for many software engineering activities, e.g. release planning. Companies document features in Issue Tracking Systems (ITS) and store feature code in Version Control Systems (VCS). *Question/Problem*: However, companies do not always manage features systematically. This issue hinders e.g. the prioritizing of features for release planning. *Principal ideas/results*: We want to provide insights into practice regarding feature management. We have developed first ideas on lightweight feature management using tags. We conducted semi-structured interviews with eight experts to get insight into practice and an early evaluation of our idea. *Contribution*: The interviews showed that fuzzy feature descriptions, insufficient traceability, and fragmentation of feature knowledge are major practice problems. The interviews thus confirm the need for a method for managing features across ITS and VCS. We propose our lightweight method for feature management and describe future research regarding our approach.

Keywords: Feature management · Tagging · Issue tracking systems · Version Control Systems · Expert interviews

1 Introduction

Features are important for many software engineering activities, e.g. release planning [6]. Feature knowledge such as the requirements related to a feature need to be known and prioritized [3] prior to release planning. In Issue Tracking Systems (ITS) feature knowledge is managed in terms of feature requests, bug reports, and development tasks [2], and is often difficult to identify [8]. Furthermore, establishing trace links between feature knowledge from ITS and code in Version Control Systems (VCS) is labor-intensive. Thus, a lightweight approach for systematic and explicit feature management in such systems is needed.

Tagging is an effective and lightweight approach for establishing links [12] for other purposes. For example, Anvik and Storey [1] propose a tool to document

P. Grünbacher and A. Perini (Eds.): REFSQ 2017, LNCS 10153, pp. 174–180, 2017.
DOI: 10.1007/978-3-319-54045-0_13

and link details of work-items from ITS in code. Developers specify details of work-items, e.g. subtasks, directly in the code using tags. The tool associates the tags to work-items. Hindle et al. [4] propose a semi-automatic tagging approach to link requirements from ITS to code commits in VCS. The approach uses Latent Dirichlet Allocation to extract topics from requirements and log messages from code commits. The topics are used to relate requirements and code commits.

Our goal is to assess whether a lightweight approach based on tagging is a viable alternative to common approaches for feature management. We define a **feature** as a functional or non-functional property of a software system. Examples are functional properties such as *user management* or non-functional properties such as *interoperability for user authorization*. We use **feature knowledge** to denote feature descriptions and all related elements such as requirements, work items, and code. We define **feature management** as a process comprising the following activities: (I) Creation, quality assurance, and change of feature descriptions, (II) Management of traceability between feature knowledge, (III) Prioritization of features, and (IV) Utilization of the feature knowledge. It is worth noting that the creation, quality assurance, and management of the related elements is not part of feature management.

In this paper, we describe the state of practice with respect to feature management in Sect. 2. We describe our approach for lightweight feature management and our future research in Sect. 3. Finally, Sect. 4 concludes this paper.

2 State of Practice

2.1 Research Method and Threats to Validity

We conducted a series of qualitative semi-structured interviews [9] with eight experts to understand current practices and problems of using features in ITS and VCS. We developed a role description prior to contacting possible experts in order to ensure the right target group. We contacted 36 experts via mail using the role description and information about our research area. Overall, we could attain eight experts for our interview study. Each expert reported her/his experience from one project in detail. Two interviews were done in person and the other six interviews were conducted via telephone. The interviews were recorded with the permission of the interviewees, transcribed, and coded for analysis [11]. We did an upfront mapping of the interview questions to the research question RQ2 (cf. Sect. 3).

According to Runeson et al. [10], we discuss the four threats: construct validity, internal validity, external validity, and reliability. We used open questions to elicit as much information as possible from the experts minimizing prior bias. The majority of interviews were conducted by phone, which is a possible threat to construct validity. However, all experts allowed us to record the interviews. We used our personal relationship to contact experts, which can be a threat to internal validity. However, we also used data from open source projects to contact experts. The number of interviewed experts is relatively small, which hinders external validity and thus the extent to which our results can be generalized.

However, due to the diversity of projects we believe that our results are also representative for other projects. The average project length was 5.4 years, with a minimum of one year and a maximum of 20 years. The projects were located in the domains: agriculture, e-commerce, insurance, logistics, pharma, public sector, semiconductor, and telecommunication. Six projects applied an agile development method and two projects used waterfall as development method. Finally, the interviews and coding was completed by one researcher, which can be a threat to reliability, but ensured consistency.

2.2   Usage and Benefits of Features in Projects

We describe the results according to the activities of feature management.

Creation of Feature Descriptions: Five projects use separate feature descriptions and three projects use user stories as feature descriptions. We call the latter US-projects. Three non-US-projects use general-purpose tools such as Word. They describe features as business use cases using templates in two projects, or as prose in one project. The remaining two non-US-projects describe features in JIRA using a customized issue type, or as prose in Sharepoint.

Quality Assurance of Feature Descriptions: In all projects reviews performed by quality managers, project managers/leaders, and developers ensure the quality of feature descriptions. Two of the US-projects ensure the quality by using the Connextra template.

Change of Feature Descriptions: In all projects changes to feature descriptions are made by all project participants. Changes are applied following an iterative process in seven projects, or after consulting the change control board in one project. In two projects, slight adaptations to feature descriptions can be made without consulting the customer as long as the feature was not prioritized.

Management of Traceability: We describe the traceability for each project. Projects 1–5 are the five non-US-projects and projects 6-8 are the US-projects. The projects 1–3 store refining requirements in JIRA. Project 1 uses tracing in JIRA to link features and requirements. Project 2 and 3 use manually assign IDs to link features and requirements. The projects 1–3 link work-items to requirements using tracing in JIRA. Project 4 stores refining requirements in Bugzilla and uses manually assign IDs to link features and requirements. In addition, the project links work-items to requirements using tracing in Bugzilla. Project 5 stores refining requirements in Team Foundation Server. The project uses tags to link work-items to features and to requirements, and to link features to requirements. The projects 6-8 link work-items to requirements using tracing in JIRA. Project 6 links requirements to wiki pages which document additional information for features, e.g. supported payment methods. Project 7 links user stories to wiki pages which document external specifications. Furthermore, the project uses epics to group user stories. Epics are larger work-items relevant to more than one sprint. All projects except project 5 link code commits to work-items by providing the work-item-ID in the commit message. Project 5 does not trace work-items to code. No project traces features or requirements directly to code.

Prioritization of Features: Features are prioritized according to the expected business value in all projects. In addition, three projects consider dependencies between features for prioritization. Customers and project managers prioritize features in four projects and in two projects, respectively. Change control boards prioritize features in the remaining two projects. Three projects prioritize features for the next release. Two projects prioritize features for the next two releases. The remaining three projects prioritize features for the next sprint, a quarter, or the next half year.

Utilization of Feature Knowledge: The experts confirmed the importance of feature knowledge documentation for a variety of activities. All experts stated that release planning benefits from feature management. Seven experts stated that effort estimation benefits from feature management. The experts utilize feature knowledge for a variety of activities. Three experts use feature knowledge to perform completeness checks. Furthermore, feature knowledge is used to perform impact analysis, to migrate legacy system, to track feature processes, or to understand changes during development. Two experts mentioned each activity.

2.3 Problems for Features in Projects and Solution Ideas

The experts stated many problems regarding features. Due to the page limit we focus on the three major problems. The first problem are **P1 fuzzy feature descriptions**. Six experts mentioned the problem. Among others, time pressure to collect and document feature-relevant information, missing formalization to describe features, and the customers' lack of knowledge how to write feature descriptions are the most notable reasons leading to fuzzy feature descriptions. Five experts mentioned **P2 Insufficient traceability tool-support** as a problem. The traceability is needed to preserve feature-overview and -progress, and to determine related elements (affected by changes). Four experts stated the **P3 fragmentation of feature knowledge** as a major problem in agile projects. Requirements arise continuously in agile projects and can influence existing features and thus influence existing requirements. Requirements of existing features are distributed among multiple individual user stories, which are not always consistently linked. This can lead to contradicting or duplicate requirements for features, and thus to fragmentation of feature knowledge.

The experts proposed the following solution ideas to address the problems. Four experts stated that improving communication between all project participants using workshops, training, guidelines, or reviews can provide a solution for **P1**. Two experts suggested to use (semi-)automatic traceability tool support where possible to address **P2**. One expert each mentioned rigorous documentation of (initial or early) customers' features in ITS, and the enforcement of traces between related user stories as solutions for **P3**.

2.4 Discussion

It is not surprising that experts use ITS to manage refining requirements and derived work-items, since we only searched for such experts. However, the few uses of elements for refining features is surprising. One reason could be that ITS only provide a limited amount of issue types for refining features in its standard configuration. The results showed that various activities benefit from feature management. Although all experts use reviews to ensure the quality of feature descriptions, fuzzy feature descriptions are the major challenge. The experts would like to use traceability, but the provided traceability is still difficult to use. Moreover, a major challenge in agile projects is fragmentation of feature knowledge. Overall, this confirms the need to implement a lightweight approach for feature management in practice.

3 Research Outline

We propose *TAFT*, a **T**agging **A**pproach to support **F**eature managemen**T** as shown in Fig. 1. We use one tag for each feature of a software, e.g. *UserManagement*. We relate feature descriptions, requirements, and work-items stored in Jira ITS to features by tagging them with the corresponding feature tag. A feature description is tagged with *UserManagement* if and only if it contains the definition of this feature. A requirement is tagged with *UserManagement* if and only if the requirement refines *UserManagement*. A work-item is tagged with *UserManagement* if and only if the described task addresses specification, quality assurance, or implementation of *UserManagement*. We relate code to features by tagging code files that implement a feature either on class- or method level. The tags in our approach provide an overview of the features and a lightweight mechanism to establish traces needed for feature management. The explicit feature knowledge provided by *TAFT* helps to improve communication and thus to minimize fuzzy feature descriptions. Moreover, the solution ideas to rigorously document features and enforce reasonable traces between feature knowledge are the core of *TAFT*.

In our research, we want to answer the following questions:

RQ1 What approaches exist for feature management across ITS and VCS?
1. Which elements from ITS and VCS do other approaches consider as feature knowledge?
2. How do other approaches manage the feature knowledge?
3. Which problems do other approaches address?
4. What are limitations of the approaches?

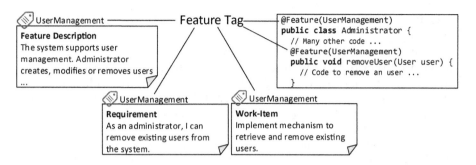

Fig. 1. TAFT approach

RQ2 What is the state of practice with regard to feature management?
1. How are features created and used in projects?
2. What is the expected benefit of using features?
3. What are problems that prevent projects from using features?
4. What do practitioners suggest to overcome these problems?

RQ3 To what extent can tagging be used to manage feature in ITS and VCS?
1. Does *TAFT* enable developers to document feature knowledge?
2. Does *TAFT* enable the use of documented feature knowledge?
3. How do developers assess the feasibility and the acceptance of *TAFT*?
4. How does feature knowledge provided by *TAFT* compares to feature knowledge provided by common trace links?

We answer RQ1 using a literature review according to Kitchenham and Charters [7]. We conducted interviews with experts from practice in order to answer RQ2. We will relate our findings for RQ2 to findings from other empirical studies. Based on the findings for RQ1 and RQ2, we develop tool support for *TAFT* in order to answer RQ3. Currently, we have implemented *TAFT* for JIRA and git. We use labels as tags in JIRA and annotations in Eclipse IDE to provide code tags in git. We have developed a dashboard that analyzes tagging information from JIRA and git in order to support utilization of feature knowledge by providing visualization of metrics related to features. We currently evaluate feasibility and acceptance of *TAFT* and the dashboard in a student project (RQ3.1–RQ3.3).

During the interviews, we also asked the experts to assess the potential of *TAFT* for feature management (RQ3.3). This early evaluation showed that *TAFT* can be a feasible and beneficial approach for managing features. The majority of experts considered the clear overview of the features and the lightweight character as the most notable benefits. However, the experts also pointed out several problems. The major problems are the effort to assign and maintain code tags manually, finding a representative tag to describe a feature, the difficulty to interpret diverse feature knowledge, and to preserve usability and consistency of tags.

In order to answer RQ3.4 we will retrospectively apply *TAFT* to the iTrust [5] project. We will incrementally refine *TAFT* during investigation of RQ3.

4 Conclusion

In this paper, we reported on the state of practice regarding feature management to provide answers for RQ2. In future work, we will perform a literature review to answer RQ1. We will relate the findings for RQ2 to findings from other empirical studies. We have started investigating RQ3.1–RQ3.3. We plan to investigate RQ3.4 in mid of 2017. We expect to finish this research by mid of 2018.

Acknowledgments. We thank all participating experts for their volunteered time and valuable feedback.

References

1. Anvik, J., Storey, M.A.: Task articulation in software maintenance: integrating source code annotations with an issue tracking system. In: 2008 IEEE International Conference on Software Maintenance, pp. 460–461, September 2008
2. Baysal, O., Holmes, R., Godfrey, M.W.: Situational awareness: personalizing issue tracking systems. In: 2013 35th International Conference on Software Engineering (ICSE), pp. 1185–1188, May 2013
3. Greevy, O., Ducasse, S., Gîrba, T.: Analyzing software evolution through feature views. J. Softw. Maint. Evol. Res. Pract. **18**(6), 425–456 (2006)
4. Hindle, A., Bird, C., Zimmermann, T., Nagappan, N.: Relating requirements to implementation via topic analysis: do topics extracted from requirements make sense to managers and developers? In: 2012 28th IEEE International Conference on Software Maintenance (ICSM), pp. 243–252, September 2012
5. iTrust: Role-Based Healthcare: http://agile.csc.ncsu.edu/iTrust/wiki/doku.php
6. Jantunen, S., Lehtola, L., Gause, D.C., Dumdum, U.R., Barnes, R.J.: The challenge of release planning. In: 2011 Fifth International Workshop on Software Product Management (IWSPM), pp. 36–45, August 2011
7. Kitchenham, B.A., Charters, S.: Guidelines for performing systematic literature reviews in software engineering (Version 2.3). Technical report, EBSE 2007-001, Keele University; University of Durham, Keele, Staffs, UK; Durham, UK (2007)
8. Merten, T., Falis, M., Hübner, P., Quirchmayr, T., Bürsner, S., Paech, B.: Software feature request detection in issue tracking systems. In: 2016 IEEE 24th International Requirements Engineering Conference (RE), pp. 166–175, September 2016
9. Myers, M.D., Newman, M.: The qualitative interview in IS research: examining the craft. Inf. Organ. **17**(1), 2–26 (2007)
10. Runeson, P., Host, M., Rainer, A., Regnell, B.: Case Study Research in Software Engineering: Guidelines and Examples, 1st edn. Wiley, Hoboken (2012)
11. Saldana, J.: The Coding Manual for Qualitative Researchers. SAGE Publications, Los Angeles (2009)
12. Storey, M.A., Ryall, J., Singer, J., Myers, D., Cheng, L.T., Muller, M.: How software developers use tagging to support reminding and refinding. IEEE Trans. Softw. Eng. **35**(4), 470–483 (2009)

From Requirements Monitoring to Diagnosis Support in System of Systems

Michael Vierhauser[1]([✉]), Rick Rabiser[1], and Jane Cleland-Huang[2]

[1] Christian Doppler Laboratory MEVSS, ISSE Johannes Kepler University Linz,
Linz, Austria
{michael.vierhauser,rick.rabiser}@jku.at
[2] Department of Computer Science and Engineering, University of Notre Dame,
South Bend, IN, USA
janeclelandhuang@nd.edu

Abstract. *Context and motivation:* Complex industrial software systems are often systems of systems (SoS) whose behavior only fully emerges during operation. Techniques such as requirements monitoring thus have to be used to observe such systems at runtime to detect deviations from their requirements. *Question/problem:* However, the focus of existing monitoring approaches is mainly on detecting violations of expected behavior, while support for subsequent diagnosis of violations is rather limited and often even neglected. Diagnosis is particularly challenging in SoS, which are characterized by complex heterogeneous architectures and a slew of different development and testing tools. *Principal ideas/results:* In this research preview paper we discuss the required capabilities for diagnosis support in SoS and outline a tool-supported framework based on a runtime artifact model and pre-defined diagnosis actions. *Contribution:* We describe our ongoing development of the framework and tools for supporting diagnosis in SoS and provide a research agenda.

Keywords: Requirements monitoring · Systems of systems · Diagnosis

1 Introduction and Motivation

Many industrial software systems today are systems of systems (SoS) characterized by decentralized control; support for multiple platforms; inherently volatile and conflicting requirements; continuous evolution and deployment; as well as heterogeneous, inconsistent, and changing elements [10]. SoS cannot fully be tested during development time: interactions between the SoS and its environment can only be checked during operation when all of its software systems, including legacy and third-party software, and the hardware interoperate for the first time. Furthermore, due to unforeseen software changes, hardware failures, or deterioration of mechanical parts, system behavior may render defined requirements invalid. Thus, SoS need to be continuously monitored during operation.

© Springer International Publishing AG 2017
P. Grünbacher and A. Perini (Eds.): REFSQ 2017, LNCS 10153, pp. 181–187, 2017.
DOI: 10.1007/978-3-319-54045-0_14

Several research communities have been developing runtime monitoring approaches for many different kinds of domains and purposes [15]. Examples include requirements-based monitoring [12], monitoring of architectural properties [8], complex event processing [18], or runtime verification [3].

Our previous experience [14] has proven that requirements monitoring is viable in SoS to detect deviations from requirements at runtime. However, most existing approaches [15] stop at detecting (and reporting) violations and do not sufficiently support diagnosis activities, such as uncovering the root cause of a requirements violation. This limits the practical usefulness of existing approaches. Particularly in SoS, due to their complexity and technological heterogeneity, developers diagnosing a requirements violation are often not familiar with all systems and requirements related to that particular violation. Thus, additional support is necessary to guide developers through the process of analyzing and remediating undesired system behavior. Providing traceability to system artifacts – such as requirements specifications, design models, or code – is essential, as requirements and their violations are related to different parts of the SoS.

For example, the SoS of our industry partner Primetals Technologies automates, optimizes, and tracks different stages of the metallurgical production process. It comprises a system that optimizes the arrangement of steel slabs on the strand in a continuous casting machine. This system in turn relies on information provided by material tracking systems. An essential requirement (monitored at runtime) specifies that certain data needs to be available from these material tracking systems before the optimization results can be calculated and that the results of the optimization calculation need to be sent to yet another component within a specified time. A violation of this requirement could, for instance, be caused by missing data from the material tracking systems – causing the optimization system to wait and take longer than anticipated to provide the results. However, it could also be the result of a database performance problem preventing completion in time, or it could be caused by a broken communication link between systems. Furthermore, it could also be the result of a defective hardware sensor not reporting the correct parameters required to start the process.

A service engineer that is notified about the violation will have a hard time finding its actual root cause. For instance, the engineer could explore related source code of the material tracking components and check the technical specification regarding the interface between material tracking and optimization. This would require the engineer to use diverse external tools not integrated with the monitoring solution – such as development IDEs, document repositories and so on. Knowing and understanding all the required tasks and tools requires a nontrivial amount of domain knowledge, which is hard to build up in an SoS context.

We are thus convinced that it is necessary to better integrate diagnosis activities and tools with a monitoring solution. Particularly, in this research preview paper we discuss the required capabilities for providing diagnosis support when monitoring SoS (Sect. 2) and describe such support (Sect. 3) we are currently developing based on an existing requirements monitoring framework for systems of systems [14].

2   Required Capabilities

Together with our industry partner we identified key capabilities for analyzing and diagnosing requirements violations. We also discuss related work and shortcomings of existing monitoring approaches regarding these capabilities.

C1 – Detailed information about requirements violations. Engineers analyzing a requirements violation require detailed information to reveal the root cause of the violation. This includes basic information such as the type of violation, the time when the violation occurred, or the involved components and systems in an SoS. Additionally, historical data – such as events, data and violations recorded in the past – is particularly useful and can help, e.g., to uncover a gradual degradation of performance. Several existing approaches provide basic support for analyzing violations. For example, Baresi and Guinea present the ECoWare framework [1], providing a Dashboard visualizing runtime data using live charts and providing an event history. Also, the Kieker monitoring framework [4] provides visualization capabilities for analyzing performance violations. Müller *et al.* [9] have presented tool support providing explanations of violations of service-level agreements in service-based systems at runtime. As also visible from their related work section, however, most existing (service-based systems) monitoring approaches do not allow a fine-grained and detailed analysis of violations. Some approaches (see related work section in [9]) provide partial explanations of violations, i.e., provide information about which service has led to the violation of a service-level agreement. Very few approaches provide a precise explanation and those that do, tend to be difficult for human users to understand, e.g., using the Event Calculus [6]. Additionally, we found [15] that existing monitoring approaches are limited to certain types of requirements (e.g., performance) or are restricted to a certain domain (e.g., service-based systems) and are thus hard to apply in systems of systems [15].

C2 – Easy access to diverse system artifacts related to a violation. Currently engineers need to investigate a violation by manually searching through source code and diverse log files, typically at multiple locations and remote machines. Finding the origin of a violation can become much simpler if trace links to diverse artifacts are available. For instance, trace links to specification documents or architectural models ease access to additional information facilitating a deeper understanding of potential root causes of a violation. While some existing monitoring approaches link requirements to higher-level models, e.g., goal models [12] or UML diagrams [4], they are unable to link violations with arbitrary system artifacts. Other approaches rely on specifying assertions directly in code [5], thus providing traceability to related code in case of violations. These approaches, however, lack trace links to higher-level artifacts.

C3 – Support for heterogeneous tool environments. Diverse tools are used for analyzing and editing system artifacts in SoS, as engineers of different systems prefer to use their established tools and methods and because there is simply no single tool satisfying the diversity of needs. Interfaces thus need to be provided to allow diverse domain-specific tools to be plugged into a monitoring infrastructure to support diagnosis. For instance, interfaces to IDEs allow inspecting and editing the source code linked to a violation. Other examples are modeling tools or document editors. While some existing monitoring approaches [4,12] allow interfacing with other tools by integrating monitoring views into an existing tool infrastructure, they do not allow triggering third-party tools, e.g., starting an IDE and automatically finding and highlighting code related to a violation.

C4 – Providing tool actions supporting diagnosis activities. Engineers will perform different kinds of diagnosis activities, e.g., depending on whether they analyze an event sequence violation or diagnose a failed data check [17]. Depending on the activities they perform they will require different computational services, i.e., actions in tools which support the respective activity. Similarly as described before in the area of Activity-Based Computing [11,13], it is necessary to provide an abstraction mechanism for describing and collecting different (diagnosis) actions and resources required for these actions. For instance, source code artifacts may be *viewed* and *edited* in an editor provided by an IDE to find out why a certain event did not occur. The reason for a failed data check might be found in configuration files or by using a debugger. For example, certain IDEs support (remote) *debugging*, allowing automatic creation of breakpoints for certain classes or methods, and establishing connections to the system that is monitored.

3   Towards Diagnosis Support for SoS

Software models are increasingly used at runtime to monitor and verify particular aspects of runtime behavior and to improve runtime decision-making [2]. We have been developing a *Requirements Monitoring Model* (RMM) [16] containing information on *Requirements* and *Constraints*, runtime *Events* and Data collected from instrumented systems, and *Monitoring Scopes* defining the components to be monitored in an SoS. Our monitoring framework REMINDS [14] builds on this model and supports development of probes for collecting events and data as well as defining and checking constraints to monitor requirements in SoS at runtime.

Based on this earlier work and the four-layered requirements monitoring framework proposed by Robinson [12] we are developing an extended tool-supported Monitoring and Diagnosis Framework (cf. Fig. 1) for SoS. Our key ideas are to collect detailed results about occurring violations (cf. *C1* from above), to relate RMM elements with system artifacts (cf. *C2*), and to provide interfaces and integrate existing tools (cf. *C3*) useful to support subsequent diagnosis activities with these artifacts (cf. *C4*).

We capture constraint check results and diagnosis data – provided by our monitoring framework [14,17] – as first-class citizens in a dedicated *runtime artifact model* (RAM). This is a prerequisite for supporting extended diagnosis beyond simple error reporting and involves maintaining a history of evaluated constraints. Revisiting such past results of checks often is of interest during diagnosis to detect points of failure or to uncover trends of gradual degradation.

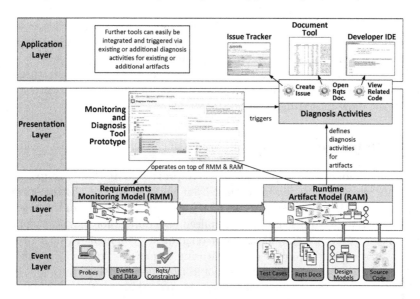

Fig. 1. Monitoring and diagnosis support along Robinson's layers [12].

In the domain of static code analysis, machine learning techniques, for example, have been used to predict potentially defective code parts [7]. Such approaches may also be adapted and employed for analyzing runtime data. For each constraint check result, additional diagnosis data can be stored in the RAM (cf. *C1*). This data typically varies, e.g., for a data constraint, details on the violated data condition such as expected vs. actual value are stored, while for an event sequence constraint information on the actual sequence, on the time between events, as well as on missing or unsuitable events is stored.

In addition to this information collected by the monitoring framework, in the RAM we explicitly describe *System Artifacts* useful for diagnosis and relate them with the elements of the RMM (cf. *C2*). Specifically, we support relating concrete artifacts such as requirements specification documents or goal models with requirements and constraints, source code and configuration files with events and probes, and architecture documentation such as UML models or diagrams with monitoring scopes. To deal with the wide variety and heterogeneity of artifacts and tools (cf. *C3*) that exist in large-scale systems – including specification documents, system administrator documentation stored in document management systems (e.g., Microsoft SharePoint), source code kept in SVN or GIT repositories, and issues collected in an issue tracking system (such as Bugzilla or Jira) – we employ a meta-modeling approach, i.e., the RAM is based on a meta-model that allows to define domain-specific artifact types with dedicated attributes.

We also allow the definition of different *Diagnosis Activities* (cf. *C4*) on top of the RAM, which can be performed depending on the type of violation. For instance, when diagnosing event sequence violations engineers may review related events or open and view related source code or documents. Documents as well as source code can be opened and viewed in an external tool. Other external actions could be the creation of an issue in a bug tracking system or starting a debugging tool for a particular piece of code related with a violation.

We are currently developing tool support based on the RAM that presents all artifacts related with a violation and additional diagnosis data together with actions that allow triggering external tools.

4   Summary and Research Agenda

Requirements monitoring in practice needs to provide more than a simple assertion about whether a requirement has been violated or not. Engineers need detailed information and assistance for diagnosing the violation. In this research preview paper we have discussed the required capabilities for diagnosis support in SoS and have briefly summarized our ongoing development of such support based on an existing requirements monitoring framework for SoS. Specifically, we extended an existing requirements monitoring model with a runtime artifact model to take into account multiple heterogeneous artifacts and diverse activities that can be performed with these artifacts in different tools.

As part of our ongoing research we plan to support different types of artifacts, trace links, and diagnosis activities and to evaluate our approach using requirements, artifacts, and tools from real-world systems. Specifically, our *research agenda* is: (1) extend the capabilities of our constraint checker [17] to capture additional data, e.g., what events actually caused a constraint to fail, and provide these details to users via the REMINDS monitoring tool; (2) develop (meta-) modeling support to define arbitrary types of artifacts and relate them with runtime elements, e.g., relate source code or requirements specifications with constraints and violations; (3) develop a framework for defining diagnosis activities and respective tool actions for different artifacts and integrate concrete actions, e.g., open an IDE and highlight source code related to a current violation, into the REMINDS monitoring tool; and (4) evaluate our diagnosis support in a case study with real users and with a concrete SoS – e.g., from our industry partner – specifically focusing on the usefulness (utility and usability) of our approach.

Acknowledgements. This work has been conducted in cooperation with Primetals Technologies and has been supported by the Christian Doppler Forschungsgesellschaft, Austria.

References

1. Baresi, L., Guinea, S.: Event-based multi-level service monitoring. In: Proceedings of the 20th International Conference on Web Services, pp. 83–90. IEEE (2013)
2. Bencomo, N., France, R., Cheng, B.H.C., Aßmann, U. (eds.): Models@run.time. LNCS, vol. 8378. Springer, Heidelberg (2014)
3. Calinescu, R., Ghezzi, C., Kwiatkowska, M.Z., Mirandola, R.: Self-adaptive software needs quantitative verification at runtime. Commun. ACM **55**(9), 69–77 (2012)

4. van Hoorn, A., Waller, J., Hasselbring, W.: Kieker: a framework for application performance monitoring and dynamic software analysis. In: Proceedings of the 3rd Joint International Conference on Performance Engineering, pp. 247–248. ACM (2012)
5. Kim, M., Viswanathan, M., Kannan, S., Lee, I., Sokolsky, O.: Java-MaC: a run-time assurance approach for Java programs. Form. Methods Syst. Des. **24**(2), 129–155 (2004)
6. Mahbub, K., Spanoudakis, G.: A framework for requirements monitoring of service based systems. In: Proceedings of the 2nd International Conference on Service Oriented Computing, pp. 84–93. ACM (2004)
7. Menzies, T., Greenwald, J., Frank, A.: Data mining static code attributes to learn defect predictors. IEEE Trans. Softw. Eng. **33**(1), 2–13 (2007)
8. Muccini, H., Polini, A., Ricci, F., Bertolino, A.: Monitoring architectural properties in dynamic component-based systems. In: Schmidt, H.W., Crnkovic, I., Heineman, G.T., Stafford, J.A. (eds.) CBSE 2007. LNCS, vol. 4608, pp. 124–139. Springer, Heidelberg (2007). doi:10.1007/978-3-540-73551-9_9
9. Müller, C., Oriol, M., Franch, X., Marco, J., Resinas, M., Ruiz-Cortés, A., Rodríguez, M.: Comprehensive explanation of SLA violations at runtime. IEEE Trans. Serv. Comput. **7**(2), 168–183 (2014)
10. Nielsen, C.B., Larsen, P.G., Fitzgerald, J., Woodcock, J., Peleska, J.: Systems of systems engineering: basic concepts, model-based techniques, and research directions. ACM Comput. Surv. **48**(2), 18:1–18:41 (2015)
11. Norman, D.A.: The Invisible Computer: Why Good Products Can Fail, the Personal Computer Is so Complex, and Information Appliances Are the Solution. MIT Press, Cambridge (1998)
12. Robinson, W.N.: A requirements monitoring framework for enterprise systems. Requir. Eng. **11**(1), 17–41 (2006)
13. Tell, P., Babar, M.A., Grundy, J.: A preliminary user evaluation of an infrastructure to support activity-based computing in global software development (ABC4GSD). In: Proceedings of the 8th International IEEE Conference on Global Software Engineering, pp. 100–109. IEEE, Bari (2013)
14. Vierhauser, M., Rabiser, R., Grünbacher, P., Seyerlehner, K., Wallner, S., Zeisel, H.: ReMinds: a flexible runtime monitoring framework for systems of systems. J. Syst. Softw. **112**, 123–136 (2016)
15. Vierhauser, M., Rabiser, R., Grünbacher, P.: Requirements monitoring frameworks: a systematic review. Inf. Softw. Technol. **80**, 89–109 (2016)
16. Vierhauser, M., Rabiser, R., Grünbacher, P., Aumayr, B.: A requirements monitoring model for systems of systems. In: Proceedings of the 23rd IEEE International Requirements Engineering Conference, pp. 96–105. IEEE (2015)
17. Vierhauser, M., Rabiser, R., Grünbacher, P., Egyed, A.: Developing a DSL-based approach for event-based monitoring of systems of systems: experiences and lessons learned. In: Proceedings of the 30th IEEE/ACM International Conference on Automated Software Engineering, pp. 715–725. IEEE (2015)
18. Völz, M., Koldehofe, B., Rothermel, K.: Supporting strong reliability for distributed complex event processing systems. In: Proceedings of the 13th International Conference on High Performance Computing & Communication, pp. 477–486. IEEE (2011)

Visualization and Representation of Requirements

On the Equivalence Between Graphical and Tabular Representations for Security Risk Assessment

Katsiaryna Labunets[1](✉), Fabio Massacci[1], and Federica Paci[2]

[1] DISI, University of Trento, Trento, Italy
{katsiaryna.labunets,fabio.massacci}@unitn.it
[2] ECS, University of Southampton, Southampton, UK
F.M.Paci@soton.ac.uk

Abstract. *Context:* Many security risk assessment methods are proposed both in academia (typically with a graphical notation) and industry (typically with a tabular notation). *Question:* We compare methods based on those two notations with respect to their actual and perceived efficacy when both groups are equipped with a domain-specific security catalogue (as typically available in industry risk assessments).
Results: Two controlled experiments with MSc students in computer science show that tabular and graphical methods are (statistically) *equivalent in quality* of identified threats and security controls. In the first experiment the perceived efficacy of tabular method was slightly better than the graphical one, and in the second experiment two methods are perceived as equivalent. *Contribution:* A graphical notation does not warrant by itself better (security) requirements elicitation than a tabular notation in terms of the quality of actually identified requirements.

Keywords: Security risk assessment method · Empirical study · Controlled experiment · Method evaluation model · Equivalence testing

1 Introduction

Risk analysis is an essential step to deliver secure software systems. It is used to identify security requirements, to look for flaws in the software architecture that would allow attacks to succeed, and to prioritize tests during test execution.

Problem. An interesting observation is that there is a difference in notation between academic proposals and industry standards for security risk assessment (SRA). Most academic approaches suggest a graphical notation, starting from the seminal work on Anti-Goals [35] to [6] and more recently [19]. Industry opts for tabular models like OCTAVE [1], ISO 27005 and NIST 800-30. Microsoft STRIDE [9] is the exception on the industry side and SREP [22] is the exception on the academic side.

The initial goal of our long term experimental plan in 2011 [21] was to empirically prove that (academic) SRA methods using a graphical notation (for short

© Springer International Publishing AG 2017
P. Grünbacher and A. Perini (Eds.): REFSQ 2017, LNCS 10153, pp. 191–208, 2017.
DOI: 10.1007/978-3-319-54045-0_15

"graphical methods") were indeed superior to risk assessment methods using a tabular notation (for short "tabular methods"). We struggled to prove difference in our previous experiments [15,16], then maybe we should prove equivalence. Thus, our study aims to answer the following research questions (RQs):

RQ1: Are tabular and graphical SRA methods equivalent w.r.t. actual efficacy?
RQ2: Are tabular and graphical SRA methods equivalent w.r.t. perceived efficacy?

Approach. We ran two controlled experiments with 35 and 48 MSc students who worked in groups of two participants. They applied both methods to four different security tasks (i.e. 2 tasks per each method) for a large scale assessment lasting 8 weeks. In the first experiment groups analyzed security tasks for the Remotely Operated Tower (ROT) for Air Traffic Management (ATM). To prevent learning effect between two experiments, in the second experiment we asked groups to perform the same security tasks but for a different ATM scenario, namely Unmanned Aerial System Traffic Management (UTM).

We measured *actual efficacy* as the quality of threats and security controls identified with a method as rated by domain-experts. *Perceived efficacy* is measured in terms of *perceived ease of use* (PEOU) and *perceived usefulness* (PU) of the methods through a post-task questionnaire administered to participants. The independent variables were methods and security tasks to assess.

A key difference with our previous studies[1] is that we provided to both groups a industry catalogue with hundreds of domain-specific threats and security controls. In this setting, using the number of identified threats and control as a measure of quality (as we did in SG2013 study) would have been inappropriate as anybody could obtain a large number of (potentially irrelevant) threats or controls just by looking up into the catalogue. So we employed several domain security experts to rate the result of the students.

We also replaced the academic tabular method SREP [22] which we used in SG2013 study by a method used in the industry SecRAM [28] which had very similar tables but a nimbler process, designed by risk-assessment industry experts to simplify SRA, in the same fashion that the graphical method was designed by SINTEF to be simple to use in its industry consultancies [19].

Key Findings and Contribution. Our main findings — as unpalatable as they might be — are that, given the same conditions, the *tabular and graphical methods are equivalent* to each other with respect to the actual and perceived efficacy. Both results are *statistically significant* when compared with two one-sided tests (TOST) [23,27] which allows for testing for equivalence of outcomes.

Our study shows that representation by itself is not enough to warrant the superiority of a graphical model over a tabular model while the presence of clear process may improve method's perception.

---

[1] For simplicity, we name our previous experiments as "SG2013" [14] and "SG2014" [16], where *SG* stands for Smart Grid domain used in the experiments.

2   Background and Related Work

From an academic perspective, we have seen a significant development in requirements engineering towards graphical methods to identify security requirements.
Some were backed up by formal reasoning capabilities [6,35], others offered variants of graphical notation [8,18,19,24], or minimal model based transformation
analysis [4]. An epiphenomena of this trend was the RE'15 most influential paper
award to the RE'05 paper introducing a graphical notation and sophisticated
reasoning capabilities to verify security properties [6].

In contrast, industry standard development bodies doggedly use tabular representations for the elicitation of threats and security requirements. NIST 800-30
and ISO 27005 standards both use tables. Domain specific methodologies such
as SecRAM [28], designed for risk assessment in ATM, also use tables. Most of
tables use essentially the same wordings, with major differences being mostly on
the process (some suggesting to analyze threats first, others suggesting to start
the analysis from assets). Such preference could be due to simplicity, or the need
to produce the documentation (in forms of table) that is often need to achieve
compliance (as opposed to actual security).

As mentioned, our research goal since 2011 [21] has been to prove that graphical methods were actually superior to tabular methods. In all our experiments,
in order to make the comparison fair, the difference between the methods was
purely in the notation and the accompanying modeling process: graphical notation on one side, tabular on the other side. The formal reasoning capabilities
supported by some methods [6] were never called into play.

This was never considered to be a problem, as the RE trend since 2005 has
"revealed the emergence of new techniques to visualize and animate requirements models [...] beautifully simple but potentially very effective" [20]. Such
folk knowledge assumes that a graphical RE model would be anyhow better. This
seemed to be partly confirmed by our initial experiment "SG2013". Yet, our other
experiments failed to produce strong, conclusive evidence in this respect [15,16].

Empirical Comparison of Graphical and Tabular Representations
Graphical and textual notations were empirically investigated in different
domains. In this discussion we focused on the works similar to ours that investigate these representations in security requirements engineering.

Opdahl and Sindre [25] compared misuse cases with attack trees in a controlled experiment with students and repeated it with industrial practitioners
in [11]. Both studies used Wilcoxon signed-ranks test for difference between two
methods. The results showed that attack trees help to identify more threats than
misuse cases, but both methods have similar perception. Stålhane et al. have conducted a series of experiments to evaluate two representations of misuse cases: a
graphical diagram and a textual template. In these experiment authors used t-
tests to compare two representations. The results reported in [29] revealed that
textual use cases helped to identify more threats than use-case diagrams. In
more recent experiments [30–32], Stålhane et al. compared textual misuse cases
with UML system sequence diagrams. The results showed that textual misuse

cases are better than sequence diagrams in identification of threats related to required functionality or user behavior. In contrast, sequence diagrams outperform textual use cases in the identification of threats related to the system's internal working. Scandariato et al. [26] evaluated Microsoft STRIDE [9], which is a mix of graphical (Data Flow Diagrams) and tabular notations. The authors used Wilcoxon test to compare different aspects of the methodology. The results showed that STRIDE is not perceived as difficult by the participants but their productivity in threats identified per hour was very low. Besides, the correctness of the threat is good because the participants identified only few incorrect threats but the completeness was low because they overlook many threats.

To answer our research questions we cannot use the standard statistical tests (e.g. t-test, Wilcoxon, etc.) as they attempt to prove difference and the lack of evidence for difference is not the same as evidence for equivalence.

3   Research Design

We use **equivalence testing** – TOST, which was proposed by Schuirmann [27] and is widely used in pharmacological and food sciences to answer the question whether two treatments are equivalent within a particular range δ [5,23]. We summarize the key aspects of TOST as it is not well known in SE and refer to the review paper by Meyners [23] for details. The problem of the equivalence test can be formulated as follows:

$$H_0 : |\mu_A - \mu_B| > \delta \quad \text{vs} \quad H_a : |\mu_A - \mu_B| \leq \delta. \tag{1}$$

where μ_A and μ_B are means of methods A and B, and δ corresponds to the range within which we consider two methods to be equivalent.

Such question can be tested as a combination of *two* tests, as:

$$\begin{aligned} &H_{01} : \mu_A < \mu_B - \delta \quad \text{or} \quad H_{02} : \mu_A > \mu_B + \delta \\ &H_{a1} : \mu_A \geq \mu_B - \delta \quad \text{and} \quad H_{a2} : \mu_A \leq \mu_B + \delta, \end{aligned} \tag{2}$$

The p-value is then the maximum among p-values of the two tests (see [23] for an explanation on why it is not necessary to perform a Bonferroni-Holms correction). The underlaying statistical test for each of these two alternative hypothesis can then be any difference tests (eg. t-test, Wilcoxon, Mann-Whitney etc.) as appropriate to the underlying data.

For variables collected along a 1–5 Likert scale, a percentage test [5] may grant statistical equivalence too easily and, therefore, we ran an absolute test with narrower range of $\delta = \pm 0.6$. A statistical difference would then correspond to a clear practical difference: a gap in the perception of two methods bigger than > 0.6 means that around 2/3 of participants ranked one method at least one point higher than the rank of the other method. For the qualitative evaluation of the security assessment by the experts it means that, e.g., two out of three experts gave one point higher to SRA performed with one method comparing to the results of the other method. It corresponds to 20% range on a 5-item scale with mean value equal to 3.

Table 1. Experimental variables

Type	Name	Description
Treatment	Tabular, Graphical	The method used to conduct SRA for a security task: SESAR SecRAM (Tabular) or CORAS (Graphical)
	IM, AM, WebApp/DB, and Network	The groups have to conduct SRA for each of four security tasks: *(1)* Identity Management (IM) and *(2)* Access Management (AM) Security, *(3)* Web Application and Database Security (WebApp/DB), and *(1)* Network and Infrastructural Security (Network)
	Experiment X	The study consisted of two controlled experiments: ROT2015 and UTM2016
Actual efficacy	Q_T, Q_{SC}	The overall quality of threats (Q_T)and security controls (Q_{SC}) based on the evaluation from three independent security experts
Perceived efficacy	PEOU, PU	Mean of the responses to the eight questions about perceived ease of use (PEOU) and nine questions about perceived usefulness (PU)

As treatments we had two methods, four security tasks, and two experiments. As dependent variables we had quality of threats and security control as a measure of actual efficacy, and PEOU and PU as a measure of method's perception.

Study Design and Planning. We chose a *within-subject design* where each group applied both methods. To avoid limitations due to domain security knowledge, each group was also given a professional-level domain-specific catalogue. We showed that catalogues are effective in equalizing non-security experts and security experts (without a catalogue) in [7]. To avoid learning effects, each group was asked to perform SRA for a different security task in the same domain. Table 1 summarizes *treatment variables* that we used in our study.

In our study each group performed the risk analysis of four security tasks (see Table 1). To control the effect of security tasks on results we split groups into two types: type A groups started by using the graphical method on IM, then the tabular method on AM and so on, alternating methods, while type B groups did the opposite. Each group was randomly assigned to either type A or B.

Experimental Protocol. Our protocol consists of three main phases:
Training. Participants were administered a short demographics and background questionnaire. For each SRA method and application scenario participants attended 2 h lecture given by an author of the paper. Each lecture on method was followed by a practical exercise on a toy scenario demonstrating application of the corresponding method. Next, participants were divided in groups of two and received training materials including EUROCONTROL EATM security catalogues and scenario description. Since catalogues and ROT description are

confidential materials for EUROCONTROL, participants received only a paper version of the documents and had to sign a non-disclosure agreement.

Application. Once trained on the scenario and methods, groups had to apply each method to four different tasks (two per method). For each task, groups:

- Attended a two hours lecture on the threats and possible security controls specific to the task but not specific to the scenario.
- Had 2 weeks to apply the assigned methods to identify threats and security controls specific for the task.
- Delivered an intermediate report.
- Gave a short presentation about the preliminary results of the method application and received feedback from one of the authors of this paper.

Evaluation. Three experts independently evaluated the quality of threats and security controls identified by groups and the overall quality of the report, providing marks and justifications. Participants received experts' assessments and the course final mark. Finally, they were asked to answer the post-task questionnaire to collect their perception of the methods taking into account the feedback.

Data Collection. Table 1 reports *dependent variables* for actual and perceived efficacy. To answer *RQ1* we measured a method's *actual efficacy* by asking external security experts to independently evaluate the quality of identified threats and security controls for each security task on a five-item scale: *Bad* (1), *Poor* (2), *Fair* (3), *Good* (4), and *Excellent* (5). Such choice is motivated by several factors. At first, the quality of results is considered to be more important in practice: "the security risk assessment report is expected to contain adequate and *relevant* evidence to support its findings, clear and *relevant* recommendations" [17] (Our emphasis). Second, as all participants were provided with a catalogues, they could easily produce a large number of threats and control, irrespective of the method used. Further, [25] have also reported that different methods might help to generate outcomes of difference quality: participants using attack trees identified mainly generic threats, while misuse cases helped to identify more domain-specific threats.

To answer *RQ2* we collected participants' opinion PEOU and PU of both methods using a post-task questionnaire at the very end of our study. The post-task questionnaire was inspired by the Technology Acceptance Model (TAM) [3] and a similar questionnaire used in [16,25]. The questions were formulated in one sentence with answers on a 5-point Likert scale (1 - Strongly agree; 2 - Agree; 3 - Not certain; 4 - Agree; 5 - Strongly agree)[2]. We followed the approach by Karpati et al. [11] and used the mean of participants' responses to PEOU and PU questions as a consolidated measure of their PEOU and PU. This approach seems to be more robust against the possible fluctuation of the responses within the same category.

---

[2] To prevent participants from "auto-pilot" answering, a half of the questions were given in a positive statement and another half in a negative statement.

Data Analysis. To test for statistical difference, we used the following underlying non-parametric tests for difference as our data is ordinal and not normal:

- Mann-Whitney (MW) test to compare two unpaired groups (eg. quality of threats in two experiments).
- Wilcoxon signed-rank test to compare two paired groups (eg. participants' perception of two methods).
- Kruskal-Wallis (KW) test to compare more than two unpaired groups (eg. quality of threats in four security tasks).
- Spearman's rho coefficient for correlation.

For the hypotheses about equivalence of two treatments we applied TOST with Wilcoxon test as the underlying test. The TOST and selection of the equivalence range is discussed in Sect. 3. For all statistical test we adopted 5% as a threshold for α (i.e. probability of committing Type-I error) [36].

4   Study Realization

The study consisted of two controlled experiments: ROT2015 and UTM2016. The participants of the study were MSc students enrolled to Security Engineering course taught by one of the author in Fall semesters of 2014–2015 and 2015–2016 academic years at the University of Trento, Italy. Experiments involved 35 and 48 participants correspondingly. Participants worked in groups of 2 members, except one participant in ROT2015 who did not have a partner. We had to discard the results from 5 participants in ROT2015 and 2 participants in UTM2016 because they failed to complete all necessary steps of the study or provide inconsistent responses to a post-task questionnaire. If the problem was only with post-task questionnaire, we discarded the results only from *RQ2* analysis and kept the group's results in the analysis for *RQ1*.

Table 2 reports participants' demographics in ROT2015 (above) and UTM2016 (below). A half of the participants (53.3%) in ROT2015 and most participants (76.7%) in UTM2016 reported that they had working experience. In ROT2015 the participants had basic knowledge of security, while in UTM2016 the participants reported good general knowledge of security. In both experiments the participants had basic knowledge of modeling languages and limited background in the application scenario.

Application Scenario Selection. In ROT2015 as an application scenario we selected the Remotely Operated Tower (ROT) which was developed for and used in our previous study [7]. ROT is a new operational concept proposed by SESAR in order to optimize the air traffic management in the small and remote airports. The main idea is that control tower operators will no longer be located at the airport. The air traffic controllers will use a graphical reproduction of the out-of-the-window view by means of cameras with a 360-degree view which overlaid with information from other sources like surface movement radar, surveillance

Table 2. Overall participants' demographic statistics

Experiment ROT2015			
Variable	Scale	Mean/median	Distribution
Age	Years	23.1	43.3% were 19–22 years old; 43.3% were 23–25 years old; 13.3% were 26–31 years old
Gender	Sex		75.8% male; 24.2% female
Work experience	—	1.3	46.7% had no experience; 36.7% had 1–2 years; 13.3% had 3–5 years; 3.3% had 6 years
Expertise in security	0(Novice)- 4(Expert)	1 (median)	26.7% novices; 60% beginners; 13.3% competent users
Expertise in modeling languages	—	1 (median)	26.7% novices; 26.7% beginners; 40% competent users; 6.7% proficient users
Expertise in ATM	—	0 (median)	93.3% novices; 6.7% beginners
Experiment UTM2016			
Variable	Scale	Mean/median	Distribution
Age	Years	24.4	32.6% were 21–22 years old; 34.9% were 23–25 years old; 32.6% were 26–30 years old
Gender	Sex		78.3% male; 21.7% female
Work experience	—	2.1	23.3% had no experience; 44.2% had 1–2 years; 23.3% had 3–5 years; 9.3% had 6–10 years
Expertise in security	0(Novice)- 4(Expert)	1 (median)	30.2% novices; 41.9% beginners; 11.6% competent users; 11.6% proficient users; 4.7% experts
Expertise in modeling languages	—	1 (median)	11.6% novices; 41.9% beginners; 30.2% competent users; 16.3% proficient users
Expertise in ATM	—	0 (median)	69.8% novices; 27.9% beginners; 2.3% competent users

radar, and others. The first implementation of ROT has been done by LFV and Saab in Sweden in 2015 [3].

To control the possible "learning effects" between different experiments, in UTM2016 we switched to the application scenario on the Unmanned Aerial System Traffic Management (UTM) based on the documents from NASA [12],

---

[3] LFV: RTS - One Year In Operation. Available: http://news.cision.com/lfv/r/rts---one-year-in-operation,c9930962.

Amazon's memorandum for commercial interests [13], and the thesis on the integration of drones into the national aerospace system [34].

Tasks. For both application scenarios we asked our groups to conduct SRA for each security task (see Table 1) using the corresponding method according to the predefined order. For example, in WebApp/DB task they could identify threats like SQL injection or DoS attack and propose controls to mitigate them.

Methods Selection. In this study we continued our work reported in [14, 16]. Thus, as an instance of graphical method we kept CORAS method *(a)* in order to have a common point of comparison with the previous studies and *(b)* because it provides a clear process to conduct SRA. CORAS was design by SINTEF [19], a research institution in Norway. They use this method to provide consulting services to their clients. CORAS is a *graphical method* whose analysis is supported by a set of diagrams that represent assets, threats, risks and treatments. This method supports both the ISO 27005 and ISO 31000 standards and provides guidance through 8-steps SRA process: *(1)* preparation for the analysis, *(2)* customer presentation of the target, *(3)* approval of the target description, *(4)* refining the target description, *(5)* risk identification, *(6)* risk estimation, *(7)* risk evaluation, and *(8)* risk treatment.

As a tabular methods we selected another ATM Security Risk Assessment Method (SecRAM) developed by SESAR (Single European Sky ATM Research Program) within 16.02.03 project[4]. The method was used by professionals in the SESAR program to conduct SRA. This method was designed as an easy to use step-wise method that can be applied to any operational focus ares of SESAR. Further when we use SecRAM we refer to SESAR SecRAM unless otherwise stated. SecRAM process includes 7 main steps: *(1)* primary assets identification and impact assessment, *(2)* supporting assets identification and evaluation, *(3)* vulnerabilities and threats identification, *(4)* likelihood evaluation, *(5)* impact evaluation, *(6)* risk level evaluation, and *(7)* risk treatment. SecRAM uses tables to represent results of each step.

5   Results

First, we performed an analysis on the various experimental factors (i.e. experiments and tasks) to determine whether there was a significant difference. Factors without a significant difference in outcomes were aggregated, whereas outcomes for factors with a significant difference were reported separately.

Factor - Security Task: The results of pairwise TOST with Wilcoxon test confirmed the equivalence of each pair of tasks for the quality of threats ($p < 0.021$ in ROT2015 and $p < 0.002$ in UTM2016) and controls ($p < 0.004$ in ROT2015 and $p < 2 * 10^{-5}$ in UTM2016). Therefore, we can use the mean

---

[4] SESAR Project 16.02.03 - ATM Security Risk Assessment Methodology, February 2003. Project aims to analyze existing security risk assessment approaches and adopt them to the ATM domain.

quality of threats and controls identified for two tasks as a measure of actual efficacy for a method. In this way we can eliminate a possible effect of task order on the results of Wilcoxon test and compare paired data.

Factor - Experiment: The results of TOST confirmed the equivalence of two experiments for the mean quality of threats and controls for both methods (TOST $p < 0.005$). However, TOST failed to reject the hypothesis about non-equivalence of two experiments for the mean participants' PEOU (TOST $p = 0.21$) and PU (TOST $p = 0.07$) for graphical method. Hence, we report the results of the two experiments separately.

Factor - Background: In both experiments the KW test did not revealed any statistically significant effect of background variables (see Table 2) on the quality of threats and controls or mean participants' PEOU and PU.

RQ1: Actual Efficacy. Figure 1 reports the mean of experts assessment of threats and security controls identified by groups. In ROT2015 and UTM2016 we had 18 and respectively 24 groups that successfully delivered the final report and were evaluated by the experts. In total we collected 72 methods applications in ROT2015 and 96 in UTM2016. The overall quality of the identified threats and security controls was "fair" or "good".

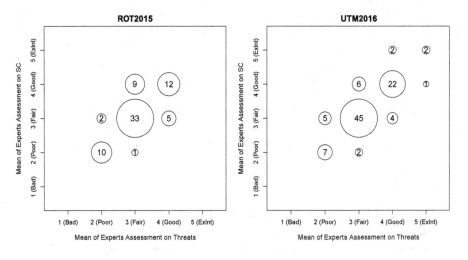

Fig. 1. Experts assessment by methods and experiments (The figures report experts overall quality assessment of the threats and controls identified for four security tasks in ROT2015 (left) and UTM2016 (right). The majority of the groups delivered threats and controls of "fair" and "good" quality. Only limited number of the reports delivered "poor" threats and security controls. The quality of the results was better than in SG2014 study and we did not split groups into "good" and "bad".)

To provide an idea on the scale of results produced by groups, we report the number of threats and security controls identified by one of the best groups for each experiment. In ROT2015 the best group identified in total 49 threats and 120 security controls which composed 178 pairs as some controls can be used to mitigate different threats. In UTM2016 the best groups identified totally 53 threats and 36 security controls which composed 64 pairs.

Table 3 presents the descriptive statistics, p-values of the TOST with Wilcoxon test for the equivalence in the mean quality of threats and controls by experiment and method. In ROT2015 tabular method helped to identify threats and controls of a slightly better quality than the graphical one. In UTM2016 both methods helped to produce same quality results. For both experiments the TOST results confirmed *the equivalence of two methods in threats and controls quality*.

Table 3. Average quality of threats and sec. controls by experiments and methods

	Actual	Tabular			Graphical			δ_{mean}	TOST
	Efficacy	Mean	Median	St. dev.	Mean	Median	St. dev.	Tab - Graph	p-value
ROT2015	Threats	3.17	3.08	0.53	2.95	2.92	0.53	+0.22	0.0009
	Sec. Ctrls	3.28	3.25	0.53	2.97	2.92	0.51	+0.31	0.001
UTM2016	Threats	3.28	3.17	0.58	3.24	3.17	0.57	+0.04	$6.3 \cdot 10^{-6}$
	Sec. Ctrls	3.31	3.25	0.67	3.29	3.25	0.62	+0.02	$2.4 \cdot 10^{-7}$

Tabular and graphical methods produces very similar quality of threats and controls in both experiments. The quality of the produced threat is within a 10% range around the mean quality range (3 - fair). For both experiments this is statistically significant with a TOST for an effect size of $\delta = \pm 0.6$ corresponding to less than two experts having a different rate of the outcome of the risk assessment.

Table 4. Average perception of tabular and graphical SRA methods

	Perceived	Tabular			Graphical			δ_{mean}	TOST
	Efficacy	Mean	Median	St. dev	Mean	Median	St. dev	Tab - Graph	p-value
ROT2015	PEOU	3.63	3.75	0.59	3.20	3.12	0.64	+0.43	0.08
	PU	3.54	3.72	0.84	3.05	3.17	0.83	+0.37	0.18
UTM2016	PEOU	3.74	3.75	0.40	3.60	3.69	0.71	+0.14	$2.6 \cdot 10^{-5}$
	PU	3.67	3.78	0.58	3.29	3.44	0.99	+0.38	0.03

ROT2015 results showed that the participants reported higher PEOU and PU for the tabular method than for the graphical one. However, TOST results did not reveal any equivalence of two methods and Wilcoxon results did not confirm stat. sig. of the difference. UTM2016 results revealed that two methods are equivalent with respect to PEOU (stat. sig. with a TOST for an effect size of $\delta = \pm 0.6$).

RQ2: Perceived Efficacy. Table 4 reports the descriptive statistics, p-values of TOST with Wilcoxon test for the equivalence in participants' PEOU and PU by experiment and method. In ROT2015 the participants reported better perception of the tabular model over the graphical one for PEOU and PU. Such difference in mean was lower than our TOST practical significance threshold of $\delta = \pm 0.6$. TOST failed to reject the hypotheses about non-equivalence between two methods for PEOU and PU. In UTM2016 the perception of the graphical method significantly increased comparing to ROT2015. So, the two methods have equivalent PEOU and PU which confirmed by TOST results.

6 Retrospective Analysis

In the previous studies (SG2013 and SG2014) we compared graphical method CORAS with different tabular methods. In SG2013 as a tabular method we chose SREP [22] proposed by University of Castilla–La Mancha and used by CMU Software Engineering Institute in their tutorials. The participants worked in groups of two and conducted SRA of four security tasks from SmartGrid scenario using both methods. The division of groups on good and "not good" was done based on security experts assessment of the final reports quality. In SG2014 we used tabular method from industry proposed by EUROCONTROL, SecRAM. The participants individually conducted SRA of two tasks from SmartGrid scenario using both methods.

In these experiments we followed the approach by Opdahl and Karpati [25] and used the number of threats and controls identified using a method as a measure of the actual efficacy. Thus, we cannot compare current results with the results from [14,16], but this comparison can be done for the perception variables.

We re-ran hypothesis testing for the equivalence of two methods in participants' PEOU and PU using TOST with MW test. We chose MW test to have comparable results across all experiments as we cannot used Wilcoxon test when we analyze the results of good groups where the samples can be unpaired.

The results of the retrospective analysis supports findings of [14]. For good groups TOST failed to reject the hypothesis about non-equivalence in mean PEOU ($p = 0.25$) and PU ($p = 0.27$). For all groups TOST results confirmed the equivalence of two methods w.r.t. mean PEOU ($p = 0.051$) and PU ($p = 0.003$).

The retrospective analysis of SG2014 for all participants revealed: *(a)* 10% significantly better mean PEOU in favor of graphical method (MW $p = 0.06$) and *(b)* 10% significant equivalence of two methods in mean PU (TOST $p = 0.08$). For good participants TOST failed to reject hypothesis about non-equivalence of two methods in mean PEOU ($p = 0.85$) and PU ($p = 0.43$).

For SG2014 the difference between the results for the perception reported in [16] and the results of the retrospective analysis can be due to the different data collection approach which is discussed in Sect. 3.

The differences between presented experiments can be due to the changes in treatments. In SG2013 textual and graphical methods have quite clear processed and textual method is good in security controls identification, while graphical one is better for threats identification (see [16, Table III]). In SG2014 the textual method has less clear process which led to better PEOU in favor of graphical method, while both methods have similar PU. In the current experiments (ROT2015 and UTM2016) both textual and graphical method have similar PEOU as they provide clear process. The difference in PU between ROT2015 and UTM2016 can be explained by the change of application scenario. In ROT2015 we used the ROT scenario that was designed by the same organization which designed tabular method and security catalogues. Possibly this combination is a "good fit" which led to better perception of the tabular method. In UTM2016 we used UATM scenario by NASA that might be "not a good fit" to the same combination of tabular method and security catalogues. This could result in a similar perceived ease of use and usefulness.

7 Threats to Validity

Regarding **internal validity**, the main concern is that the relations between the treatment and the outcome are causal and the effects of possible factors are either controlled or measured. To mitigate this we randomly assigned groups to the order of methods application. The results of two experiments were reported and discussed separately to alleviate the possible effect of the differences in experiments execution. The results of KW test did not reveal any statistically significant effect of participants' background and experience on the results.

Another possible factor that could make the difference between two experiment is changes in the feedback process between experiments. In UTM2016 we provided *feedback on typical mistakes* that the participants did in the *warm-up SRA* of a toy application scenario that was a part of the training. So, the groups were able to better understand the methods and avoid mistakes from the very first deliverable. In ROT2015 such feedback on the warm-up exercise was not provided. Also in ROT2015 the public discussion of groups' deliverables was *at will* and it might happened that not all groups decided to use their possibility to discuss the work. Besides the discussion in the class, each group received *individual feedback* on the mistakes of method application found in their deliverables. In contrast, in UTM2016 we allocated 15 min slots and asked groups to register for the open feedback session in advance. Each group participated in *at least one feedback session* and gave a 5 min presentation on the intermediate results. Besides the discussion by groups, for each deliverable we provided groups with *the summary of the typical problems* in the application of both methods. To mitigate this threat we report and analyze the two experiments separately.

The main threats to **construct validity** are the definition and interpretation of the metrics that we used to measure the theoretical constructs. We measured the *actual efficacy* of a method as the quality of threats and security controls identified using a method. The relevance of results quality for an SRA is discussing in Sect. 3. To measure the *perceived efficacy* we designed the post-task questionnaires following TAM [3]. The questionnaire includes 8 questions about PEOU and 9 questions about PU, which were adapted from [14,16].

A main threat to **conclusion validity** is related to *low statistical significance* of the findings. The effect size for the equivalence test was set to $\delta = \pm 0.6$ which corresponds to 20% difference in actual or perceived efficacy. The practical meaning of this threshold is discussed inSection 3.

In regard to **external validity**, the main threat to the generalizability of the results are the *use of students instead of practitioners* and the use of *simple* *scenarios* to apply the methods under evaluation [2]. The use of MSc students in empirical studies is still question of debate. However, some studies have argued that students perform as well as professionals [10,33]. Regarding the use of simple scenarios, in our studies we mitigated this threat by asking the participants to analyze two new operational scenarios introduced in the ATM domain.

8 Discussion

If we consider the threats to validity sufficiently mitigated we obtained the following results:

RQ1: Tabular and graphical methods are equally good w.r.t actual efficacy (i.e. quality of identified threats and security controls).

RQ2: If there is no fit between SRA components (i.e. method, catalogues, and application scenario) and methods have equally clear processes then there will be no difference in perceived efficacy of these methods.

Implication for Research. The research community can benefit from the following results of our work:

Equivalence Test. Many works in Empirical Software Engineering to compare different treatments look for the difference between them and use standard statistical tests (e.g. t-test, Mann-Whitney, Wilcoxon, and etc.) However, they do not define the range that is sufficient to proof the difference between treatments. In our study for values of 5-item scale we used $\delta = \pm 0.6$ meaning that the difference between treatments A and B is statistically significant if, for example, mean quality delivered by A is 2.8 and 3.5 for treatment B. To test for the equivalence between our treatments we used TOST approach.

Actual Efficacy: Quantity vs. Quality. The investigation of the full application of security risk assessment requires more thorough tool to measure the actual efficacy of a method. In the first experiments on the security methods comparison we measured actual efficacy of methods in terms of number of identified threats and controls. However, this approach is not precise as, first, it is important to identify the most critical threats and provide effective mitigations to them rather to identify any possible threat and control and, second, the quantitative measure can be biased by use of security catalogues.

Ease of Use. Both tabular and graphical methods can help analysts to produce SRA of a similar quality, but if a method does not have a clear process it may affect people's perception how ease to use is the method. This can be tested by another controlled experiment where participants apply same process (e.g. from CORAS method) with tabular and graphical notation, i.e. classical CORAS as an instance of graphical method and tabular CORAS where tables substitute the diagrams.

Learning Curve of graphical method is much steep comparing to the tabular one. The participants had more questions during the warm-up illustrative exercise for graphical method then for the tabular one. Our observation of groups' intermediate results showed that even after illustrative exercise many groups had difficulties to produce correct diagrams. Tabular notation had a few challenges related to understanding the concepts of primary and supporting assets.

Implications for Practice. The main implication of our study for practitioners is that both tabular and graphical- based methods can provide *similar support for SRA*. The most important is that method should provide a *clear process* supporting analyst in identification of *(a)* major threats specific to the scenario and *(b)* effective security controls to mitigate them.

The results of retrospective analysis of the previous experiments supports these findings. In SG2013 study graphical and tabular methods have similar PEOU and PU as both methods have clear process. In contrast, in SG2014 study the graphical method has higher PEOU than the tabular one because graphical method has significantly clearer process comparing to the tabular method.

Also an important role plays the *fit between SRA components*, i.e. that method and security catalogues are appropriate to the domain of the scenario. In ROT2015 experiment we observed slightly better participants' PEOU and PU, but the results failed to reveal any statistically significant equivalence nor difference between two methods in these variables. At the same time, in UTM2016 tabular and graphical methods were found to be statistically equivalent in terms of participants' PEOU and PU. The possible explanation is that tabular method, scenario, and catalogues for ROT2015 were designed by the same organization and became a "good fit", while in UTM2016 application scenario was changed to UATM scenario by NASA that might be "not a good fit" to same method and catalogues.

9 Conclusion

This paper reported the results of two controlled experiments on comparison of graphical and tabular methods for security risk assessment. The experiments involved 35 and 48 MSc students enrolled to Security Engineering course at Fall 2015 and 2016 at the University of Trento.

In this paper we studied how similar are security methods w.r.t. actual and perceived efficacy. For quality/perception value on 5-item Likert scale we defined the equivalence range $\delta = \pm 0.6$. It means, for example, that tabular and graphical methods are equivalent in terms of threats quality if $|Q(T_{graph}) - Q(T_{tab})| < \delta$.

The results of the experiments revealed that tabular and graphical methods are equivalent in terms of *actual efficacy* (*RQ1*). The groups were able to identify threats and controls of a fair quality with both methods.

Regarding the difference in *methods' perception* (*RQ2*), the data analysis results showed that participants perceived tabular method to be slightly better with respect to *perceived ease of use and usefulness* than the graphical one in the first experiments, and in the second experiment the two methods were found to be statistically equivalent with respect to perception variables.

To summarize, the study shows that tabular and graphical methods for (security) requirements elicitation and risk assessment are very similar with respect to actual and perceived efficacy. Graphical representation only does not guarantee the better quality of security requirements analysis in comparison to a tabular method.

Acknowledgment. This work has been partly supported by the SESAR JU WPE under contract 12-120610-C12 (EMFASE).

References

1. Caralli, R., Stevens, J., Young, L., Wilson, W.: Introducing OCTAVE allegro: improving the information security risk assessment process. Technical report, Software Engineering Institute, Carnegie Mellon University (2007)
2. Carver, J.C., Jaccheri, L., Morasca, S., Shull, F.: A checklist for integrating student empirical studies with research and teaching goals. Empir. Softw. Eng. **15**(1), 35–59 (2010)
3. Davis, F.D.: Perceived usefulness, perceived ease of use, and user acceptance of information technology. MIS Q. **13**, 319–340 (1989)
4. Deng, M., Wuyts, K., Scandariato, R., Preneel, B., Joosen, W.: A privacy threat analysis framework: supporting the elicitation and fulllment of privacy requirements. Req. Eng. **16**(1), 3–32 (2011)
5. Food, D.A.: Guidance for industry: statistical approaches to establishing bioequivalence (2001)
6. Giorgini, P., Massacci, F., Mylopoulos, J., Zannone, N.: Modeling security requirements through ownership, permission and delegation. In: Proceedings of RE 2005, pp. 167–176. IEEE (2005)
7. de Gramatica, M., Labunets, K., Massacci, F., Paci, F., Tedeschi, A.: The role of catalogues of threats and security controls in security risk assessment: an empirical study with ATM professionals. In: Fricker, S.A., Schneider, K. (eds.) REFSQ 2015. LNCS, vol. 9013, pp. 98–114. Springer, Heidelberg (2015). doi:10.1007/978-3-319-16101-3_7
8. Haley, C., Laney, R., Moett, J., Nuseibeh, B.: Security requirements engineering: a framework for representation and analysis. IEEE Trans. Softw. Eng. **34**(1), 133–153 (2008)
9. Hernan, S., Lambert, S., Ostwald, T., Shostack, A.: Threat modeling-uncover security design flaws using the stride approach. MSDN Magazine-Louisville, pp. 68–75 (2006)
10. Höst, M., Regnell, B., Wohlin, C.: Using students as subjects: a comparative study of students and professionals in lead-time impact assessment. Empir. Softw. Eng. **5**(3), 201–214 (2000)
11. Karpati, P., Redda, Y., Opdahl, A.L., Sindre, G.: Comparing attack trees and misuse cases in an industrial setting. Inform. Soft. Technol. **56**(3), 294–308 (2014)
12. Kopardekar, P.H.: Unmanned aerial system (UAS) traffic management (UTM): Enabling low-altitude airspace and UAS operations. Technical report (2014)
13. Kopardekar, P.H.: Revising the airspace model for the safe integration of small unmanned aircraft systems. Technical report (2015)
14. Labunets, K., Massacci, F., Paci, F., Tran, L.M.S.: An experimental comparison of two risk-based security methods. In: Proceedings of ESEM 2013, pp. 163–172. IEEE (2013)

15. Labunets, K., Paci, F., Massacci, F., Ragosta, M., Solhaug, B.: A first empirical evaluation framework for security risk assessment methods in the ATM domain. In: Proceedings of SIDs 2014. SESAR (2014)
16. Labunets, K., Paci, F., Massacci, F., Ruprai, R.: An experiment on comparing textual vs. visual industrial methods for security risk assessment. In: Proceedings of EmpiRE Workshop at RE 2014, pp. 28–35. IEEE (2014)
17. Landoll, D.J., Landoll, D.: The Security Risk Assessment Handbook: A Complete Guide For Performing Security Risk Assessments. CRC Press, New York (2005)
18. Li, T., Horkoff, J.: Dealing with security requirements for socio-technical systems: a holistic approach. In: Jarke, M., Mylopoulos, J., Quix, C., Rolland, C., Manolopoulos, Y., Mouratidis, H., Horkoff, J. (eds.) CAiSE 2014. LNCS, vol. 8484, pp. 285–300. Springer, Heidelberg (2014). doi:10.1007/978-3-319-07881-6_20
19. Lund, M.S., Solhaug, B., Stolen, K.: A guided tour of the CORAS method. In: Lund, M.S., Solhaug, B., Stolen, K. (eds.) Model-Driven Risk Analysis, pp. 23–43. Springer, Heidelberg (2011)
20. Maiden, N., Robertson, S., Ebert, C.: Guest editors' introduction: shake, rattle, and requirements. IEEE Softw. 22(1), 13 (2005)
21. Massacci, F., Paci, F.: How to select a security requirements method? A Comparative study with students and practitioners. In: Jøsang, A., Carlsson, B. (eds.) NordSec 2012. LNCS, vol. 7617, pp. 89–104. Springer, Heidelberg (2012). doi:10.1007/978-3-642-34210-3_7
22. Mellado, D., Fernández-Medina, E., Piattini, M.: Applying a security requirements engineering process. In: Gollmann, D., Meier, J., Sabelfeld, A. (eds.) ESORICS 2006. LNCS, vol. 4189, pp. 192–206. Springer, Heidelberg (2006). doi:10.1007/11863908_13
23. Meyners, M.: Equivalence tests a review. Food Qual. Prefer. 26(2), 231–245 (2012)
24. Mouratidis, H., Giorgini, P.: Secure tropos: a security-oriented extension of the tropos methodology. Int. J. Inform. Syst. Model. Des. 17(02), 285–309 (2007)
25. Opdahl, A.L., Sindre, G.: Experimental comparison of attack trees and misuse cases for security threat identification. Inform. Soft. Tech. 51(5), 916–932 (2009)
26. Scandariato, R., Wuyts, K., Joosen, W.: A descriptive study of Microsoft's threat modeling technique. Req. Eng. 20, 1–18 (2014)
27. Schuirmann, D.: On hypothesis-testing to determine if the mean of a normal distribution is contained in a known interval. In: Biometrics. vol. 37, pp. 617-617. International Biometric Soc (1981)
28. SESAR: ATM Security Risk Assessment Methodology. SESAR WP16.2 ATM Security, February 2003
29. Stålhane, T., Sindre, G.: Identifying safety hazards: an experimental comparison of system diagrams and textual use cases. In: Bider, I., Halpin, T., Krogstie, J., Nurcan, S., Proper, E., Schmidt, R., Soffer, P., Wrycza, S. (eds.) BPMDS/EMMSAD -2012. LNBIP, vol. 113, pp. 378–392. Springer, Heidelberg (2012). doi:10.1007/978-3-642-31072-0_26
30. Stålhane, T., Sindre, G.: Identifying safety hazards: an experimental comparison of system diagrams and textual use cases. In: Bider, I., Halpin, T., Krogstie, J., Nurcan, S., Proper, E., Schmidt, R., Soffer, P., Wrycza, S. (eds.) BPMDS/EMMSAD -2012. LNBIP, vol. 113, pp. 378–392. Springer, Heidelberg (2012). doi:10.1007/978-3-642-31072-0_26
31. Stålhane, T., Sindre, G.: An experimental comparison of system diagrams and textual use cases for the identification of safety hazards. Int. J. Inform. Syst. Model. Des. 5(1), 1–24 (2014)

32. Stålhane, T., Sindre, G., Bousquet, L.: Comparing safety analysis based on sequence diagrams and textual use cases. In: Pernici, B. (ed.) CAiSE 2010. LNCS, vol. 6051, pp. 165–179. Springer, Heidelberg (2010). doi:10.1007/978-3-642-13094-6_14

33. Svahnberg, M., Aurum, A., Wohlin, C.: Using students as subjects - an empirical evaluation. In: Proceedings of ESEM 2008, pp. 288–290. ACM (2008)

34. Theilmann, C.A.: Integrating autonomous drones into the national aerospace system. Ph.D. thesis, University of Pennsylvania, PA, US, April 2015

35. Van Lamsweerde, A.: Goal-oriented requirements engineering: a guided tour. In: Proceedings of RE 2001, pp. 249–262. IEEE (2001)

36. Wohlin, C., Runeson, P., Host, M., Ohlsson, M.C., Regnell, B., Wesslen, A.: Experimentation in Software Engineering. Springer, Heidelberg (2012)

Visualization of Quality of Software Requirements Specification Using Digital Elevation Model

Diding Adi Parwoto[✉], Takayuki Omori, Hiroya Itoga, and Atsushi Ohnishi[✉]

Ritsumeikan University, Kusatsu, Japan
diding.parwoto@gmail.com,
{tomori,itoga,ohnishi}@is.ritsumei.ac.jp

Abstract. *Context and motivation:* Software Requirements Specification (SRS) is an important document in software development process. In order to produce high quality software and reduce development cost, SRS should be correctly written. Several studies have been done in how to measure the quality of SRS and most of them gave values for every characteristic a numerical value from 0 to 1. *Question/Problem:* It is needed to help a user by giving a better point of view of quality of SRS and show to the user which parts of SRS need to be improved. *Principle ideas/result:* The purpose of this research is to visualize the quality of SRS using a Digital Elevation Model (DEM) metaphor. In this research, Mountain Fuji is selected as a metaphor since it is a prominent landscape for Japanese people. Among several SRS characteristics, this research visualizes three main important characteristics; unambiguity, completeness, and consistency. *Contribution:* This visualization is expected to give an improved point of view of the SRS quality to the user so they can understand and revise the document faster and more accurate. Moreover, the methodology of this research could be a base model of other prominent metaphor in different culture or country.

Keywords: Visualization · Software requirements specification · Quality of SRS · Digital Elevation Model

1 Introduction

Software requirements specification (SRS) is a specification for a particular software product, program, or set of programs that performs certain functions in a specific environment [1]. SRS is a very important document in software development process. The quality of SRS directly affects the final result of the quality of developed software and the main important aspect to achieve success in software development process [2].

Quality of SRS is based on several characteristic attributes that are used to assess the SRS. A good SRS should be unambiguous, complete, correct, consistent, stable, verifiable, modifiable and traceable [1].

P. Grünbacher and A. Perini (Eds.): REFSQ 2017, LNCS 10153, pp. 209–215, 2017.
DOI: 10.1007/978-3-319-54045-0_16

Several studies have been conducted to assess the quality of SRS by measuring the quality of characteristic attributes of the SRS. To easily assess and understand the quality of SRS better, software metric is usually used [2–4]. A software metric is a measurement derived from a software product, process, or resource. All the three studies above give value for the quality of SRS characteristics from 0 to 1. These values show the quality of each SRS characteristics for the whole document, but does not provide users ability to explore qualities of each sections, subsections, even for paragraph and sentences.

This research is conducted to visualize the quality of SRS using Digital Elevation Model (DEM) as metaphor. Hence, the contributions of this paper are proposing a framework to understand the quality of SRS faster and more accurate, accentuate the existing numeric quality by prominent metaphor, and proposing a tool to easily and attractively show where the errors or imperfectness in SRS are.

2   Background

2.1   Related Works

Some related works have been examined to point out the distinctiveness of this research. Davis et al. [2] defined 24 qualities that SRS should exhibit and provided a metric for 18 cases. Siegemund et al. [3] used an ontology reasoning technique to detect and repair faulty information and proposed a set of metrics that facilitate automatic calculation of the quality of the SRS. Saavedra et al. [4] explained that software metrics are necessary to effectively manage software development.

Metaphors and analogies are commonly voiced as key tools for enhancing creative design. Both compare a situation in one domain with the situation in another [6]. Colburn and Shute [7] characterized metaphor as "a description of an object or event using concepts that cannot be applied to the object or event in a conventional way".

DEM can be described as digital cartographic/geographic dataset of elevations in xyz coordinates. DEM is widely used to visualize topography map. Skupin has demonstrated the possibility of creating large format knowledge domain visualizations that emulate many aspects of traditional geographic depictions [5].

2.2   Visualization Technique

Visualization technique is used by Saito et al. [9] to provide a visual representation of requirements evolution history. They prove that visualization technique improves the speed and accuracy of identification of affected artefacts of requirements evolution.

Moody has clearly defined ten principles for designing effective visual notations in software engineering. These principles can be used to evaluate, compare and improving existing visual notations as well as to construct a new one [13]. He also said that visual representations are effective because it uses the capabilities of human visual system.

3 Methodology

3.1 Visualization of Qualities

Three-dimension (3D) model of Mountain Fuji is drawn in a web based environment. A DEM data is used as a source data for creating the metaphor. Mountain Fuji area was selected to be the metaphor in this research because it is very famous to Japanese people. However, the system is designed to be able to draw other mountains DEM data. Using geographic object, Mountain Fuji in this research, as metaphor has not been proved suitable for visualizing quality of SRS. This issue will be discussed later in future work.

The source of data is Shuttle Radar Topography Mission (SRTM). The SRTM provides a major advance in the accessibility of high quality elevation data for large portions of the tropics and other areas of the developing world [11]. A 1 arc second SRTM data was produced, but is not available for all countries [10]. The Mountain Fuji metaphor is drawn based on SRTM DEM data.

SRTM data used in this research has resolution of 1 Arc-Second, 1 elevation point of data represent elevation of 30 m × 30 m area of earth's surface. The data is formatted in a Band Interleaved by Line (BIL) format. BIL is a binary raster format with an accompanying header file which describes the layout and formatting of the file. File size is approximately 3.4 Megabytes containing 1290 × 1320 elevation points of Mountain Fuji area.

3.2 Metaphor for Emphasizing

The characteristics of SRS that selected to be analyzed are unambiguity, completeness and consistency. These characteristics were chosen because they are the important characteristics and also are late timing measured [8]. More specifically, from eight characteristics of an SRS which are introduced [14], the incorrectness, inconsistency, incompleteness and ambiguity are strongly related to errors of an SRS. However, the correctness of a requirement can be correctly checked by a stakeholder who gives the requirement. In other words, it is difficult for other people to judge the correctness of the requirement. So, this research focuses on the consistency, completeness, and unambiguity.

These values of quality will be shown as imperfectness in the model. By selecting the imperfectness part on the model, a user will be directed to the error on the SRS as shown in Fig. 1.

This research focuses on Sect. 3, the most important section of SRS which contain requirements specifications, based on standard structure of an SRS [14]. Area of the metaphor is divided into several parts as the number of sub area. This region is used as a specific area to show the imperfectness of corresponding part in SRS. Figure 2 shows the example division of the metaphor area in several regions, assuming there are eight sub area needed. This is a pie cart like division to maintain equality of area of the mountain, top area and bottom area, for each sub area, so sub area consists of top to bottom of mountain.

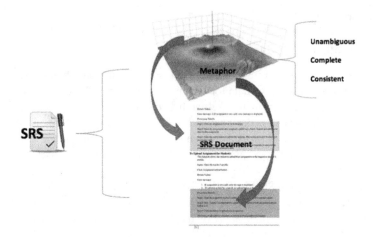

Fig. 1. Illustration of the system

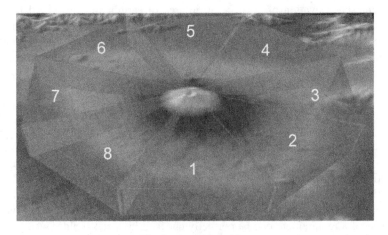

Fig. 2. Region division

In order to reduce the complexity when dealing with a big SRS that has many subsection and has huge number of paragraphs on Sect. 3, the metaphor would be designed as a nested one. Each section, subsection and paragraph will have its own metaphor.

This modularization reduces the amount of information presented at a time to within the limitation of working memory, so it improves speed and accuracy of understanding [13]. As a test case, this research used an example SRS called test case SRS that has structure as shown in Fig. 3. So, each node in Fig. 3 will have its own metaphor, same metaphor but different region division of its subsection and different qualities to show. Except for paragraph level (level 3 on Fig. 3), the division of metaphor area is based on the number of sentences. So, the qualities shown on this level is sentence quality.

Fig. 3. Modularization of metaphor

Focus of this research is to visualize quality of three characteristics of SRS using metaphor, unambiguity, completeness and consistency. These quality characteristics and errors in the each of quality characteristics are treated equally. This research assumed that the values of those characteristics are measured by other tools. This work postulates such metrics calculation tools.

There are several metrics for quality of SRS [2–4]. Using our method, we can visualize the metrics and provide quality of an SRS more understandably.

Quality projection to the metaphor can be seen on Table 1. These are the projection notations that the SRS's characteristics qualities have direct correlation with how the metaphor is drawn.

Table 1. Primary notations of quality projection

SRS's characteristic	Quality	Metaphor
Unambiguous	0–1	0% visible–100% visible (covered by fog)
Complete	0–1	0% mountain height–100% mountain height
Consistent	0–1	0–100% color consistency

To show the imperfectness on the SRS, ambiguity will be drawn as fog covering the whole area decreasing the visibility of the metaphor, incompleteness as incomplete part in particular area, especially the height of the mountain and inconsistency as wrong color on the respective height.

To help users that are not familiar with the model used as metaphor, users are given ability to see the perfect metaphor so they can get impression of how much the quality affect the metaphor.

4 Experimentation

An initial attempt to produce visualizations has been conducted to test the metaphor. Overall ambiguity is displayed by fog covering the whole area with 80%, 60% and 40% visibility of 0.8, 0.6 and 0.4 quality as shown in Fig. 4. Completeness quality is easily detected by unfinished drawing of the mountain Fuji. Mountain Fuji is drawn 80%, 60% and 40% according to the completeness quality of 0.8, 0.6 and 0.4 as shown

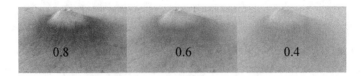

Fig. 4. Unambiguity on metaphor

in Fig. 5. For this experimentation, consistency quality is visualized by inconsistent color especially for snow on the top of the mountain. The white color of snow gradually become black as the quality decreased as shown in Fig. 6.

Fig. 5. Completeness on metaphor

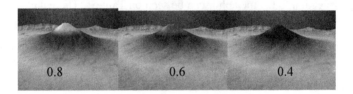

Fig. 6. Consistency on metaphor

This experimentation is going to be applied in the methodology above to produce Mountain Fuji metaphor. This metaphor is expected not only show the quality of the SRS, but significantly give new impression of the quality to the user.

5 Conclusions and Future Work

This research uses three main important characteristics of SRS to be visualized in metaphor. Using DEM as metaphor gives better understanding of the quality of SRS as it emphasizes the quality of each characteristic of the SRS. This metaphor also gives ability to user to explore the quality to sentence level so they can revise the SRS easier and more accurate. However, it is still needed to conduct an analysis to measure the effectiveness of understanding and revising SRS using this metaphor.

The advantages of using geographic object, Mountain Fuji in particular, as a metaphor should be evaluated by comparing with different visualizations. In addition, as this research is expected to be a base framework for other spatial earth contours, it is needed to examine and improve the methodology to be suited on any shape of mountain or spatial contour.

Another research on Requirement Management Measures by Loconsole [12] said that requirement development is a learning process rather than a gathering process. She studied stability and volatility of requirements and change requests. It would be a good approach if this metaphor could be extended so it could track requirements changing on software development process based on Loconsole's work.

References

1. ISO/IEC/IEEE International Standard - Systems and software engineering – Life cycle processes –Requirements engineering, ISO/IEC/IEEE 29148:2011(E) (2011)
2. Davis, A., Overmyer, S., Jordan, K., Caruso, J., Dandashi, F., Dinh, A., Kincaid, G., Ledeboer, G., Reynolds, P., Sitaram, P., Ta, A., Theofanos, M.: Identifying and measuring quality in a software requirements specification. In: 1st International Software Metrics Symposium, pp. 141–152 (1993)
3. Siegemund, K., Zhao, Y., Pan, J.Z., Aßmann, U.: Measure software requirement specifications by ontology reasoning. In: 8th International Workshop on Semantic Web Enabled Software Engineering (SWESE 2012) (2012)
4. Saavedra, R., Ballejos, L.C., Ale, M.: Quality properties evaluation for software requirements specifications: an exploratory analysis. In: WER (2013)
5. Skupin, A.: The world of geography: visualizing a knowledge domain with cartographic means. Proc. Natl. Acad. Sci. U.S.A. **101**, 5274–5278 (2004)
6. Hey, J., Linsey, J., Agogino, A.M., Wood, K.L.: Analogies and metaphors in creative design. Int. J. Eng. Educ. **24**(2), 283 (2008)
7. Colburn, T.R., Shute, G.M.: Metaphor in computer science. J. Appl. Logic **6**(4), 526–533 (2008)
8. Farbey, B.: Software quality metrics: considerations about requirements and requirement specifications. Inf. Softw. Technol. **32**(1), 60–64 (1990)
9. Saito, S., Iimura, Y., Tashiro, H., Massey, A.K., Antón, A.I.: Visualizing the effects of requirements evolution. In: Proceedings of the 38th International Conference on Software Engineering Companion, pp. 152–161. ACM (2016)
10. Pillot, B., Muselli, M., Poggi, P., Haurant, P., Dias, J.B.: Development and validation of a new efficient SRTM DEM-based horizon model combined with optimization and error prediction methods. Sol. Energy **129**, 101–115 (2016)
11. Jarvis, A., Reuter, H.I., Nelson, A., Guevara, E.: Hole-filled SRTM for the globe Version 4, available from the CGIAR-CSI SRTM 90 m Database (2016). http://srtm.csi.cgiar.org
12. Loconsole, A.: Empirical studies on requirement management measures. In: Proceedings of the 26th International Conference on Software Engineering, pp. 42–44 (2004)
13. Moody, D.: The "physics" of notations: toward a scientific basis for constructing visual notations in software engineering. IEEE Trans. Softw. Eng. **35**(6), 756–779 (2009)
14. IEEE Recommended Practice for Software Requirements Specifications. IEEE Standard 830-1998 (R2009) (2009)

Agile Requirements Engineering

Quality Requirements in Large-Scale Distributed Agile Projects – A Systematic Literature Review

Wasim Alsaqaf[✉], Maya Daneva, and Roel Wieringa

University of Twente, Enschede, The Netherlands
{w.h.a.alsaqaf,m.daneva,r.j.wieringa}@utwente.nl

Abstract. *Context and Motivation*: Agile development methods have become increasingly popular in the last years. However, these methods hardly pay attention to quality requirements (QRs), which could undermine the profits of fast delivery by introducing high rework efforts later on. This risk is high especially in agile large-scale distributed settings. *Question/problem*: Although several publications reported on the insufficient attention to quality requirements in agile methods, still little is known about agile requirements engineering practices and their impact on quality requirements in large-scale distributed settings. However, companies increasingly use agile methods in those settings, where the negative impact of ignoring quality requirements is large. Hence, the goal of this study is to identify the challenges in the engineering of quality requirements in large-scale distributed agile projects that have been researched so far, the agile practices that have contributed to the emergence of these challenges, and the proposed solutions. *Principle ideas/results*: Following an evidence-based research method, we examined 60 papers on quality requirements in agile. We found that, while there are multiple proposals to engineer quality requirements in agile, none of those has been tried out in real-life settings. Evaluating scalability of these proposals, therefore, is a priority for future research. *Contribution*: This paper identified 12 challenges in agile projects that harm the quality requirements. Besides, we identified and evaluated 13 proposals for dealing with quality requirements in agile projects, along with implications for practice and research.

Keywords: Agile requirements engineering · Quality requirements · Non-functional requirements · Large-scale distributed agile projects · Systematic literature review

1 Introduction

Quality requirements (QRs) are those requirements describing the qualities of the system (e.g. performance requirements, maintainability requirements) [1]. In the requirements engineering (RE) literature, there is a consensus that the success or failure of a system is not only decided by the correct implementation of the right functional requirements, but also by the correct implementation of the QRs [2, 3]. For example, if the response time of the system does not meet the customer expectations, we cannot say that the system delivers quality [2].

© Springer International Publishing AG 2017
P. Grünbacher and A. Perini (Eds.): REFSQ 2017, LNCS 10153, pp. 219–234, 2017.
DOI: 10.1007/978-3-319-54045-0_17

A recent systematic literature review (SLR) on agile RE [4] reported that QRs are neglected in agile RE processes. This may result in systems that do not satisfy the user expectations. In small co-located projects, this can be repaired relatively easily by adapting the next batch of requirements and fixing the part of the product already delivered. This is however not possible in agile large-scale distributed (ALSD) projects where the teams are spread over multiple locations and there are no possibilities for ad hoc coordination and communication among team members and with clients.

In response to that problem, we initiated an empirical research project [5] to develop best practices to help agile practitioners identifying, implementing and testing QRs in ALSD projects. As a first step, we identified the challenges that agile practitioners are facing concerning QRs and reviewed existing approaches to engineer QRs in agile projects. We performed a SLR based on the guidelines of Kitchenham et al. [6], which we present in this paper.

The main contribution of our SLR is twofold: first, we shed light on the empirical evidence of engineering the QRs in ALSD. As we will see, our review identifies those agile practices used in ALSD settings that are actually harming the engineering of QRs. Second, we summarize the reported solutions in literature to cope with engineering QRs. Our findings indicate that there are some specific solutions proposed and evaluated for treating one specific type of QRs (be it security, usability or compliance) however considering this respective type of QRs in isolation from other types of QRs that may be relevant in a project (e.g. in many projects, QRs are interdependent and need to be traded off [7]). Also, we found that there is still no general approach to engineer the QRs (regardless of type) in ALSD settings that has been evaluated in real-life projects.

This paper is organized as follows: Sect. 2 is on related work. Section 3 presents our research questions and our research method. Section 4 describes our findings and answers the research questions. Section 5 discusses the results and some implications for research and practice. Section 6 is on limitations. Section 7 concludes.

2   Related Work and Motivation

As a preparation of our work, we searched for SLRs on agile methods in general. We used the Scopus digital library (www.scopus.com) and identified a large number of both mapping studies and SLRs on topics pertaining to agile software development and project management. From those, we selected the ones investigating the RE process of agile methods to form our related work.

We deliberately did not limit our choice for related work to the context of ALSD because we did not want to miss any insight that could be brought by studying agile RE in other contexts. Moreover, reviews that do not mention RE in agile projects explicitly, are not selected as directly related work because they do not include the main topic of our investigation.

Based on this selection we have identified three SLRs as directly related to our work, namely those of Inayat et al. [4], Medeiros et al. [8], and Heikkilä et al. [9]. However, these reviews differ from our SLR in research questions, goal, research method, search period and primary papers. Medeiros et al. [8] conducted a mapping study on agile RE techniques used in industry. They reported user stories as the most used elicitation technique. Frequent changes of requirements and low customer involvement were indicated as the main sources of challenges. Heikkilä et al. [9] performed a systematic mapping of RE in agile software development. They aimed to identify the strong areas and the knowledge gaps of the subject. The study reported that the role of agile RE is still vague and needs more research. The study also indicated that the most documented challenges were related to the use of agile in large and complex projects and organizations. Moreover, the study concluded that the proposed solutions for the identified challenges were weak in general and not empirically evaluated. Inayat et al. [4] investigated RE practices embraced by agile teams, challenges that the agile teams face when using those practices and traditional RE challenges that were solved by the use of agile practices. The study concluded that the role of RE in ALSD projects demands more attention by researchers.

Alongside to these three reviews, we have identified seven other reviews on distributed agile [10–16] which we checked for information on RE, and specifically on QRs. The number of reviews found indicates that the community of researchers on agile software engineering works hard on consolidating the empirical evidence regarding the strengths and the weaknesses of agile approaches. In particular, a large part of the above-cited reviews concerns global software development. One review [12] states explicitly 'distributed development' as its focus. While the context of global projects is recognized as highly important and some papers do report the engineering of QRs as a problematic sub-area of agile RE [4,17], no study indicates specific challenges in QRs or solution strategies to solve these challenges in the context of distributed development. This motivated us to initiate the present review.

3   Research Method

The key steps in our research process used the evidence-based guidelines by Kitchenham et al. [6] and are described in the subsections below.

3.1   Research Questions

As indicated in the Introduction, our review's focus is on practices in ALSD and proposed approaches to cope with QR challenges in ALDS. We are set out to answer three research questions: **RQ1:** *What are the agile practices used to engineer QRs in ALSD settings, according to published literature?* **RQ2:** *What QRs challenges have been reported in agile projects, in general?* **RQ3:** *What are the existing solutions to cope with neglected QRs in agile RE in general (not only in ALSD), as per RE literature?* The purpose of RQ1 is to uncover the practices used in ALSD settings to engineer the QRs. RQ2 is expected to shed light on those challenges reported in literature regarding the implementation of the QRs in these settings. RQ3 will identify proposed solutions as per literature and evaluate their fitness in solving the identified challenges.

3.2   Search and Selection Strategy

To avoid doing a work that already has been done, we searched for existing SLRs that might have answered our questions. To collect the papers, we chose to use Scopus. Scopus provides access to high quality peer reviews research abstracts that have been published by a wide range of prominent publishers like Elsevier, Springer and IEEE computer society [9,18]. Elsevier even claims that Scopus is the most comprehensive database of peer-reviewed research.[1] After concluding that our specific questions have not been answered yet, we started extracting research keywords from our research questions. This was an iterative process. To cover the whole spectrum of candidates of keywords, we experimented with strings including the terms "requirements engineering", "RE", "Agile", "agility", "non-functional requirements", "quality requirements", "quality", "quality attributes", "scaled", "outsourced", "distributed". The keywords related to "large-scale distributed" settings were eventually removed from the search string because we did not want to miss any knowledge that could be lost if we restricted our search to a particular setting. Our final string was:

"((Agile OR agility) AND (Requirements OR non-functional requirements OR non-functional OR quality requirements OR quality attributes OR quality))".

We formulated the following inclusion criteria: (I1) The paper is peer-reviewed. (I2) The paper is in English. (I3) The paper discusses two or more of the following topics: Agile, RE, QRs, distributed and large-scale projects. (I4) The paper is published between Jan'02 and April'16. Next, we used the following exclusion criteria: (E1) The paper does not focus explicitly on agile. (E2) The paper does not discuss RE as their central topic; (E3) The paper is not available for download.

3.3   Conducting the Review

3.3.1   Search and Application of the Inclusion/Exclusion Criteria

We fired our search query on Scopus, which yielded an overwhelming number of publications: 2830. To reduce this number to a manageable size, we have limited our search to the 'Computer Science' subject in Scopus, which resulted in 612 papers. The first author has then read the abstracts of these papers to apply the inclusion and exclusion criteria. He manually removed 446 papers. The reasons for the removal of those papers were that these papers (1) either did not meet the inclusion criterion I3, or (2) meet the exclusion criterion E2. The application of the inclusion and exclusion criteria reduced the number of papers to166. The second author checked the removed papers separately to ensure that no papers were mistakenly removed. The number of papers remained intact. After this step, the first two authors have re-read and analysed the title, keywords, abstract, introduction and conclusion of all the 166 papers in order to assess their relevance to our topics of interest. We considered a paper 'relevant' if it provides "enough" information to answer one or more of our research questions. The papers that we deemed 'relevant' turned out to be: (i) empirical studies that treated the RE process within agile methods and papers that compared agile and traditional RE

---

[1] https://www.elsevier.com/solutions/scopus.

processes – 6 papers in total, (ii) papers that proposed approaches to QRs in agile context – 18 papers, (iii) papers on the use of agile methods in distributed context – 15 papers, and (iv) papers that discussed two or more of the aforementioned options – 12 papers. This totalled to 51 papers. The papers that we found irrelevant were either SLRs (16 in total), or papers in which agile, QRs, RE, were part of the context in the papers but not central to the research reported in them (99 papers were of this nature). An additional 9 papers were added to the selected primary papers based on the 'snowball effect' [6] which brought the final number of primary papers to 60. The full referenced list with primary papers is available at this website: https://wasimalsaqaf.files. wordpress.com/2016/12/primary-papers1.docx. We do not include it here, to save space. In this website, a reference to a primary paper is labelled with the letter P (e.g. P1, P2, P3,...,P60). In this paper, we will use the labels P1, P2,...,P60, whenever we refer to a paper in our list of primary papers.

3.3.2 Thematic Synthesis

Once the primary papers were identified, the process of systematically extracting data from them started. We used thematic analysis for this purpose [19]. We read the papers multiple times, first to extract the relevant information – publication information, context information and findings, and then to do coding based on it. The coding process has been done by inductively applying descriptive labels (called codes) to segments of texts of each paper. We have followed Saldana's open coding approach [20] in which we assigned codes inductively as we did not want to force any preconceived outcomes. The process of open coding has resulted in identifying 182 segments of text which describe the main outcomes of the selected papers. The identified segments were coded based on their content using 30 codes. Thereafter the codes were categorized based on their similarity into 7 themes, namely: Process, People, Challenges, Scope, Characteristics, Learning and Challenges. The process of extracting and analysing the data was conducted using Microsoft Excel 2016 program. We also used it to generate Figs. 1 and 2. Table 1 provides two examples of how the process of identifying and

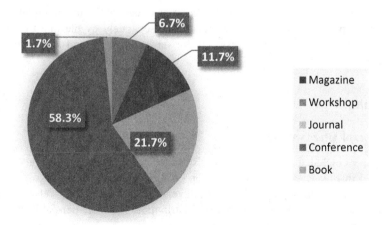

Fig. 1. Distribution of papers according to publication categories

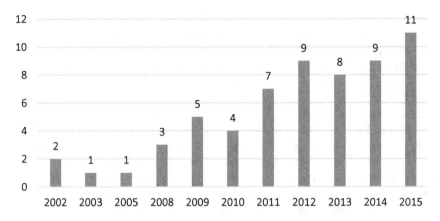

Fig. 2. Number of publications per year

Table 1. Text and codes

Original text	Theme and code
"Our project still faced challenges in practicing TDD (Test Driven Development) and the development team agreed that the method should have been utilized more than it was. Quality assurance was sometimes lacking and many bugs were only found after completing a feature" [P4]	Theme: Challenges Code: Validation
"The requirements engineering techniques used in Agile is some-times not clearly defined so the actual implementation is dependent on developer. In Agile we need skilled person as developer. While traditional techniques provide a clear view to the developer" [P5]	Theme: People Code: Developer

coding a segment of text was conducted. In order to ensure the internal quality of the data analysis process, the process has been done separately by the first two authors. Thereafter, the results of both researchers were compared and differences were re-solved.

4   Results

4.1   General Observations

The 60 papers included in our SLR were distributed according to publication categories as depicted in Fig. 1. For more information on the venues in each category, we refer interested readers to download the full venues list from the website: https://wasimalsaqaf.files.wordpress.com/2016/12/distribution-of-papers-per-publication-source3.docx.

The conference that published the highest number of papers is SoutheastCon Conference (www.ewh.ieee.org/reg/3/southeastcon/) with 6 publications. The international conferences on Requirements Engineering (RE) and on Global Software Engineering published 3 papers each. The Malaysian Software Engineering conference published 2 papers, whereas all other conference venues (21 conferences in total) are represented by one publication each. Regarding magazine papers, IEEE Software was the only one that published papers included in our SLR (3 in total). In terms of journal papers, the Journal of Systems and Software published the most (3 papers), followed by Information and Software Technology (2 papers).

Regarding the year of publication, we found that 53 papers were published after 2008, whereas 7 papers were published in the period of 2002–2008. This indicates that the topic of our study gained more attention in the past seven years. 2015 was the most productive year with 11 published papers (Fig. 2).

4.2   Answers to the Research Questions

4.2.1   RQ1: What Are the Agile Practices Used to Engineer QRs in ALSD Settings According to Published Literature?

Although we did not deliberately search for agile practices concerning specific types of QRs, we however did find papers that looked at four types of QRs: security [P6][P7] [P8], safety [P9], compliance [P10] and usability [P11]. Each of these papers focused on the specific practices currently used for engineering the respective type of QRs discussed in the paper, independently from other QRs. In essence, these specific practices suggest (as we would see below) either introducing a new artefacts into agile RE, or a new role, or new social behaviour, or a new tool, or a combination of those.

Baca et al. [P6] reported about the Security-Enhanced Agile Process that introduced into the agile RE process two new artefacts − security metrics and risk analysis reports, as well as three new roles − security manager, security master and security architect. It was developed and evaluated in an ALSD project delivering a mobile money transfer system. Next, Savola et al. [P7] presented an approach also based on artefacts: risk-driven security metrics and visualization. Its pilot evaluation was a project case of a well-established telecommunication product. Last, Baca and Carlsson. [P8] presented a set of artefact-based practices: writing security requirements, creating a security matrix and documenting abuse cases. These practices were evaluated in a large telecommunication project.

Concerning safety, Gary et al. [P9] report on an open source distributed project delivering an image-guided surgical environment, for which safety was the most important QR. The project deployed the practices of: (1) requirements traceability management practices linked to code management, (2) safety-by-design practices, (2) continuous integration and (4) architecture validation that involved extracting models from source code. The project used quality attribute utility trees and scenarios for specifying the QRs of safety, plus testability and usability −as related to safety.

Regarding compliance requirements, Fizgerald et al. [P10] report on a large distributed organization delivering a life science application (that is subjected to auditing by the Food and Drug Administration, ISO, and the Society of Pharma Engineering).

Their project introduced the role of the so-called Product Counsel (group of senior managers who steer the compliance requirements process), the use of compliance templates, and the practices of continuous compliance related to each iteration, of 'living traceability' of compliance requirements, of using risk as the prioritization criterion for user stories, and the use of various tools (e.g. JIRA, Bamboo, Confluence) to help with the implementation of these practices.

Concerning usability QRs, Wale-Kolade [P11] presents a large scale distributed project developing a Scandinavian country's pension handling system, where usability roles and artefacts were integrated into agile. The specific practices instrumental to the project were: integrating a usability design head and usability designers into the developers' team, using personas and sketches, engaging expert users, and diffusing designs.

Although we could not find any paper that examined the ways in which QRs as a whole are treated in agile projects, there were papers that contained descriptions of practices that can be interpreted as ways of coping with QRs. To identify these papers, we looked at the descriptions of context provided in the primary papers. Out of the 60 papers included in our review, 29 were empirical studies. Out of those 29, 21 described explicitly their own context settings as "large-scale" and/or "distributed". In those 21 studies, the authors described agile RE practices that hint to practices of coping with QRs. A summary of those practices can be found in Table 2, where the rightmost column of the table indicates if the practice concerns artefacts, tools, roles, or social behaviour (concerning behaviour, see the first and last row in Table 2).

4.2.2   RQ2: What QRs Challenges Have Been Reported in Agile Projects in General?

Twenty-six papers reported explicitly and implicitly the neglect of QRs in agile projects. Table 3 summarizes 12 specific challenges caused by agile practices regarding QRs in general, according to these papers. The identified challenges refer to almost the whole spectrum of RE activities and lead consciously or subconsciously in the neglect of QRs.

Table 3 suggests that some characteristics of agile RE pitched as strengths in agile textbooks (e.g. the role of the product owner, the use of user stories) can be considered in fact as inhibitors to engineering of QRs. Four of the 12 challenges relate to the product owner's role. In this respect, 11 papers point out to various aspects associated to that role as conductive to QRs difficulties, e.g. insufficient knowledge on product quality's side regarding QRs, being overloaded yet serving as a single point of contact on QRs. This observations agrees with the SLR of Medeiros et al. [8] that pinpoints to the product owner as a potential source of RE challenges.

4.2.3   RQ3: What Are the Existing Solutions to Cope with Neglected QRs in Agile RE in General (not Only in ALSD), as Per RE Literature?

We found several solution proposals that however are in their early stage and, in turn, are not empirically validated. This agrees with the conclusion of Inayat et al. [P30] that observed a lack of knowledge about the effectivity of solution proposals. Table 4 summarizes our findings. The rightmost column indicates if agility has been considered explicitly in the design of the proposal. Qumer et al. [P46] stated that for a software

Table 2. Agile practices regarding RE in ALSD settings

Practice	Description	References	Type of practice
Face-to-face communication	Communication sessions between development team and the Product Owner (PO) to identify the requirements	P2, P4, P12, P13, P14, P15, P16	Social behaviour based
Iterative emergence of requirements	The requirements emerge during the development process instead of defining them up-front	P2, P4, P12, P17, P18	Artefact based
Frequent prioritization	Continuously prioritizing the user stories based on the changing business values	P2, P19	Artefact based
User stories	Short and abstract description of the requirements used to encourage the face-to-face communication	P2, P4, P14, P17, P20, P21, P22, P23, P24, P25	Artefact based
Product grooming	Continuously revisiting the set of user stories to remove obsolete stories, create new stories and re-assessing their relative priority	P14	Artefact based
Delivery story	Extended user story with additional information such as functional specification, quality requirement's high level design and test scenarios	P19	Artefact based
Wiki	Online tool that can be accessed by all team members to communicate the user stories	P24, P26	Tool based
Evolutionary prototyping	A prototype that is built iteratively to be finally used in Production	P2, P4	Artefact based
Unit testing	A test that is written to test a single isolated small unit of the code	P27	Artefact based
Test driven development	The requirements first of all are turned into test cases, then the necessary code is written to pass the test cases	P2, P14, P28	Artefact based
Continuous integration	All product copies of all team members are merged several times a day to validate the correct working of the product	P14, P28, P29	Artefact based
Refactoring	Just before the end of each iteration the internal structure of the product is getting restructured to enhance the internal quality	P14	Artefact based
Pair programming	Two developers are sitting together behind one screen. One is programming and the other is controlling and validating the code	P14	Social behavior, artefact based

Table 3. Reported challenges regarding QRs

Challenge	References
Agile does not provide a widely accepted technique for gathering the QRs	P32, P34, P37
Focusing on delivering functionality at the cost of architecture flexibility	P2, P20, P31, P36, P38, P39, P40
Ignoring predictable architecture requirements	P38, P39
Inability of user stories to document QRs	P19, P21, P35, P36
Inability of user stories to document requirements dependencies	P19, P34, P36
Validating QRs occurs too late in the process	P4, P19, P10, P27, P41
The lack of requirements traceability mechanism	P10, P30, P32, P33, P42, P43, P44
Product Owner's lack of knowledge	P14, P16, P19, P36, P38
Product Owner's heavy workload	P14, P16
Insufficient availability of the Product Owner	P17
Insufficient requirements analysis	P40, P45
Dependence on the product owner as the single point to collect the requirements	P33, P38, P40

method to be considered Agile, the degree of its agility should be evaluated based on the presence of five key elements, namely: flexibility, speed, leanness, learning and responsiveness. Proposals that did not describe the degree of their agility were not considered as agile.

As Table 4 indicates, some of the presented solutions introduced several new artefacts to agile (e.g. [P49][P50][P51][P52][P53][P54]). For example, the authors of the NERV approach [P49] suggest to introduce six new artefacts: NFR Elicitation Taxonomy, NFR Reasoning Taxonomy, NFR Quantification Taxonomy, NFR Trigger Card, NFRusCOM Card (Non-Functional Requirements User Story Companion Card) and NAI (NERV Agility Index, which is essentially a set of metrics). However, one might think that introducing new artefacts could result in making agile a heavy documented approach which is misaligned with the second principle of the agile manifesto, namely "Working software over comprehensive documentation" [21].

Our reviewed literature also reported solutions [P12][P44][P57] that were focused on integrating specific QRs types in agile. Below (Table 5) we describe them. We note that those solutions came from the papers only that were returned by our search string, since we did not look explicitly for solutions to particular QR's types. Among the proposals in Table 5, only one [P12] considered the agility factor.

Our review suggests that researchers generated an abundant number of proposals, some of which focused on integrating specific QRs types in agile. However, if a solution for every single type of the QRs is proposed and adopted, we would eventually end up with a huge number of approaches proliferation. Amplifying agile with tools, rols and/or practices needed to integrate each type of QRs will definitely result in a heavy approach that does not meet the agile principles defined in the agile manifesto [21].

Table 4. Reported solutions

Ref.	Proposal in summary	Agility factor considered?
P47	A suggestion to use todays' technologies to cope with agile poor documentation of requirements	No
P5, P38	A suggestion to combine agile and traditional methods in a hyper approach to deliver successful projects	No
P34	A solution proposal to cope with uncomplete requirements such QRs during the RE process	No
P40	The solution proposal to cope with agile weaknesses such as requirements analysis by combining the strengths of agile and traditional methods in a hybrid solution	No
P35	Proposes SENoR workshop sessions to collect the QRs and documenting them using use cases	No
P48	Combines two QRs analysis approaches in one namely: (1) Four layered approach to QR analysis and (2) Quantitative assessment of QRs. by leveraging their strengths and eliminating their weaknesses	No
P49	Tackles the neglect of QRs in agile by providing several artefacts to be used in different requirements activities	No
P50, P51, P52 P53, P54	Proposes several artefacts to identify, model and link QRs to functional requirements	No
P55	An extension to [P49] and [P50] to include the extraction of QRs from images	No
P56	Proposed the ACRUM framework to cope with the neglect of QRs in SCRUM	Yes

Table 5. Reported solutions concerning particular QRs types

Ref.	Proposal in summary	Agility factor considered?
P44	Proposes a traceability model to trace functional requirements and QRs regarding security and performance issues	No
P12	Proposed a little design up front approach to provide as much user design information as needed to support the integration of usability in the agile iterations	Yes
P57	Introduces the security backlog artefact and the security master role in SCRUM to cope with the neglect of security requirements	No

5 Discussion

We found no study that was dedicated on QRs as a whole. This observation concurs the statements of other authors indicating the lack of empirical evidence on how agile projects handle QRs systematically, in their entirety [P2][P16][P21][P25][P26][P30] [P31][P58]. The fact that there were quite a few proposals without any empirical evaluation and that the proposals have been put forward by researchers without practitioners' participation might well be a signal that incorporating QRs in agile in a seamless way that is also repeatedly successful, is far from straightforward. Another explanation would be to assume that agile projects more often than not do neglect QRs in agile settings and agile practitioners so far have not resolved the difficult task of handling QRs systematically. This agrees with the observation of many authors [P2][P4] [P30] [P31][P32][P33][P34][P35][P36] who mention the developers' neglect of QRs.

We also observe that organisations using large scale agile software development, introduce new roles in order to engineer QRs ([P6][P11]). This indicates that the Product Owner role is not enough in this context. One might think that these new roles (e.g. usability head, security master) imply an anti-pattern, as the Product Owner's role as a single empowered/engaged individual is fundamental in Scrum [P14][P16]. However, we do not think this finding is surprising, because large organizations usually attempt to come up with a mix of agile and 'traditional' practices – just because they want to hedge the risk of adopting agile methods in a project with a broad range of stakeholders, conflicting requirements and needs for explicit knowledge-sharing [P19].

An interesting observation is that no study of those that suggest a security, safety or usability QRs approach, mentions the role of the requirement engineer or the software architect. Instead of these general job titles, the papers use specialists' roles (security master, usability head). This is in contrast with previously published papers on engineering QRs [P1] that suggested the software architects' involvement in eliciting, documenting, negotiating and validating QRs. Do agile methods eliminate those roles? May we assume that people with these job titles, are part of the development team? We think this could be an interesting line for future research. More empirical studies in large scale contexts are needed to understand how these roles submerge and what the individual contribution of each one is to engineering the QRs in a systematic way.

Another interesting observation regarding agile practices is that practitioners are not totally agree on how to engineer architectural related requirements (e.g. QRs).in ALSD. While the co-author of the agile manifesto claims that Just-In-Time (JIT) requirements [22] is the way to be agile and anticipate on requirements changes, an industrial experience working paper [23] claims that the agile community encourages the use of the so-called "Architecture spike" for large-scale projects. The architecture spike was described in the working paper as a small design upfront to identify and implement the architectural related requirements. However, the working paper recognized the architecture spike's lack of an overall vision on crucial product qualities (e.g. QRs).

The role of the PO was observed as a weakness in agile. We found that. insufficient knowledge of PO on product quality's side regarding QRs, the heavy workload and her act as a single point of contact on QRs are challenges in agile. This observation was confirmed by an industrial experience article written by an agile practitioner [24].

We observed that organizations adopt social-behaviour-based practices for the purpose of QRs engineering. This is in line with the agile manifesto [21] which suggests that people take priority over process. We think this may also be considered an enrichment to the current approaches to QRs (e.g. security, safety) as described in empirical studies because too often empirical RE papers on these requirements focus on their respective method itself and not on the social context in which the method is applied.

Our results indicate that QRs engineering may well imply introduction of additional artefacts and tools. This is not surprising because large and distributed systems delivery organizations share knowledge through artefacts and tools for their management. However, we think that to keep a process agile, there should be possibly a limit to the number of artefacts that could be added. What this limit could be is a line for future research.

We compared our results with the three SLR in Sect. 2. Our finding about the lack of an empirically evaluated method for QRs agrees with the findings of the three SLRs. In contrast to these reviews, we found that some of the RE practices that are supposed to "help" with requirements and overcome challenges in traditional RE (e.g. frequent requirements change), may well be counterproductive in regard to QRs. For example, while the product owner is found by Inayat et al. [4] to be instrumental to agile RE, the primary papers in our review indicated quite a few QR challenges arising out of the product owner's role, e.g. insufficient knowledge, massive overload and unavailability.

Our review has some practical implications. First, we found that agile practices no matter how critical for business value generation, could lead to the detriment of QRs and ultimately increase the total cost of ownership of a system. Practitioners should therefore be extremely conscious about treating QRs early enough in their projects. It might be possible that experienced agile practitioners have accumulated much knowledge in managing risk related to QRs, however this knowledge so far remained tacit and needs to be explicated and properly documented in literature, should we want to build upon it for the purpose of improving QRs in agile in the long run.

Second, existing QR-methods make the tacit assumption that it is generally a good idea for practitioners to add more tasks (those related to QRs) to their work, be it adding a new artefact, adopting new behaviours, or introducing a new tool. While this assumption sounds reasonable, it may not be realistic in all cases, just because companies and development organizations vary in their understanding of how much agility and waterfall is a healthy combination for their context. Adding more tasks that would inject waterfall aspects in the agile process may not be attractive to many organizations.

Third, we would like to note that some QR methods are proposed to tackle the downside of another method. This can result in a situation where one method's disadvantage is other method's advantage. However, empirical evaluations are needed to check if the presumed advantages and limitations of each proposal are in fact observable in real-life settings. Only then, practitioners could receive a recommendation on which method would be a good addition to their toolbox in their organizational and project settings.

6 Limitations

We evaluated the possible limitations to our review. First, it might be possible that we passed selection bias into the process of evaluating the papers for inclusion. This is because the second author contributed to one of the SLRs on agile RE [4] and also because she knows in person some of the authors of agile RE case studies. However, to reduce this bias, the first author did apply the selection criteria on his own and the second author did so only regarding the papers whose authors were not in professional relationship with her.

Through snowballing, we found 9 more papers that we added to our list for inclusion. This could be traceable to our search string, which was limited only to the 'Computer Science' subject area in Scopus. Due to the fact that the term "agility" is used by other disciplines (e.g. business and management sciences) that publish papers on agile delivery and project management of complex information systems, it might be possible that we missed some relevant papers. Also, we limited the years to 2002–2016. This choice however is justified by the fact that the agile manifesto [21] was created in 2001.

Furthermore, our review included ten papers that took the perspective of a specific type of QRs - namely - security [P6][P7][P8][P45][P57][P59], usability [P12][P60], safety [P9][P10], and compliance [P10]. They signalled the inability of agile methods to handle those respective types of QRs. We assume that there may well be many more publications that took such a specific QRs perspective, however we did not hit them in Scopus because our search string was not designed for this purpose. As we wanted to find published approaches to engineering QRs in general, we deliberately avoided including specific terms (such as e.g. security, usability) that name a specific type of QRs.

It might be possible that in our coding process we might have misunderstood some contextual details that we found in the primary papers concerning agile RE. We mitigated this by coding the papers independently by the first two authors, both with experience as practicing software engineers and consultants, and integrating the results later.

Last, we looked at scientific literature, while it might be the case that industry events that do not result in papers available in scientific libraries, offer in fact valuable insights into industrial practices regarding QRs and ALSD projects. It might be therefore a good idea to include the so-called "grey literature"[2] to our review. We however did not plan such a step, given our resources available.

7 Conclusion

This review shows that very little is known about the evolution of QRs in ALSD setting. While there are proposals of researchers, very little empirical work has so far been done to evaluate these proposals' scalability to real-life settings. More research is needed to understand the contexts in which these approaches would fit and add value.

---

[2] http://www.greylit.org/about.

While the neglect of QRs in agile projects is already known, this study points out which agile practices may actually complicate the engineering of QRs, or at least affect them in a suboptimal way. Table 3 revealed that 12 different elements of the agile process decrease the focus on QRs. A combined effect of those elements in a project may result in neglecting the QRs at almost all iterations of the RE process. We therefore think that more research is needed to fully understand the scope of the potentially damaging effects of agile on QRs.

Regarding the extent of agility in the proposed approaches, it was a surprise that the most of the proposals did not go through an agility assessment to ensure the agility factor remains intact during the application of those solutions. After all an agile solution should keep the process agile. If the proposed approaches lack agility, these would not appeal to practitioners to try them out in their projects. An implication is then that we as a community should develop our proposals together with practitioners for industry. So, more research via company-university collaborations seems to be beneficial.

References

1. Lauesen, S.: Software Requirements: Style and Techniques. Pearson Education, London (2002)
2. Blaine, J.D., Cleland-Huang, J.: Software quality requirements: how to balance competing priorities. IEEE Softw. **25**, 22–24 (2008)
3. Kazman, R., Bass, L.: Toward deriving software architectures from quality attributes. Softw. Eng. Inst. 1–44 (1994)
4. Inayat, I., Salwah, S., Marczak, S., Daneva, M., Shamshirband, S.: A systematic literature review on agile requirements engineering practices and challenges. Comput. Human Behav. **51**, 915–929 (2014)
5. Alsaqaf, W.: Engineering non-functional requirements in large scale distributed agile environment. In: REFSQ-JP 2016, p. 7 (2016)
6. Kitchenham, B.A., Budgen, D., Brereton, P.: Evidence-Based Software Engineering and Systematic Reviews. Chapman and Hall/CRC, London (2015)
7. Daneva, M., Buglione, L., Herrmann, A.: Software architects' experiences of quality requirements: what we know and what we do not know? In: REFSQ, pp. 1–17 (2013)
8. Medeiros, J.D.R.V., Alves, D.C.P., Vasconcelos, A., Silva, C., Wanderley, E.: Requirements engineering in agile projects: a systematic mapping based in evidences of industry. In: CibSE, pp. 460–473 (2015)
9. Heikkilä, V.T., Lassenius, C., Damian, D., Paasivaara, M.: A mapping study on requirements engineering in agile software development. In: Euromicro DSD/SEAA, pp. 199–207 (2015)
10. Razavi, A.M., Ahmad, R.: Agile development in large and distributed environments: a systematic literature review on organizational, managerial and cultural aspects. In: MySEC, pp. 216–221 (2014)
11. Jalali, S., Wohlin, C.: Agile practices in global software engineering – a systematic map. In: ICGSE, pp. 45–54 (2010)
12. Saeeda, H., Ahmed, M., Khalid, H., Sameer, A.: Systematic literature review of agile scalability for large scale projects. Int. J. Adv. Comput. Sci. Appl. **6**, 63–75 (2015)

13. Rizvi, B., Bagheri, E., Gasevic, D.: A systematic review of distributed agile software engineering. J. Softw. Evol. Process. **27**, 723–762 (2015)
14. Šmite, D., Wohlin, C., Gorschek, T., Feldt, R.: Empirical evidence in global software engineering: a systematic review. Empir. Softw. Eng. **15**, 91–118 (2010)
15. Jalali, S., Wohlin, C.: Global software engineering and agile practices: a systematic review. J. Softw. Evol. Process. **24**, 643–659 (2012)
16. Hossain, E., Babar, M.A.: Using scrum in global software development: a systematic literature review. In: ICGSE, pp. 175–184 (2009)
17. Ramesh, B., Cao, L., Baskerville, R.: Agile requirements engineering practices and challenges: an empirical study. Inf. Syst. J. **20**, 449–480 (2010)
18. Daneva, M., Damian, D., Marchetto, A., Pastor, O.: Empirical research methodologies and studies in requirements engineering: how far did we come? Editorial for the JSS special issue on empirical RE research and methodologies. J. Syst. Softw. **95**, 1–9 (2014)
19. Cruzes, D.S., Dyba, T.: Recommended steps for thematic synthesis in software engineering. In: 2011 International Symposium on Empirical Software Engineering and Measurement, pp. 275–284 (2011)
20. Saldaña, J.: The Coding Manual for Qualitative Researchers. SAGE Publications Ltd., California (2012)
21. Alliance, A.: Manifesto for Agile Software Development (2001)
22. Robert, C.M., Micah, M.: Agile Principles, Patterns and Practices in C#. Prentice Hall, New Jersey (2006)
23. Philippus, E.: Architecture Spikes (2009)
24. Vlietland, J.: Waarom Product Owner de meest ingewikkelde rol is in het scrum team. http://www.agilepractice.nl/story/product-owner-scrum-team/

Improving User Story Practice with the Grimm Method: A Multiple Case Study in the Software Industry

Garm Lucassen[(✉)], Fabiano Dalpiaz,
Jan Martijn E.M. van der Werf, and Sjaak Brinkkemper

Utrecht University, Utrecht, The Netherlands
{g.lucassen,f.dalpiaz,j.m.e.m.vanderwerf,s.brinkkemper}@uu.nl

Abstract. *Context and motivation*: Previous research shows that a considerable amount of real-world user stories contain easily preventable syntactic defects that violate desired qualities of good requirements. However, we still do not know the effect of user stories' intrinsic quality on practitioners' work. *Question/Problem*: We study the effects of introducing the Grimm Method's Quality User Story framework and the AQUSA tool on the productivity and work deliverable quality of 30 practitioners from 3 companies over a period of 2 months. *Principal ideas/results*: Our multiple case study delivered mixed findings. Despite an improvement in the intrinsic user story quality, practitioners did not perceive such a change. They explained, however, there was more constructive user story conversation in the post-treatment period leading to less unnecessary rework. Conversely, project management metrics did not result in statistically significant changes in the number of comments, issues, defects, velocity, and rework. *Contribution*: Introducing our treatment has a mildly positive effect but a larger scale investigation is crucial to decisively assess the impact on work practice. Also, our case study protocol serves as an example for evaluating RE research in practice.

Keywords: User stories · Requirements engineering · Agile development · Empirical study · Multiple case study

1 Introduction

Thanks to the rapid adoption of agile development practices, approximately 50% of software practitioners capture requirements using the semi-structured natural language (NL) notation of *user stories* [8,12,25]: "As a ⟨*role*⟩, I want ⟨*goal*⟩, so that ⟨*benefit*⟩".

Despite the simplicity and wide-spread adoption of this requirements engineering (RE) method, practitioners make many mistakes when creating user stories. In previous work, we analyzed 1,000+ real-world user stories and found that 56% contain easily preventable syntactic defects [13]. Examples include the

© Springer International Publishing AG 2017
P. Grünbacher and A. Perini (Eds.): REFSQ 2017, LNCS 10153, pp. 235–252, 2017.
DOI: 10.1007/978-3-319-54045-0_18

use of a non-standard template and the specification of multiple features in one user story.

Our solution for practitioners to create high-quality user stories was to introduce two artifacts: the Quality User Story (QUS) framework and the computational linguistics tool Automatic Quality User Story Artisan (AQUSA) [13]. Although we have empirically confirmed that numerous real-world user stories violate QUS characteristics [13], we still lack evidence of the impact of QUS and AQUSA on practitioners' work.

This paper studies the impact of QUS and AQUSA on team communication frequency, team communication effectiveness, work deliverable quality, and work productivity. We do this via a multiple case study where we compare the pre-treatment period with the experimental period (2 months each) with 30 practitioners from 3 companies.

The participants first attended a 2 h training, received a summary of the training's content and applied their new skills in a training workshop. After we integrated AQUSA with the company's issue tracker, the participants applied QUS and AQUSA in their work activities for two months. During this period, we collected software development process metrics, practitioner perception of the impact, and inherent user story quality. To determine the effect of our treatment, we compared the results against data taken from the issue tracker in the preceding two months.

The results of our empirical study are summarized by the following findings:

- The intrinsic user story quality generally increased after the treatment, resulting in fewer violations of the user story qualities prescribed by the QUS framework;
- The perception on quality by practitioners shows a marginal improvement but without reaching statistical significance;
- Despite our accurate measurements of the impact on work practices, we could not identify any significant change, also due to changes in the organizational context.

The next section of this paper outlines the research method. We then present the results in Sect. 3 and review related literature in Sect. 4. Finally, Sect. 5 presents a discussion of the findings and concludes this paper with an outline of future work.

2   Research Method

We study the impact of introducing a tool-supported quality framework for user stories in agile development. We do this through a multiple case study with three software product organizations. Over a span of two months, these organizations incorporated two artifacts into their user story practices: QUS and AQUSA.

QUS [13] defines the quality of user stories via three types of criteria: (i) *syntactic* (e.g., atomic and well-formed), concerning the textual structure of a user story; (ii) *semantic* (e.g., problem-oriented and unambiguous), which focus on the meaning of user stories; and (iii) *pragmatic* (e.g., unique and uniform), referring to how user stories are being used in RE. AQUSA automatically verifies some QUS criteria using computational linguistics algorithms. In particular, AQUSA supports those criteria for which we can reach close to 100% recall: unique, minimal, well-formed, uniform and atomic.

We combine QUS and AQUSA into a package called *Grimm Method*, which provides an easy-to-remember term for practitioners and explains our artifacts' use during user story creation, poker planning, and software development.

We investigate the impact of the Grimm Method (our independent variable) by presenting data that test the following four hypotheses (each defining one dependent variable): *"Applying the QUS framework accompanied by the AQUSA tool"* . . . :

H1 - *"increases communication frequency"*
H2 - *"fosters more effective communication"*
H3 - *"improves work deliverable quality"*
H4 - *"increases work productivity"*

2.1   Grimm Method Treatment Design

To minimize threats to the internal validity of our study and to ensure uniform data collection, we devised a stepwise treatment design. All the physical materials described in each of the steps below are available online [11]. Also, video/audio-recordings of the training sessions can be made available upon request.

1. **Baseline measurement -** Two months before applying the treatment we start collecting software development process metrics. We refer to this time frame as the pre-treatment period.
2. **Intake survey -** On the treatment application day, each experiment participant fills out a brief intake survey to learn more about his/her knowledge of user stories and professional experience.
3. **Training -** The experimental treatment consists of a 2-h training session during which the participants: (1) attend a presentation by the first author on the Grimm Method [11], (2) discuss analysis of their stories by AQUSA, (3) apply the QUS framework in a training workshop and (4) receive a summary of the training's content as reference material.
4. **Experimental period -** Upon completing the training, the team kicks off the two-month experimental period by integrating AQUSA with their issue tracker. From this moment, the team applies QUS in their daily work activities, supported by AQUSA that automatically analyzes any updated or newly added user stories and collects data on company's software development processes.
5. **Exit survey -** At the end of the experimental period each team member completes an exit survey on the impact of introducing the Grimm Method. The exit survey consists of 24 questions to capture the participant's perception of H1–H4, subdivided in four distinct parts. The first and second part

include questions on the pre-treatment period and experimental period in isolation, the third part has questions that directly compare the two periods, and the fourth part includes four open questions for respondents to provide further feedback.

6. **Project Manager Evaluation -** Together with the team's project manager we evaluate the experimental period. The goal of this conversation is to validate our interpretation of the data. In particular, we ask the project manager to clarify outliers and to explain context-specific responses to the exit survey.

7. **Interviews -** We go through the responses to the exit survey to identify participants who give inconsistent, particularly positive, remarkably negative and/or opinionated answers. We invite these participants to clarify their responses in a follow-up interview to gather in-depth qualitative data.

These steps result in three types of data to test the hypotheses: (1) the intrinsic user story quality as reported by AQUSA, (2) the practitioners' perception of the Grimm Method's impact on work processes and user story quality, and (3) metrics about the software development process. We detail each data type in the following subsections. We employ methodological triangulation to reduce bias and to strengthen the validity of our results to form a more detailed and balanced picture of the actual situation [18].

2.2   Measures

User Story Quality. The first type of collected data is the intrinsic user story quality reported by AQUSA. As a direct measure of the impact of introducing the Grimm Method, the results indicate whether the experiment participants actually started creating syntactically better user stories. We apply AQUSA analyses to user stories created during the pre-treatment period and experimental period to detect the total number of violations for five quality criteria: well-formed, atomic, minimal, uniform and unique [13]. Note that this is a subset of the full QUS framework based on the characteristics that can be automatically checked with high precision and recall accuracy. We expect the total number of violations to decrease after introducing the Grimm Method.

Perceived Impact on Work Practice. We collect the second type of data by means of the exit survey and follow-up interviews. In both cases, the experiment participants self-report how they perceive the impact of the Grimm Method on their work. In total, the exit survey includes 12 Likert-Type statements on whether the respondents perceive the user stories to contribute to H1, H2, H3 and H4. Examples include "The user stories improved my productivity" and "User story conversation occurs more frequently since the Grimm Method training". Furthermore, the survey contains 4 questions and statements on respondents' perception of the intrinsic quality of the user stories themselves such as "How would you rate the quality of the user stories?" and "The quality of our user stories is better since the Grimm Method training". For the complete list of survey questions we refer the reader to the online materials [11]. Note that similar to our previous work [12], the survey relies on the participants' own understanding of *productivity* and *work deliverable quality* rather than enforcing our own definition.

Process Metrics. Over the years, a large corpus of software development metrics has been proposed in the literature. The available metrics span from inherent code quality metrics such as *cyclomatic complexity* [15] to team well-being metrics like the *Happiness Index* [10]. For RE alone, a literature review by Holm et al. [6] distilled 298 unique dependent variables from 78 articles. In RE research, however, it is unclear when and why which specific metrics are applicable [6].

Although the quality of user stories can potentially impact code quality metrics, the primary intention of user stories is to streamline the processes facilitating software development. By capturing and communicating the discussion around the features to be implemented, user stories aim to enable developers to produce software that stakeholders actually want [2] and practitioners perceive a key quality of user stories to be enabling creation of the *right software* [12]. For this reason this study looks at a specific type of metrics related to the (human) *processes* around software development [14].

We select the following five metrics from literature for their relevance to our hypotheses and their availability from project management software like Jira[1]:

Formal communication - We measure the frequency of communication in a team (H1) as the number of comments added to the stories completed in a 2-week sprint.

Rework - We measure the amount of rework in a project by calculating the *recidivism rate*: the rate at which user stories move backward in the software development process [4]. When a developer assigns the status 'done' to a user story, but it is not complete or has bugs, it is re-assigned 'to-do' or 'in progress', causing the recidivism rate to go up. A high recidivism rates is an indicator of ineffective communication causing misunderstanding among the stakeholders. We calculate recidivism rate as: $200 * (Backward/(Forward + Backward))$. Note that we include a multiplier of 200 to get a natural 0–100% range, instead of 0–50 as in [4]. This metric measures communication effectiveness thereby relating to H2.

Pre-release defects - The number of bugs added to the issue tracker during a 2-week sprint. Inspired by defect prediction literature [19,20,26], which base their metrics on all the defects in a six-months period before a new release. Unlike these works, we focus on the narrow 2-week period of a sprint as Scrum prescribes every sprint to be a potentially *releasable* increment. This metric measures work deliverable quality, which is used to assess if H3 holds.

Post-release defects - The number of bugs related to user stories in a sprint, as reported in the two sprints after that sprint. This choice is inspired by defect prediction literature, which counts all defects in the first six months

---

[1] https://www.atlassian.com/software/jira.

after a release. Again, we substantially shorten this time-frame because of Scrum's quick feedback cycle. Moreover, summing the defects as reported in twelve sprints would make the defect count differences between consecutive sprints negligibly small. This metric measures work deliverable quality that is used to test H3.

Team productivity - To measure the productivity of the development team (H4) we sum the story points a team completes in a sprint: the so-called *velocity* [2].

2.3   Experiment Participants

We announced the experiment within our professional networks. Based on organizational details and selection criteria such as development sprint length and compatibility of the issue tracker with AQUSA, we invited 11 companies to participate and sent them the exact details of the experiment. 5 companies with headquarters in the Netherlands registered for participation. Unforeseen technical difficulties integrating AQUSA with firewalled enterprise editions of Jira reduced the number of companies to 3.

eCommerce Company is a large company with over 2000 employees. One team working on a next generation edition of the platform consisting of 6 developers, 2 UX designers and 3 project managers participated in the study.

Health Company is a medium-sized software producing organization that has multiple products for delivering digital healthcare. A team working on a new product consisting of 4 software developers, 1 software architect, 1 UX designer, 1 scrum master and 1 project manager participated in the study.

RealEstate Company is a medium-sized software producing organization that develops a product for a housing cooperative. The participating team of 11 employees has 6 software developers, 3 testers, one product owner and one product manager.

In total, 30 practitioners from six different countries participated in the experiment. The roles of these participants are: 16 software developers, 7 managers, 3 testers, 3 UX designers and 1 CTO. All the teams use Scrum as their primary software development method and employ user stories. All practitioners report they capture user stories in the Connextra template *"As a ⟨role⟩ , I want ⟨goal⟩, [so that ⟨benefit⟩]"*, 11 of which ensure their quality by applying the INVEST framework, while 8 defined their own guidelines instead and the remaining 11 participants do not use any guidelines. Note that the majority of practitioners from RealEstate company indicated they did not use quality guidelines, while 2 selected INVEST and 2 others chose self-defined guidelines. For the eCommerce company, it was a tie between INVEST and self-defined guidelines with 4 each, followed by 3 saying they are not aware of any guidelines. The Health company participants are more in agreement with 6 employing INVEST and just 1 each choosing self-defined or no guidelines at all. The average participant has 3.1 years of experience in working with user stories while his or her organization has 4.7

years of experience. Concerning their expertise with user stories, 2 participants indicate they are at the novice stage, 5 are beginner, 15 are intermediate and 8 are advanced.

3 Results

This section presents the results of our multiple case study. We first look at the change in intrinsic quality between the pre-treatment period and the experimental period (Sect. 3.1). We then investigate the participants' perception of the effectiveness of the Grimm Method (Sect. 3.2). Finally, we analyze the software development process itself by comparing the metric computed on the basis of issue trackers data (Sect. 3.3).

3.1 Intrinsic User Story Quality

We collected all user stories created by the companies during the pre-treatment period and the experimental period. We analyzed them running AQUSA's defect detection algorithms. We observe a reduced number of defects in the second period in Table 1.

In particular, there are 38.3% fewer defects per user story (see the last row) for eCommerce company and 47.5% fewer defects for RealEstate company in the experimental period. The number of defects remained practically stable for Health company (one additional defect: 23 instead of 22) (4.5% more). Aggregating all the results, the post-period reveals 116 fewer defects for nearly as many user stories. The companies produced 241 user stories in the pre-treatment period with 266 defects versus 239 user stories with 150 defects in the experimental period. Due to the small number of defects for Health company, there is a substantial difference between the 27% macro-average and 43.14% weighted micro-average defect reduction [22].

Looking beyond the averages, the distribution of defects mostly remained the same for eCommerce and RealEstate companies, while they changed for Health company. The number of uniformity and uniqueness defects (almost) doubled whereas the number of well-formed and atomic defects (more than) halved.

The results suggest that applying the Grimm Method treatment generally had a positive effect on the intrinsic quality of user stories. On the other hand, the improvement is to be expected considering we measure quality with the exact same criteria as prescribed by the treatment. To further test the quality of the textual requirements, we considered using algorithms that assess single sentence complexity. Unfortunately, this field is still immature [24]; while many metrics for readability of texts exist, they require passages of text with 100+ words. Nevertheless, we applied multiple readability metrics to our user story collections but found no substantial change between the pre-treatment period and the experimental period. For example: the *Gunning fog indexes* [5] of our three sets are 11.0 vs. 10.8, 12 vs. 12.1, and 9.3 vs. 8.7, while the *New Dale-Chall* scores [1] are 5 vs. 5.3, 5.3 vs. 5.4, and 5.5 vs. 4.9 for eCommerce, Health and RealEstate, respectively.

Table 1. Intrinsic user story quality analysis by AQUSA, comparing the pre-treatment period (*pre*) and the experimental period (*exp*).

Number of user stories	eCommerce		Health		RealEstate	
	Pre	Exp	Pre	Exp	Pre	Exp
	105	71	33	33	103	135
Defects breakdown						
- *Well formed*: each story has at least a role and a means	63	27	7	4	33	22
- *Atomic*: each story expresses a requirement for *one* feature	10	1	6	2	6	8
- *Minimal*: each story contains only role, means, and ends	20	11	0	0	30	16
- *Uniform*: all written stories employ the same template	38	19	7	13	24	18
- *Unique*: each story is unique, duplicates are avoided	20	5	2	4	0	0
Total defects	151	63	22	23	93	64
Defects per user story	1.44	0.89	0.67	0.70	0.90	0.47

3.2 Participant Perception

At the end of the experimental period each participant completed an exit survey on the perceived impact of introducing the Grimm Method. 27 participants submitted a complete and valid survey. Due to the limited sample size we mostly report on the aggregate answers of all respondents; a per-company discussion is presented at the end of the subsection. We first analyze the participants' responses, illustrated with quotes from 6 follow-up interviews. After perceived user story quality, we focus on the treatment's impact (H1–H4). Note that we use H#a to highlight questions that directly compare the pre-treatment and experimental periods, and H#b for questions on an individual period.

User Story Quality. The exit survey asks the participants to rate user story quality on a scale from 0–10 twice: first for the pre-treatment period and then again for the experimental period. Overall, the responses show a small user story quality improvement after applying the treatment: an average score of 6.96 vs. 7.15 with standard deviations of 1.34 vs. 1.29. In total, 9 respondents report a positive user story quality change after the experimental period, 12 report no change at all and 6 indicate the quality of the user stories decreased. However, when analyzing the distribution of responses via a Wilcoxon signed-rank test, we obtain no statistically significant difference between the two periods ($Z = -.984, p = .325$). Thus, concerning the introduction of the Grimm Method's QUS and AQUSA, we could not observe statistically significant changes in practitioner's perception of user story quality.

Yet, when asked to directly compare the pre-treatment period with the experimental period the responses are less neutral. The majority of respondents (16 or 59%) state they agree with the Likert-Type statement "The quality of our user stories is better since the Grimm Method training", while 10 respondents neither agree nor disagree (37%) and just 1 respondent disagrees (4%). Also, 14 respondents (52%) agree with the statement "My satisfaction of our user stories is higher since the Grimm Method training", 11 neither agree nor disagree (41%) and 2 respondents disagree (7%).

In follow-up interviews, we asked respondents to motivate their answers and to explain why they did not report a change in the user story quality score, yet they do agree that the quality of their user stories improved. Two eCommerce Company and two RealEstate Company interviewees emphasize that their reported increase in user story quality was moderate, if present at all. They indicate that introducing the Grimm Method did not result in a meaningful, lasting process change, but that they themselves and their colleagues did become more aware of the relevance of capturing user stories in a diligent manner. The UX designer from eCommerce Company notes *"I believe that someone coming from outside the organization to tell us how you are supposed to do this has had the most influence. It aligns everyone's ideas on user stories. It helps that the method presents everything in a piecemeal fashion."*

These results reveal a discrepancy between the *intrinsic* and *perceived* change in user story quality. While the number of defects dropped by 43.14%, just 9 participants reported a (marginal) positive change in user story quality. Although respondents did respond positively to the Likert-Type statements, follow-up interviews clarified that the respondents do not believe user story quality improved substantially.

One possible explanation for this mismatch is AQUSA's focus on highlighting simple, easy to detect issues. This results in highly accurate yet seemingly trivial output. The importance of fixing a uniformity mistake, for example, can be difficult to comprehend, and those improvements may be regarded as too small to lead to an improvement.

Communication Frequency and Communication Effectiveness. We study participants' perception of conversation by breaking it down into two dimensions: frequency and constructiveness. Respondents do not report a significant change in H1b: communication frequency between the pre-treatment period and experimental period (see Fig. 2). 21 respondents did not change their answer after the training (78%), 4 reported a decrease in conversation frequency (15%) and 2 reported an increase (7%). The majority of respondents still experienced excessive communication around user stories; however, 3 out of the 4 participants from eCommerce Company that reported a communication decrease did no longer perceive the amount of conversation to be *excessive*.

The number of respondents that agree with statement H2b "The user stories contributed to constructive conversation concerning the software to be made" after the treatment grew from 14 to 18 (52% to 67% as per Fig. 2). Notably, the respondent that indicated he strongly disagreed with the statement for the pre-treatment period agreed with the statement after the treatment. When directly comparing the pre-treatment period with the experimental period, most respondents agreed that conversation was more frequent (H1a, 13 or 48%) *and* was more effective (H2a, 14 or 52%, see Fig. 1).

Again, the data exhibits a discrepancy. Participants self-report small communication differences between the pre-treatment period and experimental period, yet agree with statements that communication frequency and effectiveness improved after attending the Grimm Method training. Follow-up interviewees gave diverse motivations of their answers and clarifications of this discrepancy. The answers regarding whether conversation frequency increased or decreased after applying the treatment varied in particular. One respondent indicated the amount of conversation increased by up to 40% while another thought the amount of conversation decreased substantially.

Regardless of the increase or decrease, however, the interviewees agreed on the positive impact on conversation effectiveness. The same UX designer from eCommerce Company reported a positive change in communication frequency and effectiveness: *"Previously we lost a lot of time talking about trivial things. By trying to create better user stories as a team the discussion became more focused which resulted in more in depth conversation on why and how to approach a problem. Although this means more conversation it also saved time"*.

A software developer from eCommerce Company who contributed to the exhibited discrepancy explained his choice as follows: *"I think the conversation effectiveness did change positively, but the Grimm Method training made me more critical of what to expect from user story conversation in terms of effectiveness"*. This explanation highlights an unexpected phenomenon: although the treatment achieved its intended effect, it simultaneously influenced the way we measure that effect. These consequences cancel each other out, leading to a nullification of the impact measurement.

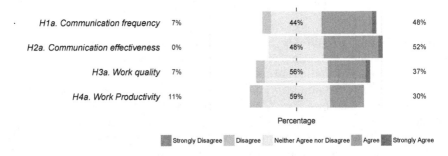

Fig. 1. Answers to Likert-Type statements directly comparing pre-treatment and experimental periods. The shown percentages (left-to-right) refer to Strongly Disagree + Disagree, Neither Agree nor Disagree and Agree + Strongly Agree, respectively.

Work Deliverable Quality and Work Productivity. Although respondents reported little change in work deliverable quality (H3b) after the experimental treatment in Fig. 1, 10 respondents (37%) agreed with H3a "The quality of my work deliverables is better since the Grimm Method training" in Fig. 2. In follow-up interviews, we asked respondents to clarify this discrepancy. Interviewees' responses were unanimous: the technical quality of the developed software did not improve, whereas the treatment clarified the goals of user stories thereby making it easier to develop software with less rework. This sentiment is illustrated by a software engineer from RealEstate Company: *"More effective and efficient conversation on user stories has reduced the amount of surprises later on. As a developer you have the responsibility to continue posing questions until you know what you are working on. The actual work deliverable quality is the same."*

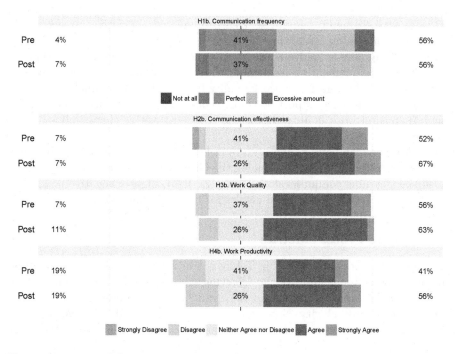

Fig. 2. Answers to Likert-Type statements for pre-treatment and experimental periods.

Responses were more consistent for work productivity. For H4b, 7 respondents indicated a positive change (26%), 16 did not change their answer (59%) and 4 experienced a decrease in work productivity (15%). Similarly, 8 or 30% of respondents agreed with H4a "My work productivity is higher since the Grimm Method training" (Fig. 2). Again, interviewees did not find user stories to have a direct impact on developers productivity because programming tasks do not substantially change due to better user stories. The interviewees, however, perceived more efficient processes around software development. The product manager of Health Company says *"I do not think the productivity itself increased, but we are more efficient in getting to the stage of being productive"* and a software developer from eCommerce Company *"I do not think my personal productivity increased, but for the entire team it did. As a team you can collaborate and communicate more efficiently and effectively which improves productivity"*.

Note that we found no correlation between a participant's role and his or hers perceived change in work deliverable quality and work productivity. It is likely, however, that this is due to the study's sample size. A future study at a larger scale could confirm our earlier results [12] that project managers perceive a more positive impact than software developers. Similarly, there is no statistically significant difference between the three case companies concerning their change in perception due to the limited sample size. Inspecting the Likert-Type graphs per company available online [11] reveals that:

- **RealEstate** Company employees clearly indicated a positive impact in all questions concerning both H#a and H#b.
- **Health** Company employees are mostly neutral concerning H#a: slightly positive on communication frequency (H1a) and communication effectiveness (H2a), and mildly negative on work quality (H3a) and work productivity (H4a). In H#b questions, they report no change concerning communication effectiveness (H2b) and work quality (H3b), and a minor positive change about work productivity (H4b).
- **eCommerce** Company employees are in between. They report both positive and negative change after introducing the Grimm Method, with more positive results concerning communication (H1a, H2a, H2b), slightly negative results on work quality (H3b), and neutral results for the other questions.

3.3 Software Process Metrics

The raw metric data is presented in Tables 2, 3 and 4, one for each participating company. The columns capture the following data: sprint identifier, number of comments, issues and defects within the sprint, number of post-release defects, recidivism rate and velocity. Note that we separate each table in two: the pre-treatment period corresponds to sprints 1–4 and the experimental period spans across sprints 5–8.

A visual, qualitative inspection of the results reveals three main concerns:

1. The total number of comments, issues, defects and velocity varies greatly between companies; compare, for example, the number of comments in the eCommerce company and in the Health company.
2. Some sprints include data outliers such as the number of defects in RE7.
3. The impact of the Grimm Method is likely to be small and can hardly be detected by visual inspection.

Table 2. eCommerce metric data

Sprint	Issues	Comments	Def	Post Def	Recidivism	Velocity
EC1	50	1	15	24	0.00	24
EC2	67	1	12	18	4.11	34
EC3	59	2	11	10	4.62	8
EC4	71	3	8	6	2.21	15
Treatment applied						
EC5	21	6	3	7	8.00	18
EC6	21	4	2	22	0.00	18
EC7	28	14	4	21	4.84	16
EC8	48	9	17	6	3.06	16

Table 3. Health metric data

Sprint	Issues	Comments	Def	Post Def	Recidivism	Velocity
HE1	56	54	2	7	14.32	47
HE2	42	64	4	4	9.36	63
HE3	17	26	4	2	3.23	23
HE4	19	46	1	5	7.96	33
Treatment applied						
HE5	20	24	1	12	3.69	32
HE6	21	56	3	12	0.93	50
HE7	30	36	9	3	2.56	37
HE8	26	40	1	0	9.55	42

To learn the actual impact of the Grimm Method we investigate whether the pre-treatment period and experimental period produce statistically different means. To reduce the numbers' variety we normalize them to a 0 to 100 scale, where 100 is the highest score per columns per company. For example: eCommerce Company's sprint EC7 has the most comments, 14, and is assigned 100. EC6 has 4 comments and gets normalized to $4/14 * 100 = 28.57$.

Table 4. RealEstate metric data

Sprint	Issues	Comments	Def	Post Def	Recidivism	Velocity
RE1	130	5	9	15	3.57	18
RE2	136	7	1	15	4.05	14
RE3	137	10	4	15	8.23	7
RE4	117	5	2	44	6.67	8
Treatment applied						
RE5	113	12	8	106	3.31	22
RE6	96	2	18	94	7.14	18
RE7	268	18	59	85	8.13	33
RE8	230	9	20	27	6.77	22

Table 5. Wilcoxon signed-rank tests

	Issues	Comments	Def	Post Def	Recidivism	Velocity
Z	−1.177	−1.490	−.178	−1.557	−.275	−.628
Sig.	.239	.136	.859	.120	.784	.530

To test if the mean ranks differ between the pre-treatment and the experimental period we apply the Wilcoxon signed-rank test for non-parametric data (see Table 5). None of the tests produce a significant difference between the pre-treatment period and experimental period groups with all $Z < \pm1.960$. This indicates that introducing the Grimm Method and Tool did not produce a statistically significant change in number of comments, issues, pre-release defects, post-release defects, recidivism rate nor velocity.

Although no statistically significant effect is observable, outliers in the data suggest that some change did occur. The outliers' significant divergence from the means make them eligible for removal in case the data has been unfairly influenced. For instance: the number of pre-release defects in EC7 is 3 times as high as the second highest value. We asked the in-charge project managers to clarify the outliers in their data. Their explanations reassured us of their validity. Two of the three project managers attribute the outliers to company-specific irregularities. In summary:

- The eCommerce company team lost productivity starting from EC3 due to internal discussions concerning the product direction.

– For the RealEstate company the merger of two project teams into one in RE3 resulted in productivity loss. Furthermore, an upcoming release in RE7 resulted in the reporting of many defects.
– The Health company project manager did notice a steady increase in productivity during the experimental period. However, he did not believe the Grimm Method has been the primary driver of this improvement, which he attributed to how the team started achieving what it is capable of after a period of under performance.

Yet, each project manager agreed that the frequency and effectiveness of user story conversation improved after the Grimm Method training. A replication of this study on a larger scale is necessary to confirm whether the phenomenon of experiencing a positive change without actively attributing it to the treatment is universal.

4   Related Literature

Although many evaluations exist on the impact of new RE methods, we could not identify any study where an RE treatment was experimented by comparing months-long periods with companies. A review of empirical papers on software process improvement [23] shows that just 8 out of 148 studies applied experimentation as their research method. None of these 8 both (1) relate to RE and (2) apply a pre-post comparison. However, the literature includes several closely related case study reports.

Kamata and Tamai investigated the relationship between requirements quality and project success or failure [7]. They analyzed 32 projects completed in a Japanese company which produces thorough quality reports for all requirements. They detected a weak relationship between SRS quality and project outcome, with five SRS criteria having a strong impact: overview, product perspective, apportioning of requirement, functions and purpose. Similarly, Knauss et al. found that in 40 student projects', success relates to the quality of the SRS they produce. For their specific context, they were even able to define a quality threshold that can be used to predict risk of failure [9].

Damian et al. introduced a formal RE process to the daily work processes of 31 project members of one Australian company [3]. They collected data over 6 months via a questionnaire, interviews and document inspection to measure practitioner's perception and development performance in terms of estimated effort vs. expended effort. Their analysis of the data indicated a positive effect of improving requirements management process in industry on downstream software development, especially in terms of more accurate estimations, improved project planning, and enhanced project scoping.

Sommerville and Ransom investigated whether improvements in RE process maturity lead to business improvements [21]. Over a period of 18 months, 9 case study companies incorporated advice on RE process improvement and self-reported on business key performance indicators (KPIs). After the experimental period, for each company both the RE process maturity and relevant business

KPIs had improved. In spite of this, the authors could not statistically correlate the two due to incompatible KPIs.

Napier et al. explored the feasibility of an RE improvement process based on the RE Good Practice Guide that considers stakeholders' perception of which problems are most relevant [17]. The authors evaluate this method during a three-year action research process with one company. The results show a 69% increase in the number of implemented RE guidelines and unanimous positive perception by the participants.

Méndez Fernández and Wagner [16] explored the effect of the RE improvement approach *ArtREPI* that applies the RE best practice database AMDiRE. The impact of ArtREPI in two case studies is measured via two post-treatment questionnaires: one on the support of process engineers and one about project participants' rating of ArtREPI's output. ArtREPI meets practitioners' process improvement needs when problem and artifact orientation are important, but the authors call for larger-scale replications.

Our research incorporates elements from each of the aforementioned studies. We consider the relevance of little direct author involvement [16], allow the companies to choose themselves which quality criteria to apply [17], introduce our treatment to multiple companies [21] and collect both qualitative perception data and quantitative metrics [3]. Differently from Damian's study [3], our metrics include quantitative and qualitative data on indirectly related human processes around software development.

There are many other possible metrics. Holm et al.'s systematic literature review [6] provides an overview of how previous literature conceptualizes and operationalizes RE. Their examination of 78 studies reveals that in total researchers used 298 dependent variables corresponding to 37 unique classes and they find there is no agreement on how to measure RE success and unclarity in the choice of the variables. However, RE validation studies like ours do perform best: 60% of all dependent variables are of the type *defects found* and the majority of dependent variables include a motivation.

5 Discussion and Outlook

We studied the effect of applying the Grimm Method's QUS framework and the AQUSA tool into existing user story practices through a multiple case study. Although the number of user story quality defects decreased by 43.14% after applying the treatment, participants did not perceive a meaningful change in user story quality. Yet, the respondents agreed that communication frequency and effectiveness improved.

On the negative side, we found no statistically significant difference in communication frequency, communication effectiveness, work quality and work productivity perception between the pre-treatment and experimental periods. Furthermore, our study of the impact on work practices by measuring software process metrics (number of comments, issues, defects, velocity and recidivism rate) did not lead to statistically significant results, perhaps also due to organizational changes between the two periods.

Taking our results into account, we cannot accept our hypotheses H1–4 from Sect. 2. Further investigation is required to obtain more decisive results. However, the results make us hypothesize that improving user stories' intrinsic quality in itself is not essential, but that highlighting quality criteria defects seems to stimulate relevant and meaningful discussion around user stories (a key activity according to Cohn [2]). For example, the quality criterion *minimal* is seldom resolved by simply removing the text between two brackets, as the in-brackets text is often important: during Grimm Method workshops, defects of this type often indicated an insufficiently refined user story to be further discussed prior to assigning it to the sprint backlog. The consequence of these dynamics is not necessarily a higher quality user story or a direct increase in productivity, but a team that may more quickly agree upon the requirements.

Another explanation for the outcome is that the treatment is wrong, incomplete or even overcomplete. Although the QUS framework describes 13 quality characteristics, the individual relevance is unknown. Replacing or removing some criteria could improve the results. Also, in this study we focused on just the 5 (out of 13) characteristics that the AQUSA tool automatically detects. It would be interesting to conduct a study on all of QUS framework's criteria and to assess their individual impact.

Threats to Validity. Multiple human factors should be considered and many aspects of the study design are hard to control for. Two important internal validity threats are the *Hawthorne Effect* and *good participant response bias* which causes participants that are aware of being observed to (sub)conciously modify their behavior. Related is the first *confounding* variable: simply instructing participants to pay attention to user story quality when creating them could be enough to explain the change in intrinsic user story quality. Additionally, there is a risk of *regression toward the mean*: if the user stories' quality was very poor, they would have improved regardless of the applied quality criteria. Although we tried to control for the latter two validity threats by selecting case companies with multiple years of user story experience, their relevance persists due to the absence of control groups. Note that all four of these threats could explain why we did not detect statistically significant positive changes, yet participants do agree that communication frequency and effectiveness improved after applying the treatment.

Our application of the treatment and measurement of the results introduce two other validity threats. After attending the training, the participants could have attempted *hypothesis guessing*: knowing the desired result changes their actions. In a larger scale study it is possible to control for this threat by leaving participation in the study open ended and not informing participants of data collection. A large scale study also allows taking into account other potentially confounding variables such as the number of people in the project or the company size. For example, in the large eCommerce company, frequent team composition changes could influence the team's acceptance of new methods. Furthermore, there is an evident *history* threat: events outside of the researchers' control affect the outcome of the results. In the chaotic environment of software companies, many unforeseen events occur over a two month period that can affect the collected data. Although unavoidable in empirical research, substantially increasing the scale of the study is likely to reduce the impact of on the data.

Finally, there is a potential *bias in the experimental design*: the number of comments in Jira is not sufficient to measure the intended effect of increasing communication. In agile software development, much of the communication is verbal and informal. Unfortunately, it is extremely hard to accurately measure and record verbal communication.

Future Work and Outlook. The mildly positive participant perception is not confirmed by software development process metrics. As in similar studies [16, 21], a large scale replication is necessary to generalize our conclusions, also to reduce threats to validity by controlling for confounding variables as company and project size. Additionally, we want to study the implications of specific quality criteria; what are the consequences of a minimality or uniformity defect in isolation? Also, we aim to devise tools that learn how to suggest improvements based on the most common resolution strategies.

Finally, we invite the RE community to undertake similar studies with the aim of measuring the *actual* effect of RE methods on work practices; our mixed results emphasize the importance of replication studies but also highlight some of the problems that other researchers could encounter in the evaluation of their own solutions.

References

1. Chall, J.S., Dale, E.: Readability Revisited: The New Dale-Chall readability formula. Brookline Books, Brookline (1995)
2. Cohn, M.: User Stories Applied: For Agile Software Development. Addison Wesley, Boston (2004)
3. Damian, D., Chisan, J., Vaidyanathasamy, L., Pal, Y.: Requirements engineering and downstream software development: Findings from a case study. Empir. Softw. Eng. **10**(3), 255–283 (2005)
4. Davis, C.W.H.: Agile Metrics in Action: Measuring and Enhancing the Performance of Agile Teams, 1st edn. Manning Publications Co., Greenwich (2015)
5. Gunning, R.: Technique of Clear Writing. McGraw-Hill, New York (1968)
6. Holm, H., Sommestad, T., Bengtsson, J.: Requirements engineering: the quest for the dependent variable. In: Proceedings of IEEE International Requirements Engineering Conference (RE), pp. 16–25 (2015)
7. Kamata, M.I., Tamai, T.: How does requirements quality relate to project success or failure? In: Proceedings of IEEE International Requirements Engineering Conference (RE), pp. 69–78 (2007)
8. Kassab, M.: The changing landscape of requirements engineering practices over the past decade. In: Proceedings of International Workshop on Empirical Requirements Engineering (EmpiRE), pp. 1–8. IEEE (2015)
9. Knauss, E., Boustani, C., Flohr, T.: Investigating the impact of software requirements specification quality on project success. In: Bomarius, F., Oivo, M., Jaring, P., Abrahamsson, P. (eds.) PROFES 2009. LNBIP, vol. 32, pp. 28–42. Springer, Heidelberg (2009). doi:10.1007/978-3-642-02152-7_4

10. Kniberg, H.: What is Crisp? (2010). http://blog.crisp.se/2010/05/08/henrikknib erg/what-is-crisp. Accessed 25 May 2016

11. Lucassen, G.: Experimental materials QUS and AQUSA evaluation (2016). http:// www.staff.science.uu.nl/lucas001/qus_aqusa_eval_materials.zip. Accessed 02 Oct 2016

12. Lucassen, G., Dalpiaz, F., Werf, J.M.E.M., Brinkkemper, S.: The use and effectiveness of user stories in practice. In: Daneva, M., Pastor, O. (eds.) REFSQ 2016. LNCS, vol. 9619, pp. 205–222. Springer, Heidelberg (2016). doi:10.1007/978-3-319-30282-9_14

13. Lucassen, G., Dalpiaz, F., van der Werf, J.M.E.M., Brinkkemper, S.: Improving agile requirements: the quality user story framework and tool. Requir. Eng. 21(3), 383–403 (2016)

14. Madeyski, L., Jureczko, M.: Which process metrics can significantly improve defect prediction models? An empirical study. Softw. Qual. J. 23(3), 393–422 (2015)

15. McCabe, T.J.: A complexity measure. IEEE Trans. Softw. Eng. SE-2(4), 308–320 (1976)

16. Méndez Fernández, D., Wagner, S.: A case study on artefact-based re improvement in practice. In: Abrahamsson, P., Corral, L., Oivo, M., Russo, B. (eds.) PROFES 2015. LNCS, vol. 9459, pp. 114–130. Springer, Heidelberg (2015). doi:10.1007/978-3-319-26844-6_9

17. Napier, N.P., Mathiassen, L., Johnson, R.D.: Combining perceptions and prescriptions in requirements engineering process assessment: an industrial case study. IEEE Trans. Softw. Eng. 35(5), 593–606 (2009)

18. Runeson, P., Höst, M.: Guidelines for conducting and reporting case study research in software engineering. Empir. Softw. Eng. 14(2), 131–164 (2009)

19. Schröter, A., Zimmermann, T., Premraj, R., Zeller, A.: If your bug database could talk. In: Proceedings of International Symposium on Empirical Software Engineering (ISESE), pp. 18–20 (2006)

20. Shihab, E., Jiang, Z.M., Ibrahim, W.M., Adams, B., Hassan, A.E.: Understanding the impact of code and process metrics on post-release defects: a case study on the Eclipse project. In: Proceedings of International Symposium on Empirical Software Engineering and Measurement (ESEM), pp. 4:1–4:10. ACM (2010)

21. Sommerville, I., Ransom, J.: An empirical study of industrial requirements engineering process assessment and improvement. ACM Trans. Softw. Eng. Methodol. 14(1), 85–117 (2005)

22. Tague-Sutcliffe, J.: The pragmatics of information retrieval experimentation, revisited. Inf. Process. Manag. 28(4), 467–490 (1992)

23. Unterkalmsteiner, M., Gorschek, T., Islam, A.K.M.M., Cheng, C.K., Permadi, R.B., Feldt, R.: Evaluation and measurement of software process improvement - a systematic literature review. IEEE Trans. Softw. Eng. 38(2), 398–424 (2012)

24. Vajjala, S., Meurers, D.: Readability-based sentence ranking for evaluating text simplification (2016). arXiv e-prints arXiv:1603.06009

25. Wang, X., Zhao, L., Wang, Y., Sun, J.: The role of requirements engineering practices in agile development: an empirical study. In: Zowghi, D., Jin, Z. (eds.) Requir. Eng. CCIS, vol. 432, pp. 195–209. Springer, Heidelberg (2014). doi:10.1007/978-3-662-43610-3_15

26. Zimmermann, T., Premraj, R., Zeller, A.: Predicting defects for Eclipse. In: Proceedings of PROMISE 2007 Workshop (2007)

Natural Language Processing, Information Retrieval and Machine Learning

Semi-automatic Software Feature-Relevant Information Extraction from Natural Language User Manuals

An Approach and Practical Experience at Roche Diagnostics GmbH

Thomas Quirchmayr[1(✉)], Barbara Paech[1], Roland Kohl[2], and Hannes Karey[2]

[1] Institute for Computer Science, University of Heidelberg, Heidelberg, Germany
{thomas.quirchmayr,barbara.paech}@informatik.uni-heidelberg.de
[2] Roche Diagnostics GmbH, Mannheim, Germany
{roland.kohl,hannes.karey}@roche.com

Abstract. *Context and motivation*: Mature software systems comprise a vast number of heterogeneous system capabilities which are usually requested by different groups of stakeholders and which evolve over time. Software features describe and bundle low level capabilities logically on an abstract level and thus provide a structured and comprehensive overview of the entire capabilities of a software system. *Question/problem*: Software features are often not explicitly managed. Quite the contrary, feature-relevant information is often spread across several software engineering artifacts (e.g., user manual, issue tracking systems). It requires huge manual effort to identify and extract feature-relevant information from these artifacts in order to make feature knowledge explicit. *Principal ideas/results*: Our semi-automatic approach allows to identify and extract atomic software feature-relevant information from natural language user manuals by means of a domain glossary, structural sentence information, and natural language processing techniques with a precision and recall of over 94% and 96% respectively. *Contribution*: We provide an implementation of the atomic software feature-relevant information extraction approach together with this paper as well as corresponding evaluations based on example sections of a user manual taken from industry.

Keywords: Software feature · Information extraction · Natural language processing

1 Introduction

The necessity of feature-based software system descriptions is manifold: release planning in software product management (see, e.g., [41], software product line engineering (see, e.g., [5]), requirements feature interaction detection (see, e.g., [36]), stakeholder communication (see, e.g., [35]), as well as software product

P. Grünbacher and A. Perini (Eds.): REFSQ 2017, LNCS 10153, pp. 255–272, 2017.
DOI: 10.1007/978-3-319-54045-0_19

comparison (see, e.g., [16]). However, features are often not explicitly managed, at least not from scratch. Rather, feature-relevant (FR) information is spread across several software engineering (SE) artifacts. Thus, these artifacts need to be searched in order to uncover FR information. In our prior paper [34], we pointed out that user manuals can serve as an appropriate source to gather FR information from a user workflow-driven perspective. Depending on the size of the software system and thus the size of the corresponding user manual, manual FR information extraction is cumbersome, error-prone, and costly (see, e.g., [38]). As a consequence, our overall research goal is to provide automated support to extract features and related FR information from natural language (NL) user manuals.

In this paper, we report on an approach which semi-automatically extracts atomic FR information from NL user manuals based on lexical and syntactic text characteristics. Furthermore, we evaluate our approach based on data of a user manual of a bespoke in-house customer relationship management (CRM) software system of Roche Diagnostics GmbH (in the following *Roche*). Roche is a globally operating company with more than 5000 employees. The in-house development department focuses on the implementation of bespoke software systems and the customization of buy-in standard software. The CRM software system is called Global Deal Calculator (GDC) and it supports contract life cycle management. Roche started to manage features for GDC recently. However, they do not have a complete feature-based description of the entire GDC. Therefore, Roche wants to complete the GDC features with minimal manual effort from the existing and up-to-date GDC user manual retrospectively.

We did a first exploration of Roche's user manual. It showed, that it is impossible to extract features directly from the user manual, because (1) features are often only implicitly mentioned (e.g., the sentence *"The quantificator calculates materials."* describes the feature *price calculation* only implicitly as the term "price" is not mentioned in the sentence) and (2) relevant information is spread across the entire user manual. Therefore, we follow a bottom-up approach, that is to extract atomic FR information and cluster it logically into features afterwards.

The remainder of this paper is structured as follows: Sect. 2 gives an overview of the feature concept as well as insight into natural language processing techniques used in our approach. Section 3 describes our approach for atomic FR information extraction and Sect. 4 provides an evaluation based on example data from the GDC user manual. Section 5 discusses threats to validity followed by a discussion of related work in Sect. 6. Finally, Sect. 7 concludes the paper and discusses future contributions.

2   Background

The term *feature* is widely used in computing: from image processing (e.g., image structure [33]), signal processing (e.g., aiming to capture specific aspects of audio signals in a numeric way [33]) to computer linguistics (e.g., property of a class of linguistic terms which describes individual members of this class [15]), machine learning (e.g., specification of an attribute and its value [8]), and software engineering (e.g., characteristic of a software item [20]). Even within the domain of software engineering, there is neither a common understanding nor a precise definition of a feature in literature (see, e.g., [4,14,30]) as well as in practice. Therefore, in the context of this paper, we define a feature as follows (inspired by [9,17]):

> A **feature** describes an abstract unit of behaviour of a software system at a high level and bundles atomic information which describe the unit of behaviour at a detail level. The latter is called atomic feature-relevant information.

As an example, *"Quantificator calculates materials"* is an atomic FR unit of information of the feature *"Price Calculation"*. An atomic unit of information, in contrast to combined information, cannot be broken down into other simpler units of information without losing information (see, e.g., [11,24]). In short, we want to extract smallest bits of information. Based on the requirement of information *atomicity*, we define a **linguistic information model** (LIM) for atomic FR information (see Fig. 1).

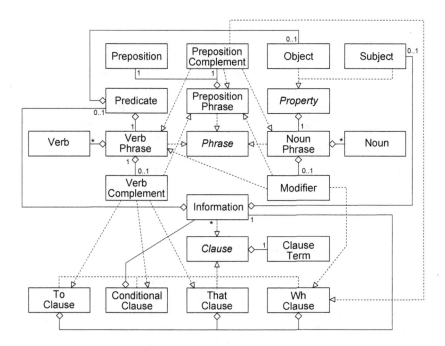

Fig. 1. Linguistic information model (LIM)

An atomic unit of *Information* is a *Clause* and comprises at most one *Subject* and one *Predicate*. A *Clause* contains one *Clause Term* and is either a *To Clause*, a *Conditional Clause*, a *That Clause*, or a *Wh Clause*. Additionally, Clauses comprise Information. In contrast to the other Clauses, a Conditional Clause might contain more than one atomic unit of Information as combined conditions (e.g., *If the quantificator runs AND the error is shown*) cannot be separated. A *Predicate* requires a *Verb Phrase* which comprises at least one *Verb* and optional *Verb Complements*. Furthermore, a *Predicate* might include an *Object*. Both *Subject* and *Object* are a *Property*, which contains a *Noun Phrase*. A *Noun Phrase* consists of *Nouns* and *Modifiers*. For simplification, adverbs are included in *Verbs*, and adjectives are included in *Nouns*. Figure 2 depicts some components of the LIM based on two example sentences.

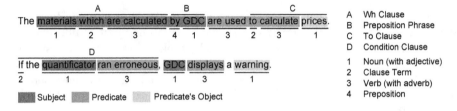

Fig. 2. LIM components based on 2 example sentences

Our approach utilizes NL processing (NLP) techniques (see, e.g., [21]) in order to extract FR information on detail level and split them into atomic units of FR information. Basically, we use a part-of-speech (POS) parser (see, e.g., [21]) in order to determine the syntax of NL texts. A POS parser determines the syntax of a sentence providing a parse tree as output. A parse tree is a rooted and ordered tree which represents the syntax of a given textual sentence based on some context-free grammar (see, e.g., [12]). In order to measure the performance of a POS parser, we refer to the *accuracy* as the ratio of the amount of correct parse trees ($|PT_c|$) and the total amount of parse trees ($|PT|$) as output of a POS parser:

$$\text{accuracy} = \frac{|PT_c|}{|PT|}, \ PT_c \subset PT$$

3   Atomic Feature-Relevant Information Extraction

In general, gathering and extracting FR information from NL user manuals poses the challenge, that the manual's textual content is usually not structured along features. More precisely, these documents lack FR meta data [2]. The analysis of the GDC user manual showed that we are able to identify potentially FR sentences by means of domain terms: each sentence which contains at least one domain term is considered to potentially contain FR information.

Figure 3 shows our approach to semi-automatically extract atomic FR information. Each process step is described in detail in the following.

User Manual Revision (*manual, optional*): NLP techniques require a syntactically correct textual basis in order to deliver correct results. Therefore, in a

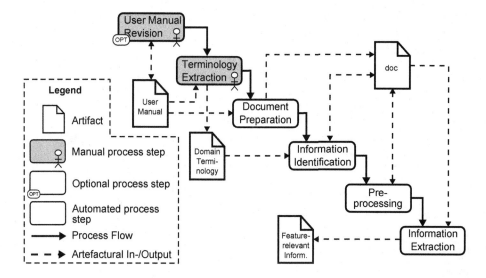

Fig. 3. Atomic feature-relevant information extraction process

first step, a user manual revision might be performed in order to ensure syntactical correctness. In case the user manual is already syntactically correct, this process step can be skipped. When our approach is fully developed, this will be the only manual step in the approach. Clearly, the effort depends on the quality of the user manual. In any case, this revision can be done by a non-expert (e.g. we asked a student helper from translation studies for support). Thus, the effort is acceptable.

Terminology Extraction (*manual*) deals with the extraction of domain-specific terms (domain terms in short) from the user manual. The domain terms are required to further identify potentially FR sentences (see, e.g., [39]). At the current state of our research, this step is still a manual task: domain experts need to extract a set of domain-specific terms (*Domain Terminology*) from the user manual. In the context of our approach, the last two authors of this paper act as GDC domain experts. In the future, we plan to automatically support terminology extraction (see, e.g., [25]).

Document Preparation (*automated*) aims to automatically extract all relevant data (NL text and corresponding structural information) from a user manual as Microsoft Word document (*.docx). Compared to other document formats (e.g., *.pdf), the extraction of structural information (e.g., bullet point, heading, etc.) is easy and open source by means of available APIs (e.g., Apache POI[1]). The data are then transformed into an internal data model (*doc*) which eases further processing. This step is illustrated in Fig. 4. The contents of a users' manual might contain both text and associated images (see left hand side of Fig. 4). The text is split into paragraphs containing at least one sentence

---

[1] https://poi.apache.org/.

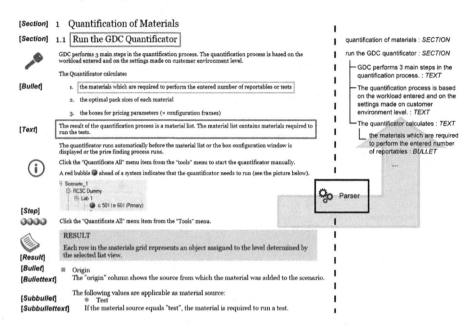

Fig. 4. Document preparation (left: user manual excerpt, right: *doc*) (Color figure online)

(see, e.g., red, green, and yellow rim). A sentence can be either complete (blue rim) or incomplete (yellow rim). In contrast to an incomplete sentence, a complete sentence contains at least a subject and a predicate. Additionally, incomplete sentences appear to convey only parts of a complete thought, lacking some components which are grammatically necessary to complete the thought [37].

The entire content of a user manual is usually structured (e.g., (sub-)sections, bullets, listings). This structural information (we call it *sentence type*) conveys additional implicit semantic information to the reader (e.g., an enumeration indicates a conjunction of the enumerated sentences). Figure 4 depicts example sentence types in blue square brackets on the left hand side (they are not part of the user manual itself). The GDC user manual comprises 8 different sentence types, namely text, bullet, bullet text, sub-bullet, sub-bullet text, step, section, and result. By means of the Apache POI API, the NL text as well as the sentence types are extracted (indicated by *Parser* in Fig. 4). Furthermore, we apply some minor automated adjustments to correct wrong sentence types (e.g., a text cannot directly be followed by a sub-bullet, therefore it is changed to a bullet automatically).

Information Identification (*automated*) determines potentially FR sentences by means of predefined exclusion patterns, the sentence type, and the extracted domain terminology. In the course of the analysis of the GDC user manual, we uncovered general lexical exclusion patterns which allow to

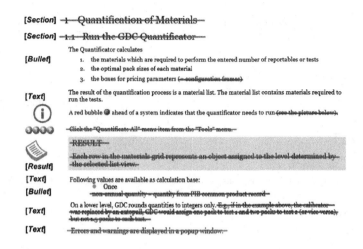

Fig. 5. Information identification example (Color figure online)

automatically identify *feature-irrelevant* sentences or phrases (part of a sentence) in sentences, namely:

- phrases in brackets, e.g., *The quantificator needs to run (see the picture below)*.
- phrases or sentences starting with "e.g."
- phrases or sentences including "section" or "figure", e.g., *Section "Quantification of Materials" describes [. . .]*.
- phrases or sentences which represent formulas, e.g., $x = 120\,pc/60\,pc * 100$

First, all feature-irrelevant sentences and phrases which match the exclusion patterns are removed in order to decrease the amount of data to be processed (see phrases crossed out with blue lines in Fig. 5). Second, sentences of the types section, result, and step are filtered (see phrases crossed out with red lines in Fig. 5). Finally, the remaining sentences are investigated regarding domain terms: each sentence which contains at least one domain term is considered to potentially contain FR information, all the others are ignored (see phrases crossed out with green lines in Fig. 5).

Preprocessing (*automated*): Our approach extracts atomic FR information based on syntactic patterns in parse trees. Thus, the approach highly depends on correct parse trees. We use the Stanford POS parser[2] [26] to generate a parse tree for each FR sentence. Without textual or parse tree based modifications, the accuracy of Stanford's POS parser is not sufficient (see Sect. 4). In order to improve the POS parser accuracy, we apply two automated preprocessing steps:

(a) **Lexical-based textual modifications (*automated*):** we apply lowercasing to the entire text. Afterwards, we search for domain terms (e.g., *material list*) and quoted terms (e.g., *"start quantificator"*) contained in the text.

---

[2] http://nlp.stanford.edu/software/lex-parser.shtml.

*the user tries to open the **material list**,*
*but **gdc** detects invalid **test** data*

```
(S
 (NP (DT the) (NN user))
 (VP
  (VP (VBZ tries)
   (S
    (VP (TO to)
     (VP (VB open)
      (NP (DT the (NN material) (NN list))))))
   (, ,)
   (CC but)
   (VP (VBP gdc)
    (NP
     (ADJP (JJ detects) (JJ invalid))
     (NN test) (NNS data)))))))
```

(a) Without textual modifications

*the user tries to open the **DTmaterialDTlist**,*
*but **DTgdc** detects invalid **DTtest** data*

```
(S
 (NP (DT the) (NN user))
 (VP (VBZ tries)
  (S
   (VP (TO to)
    (VP (VB open)
     (NP (DT the (NN DTmaterialDTlist)))))))
  (, ,)
  (CC but)
  (S
   (NP (NNP DTgdc)
    (VP (VBZ detects)
     (NP (JJ invalid) (NN DTtest) (NNS data)))))))
```

(b) With textual modifications

Fig. 6. POS parser accuracy increases with domain term (**bold**) bundling (Color figure online)

They are then equipped with prefixes and finally bundled (e.g. *material list* becomes *DTmaterialDTlist*, "*start quantificator*" becomes *QDstartQDquantificator*). As a consequence, the Stanford NLP parser treats them as single nouns instead of trying to parse the terms separately (see, e.g., [18]). Figure 6 shows the difference of the resulting parse trees: Fig. 6a treats *gdc*, which is a domain term, as verb (blue rim) which actually distorts the entire parse tree structure. Figure 6b shows the same sentence with the textual modifications applied. *DTgdc* is correctly treated as a noun (blue rim) and thus the entire parse tree becomes correct too.

(b) **Pattern-based parse tree transformations (*automated*):** In total, we identified 7 recurring patterns in parse trees which indicate incorrect parts of a parse tree. By means of Tregex [27], which is a utility for matching patterns in parse trees, the incorrect parts of a parse tree can be identified. Tsurgeon [27], which is a tree-transformation utility built on top of Tregex, allows to manipulate the identified parse trees as desired. Figure 7 shows an example of an incorrect parse tree (left hand side), which is corrected (right hand side) by means of a Tregex pattern and Tsurgeon (see upper part).

Information Extraction (*automated*): After successfully identifying potentially FR sentences and normalizing their parse trees, FR information is extracted in four iterative steps: (1) syntactic information extraction, (2) information simplification, (3) enumeration resolution, and (4) syntactical relevance determination.

(1) **Syntactic Information Extraction (*automated*):** FR information is extracted from each sentence by traversing the parse tree and determining relevant LIM-elements iteratively by means of POS patterns (e.g., a preposition following a noun phrase like "number *of reportables*" indicates a modifier of the type preposition phrase):

1. subjects (noun phrases + modifiers)
2. predicates (verb phrases + complements)
3. objects of predicates (noun phrases + modifiers)
4. conditional clauses

```
String patternString = "NP=par $+ (NP=del <+(NP) (NP < __=mov $+ __=mov2))";
TregexPattern tregexPattern = TregexPattern.compile(patternString);
String surgeryString = "[move mov >-1 par][move mov2 $- par][delete del]";
TsurgeonPattern surgery = Tsurgeon.parseOperation(surgeryString);
Tree tree = Tsurgeon.processPattern(tregexPattern, surgery, tree);
```

```
(ROOT                                  (ROOT
 (NP                                    (NP
  (NP (DT the) (JJ optimal) (NN pack))   (NP (DT the) (JJ optimal) (NN pack) (NNS sizes))
  (NP                                    (PP (IN of)
   (NP (NNS sizes))                       (NP (DT each) (NNP material)))))
   (PP (IN of)
    (NP (DT each) (NNP material))))))))
```

Fig. 7. Parse Tree Transformation Example in Java

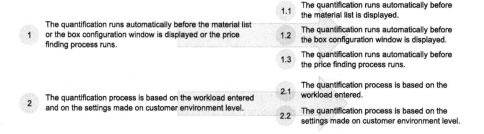

Fig. 8. Information simplification example

Each potential FR sentence results in exactly one unit of **potential** FR information which might not be atomic yet.

(2) **Information simplification (*automated*):** In order to retrieve atomic units of information, all conjunctions in phrases, clauses (except conditional clauses), complements, and modifiers are resolved; each conjunction element becomes part of a new atomic unit of information (see Fig. 8).

(3) **Enumeration Resolution (*automated*):** The user manual excerpt on the left hand side of Fig. 4 shows a paragraph with a bullet list. Paragraphs which contain bullet lists need to be resolved in order to retrieve atomic information. Resolving a bullet list means to combine the potential FR information from the introducing sentence (e.g., *The quantificator calculates*) with each potential FR information of the related bullet sentence (e.g., *the optimal pack size of each material*), depending on the corresponding syntax of the information (see Fig. 9). In total, we identified 11 different syntactical patterns which entail different combinations.

The Quantificator calculates
...
2. the optimal pack size of each material

The following materials are available:
..
- reagent

The Quantificator calculates the optimal pack size of each material.

The material reagent is available.

Fig. 9. Enumeration resolution example

(4) **Syntactical Relevance Determination (*automated*):** Finally, we differentiate between truly FR information and feature-irrelevant information based on the syntax. An unit of information is syntactically relevant (and thus FR) if its syntax (based on the LIM) equals one out of 11 predefined patterns; else it is considered syntactically irrelevant and thus feature-irrelevant. A pattern defines the LIM-elements (e.g., subject + predicate + object) which need to be present in a FR unit of information (e.g., *the quantificator calculates materials.*) On the other hand, each potentially FR information which does not match a predefined pattern (e.g., *"The quantificator runs."* contains only subject + predicate) is feature-irrelevant.

4   Evaluation

In order to evaluate the performance of our approach, we created three gold standards: the gold standards *feature-relevant sentences* as well as *atomic feature-relevant information* from the FR sentences were provided by the GDC experts. The gold standard *correct parse trees* was provided by the first author as there is no GDC-specific knowledge required.

The GDC user manual contains more than 600 pages in its current version. The example sections chosen for evaluation comprise in total 43 pages. The sections contain 1161 sentences (complete as well as incomplete). The sentences are distributed over the different sentence types as follows: 46.7% text (543 sentences), 29.6% bullet text (343), 7.9% bullet (92), 5.2% step (60), 3.9% section (45), 3.5% result (41), 2.3% sub-bullet text (27), and 0.9% sub-bullet (10). The GDC experts investigated the sentences and determined whether or not they contain FR information: 639 sentences are feature-relevant and 522 are not. Furthermore, the GDC experts extracted the atomic FR information from the 639 feature-relevant sentences. In total, they determined 849 atomic FR units of information (1.33 FR units of information per FR sentence). We evaluated the accuracy using the standard metrics precision (P), recall (R) and F_1-score (F_1). Precision is the fraction of retrieved instances which are relevant, whereas recall is the fraction of relevant instances which are retrieved. The F_1 score considers both precision and recall as their harmonic mean. They are calculated as follows:

$$P_i = \frac{TP_i}{TP_i + FP_i} \qquad R_i = \frac{TP_i}{TP_i + FN_i} \qquad F_{1_i} = \frac{P_i \times R_i}{P_i + R_i}$$

The subordinated i in precision, recall and F_1 refers to the actual type we are investigating in the corresponding evaluation context: in context of *information identification* and *information extraction*, i refers to *FR sentences* and *atomic FR information* respectively. True positives (TP_i) are instances which are classified as and actually are of type i. False positives (FP_i) are instances which are classified as but actually are not of type i. False negatives (FN_i) are instances which are classified as type $j \neq i$ but actually are of type i. Last, true negatives (TN_i) are instances which are classified as and actually are of type $j \neq i$.

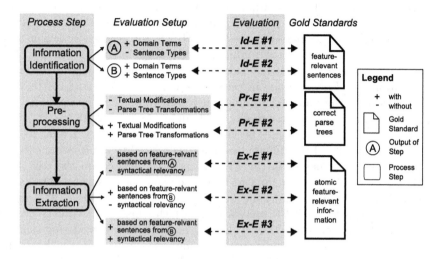

Fig. 10. Evaluation overview

Figure 10 shows an overview of the different evaluations for our approach. The left hand side depicts the selected steps of our approach (see Fig. 3 in Sect. 3) which are evaluated. The right hand side shows the three gold standards. The upper part shows two evaluations (*Id-E #1 &#2*) in context of *Information Identification*. Id-E #1 compares the FR sentences (A) identified by means of domain terms without considering sentence types with the FR sentences from the gold standard. Id-Eval #2 compares the FR sentences (B) identified by means of domain terms considering sentence types with the FR sentences from the gold standard. Regarding *Document Processing*, we provide two evaluations: the first one does not consider textual modifications and parse tree transformation (*Pr-E #1*), while the second one (*Pr-E #2*) does. *Information Extraction* is based on the identified FR sentences. Therefore, we provide three evaluations. As a basis for increasing extraction accuracy, the first evaluation (*Ex-E #1*) uses the FR sentences (A) and does not consider syntactical relevancy determination. Both, evaluation *Ex-E #2* and *#3* are based on the FR sentences (B). They differ with respect to the consideration of syntactical relevancy determination: Ex-E #2 does not consider, and Ex-E #3 considers syntactical relevancy determination.

(1) **Information Identification:** The first two columns of Table 1 represent the evaluation results for the identification of FR sentences. Initially, we only use the domain terms in order to identify FR sentences (see Id-E #1). We achieve a precision and recall of 73.54% and 98.75% respectively, which

results in a F_1 score of 84.30%. Considering sentence types and feature-irrelevant patterns (see *Information Identification* in Sect. 3) improves the precision and F_1 score to 80.69% and 88.81% respectively (see Id-E #2).

(2) **Preprocessing:** The evaluation of preprocessing is different compared to information identification and information extraction. It solely evaluates the accuracy of the POS parser related to both FR and feature-irrelevant sentences. The accuracy of the Stanford POS parser in context of the 1161 example sentences without any textual modifications and parse tree transformation (see *Preprocessing* in Sect. 3) is 76.41%. By applying the textual modifications, the sentence accuracy increased to 95.26%; by applying the parse tree modifications, we finally reach an accuracy of 98.43%.

(3) **Information Extraction:** The last three columns in Table 1 refer to the evaluation results of the different evaluations related to information extraction. Ex-E #1 is based on the FR sentences Ⓐ. Based on the 639 (631 TP + 8 FP) FR sentences from Id-E #1, our approach identifies 99.06% of all atomic units of FR information, but with a precision of 77.23% only. Based on the identified FR sentences Ⓑ which considered sentence types, the precision increased to 83.02% (Ex-E #2). Finally, by considering *syntactical relevance*, the precision remarkably increased to 94.06% which results in a final F_1 score of 95.48% (Ex-E #3). The recall decreases, because 18 units of information which are actually FR do not match our syntactical patterns (e.g., *The correction factor can be switched off*) and are therefore considered feature-irrelevant.

Table 1. Evaluation results

Metrics	Identification		Extraction		
	Id-E #1	Id-E #2	Ex-E #1	Ex-E #2	Ex-E #3
TP	631	**631**	841	**841**	823
TN	295	371	301	377	497
FP	227	151	248	172	52
FN	8	8	8	8	26
R	98.75%	**98.75%**	99.06%	**99.06%**	96.94%
P	73.54%	80.69%	77.23%	83.02%	94.06%
F_1	84.30%	88.81%	86.79%	90.33%	95.48%

5 Threats to Validity

This section discusses the threats to internal and external validity of our results and the measures taken to minimize these threats.

5.1 Threats to Internal Validity

Internal validity refers to the extent to which the procedure influenced the result. User manual revision was applied on two different sections of the user manual. The first section was revised by the first author of the paper, the second section was revised by a non-author who got instructed a priori. In order to compute precision and recall we compared the results of our approach with two gold standards (see Sect. 4). These gold standards were created by the two last authors of our paper which are domain experts. As they did not participate in the development and implementation of our approach, the gold standard is not influenced by the developed approach.

5.2 Threats to External Validity

External validity refers to the extent to whether the approach can be applied in other contexts. In the following we discuss the effort needed to adapt our approach to another context. Our approach utilizes different techniques in four iterative process steps in order to extract atomic FR information automatically. *Document Preparation* extracts NL text and sentence types from a user manual. The sentence types might differ between different user manuals, but can be simply exchanged in a configuration file of our tool after determining them manually with low effort. *Information Identification* aims to identify sentences which potentially contain FR information by means of domain terms, their sentence type and basic lexical exclusion patterns. The exclusion patterns can be defined via regular expressions in the configuration file too. These patterns refer to e.g., formulas, examples, and sections. This information is feature-irrelevant, independent of the domain. The patterns can be adapted again with low effort. *Preprocessing* generates a parse tree for each potentially FR sentence by means of a POS parser as well as automated textual and parse tree modifications; neither textual nor parse tree modifications are domain-specific. *Information Extraction*: Based on the sentence type of a sentence, the potentially FR information are then automatically extracted and simplified into atomic units of information. Finally, the FR units of information are determined based on predefined syntactical patterns. However, the results of the approach highly depend on the syntax of the natural language text provided in the user manual and furthermore the accuracy of the POS parser. This approach was developed in the context of GDC. We developed it based on one section with considerable effort. The adaptations for the next sections were minor. Thus, we believe that this approach will work well for the whole manual. We believe that this approach could work well for other domains too. However, the adaptations for other user manuals are difficult to judge without knowing the specifics. Altogether, our approach should be adaptable to other domains with acceptable effort.

6 Related Work

Berry et al. [7] define four broad categories of tools which analyze NL texts in context of requirements engineering (RE): (a) finding defects and deviations in

NL RE documents, (b) generating models from NL descriptions, (c) inferring trace links between NL RE artifacts, and (d) identifying key abstractions from NL documents. We follow a bottom-up approach, that is to extract atomic FR units of information from a user manual first and determine corresponding features (by logically clustering the atomic FR information) afterwards. Thus, our approach is related to category (b) as well as category (d). In the following, we focus on related work from both categories.

Several approaches exist which extract features and corresponding models from textual requirements documents in an automated (e.g., [28]), semi-automated (e.g., [29]), or manual (e.g., [23]) way. Besides *user manual revision* and *terminology extraction*, our approach is fully automated.

Bakar et al. [5] provide a recent overview about feature extraction. They identified several kinds of requirements documents used for feature extraction, ranging from software requirements specifications (see, e.g., [10]), to product description (see, e.g., [1]) to user comments (see, e.g., [19]), issue tracking systems (e.g., [31]), and online software reviews (e.g., [6]). In a previous work [34] we found, that user manuals provide consistent FR information. Especially for mature software systems (e.g., Roche's GDC), user manuals may often be the most up-to-date and valuable source for FR information.

Bakar et al. also identified different types of output from existing feature extraction approaches: trees or models (see, e.g., [38]), keywords (see, e.g., [10]), NL phrases (see, e.g., [32]), or clustered requirements (see, e.g., [3]). Depending on the stakeholder's viewpoint and intention regarding features, the desired level of information might differ: whilst IT managers (e.g., CIO) might want to overview abstract software features (e.g., in order to evaluate alternative software), project managers might need more detailed information (e.g., regarding communalities/variabilities), and developers might furthermore need even more detailed information (e.g., displayed columns of a screen). Therefore, we chose a bottom-up approach to hierarchically capture and provide FR information throughout different levels in the future: features (and sub-features) on higher levels and related atomic FR units of information on detailed level.

Many feature extraction approaches use NLP (see, e.g., [10]) or information retrieval techniques (see, e.g., [3,31]) to identify and extract relevant information. The range of NLP techniques used, is very broad (e.g., POS tagging, stemming, lemmatization [21]). Information retrieval techniques (e.g., clustering, classification) often utilize machine learning (ML) algorithms, most of them are supervised. Supervised algorithms in context of ML refer to algorithms which learn from labeled training data (pair of input and desired output) in order to make predictions on unlabeled data. The preparation of training data requires huge manual effort. Thus, our approach relies on (automated) process steps utilizing NLP techniques which need little - compared to supervised ML training data - manually prepared input.

Some feature extraction approaches (see, e.g., [28,32,40] require syntactically and/or lexically restricted textual input (e.g., noun + verb + noun [40]) in order to extract the desired output. Our approach uses syntactical and lexical patterns too. But in contrast, our basic lexical patterns (e.g., exclude phrases starting with "e.g.") are used as exclusion and not as inclusion criteria. Furthermore, we do not combine lexical and syntactic patterns (e.g., noun + "have" + noun) as this limits the application of an approach considerably. To the best of our knowledge, we present the first semi-automatic domain-independent approach which extracts atomic feature-relevant information by means of a domain terminology in combination with syntactical patterns.

7   Conclusion and Future Work

In this paper, we present an approach to semi-automatically extract atomic FR information from NL user manuals. Besides the process steps *User Manual Revision* (optional) and *Terminology Extraction*, our approach is fully automated. In order to evaluate the practical application and feasibility, we conduct a case study in a real-world industrial setting and report their results. Through the application of several automated textual modifications and parse tree transformations, we are able to show increasing POS parser accuracy. Based on the resulting parse trees, our approach allows to extract atomic FR information with both a precision and recall of above 94%.

The long term goal of our research is to extract related features and corresponding information from user manuals. Therefore, future work comprises three main parts:

1. **Domain Terminology Extraction:** Currently, the domain terminology must be provided by domain experts. Similar to feature extraction itself, manual terminology extraction involves a huge effort. Therefore, we plan to support terminology extraction with a pipeline of NLP-technologies (see, e.g., [22, 25]).
2. **Software Feature Clustering:** As already mentioned in Section 2, features are composed of logically related atomic FR units of information. Therefore, we need to cluster logically related FR units of information to generate superordinate features (bottom-up approach) by means of information retrieval technologies (see, e.g., [13, 28]).
3. **Application on entire GDC User Manual:** As a last step, we will apply our approach to the entire GDC user manual in order to provide a comprehensive and structured overview of the GDC features and corresponding FR information.

Acknowledgements. We would like to thank Roche Diagnostics GmbH for the financial support of this research project. Many thanks also to the GDC experts for their participation in the case study and valuable discussions of the results.

References

1. Acher, M., Cleve, A., Perrouin, G., Heymans, P., Vanbeneden, C., Collet, P., Lahire, P.: On extracting feature models from product descriptions. In: Proceedings of 6th International Workshop on Variability Modeling of Software-Intensive Systems (VaMoS 2012), pp. 45–54. ACM (2012)

2. Aggarwal, C., Zhai, C.: Mining Text Data. Springer, Heidelberg (2012)
3. Alves, V., Schwanninger, C., Barbosa, L., Rashid, A., Sawyer, P., Rayson, P., Pohl, C., Rummler, A.: An exploratory study of information retrieval techniques in domain analysis. In: Proceedings of 12th International Software Product Line Conference (SPLC 2008), pp. 67–76 (2008)
4. Apel, S., Kästner, C.: An overview of feature-oriented software development. Object Technol. **8**(5), 49–84 (2009)
5. Bakar, N.H., Kasirun, Z.M., Salleh, N.: Feature extraction approaches from natural language requirements for reuse in software product lines. Syst. Softw. **106**(C), 132–149 (2015)
6. Bakar, N.H., Kasirun, Z.M., Salleh, N.: Terms extractions: an approach for requirements reuse. In: 2nd International Conference on Information Science and Security (ICISS), pp. 1–4 (2015)
7. Berry, D., Gacitua, R., Sawyer, P., Tjong, S.F.: The case for dumb requirements engineering tools. In: Regnell, B., Damian, D. (eds.) REFSQ 2012. LNCS, vol. 7195, pp. 211–217. Springer, Heidelberg (2012). doi:10.1007/978-3-642-28714-5_18
8. Bishop, C.M.: Pattern Recognition and Machine Learning. Springer, Berlin (2006)
9. Bosch, J.: Design and Use of Software Architectures: Adopting and Evolving a Product-line Approach. ACM Press, New York (2000)
10. Boutkova, E., Houdek, F.: Semi-automatic identification of features in requirement specifications. In: Proceedings of 19th International Requirements Engineering Conference (RE 2011), pp. 313–318 (2011)
11. Chandrasekar, R., Doran, C., Srinivas, B.: Motivations and methods for text simplification. In: Proceedings of 16th Conference on Computational Linguistics (COLING), pp. 1041–1044 (1996)
12. Charniak, E.: Statistical parsing with a context-free grammar and word statistics. In: AAAI/IAAI, pp. 598–603 (1997)
13. Chen, K., Zhang, W., Zhao, H., Mei, H.: An approach to constructing feature models based on requirements clustering. In: Proceedings of 13th International Requirements Engineering Conf. (RE 2005), pp. 31–40 (2005)
14. Classen, A., Heymans, P., Schobbens, P.-Y.: What's in a feature: a requirements engineering perspective. In: Proceedings of 11th International Conference on Fundamental Approaches to Software Engineering (FASE 2008), pp. 16–30 (2008)
15. Corbett, G.: Linguistic features. Afr. Aff. **87**, 25–54 (2006)
16. Earls, A., Embury, S., Turner, N.: A method for the manual extraction of business rules from legacy source code. BT Technol. **20**(4), 127–145 (2002)
17. Eisenbarth, T., Koschke, R., Simon, D.: Locating features in source code. Trans. Softw. Eng. **29**(3), 210–224 (2003)
18. Ghosh, S., Elenius, D., Li, W., Lincoln, P., Shankar, N., Steiner, W.: Arsenal: automatic requirements specification extracting from natural language. In: Proceedings of 8th Interantional Symposium of NASA Formal Methods (NFM 2016), pp. 41–46 (2016)
19. Guzman, E., Maalej, W.: How do users like this feature? A fine grained sentiment analysis of app. reviews. In: Proceedings of 22nd International Requirements Engineering Conference (RE 2014), pp. 153–162. IEEE (2014)
20. IEEE: IEEE Standard Glossary of Software Engineering Terminology. IEEE Std, pp. 610–612 (1990)
21. Indurkhya, N., Damerau, F.J.: Handbook of Natural Language Processing, vol. 2. CRC Press, Boca Raton (2010)
22. Ittoo, A., Bouma, G.: Term extraction from sparse, ungrammatical domain-specific documents. Expert Syst. App. **40**(7), 2530–2540 (2013)

23. John, I., Dörr, J.: Elicitation of requirements from user documentation. In: 9th International Workshop on Requirements Engineering: Foundation for Software Quality (REFSQ 2003) (2003)

24. Jonnalagadda, S., Tari, L., Hakenberg, J., Baral, C., Gonzalez, G.: Towards effective sentence simplification for automatic processing of biomedical text. In: Proceedings of Human Language Technologies (NAACL HLT 2009), pp. 177–180 (2009)

25. Kim, S.N., Baldwin, T., Kan, M.-Y.: An unsupervised approach to domain-specific term extraction. In: Proceedings of Australasian Language Technology Association, Workshop, pp. 94–98 (2009)

26. Klein, D., Manning, C.D.: Fast exact inference with a factored model for natural language parsing. In: Becker, S., Thrun, S., Obermayer, K. (eds.) Advances in Neural Information Processing Systems, vol. 15, pp. 3–10. MIT Press, Cambridge (2003)

27. Levy, R., Andrew, G.: Tregex and tsurgeon: tools for querying and manipulating tree data structures. In: Proceedings of 5th International Conference on Language Resources and Evaluation (LREC 2006), pp. 2231–2234 (2006)

28. Li, Y., Guzman, E., Tsiamoura, K., Schneider, F., Bruegge, B.: Automated requirements extraction for scientific software. Procedia Comput. Sci. **51**, 582–591 (2015)

29. Loughran, N., Sampaio, A., Rashid, A.: From requirements documents to feature models for aspect oriented product line implementation. In: Bruel, J.-M. (ed.) MODELS 2005. LNCS, vol. 3844, pp. 262–271. Springer, Heidelberg (2006). doi:10. 1007/11663430_27

30. Marciuska, S., Gencel, C., Abrahamsson, P.: Automated feature identification in web applications. In: Proceedings of 14th International Conference on Software Quality (QSIC 2014), pp. 100–114 (2014)

31. Merten, T., Falis, M., Hübner, P., Quirchmayr, T., Bürsner, S., Paech, B.: Software feature request detection in issue tracking systems. In: Proceedings of 24th International Requirements Engineering Conference (RE 2016), pp. 166–175 (2016)

32. Mu, Y., Wang, Y., Guo, J.: Extracting software functional requirements from free text documents. In: Proceedings of 1st International Conference on Information and Multimedia Technology (ICIMT 2009), pp. 194–198 (2009)

33. Nixon, M.: Feature Extraction & Image Processing. Academic Press, Cambridge (2008)

34. Paech, B., Hübner, P., Merten, T.: What are the features of this software? An exploratory study. In: Proceedings of 9th International Conference on Software Engineering Advances (ICSEA 2014), pp. 114–125 (2014)

35. Pikkarainen, M., Haikara, J., Salo, O., Abrahamsson, P., Still, J.: The impact of agile practices on communication in software development. J. Empir. Softw. Eng. **13**(3), 303–337 (2008)

36. Shaker, P., Atlee, J.M., Wang, S.: A feature-oriented requirements modelling language. In: Proceedings of 20th International Requirements Engineering Conference (RE 2012), pp. 151–160 (2012)

37. Ward, L.J., Woods, G.: English Grammar for Dummies. Wiley, Hoboken (2013)

38. Weston, N., Chitchyan, R., Rashid, A.: A framework for constructing semantically composable feature models from natural language requirements. In: Proceedings of 13th International Software Product Line Conference (SPLC 2009), pp. 211–220 (2009)

39. Wimalasuriya, D.C., Dou, D.: Ontology-based information extraction: an introduction and a survey of current approaches. Inf. Sci. **36**(3), 306–323 (2010)

40. Zapata, J.C.M., Losada, B.M., Gonzalez-Calderon, G.: An approach for using pro-cedure manuals as a source for requirements elicitation. In: Proceedings of 38th Conference Latinoamericana En Informatica (CLEI 2012), pp. 1–8 (2012)
41. Zorn-Pauli, G., Paech, B., Wittkopf, J.: Strategic release planning challenges for global information systems - a position paper. In: Proceedings of 6th International Workshop on Software Product Management (IWSPM 2012), pp. 186–191 (2012)

Mining User Requirements from Application Store Reviews Using Frame Semantics

Nishant Jha and Anas Mahmoud$^{(\boxtimes)}$

The Division of Computer Science and Engineering, Louisiana State University,
Baton Rouge, LA 70803, USA
njha1@lsu.edu, mahmoud@csc.lsu.edu

Abstract. *Context and motivation*: Research on mining user reviews in mobile application (app) stores has noticeably advanced in the past few years. The majority of the proposed techniques rely on classifying the textual description of user reviews into different categories of technically informative user requirements and uninformative feedback. *Question/Problem*: Relying on the textual attributes of reviews often produces high dimensional models. This increases the complexity of the classifier and can lead to overfitting problems. *Principal ideas/results*: We propose a novel semantic approach for app review classification. The proposed approach is based on the notion of semantic role labeling, or characterizing the lexical meaning of text in terms of semantic frames. Semantic frames help to generalize from text (individual words) to more abstract scenarios (contexts). This reduces the dimensionality of the data and enhances the predictive capabilities of the classifier. Three datasets of user reviews are used to conduct our experimental analysis. Results show that semantic frames can be used to generate lower dimensional and more accurate models in comparison to text classification methods. *Contribution*: A novel semantic approach for extracting user requirements from app reviews. The proposed approach enables a more efficient classification process and reduces the chance of overfitting.

Keywords: Requirements elicitation · Application stores · Classification

1 Introduction

Mobile application markets, or app stores (e.g., Google Play and Apple App Store), represent a unique model of service-oriented business. Such platforms have created an unprecedented opportunity for app developers to directly monitor the opinions of a large population of end-users of their software [25]. Through app stores feedback services, app users can directly share their experience in the form of textual reviews and meta-data (e.g., star ratings). Analyzing large datasets of app store reviews has revealed that they contain substantial amounts of up-to-date technical information. Such information can be leveraged by app developers to help them maintain and sustain their apps in a highly-competitive

© Springer International Publishing AG 2017
P. Grünbacher and A. Perini (Eds.): REFSQ 2017, LNCS 10153, pp. 273–287, 2017.
DOI: 10.1007/978-3-319-54045-0_20

and volatile market [25]. These realizations have encouraged researchers to look for automated methods to detect such informative reviews and further classify them into fine-grained software user requirements (feature requests) and maintenance tasks (bug reports) [6,7,20,26]. Automated support is necessary to help app developers to quickly filter through *junk* reviews, identify bugs in their applications, and understand contemporary end-user requirements.

In general, app store mining techniques rely on the textual attributes of user reviews to classify them into technically informative and uninformative reviews. Such techniques range from detecting the presence/absence of certain indicator words (e.g. *"crash"*, *"bug"*), to more advanced techniques that rely on automated text classification and modeling [6,12,20,26]. While these techniques have shown decent accuracy levels, they typically suffer from several drawbacks. For instance, users tend to express their reviews using informal language which often includes colloquial terminologies. Such a broad range of words (classification features) often results in complex models, which in turn might lead to overfitting problems. In particular, due to the rapid manner in which natural language evolves online, a classifier trained using a vocabulary collected at a certain point in time might not be able to accurately generalize for newer apps [22].

To work around these limitations, in this paper, we propose a novel semantically aware approach for mining and classifying user reviews in app stores. The proposed approach is based on the notion of semantic role labeling (SRL). The primary assumption behind SRL is that words can be grouped into semantic classes, called frames. A semantic frame describes an event that occurs in a sentence along with its participants (e.g., people, objects). The main aim is to capture the meaning of the sentence at a higher level of abstraction. More specifically, by annotating words and phrases in text with various frame elements (or roles), we can generalize from specific sentences to scenarios. Such annotations can be generated using the FrameNet [2] project. FrameNet provides an online lexical repository of semantic frames and their roles.

SRL and frame semantics have been successfully exploited in a plethora of text classification tasks, such as predicting the stock market movement by analyzing the textual content of financial news articles [32], extracting social networks from unstructured text [1], question answering tasks [29], and stance classification in political debates [13]. In this paper, we follow this line of research to describe a light-weight and accurate approach for identifying informative user reviews and classifying them into different types of actionable requests that app developers can effectively utilize. Our approach is evaluated using a large dataset of user reviews, sampled from a diverse set of apps that are selected from a broad range of application domains.

The remainder of this paper is organized as follows. Section 2 reviews seminal work in app user review classification. Section 3 introduces the FrameNet project and the notion of semantic frames. Section 4 describes our experimental setup. Section 5 presents our results and discusses our main findings. Section 6 identifies the threats to the study's validity. Finally, Sect. 7 concludes the paper and discusses prospects for future work.

2   Related Work

The research on mining app reviews for software engineering purposes has notice-ably advanced in the past few years. Chen et al. [7] presented AR-Miner, a computational framework that helps developers to identify the most informative user app reviews. Uninformative reviews were initially identified and filtered out using Expectation Maximization for Naive Bayes— a semi supervised text clas-sification algorithm. The remaining reviews were then analyzed and categorized into different groups using topic modeling [3]. These groups were ranked by a review ranking scheme based on their potential information value. The proposed approach was evaluated on a manually classified dataset of app reviews col-lected from four popular Android apps. The results showed high accuracy levels in terms of precision, recall, and the quality of ranking.

Panichella et al. [26] proposed a supervised approach for classifying mobile app reviews into categories relevant to software maintenance (e.g., bug reports and user requirements). The authors extracted a set of linguistic features from each review, including most important words, the main sentiment of the review, and linguistic patterns that may represent a potential maintenance request. Dif-ferent types of classifiers were then trained using different combinations of these features. The results showed that decision trees [28], trained over recurrent lin-guistic patterns and sentiment scores, achieved the best performance in terms of precision and recall.

Carreño and Winbladh [6] proposed an approach for mining user comments to extract software requirements for future releases of software systems. The proposed approach applies topic modeling techniques and sentiment analysis classification (Aspect and Sentiment Unification Model) to identify comments relevant with regards to requirement changes. Evaluating the proposed approach over three datasets of manually classified user reviews showed promising perfor-mance levels in terms of accuracy and effort-saving.

Guzman and Maalej [12] proposed an automated approach to help devel-opers filter, aggregate, and analyze app reviews. The proposed approach used a collocation finding algorithm to extract fine-grained requirements mentioned in the review. Extracted requirements were then grouped into more meaningful high-level features using topic modeling. The author used over 32,210 reviews extracted from seven iOS and Android apps to conduct their analysis. The results showed that the proposed approach managed to successfully extract the most frequently mentioned features in these reviews. These features were also grouped into coherent coarse-grained sets of app requirements.

Maalej and Nabil [20] introduced several probabilistic techniques for clas-sifying app reviews into bug reports, feature requests, user experiences, and ratings. The authors experimented with several binary and multi-class classi-fiers, including Naive Bayes, decision trees, and maximum entropy. A dataset of 4400 manually labeled reviews from Google Play and the Apple App Store was used to evaluate the performance of these different classifiers. The results showed that binary classifiers (Naive Bayes) were more accurate for predicting the review type than multi-class classifiers. The results also revealed that review features, such as star-rating, tense, sentiment scores, and length, as well as certain text analysis techniques, such as stemming and lemmatization, enhanced the classification performance.

Iacob and Harrison [14] introduced MARA, a tool for automatic retrieval of mobile app feature requests from user reviews in app stores. The proposed approach is based on identifying sentences expressing feature requests based on a set of predefined linguistic rules. These rules were mined from analyzing most frequent keywords and linguistic patterns associated with feature requests. Such keywords were abstracted into a set of 237 linguistic rules. The approach was evaluated over a sample of 480 reviews extracted from Google Play. The results showed that 23.3% of reviews represented feature requests.

3   Frame Semantics

Housed and maintained by the International Computer Science Institute in Berkeley, California, the FrameNet project [2] provides a massive machine readable database of manually annotated sentences based on the theory of Frame Semantics [10]. This theory states that the meanings of lexical items (predicates) are best defined with respect to larger conceptual chunks, called *Frames*. Technically, the FrameNet[1] project works to identify significant frames in sentences, their frame elements, and lexical units. A semantic frame (or simply *frame*) can be described as a schematic representation of a situation (events, actions) involving various elements. A frame element (FE) can be defined as a participant entity or a semantic role in the action described by the frame. Lexical units (LU) are basically the words that evoke different frame elements. For instance, the frame COMMERCE_BUY describes a basic commercial transaction involving a buyer and a seller exchanging money and goods. This frame has the core frame elements `buyer` (can be evoked by lexical units such as *buy*) and `goods`. A core FE is an element that is necessary for the frame to occur. The frame also has other FEs such as `place`, `purpose`, `seller`, and `time`.

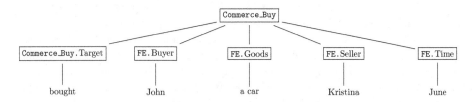

Fig. 1. Semantic annotation of the sentence *"John bought a car from Kristina in June"* under the COMMERCE_BUY semantic frame

Figure 1 shows the tree representation of the semantic annotation of the sentence *"John bought a car from Kristina in June."* under the semantic frame COMMERCE_BUY. This sentence includes the frame elements `buyer`, `goods`, `seller`,

---

[1] https://framenet.icsi.berkeley.edu/fndrupal/.

and `time`, evoked by the lexical units *John, car, Kristina,* and *June* respectively. This unique form of semantic annotation represents an invaluable source of knowledge that can be exploited to support several computational linguistic tasks. For example, the FrameNet database has been used in tasks such as semantic classification of text [11], question answering [17] and information extraction [24]. Following this line of research, in this paper, we utilize the FrameNet project to tackle the problem of app review classification. Our expectation is that FrameNet tagging will enable a deep understanding of the meaning of individual user reviews. This in turn should help in training more accurate app review classifiers. Consider, for example, the sentence *"I can't see the pictures fix it please!!"* extracted from a review of the photo-sharing app *Imgur.* Tagging this sentence using FrameNet results in the following frames:

I [can't]CAPABILITY [see]GRASP the [pictures]PHYSICAL_ARTWORKS [fix]PREDICAMENT it [please]STIMULUS_FOCUS.

The key semantic frame in this example is PREDICAMENT, which according to FrameNet data dictionary refers to a situation where *"An Experiencer is in an undesirable Situation, whose Cause may also be expressed"*. This frame can also be evoked by other words such as *problem, trouble,* and *jam.* In general, any situation of inconvenience might evoke this frame. From a classification point of view, this frame represents a feature that can be used to predict bug reports.

Another example is the two review sentences *"I wish you could add a functionality to use this app with any POP3 mailboxes"* and *"I wanted to be able to use Gmail with all POP3 mailboxes."* extracted from two different reviews of the *Gmail* app. Both sentences convey the same message, describing a user requirement for the app to support all POP3 mailboxes, but with different terminologies. Tagging these two sentences using FrameNet generates the following representations:

I [wish]DESIRING you [could]CAPABILITY [add]STATEMENT a functionality to [use]USING this app with [any]QUANTITY POP3 mailboxes.

I [wanted]DESIRING to be [able]CAPABILITY to [use]USING Gmail with [all]QUANTITY POP3 mailboxes.

In the first sentence, the words *wish, could, add, use,* and *any* evoke the frames DESIRING, CAPABILITY, STATEMENT, USING, and QUANTITY respectively. In the second sentence, the words *wanted, able, use,* and *all* evoke the frames DESIRING, CAPABILITY, USING, and QUANTITY respectively. This example shows how similar frames are evoked by different words that share the same meaning in a specific context. For instance, in the above two sentences, the words *wish* and *wanted* are two different words that share the same meaning in the given context, and therefore, evoke the same frame DESIRING. Similarly, the words *could* and *able* evoke the semantic frame CAPABILITY in both sentences.

Form a classification point of view, this kind of semantic abstraction is expected to enhance the predictive capabilities of classifiers as general meaning, rather than exact words, are considered as classification features. In particular, in text classification tasks, each individual word of the text is treated as a separate classification feature, such that the input text is represented as an unordered vector of its words. This approach, known as *Bag-of-Words*, or BOW classification, relies on the presence or absence of certain indicator terms in the text to make a decision. For instance, in the context of app review classification, words such as {*bug, crash, fix, problem, issue, defect, solve, problem, trouble*} tend to be associated with bug reporting reviews, while words such as {*add, please, would, hope, improve, miss, need, prefer, suggest, want, wish*} are typically associated with feature requests or user requirements [20]. Such words are used by text classifiers to make sense of the input text and classify it under a certain label.

The approach we present in this paper can be described as a *Bag-of-Frames*, or BOF, approach. In particular, the frames generated from each review, rather than each word, are used as classification features. Therefore, the review's text is represented as an unordered vector of frames. Our assumption is that the BOF representation of the data is expected to generate lower dimensional and more semantically abstract models, thus enabling more accurate predictions than the BOW representation. To test this assumption, we collect a dataset of app reviews from a set of apps sampled from a broad range of application domains. These reviews are semantically annotated to generate their BOF representations. Two different classifiers, including Naive Bayes (NB) and Support Vector Machines (SVM), are then used to classify these reviews into different actionable software engineering requests. Generated classifiers are evaluated over a set of unseen before reviews that were sampled from a new set apps to test for overfitting. Next is a description of our experimental analysis in greater detail.

4   Experimental Settings

In this section, we describe our experimental settings, including the dataset used to carry out our analysis, the classifiers used to classify the data, and the performance measures used to assess the performance under different classification settings.

4.1   Experimental Dataset

Our ground-truth dataset of app reviews is compiled from two external datasets and an internal dataset obtained from different sources. Using such a diverse dataset enhances the internal and external validity of our results by reducing any potential sampling bias, a problem commonly known as the app sampling problem [21]. The external datasets include the data collected by Maalej and Nabil [20] and the data provided by Chen et al [7]. Random sampling is used to select instances from these two datasets.

The internal dataset includes reviews that were locally collected from three iOS apps, including *CreditKarma*, *FitBit*, and *Gmail*. The most recent user reviews of each app were collected using the RSS feed generator of the iOS app store. These reviews, along with the reviews sampled from the two external datasets, were manually classified by the researchers into user requirements, bug reports, and others. In case of a conflict, a discussion was held to reach a consensus. Instances where agreement could not be reached were discarded. In total, 13 instances were discarded from all datasets. Table 1 summarizes the characteristics of our dataset, including the source of data, the number of bug reports, user requirements, and other instances collected from each source[2].

Table 1. The dataset used in our analysis

Source	Sampled	Discarded	Bugs	Req.	Others	Total
Internal data	705	3	170	65	467	702
Data from [20]	725	8	318	199	200	717
Data from [7]	1500	2	854	537	107	1498
Total	2930	13	1342	801	774	2917

4.2 Classifiers

To classify our data, we use two classifiers that have been showing consistently good performance in app store mining research. These classifiers include:

- **Support Vector Machines (SVM):** SVM is a supervised machine learning algorithm that is used to recognize patterns in multidimensional data spaces [5]. SVM tries to find optimal hyperplanes for linearly separable patterns in the data and then maximizes the margin around the separating hyperplane. Technically, support vectors are the critical elements of the training set that would change the position of the dividing hyperplane if removed. SVM classifies the data by mapping input vectors into an N-dimensional space, and deciding in which side of the defined hyperplane the point lies. SVMs have been empirically shown to be effective in high dimensional and sparse text classification tasks [15].
- **Naive Bayes (NB):** NB is a simple, yet efficient, linear probabilistic classifier that is based on Bayes' theorem [18]. NB is based on the conditional independence assumption which implies that the attribute values of the data are independent of each other given the class. In the context of text classification, the features of the model are the individual words of the text artifacts.

---

[2] Our data is publicly available at http://seel.cse.lsu.edu/data/refsql7.zip.

Such data is typically represented using a 2-dimensional *word x document* matrix. The entry i,j in the matrix can be either a binary value that indicates whether the document d_i contains the word w_j or not (i.e. $\{0,1\}$), or the relative frequency of the word w_j appearing in the document d_i [22].

4.3 Implementation and Classification Settings

To implement NB and SVM, we use Weka[3], a data mining software that implements a wide variety of machine learning and classification techniques. SVM is invoked through Weka's SMO, which implements John Platt's sequential minimal optimization algorithm for training a support vector classifier [27]. To evaluate our classifiers, we use 10-fold cross validation. This method of evaluation creates 10 partitions of the dataset such that each partition has 90% of the instances as a training set and 10% as an evaluation set. The evaluation sets are chosen such that their union is the entire dataset. The benefit of this technique is that the results exhibit significantly less variance than those of simpler techniques such as the holdout method (i.e., 70% for training and 30% for testing) [16].

To generate the BOF representation of our data (i.e. annotate the review sentences), we use SEMAFOR[4]— a probabilistic frame semantic parser [8]. SEMAFOR automatically processes English sentences according to the form of semantic analysis in Berkeley FrameNet. The generated annotations are represented using XML. A special parser was created to extract the semantic frames of each annotated sentence from the XML output.

For the BOW analysis, we use the Weka's stemmer `IteratedLovinsStemmer` to stem the reviews in our dataset [19]. Stemming reduces words to their morphological roots. This leads to a reduction in the number of features (words) as only one base form of the word is considered. Most common words (words that appear in all reviews) along with words that appear in one data instance (review) are removed from the data since they are highly unlikely to carry any generalizable information. English stop-words were not removed from our data. This decision was based on the previous observation that some of these words (e.g., *would, should, will*) carry important distinctive information for user requirement reviews. Therefore, removing such words typically leads to a decline in the performance. Furthermore, in our analysis, we use Multinomial NB, which uses the normalized frequency (TF) of words in their documents [22]. Multinomial Naive Bayes is known to be a more robust text classifier, consistently outperforming the binary feature model (Multi-variate Bernoulli) in highly diverse real-world corpora [22].

4.4 Evaluation Measures

Recall, precision, and the F-measure are used to evaluate the performance of the different classification techniques used in our analysis. Recall is a measure of

---

[3] www.cs.waikato.ac.nz/~ml/weka/.

[4] www.cs.cmu.edu/~ark/SEMAFOR/.

coverage. It represents the ratio of correctly classified instances under a specific label to the number of instances in the data space that actually belong to that label. Precision, on the other hand, is a measure of accuracy. It represents the ratio of correctly classified instances under a specific label to the total number of classified instances under that label. Formally, if A is the set of data instances in the data space that belong to the label λ, and B is the set of data instances that were assigned by the classifier to that label, then recall ($\boldsymbol{R}$) can be calculated as $R_\lambda = |A \cap B|/|A|$, and precision ($\boldsymbol{P}$) can be calculated as $P_\lambda = |A \cap B|/|B|$. We also use the F measure to report our results. This measure, which represents the harmonic mean of recall and precision, can be calculated as $F_\beta = ((\beta^2 + 1)PR)/(\beta^2 P + R)$. In our analysis, we use $\beta = 1$.

5   Results and Discussion

The results of our classification process are shown in Table 2. The results show that, under the BOF representation, SVM managed to outperform NB, achieving $F_{bugs} = 0.86$ and $F_{req.} = 0.74$, while NB achieved $F_{bugs} = 0.81$ and $F_{req.} = 0.70$. A similar behavior was observed under the BOW representation; SVM managed to achieve $F_{bugs} = 0.85$ and $F_{req.} = 0.75$, in comparison to NB which achieved $F_{bugs} = 0.79$ and $F_{req.} = 0.72$. In general, SVM outperforms NB, achieving almost equivalent performance under the two different representations of the data. The relatively better performance of SVM can be attributed to its overfitting avoidance tendency— an inherent behavior of margin maximization which does not depend on the number of features [4]. Therefore, it has the potential to scale up to high-dimensional data spaces with sparse instances [15], given that the right kernel is selected. Choosing a proper kernel function can significantly affect SVM's generalization and predictive capabilities [30]. In our analysis, the best results of the BOW representation was achieved using the Normalized Poly Kernel, while the BOF classifier hit a maximum using the Pearson VII function-based universal kernel (Puk) with $\sigma = 8$ and $\omega = 1$ [31].

Table 2. The performance of NB and SVM over the BOF and the BOW representations of the data in Table 1

	Bug reports			User requirements		
Classifier	p	r	F_1	p	r	F_1
BOF + NB	0.80	0.83	0.81	0.70	0.69	0.70
BOF + SVM	0.84	0.88	**0.86**	0.73	0.75	0.74
BOW + NB	0.81	0.77	0.79	0.71	0.73	0.72
BOW + SVM	0.78	0.93	0.85	0.83	0.69	**0.75**

To assess the generative capabilities of our classifiers, we test their performance on an external set of reviews that was sampled from apps that were not included in our original dataset, including *Google Chrome*, *Facebook*, and *Google Maps*. Similar to the reviews in original dataset (Table 1), the newly sampled reviews were classified manually by the researchers (See Sect. 4.1). Table 3 describes the final test dataset[5]. Our main objective is to test the ability of the generated models to generalize over unseen-before data, in other words, test for overfitting. In automated classification, overfitting refers to a phenomenon where the classifier learns separate data instances (i.e., model the training data), rather than learning general categories. Formally, the model **M** overfits the data if there exists some other model **M'**, such that, **M** has a smaller error over the training data than **M'**, however **M'** has a smaller error than **M** over the entire distribution [23].

Table 3. A test set of app reviews sampled from three apps

Source	Bugs	Req.	Others	Total
Google chrome	125	26	91	242
Facebook	56	7	32	95
Google maps	108	17	50	175
Total	289	50	173	512

To test for overfitting, the original models generated using the data in Table 1 were saved, reloaded, and reevaluated using the test set. The performance of our different classifiers on the external test set is shown in Table 4. The results show that the BOF classifiers managed to outperform the classifiers generated using the BOW representation. More specifically, BOF+SVM achieved $F_{bugs} = 0.96$ and $F_{req.} = 0.75$. In contrast, the BOW classifiers' performance has drastically dropped over the set of user requirements in the test set to $F_{req.} = 0.54$ for SVM and $F_{req.} = 0.39$ for NB, failing to match the performance levels achieved on the training dataset.

Table 4. The performance of the different classifiers over the test set (Table 3)

Classifier	Bug reports			User requirements		
	p	r	F_1	p	r	F_1
BOF + NB	0.85	0.92	0.88	0.41	0.73	0.53
BOF + SVM	0.94	0.99	**0.96**	0.62	0.96	**0.75**
BOW + NB	0.84	0.71	0.77	0.28	0.62	0.39
BOW + SVM	0.78	0.97	0.86	0.45	0.68	0.54

---

[5] http://seel.cse.lsu.edu/data/refsq17.zip.

In general, the results over the test dataset suggest that the NB and SVM classifiers trained under the BOW representation of the data suffered from over-fitting. This behavior can be attributed to the fact that the feature space (number of words) is typically very large [15]. Larger number of features causes the vector representation (BOW) of reviews to be very sparse (only very few entries with non-zero weights). This in turn forces the classifier to learn specific data instances rather than the general classification categories. The BOF representation, on the other hand, seems to be overcoming this problem by raising the level of abstraction from specific words to more abstract semantic representations. Reducing the number of features that the classifier needs to consider reduces the chances of overfitting and leads to better generalizations over unseen before data instances. For example, Table 5 shows the frames generated for the words that were semantically distinctive to our classifiers. The BOW training dataset did not have the word *desire*. As a results, the user requirement *"another window is highly desired"* in our BOW test set was miss-classified as *others*. However, under the BOF representation, this review was correctly classified as a user requirement since the word *desire* evoked the frame DESIRING, which is one of the most distinctive frames of the user requirement reviews.

Table 5. Popular frames in our dataset and their evoking words

Semantic frame	Evoking words
TEMPORAL_COLLOCATION	when, now, current
CAPABILITY	can, cannot, able, unable, capable
DESIRING	eager, hoping, want, desire
PREDICAMENT	problem, error, fix, trouble
MEASURE_DURATION	year, month, week, day, minute, time, awhile, endless

A smaller number of features not only reduces the chances of overfitting, but also speeds up the training process by reducing the computational requirements of the classifier. In our analysis, the BOF representation required 10 s to build the model and 96 s to evaluate the classifier using the 10-fold evaluation strategy, while the BOW representation required 32 s to build the model and 293 s to evaluate the classifier. This can be explained based on the fact that only 552 unique frames were used to build the BOF model, while the BOW model was built using 1592 unique words (features). On average, the BOF representation of the data saves up to 60% of space and time requirements needed to build a model using the BOW representation. The running time was measured on an Intel(R) Core(TM) i5-2500 CPU 2.3 GHz, with 8.0 GB of RAM.

In terms of operation overhead, the semantic frames approach is fully automated and requires minimum to no calibration from the user. This gives this approach an advantage over other text-reduction strategies typically applied in related research. For instance, methods that rely on mining recurrent linguistic patterns from reviews help to reduce the dimentionality of the text by using sentence templates rather than individual words (e.g., *"[someone] should try to [verb]"*). However, preparing a complete catalog of such patterns can be a laborious and time-consuming process [26] as researchers have to manually mine hundreds of reviews to capture and isolate such patterns [14]. Topic modeling has also been used as a means to classify and organize app reviews (e.g. [6,12]). The main objective is to reduce the dimentionality of the review text by grouping their words into thematic groups known as topics. However, most state-of-the-art topic modeling techniques (e.g., LDA, PLSI) require an exhaustive calibration of several parameters in order to generate meaningful output [3]. Furthermore, generated topics are often not trivial to interpret and rationalize, and going through a large number of topics (100–200) can be an exhaustive and error-prone process [6]. This level of operational complexity limits the practicality of any tools built on top of these techniques. In terms of limitations, the semantic frames approach requires downloading the FrameNet database locally. This database requires around 500 megabytes of space. However, this space overhead could be saved by using an online semantic parser[6].

6   Threats to Validity

The study presented in this paper has several limitations that might affect the validity of the results. Internal validity refers to confounding factors that might affect the causal relations established in the experiment [9]. A potential threat to the proposed study's internal validity is the fact that human judgment is used to prepare our ground-truth dataset. This might result in an experimental bias as humans tend to be subjective in their judgment. However, it is not uncommon in text classification tasks to use humans to manually classify the data. Therefore, these threats are inevitable. However, they can be partially mitigated by following a systematic classification procedure using multiple judges at different levels of experience to classify the data.

Threats to external validity impact the generalizability of results [9]. In particular, the results of our experiment might not generalize beyond the specific experimental settings used in this paper. A potential threat to our external validity stems from the datasets used in our experiment. In particular, our dataset is limited in size and was generated from a limited number of apps. To mitigate this threat, we compiled our dataset from several sources, including two external datasets that have been used before in the literature and a dataset that we collected locally. We also made sure that our reviews were selected from a diverse set of apps, covering a broad range of application domains. Other threats might stem from the tools we used in our analysis. For instance, we used Weka as our classification platform; and we used SEMAFOR to semantically annotate

---

[6] http://demo.ark.cs.cmu.edu/parse.

our review sentences. However, these tools have been extensively used in the literature and have been shown to generate robust results. Furthermore, such tools are publicly available which allows other researchers to replicate our results.

Construct validity is the degree to which the various performance measures accurately capture the concepts they purport to measure [9]. In our experiment, there were minimal threats to construct validity as the standard performance measures (Recall, Precision, and F_1), which are extensively used in related research, were used to assess the performance of different methods. We believe that these measures sufficiently quantified the different aspects of performance we were interested in.

7   Summary and Future Work

User reviews in mobile application stores represent a rich and a timely source of information for app creators. Such information can be mined to enable a more adaptive and a more responsive software engineering process. The main objective is to arrive at user satisfaction in an effective and a timely manner. Following this line of research, in this paper we presented a novel semantically aware approach for classifying users reviews in app stores. The proposed approach relies on semantic role labeling. In particular, individual user review sentences are extracted and annotated to identify the semantic roles played by the words that appear in each sentence. Such roles, known as semantic frames, capture the underlying meaning of the review. An underlying assumption is that relying on the meaning of the text enhances the predictive capabilities of the classifier.

To conduct our analysis, an experimental dataset of user reviews was compiled from three different sources, including two datasets collected by other researchers [7,20], and a dataset that was prepared locally. Individual reviews were semantically annotated using FrameNet. Annotated sentences, represented as *Bags-of-Frames* (BOF) were then classified using Naive Bayes (NB) and Support Vector Machines (SVM) and compared to standard Bag-of-Words (BOW) text classification. The results showed that, the Bag-of-Frames (BOF) approach achieved competitive results in comparison to the BOW approach on the training dataset. However, classifiers trained under the BOF representation were able to generalize better over the set of user requirements in a test set of never-seen before reviews, suggesting that the initial BOW classification models suffered from overfitting. The main advantage of the BOF approach stems from the drastic reduction in the number of features required for classification. Smaller number of features can produce lower dimensional models which can generalize better for new data.

Finally, the line of research in this paper has opened several research directions to be pursued in our future work, including:

- **Data collection:** A major part of our future effort will be devoted for preparing larger datasets collected from a more diverse set of apps. More data will enable us to better evaluate our approach and train more robust classifiers.

- **Analysis:** In our future work, other classification features (star-rating, author information, number of likes and downloads), that are often used in app store mining research will be investigated. Our objective is to identify combinations of features that can complement the BOF approach to achieve higher accuracy levels.
- **Tool support:** A working prototype which implements our findings in this paper will be developed. This prototype will enable app developers to extract, semantically annotate, and classify their apps' reviews in an effective and accurate manner.

Acknowledgment. This work was supported in part by the Louisiana Board of Regents Research Competitiveness Subprogram (LA BoR-RCS), contract number: LEQSF(2015-18)-RD-A-07.

References

1. Agarwal, A., Balasubramanian, S., Kotalwar, A., Zheng, J., Rambow, O.: Frame semantic tree kernels for social network extraction from text. In: Conference of the European Chapter of the Association for Computational Linguistics, pp. 211–219 (2014)
2. Baker, C., Fillmore, C., Lowe, J.: The Berkeley framenet project. In: International Conference on Computational Linguistics, pp. 86–90 (1998)
3. Blei, D., Ng, A., Jordan, M.: Latent dirichlet allocation. J. Mach. Learn. Res. **3**, 993–1022 (2003)
4. Brusilovsky, P., Kobsa, A., Nejdl, W. (eds.): The Adaptive Web: Methods and Strategies of Web Personalization. Springer, Heidelberg (2007). pp. 335–336
5. Burges, C.: A tutorial on support vector machines for pattern recognition. Data Min. Knowl. Discov. **2**(2), 121–167 (1998)
6. Carreño, G., Winbladh, K.: Analysis of user comments: an approach for software requirements evolution. In: International Conference on Software Engineering, pp. 582–591 (2013)
7. Chen, N., Lin, J., Hoi, S., Xiao, X., Zhang, B.: AR-Miner: mining informative reviews for developers from mobile app marketplace. In: International Conference on Software Engineering, pp. 767–778 (2014)
8. Das, D., Schneider, N., Chen, D., Smith, N.: SEMAFOR 1.0: A probabilistic frame-semantic parser (2010)
9. Dean, A., Voss, D.: Design and Analysis of Experiments. Springer, Heidelberg (1999)
10. Fillmore, C.: Frame semantics and the nature of language. In: Annals of the New York Academy of Sciences: Conference on the Origin and Development of Language and Speech, pp. 20–32 (1976)
11. Fleischman, M., Kwon, N., Hovy, E.: Maximum entropy models for FrameNet classification. In: Empirical Methods in Natural Language Processing, pp. 49–56 (2003)
12. Guzman, E., Maalej, W.: How do users like this feature? A fine grained sentiment analysis of app reviews. In: Requirements Engineering Conference, pp. 153–162 (2014)
13. Hasa, K., Ng, V.: Frame semantics for stance classification. In: Computational Natural Language Learning, pp. 124–132 (2013)

14. Iacob, C., Harrison, R.: Retrieving and analyzing mobile apps feature requests from online reviews. In: Mining Software Repositories, pp. 41–44 (2013)
15. Joachims, T.: Text categorization with support vector machines: learning with many relevant features. In: Nédellec, C., Rouveirol, C. (eds.) ECML 1998. LNCS, vol. 1398, pp. 137–142. Springer, Heidelberg (1998). doi:10.1007/BFb0026683
16. Kohavi, R.: A study of cross-validation and bootstrap for accuracy estimation and model selection. In: International Joint Conference on Artificial Intelligence, pp. 1137–1143 (1995)
17. Kumar Sinha, S.: Answering Questions About Complex Events. University of California at Berkeley (2008)
18. Langley, P., Iba, W., Thompson, K.: An analysis of Bayesian classifiers. In: National Conference on Artificial Intelligence, pp. 223–228 (1992)
19. Lovins, J.: Development of a stemming algorithm. Mech. Transl. Comput. Linguist. 11, 22–31 (1968)
20. Maalej, W., Nabil, H.: Bug report, feature request, or simply praise? On automatically classifying app reviews. In: Requirements Engineering Conference, pp. 116–125 (2015)
21. Martin, W., Harman, M., Jia, Y., Sarro, F., Zhang, Y.: The app sampling problem for app store mining. In: Working Conference on Mining Software Repositories, pp. 123–133 (2015)
22. McCallum, A., Nigam, K.: A comparison of event models for naive Bayes text classification. In: AAAI-98 Workshop on Learning for Text Categorization, pp. 41–48 (1998)
23. Mitchell, T.: Machine Learning. McGraw-Hill, New York City (1997)
24. Moschitti, A., Morarescu, P., Harabagiu, S.: Open domain information extraction via automatic semantic labeling. In: The Florida Artificial Intelligence Research Society Conference, pp. 397–401 (2003)
25. Pagano, D., Maalej, W.: User feedback in the AppStore: an empirical study. In: Requirements Engineering Conference, pp. 125–134 (2013)
26. Panichella, S., Di Sorbo, A., Guzman, E., Visaggio, C., Canfora, G., Gall, H.: How can I improve my app? Classifying user reviews for software maintenance and evolution. In: International Conference on Software Maintenance and Evolution, pp. 281–290 (2015)
27. Platt, J.: Fast training of Support Vector Machines using sequential minimal optimization. In: Schoelkopf, B., Burges, C., Smola, A. (eds.) Advances in Kernel Methods - Support Vector Learning. MIT Press, Cambridge (1998)
28. Quinlan, J.: Induction of decision trees. Mach. Learn. 1(1), 81–106 (1986)
29. Shen, D., Lapata, M.: Using semantic roles to improve question answering. In: Joint Conference on Empirical Methods in Natural Language Processing and Computational Natural Language Learning, pp. 12–21 (2007)
30. Steinwart, I.: On the influence of the kernel on the consistency of Support Vector Machines. J. Mach. Learn. Res. 2, 67–93 (2001)
31. Üstün, B., Melssen, W., Buydens, L.: Facilitating the application of support vector regression by using a universal Pearson VII function based kernel. Chemometr. Intell. Lab. Syst. 81, 29–40 (2006)
32. Xie, B., Passonneau, R., Wu, L., Creamer, G.: Semantic frames to predict stock price movement. In: Annual Meeting of the Association for Computational Linguistics, pp. 873–883 (2013)

Traceability

Using Interaction Data for Continuous Creation of Trace Links Between Source Code and Requirements in Issue Tracking Systems

Paul Hübner[(✉)] and Barbara Paech

Institute for Computer Science, Heidelberg University, Im Neuenheimer Feld 205,
69120 Heidelberg, Germany
{huebner,paech}@informatik.uni-heidelberg.de

Abstract. *Context and Motivation*: Information retrieval (IR) trace link creation approaches have insufficient precision and do not perform well on unstructured data which is typical in issue tracker systems (ITS). *Question/problem*: We are interested in understanding how interaction tracking on artifacts can help to improve precision and recall of trace links between requirements specified unstructured in an ITS and source code. *Principal ideas/results:* We performed a study with open source project data in which artifact interactions while working on requirements specified in an ITS have been recorded. *Contribution*: The results of our study show that precision of interaction-based links is 100% and recall is 93% for the first and 80% for the second evaluated data set relative to IR-created links. Along with the study we developed an approach based on standard tools to automatically create trace links using interactions which also takes into account source code structure. The approach and the study show that trace links creation in practice can be supported with little extra effort for the developers.

Keywords: Traceability · Continuous · Interaction · Requirement · Source code

1 Introduction

Existing trace link creation approaches are typically based on information retrieval (IR) and on structured requirements like use cases or user stories. Also, they often focus on links between requirements [5]. It is known that precision of IR created links is often not satisfying [14] even in the case of structured requirements. Thus, handling of false positive IR created trace links requires extra effort in practice which is even a research subject on its own [12,15,29].

Still, the research focus in RE is to improve recall, since security critical domains like the aeronautics and automotive industry require complete link sets and thus accept the effort to remove many false positives [6]. These links are created periodically, when needed for certification to justify the safe operation of a system.

© Springer International Publishing AG 2017
P. Grünbacher and A. Perini (Eds.): REFSQ 2017, LNCS 10153, pp. 291–307, 2017.
DOI: 10.1007/978-3-319-54045-0_21

However, in many companies requirements are managed in issue tracking systems [22]. For open source projects ITS are even the de facto standard for all requirements management activities [26]. In ITS the requirements text is unstructured, since ITS are used for many purposes, e.g. development task and bug tracking in addition to requirement specification. This impairs the results of IR-based trace link creation approaches [27]. Furthermore, for many development activities it is helpful to consider links between requirements and source code during development, e.g. in maintenance tasks and for program comparison [23]. If these links are created continuously, that means after each completion of an issue, they can be used continuously during the development. In these cases, large effort for handling false positives and thus, bad precision is not desirable. Therefore, a trace link creation approach for links between unstructured requirements and code is needed with good precision and recall. It is the goal of our research to develop such an approach [16] based on interaction logs and code relations. Interaction logs capture the source code artifacts touched while a developer works on an issue. We already provided a trace link creation approach based on version control system (VCS) change logs [11]. Interaction logs provide more fine-grained interaction data than VCS change logs. Code relations such as references between classes provide additional information. In this paper we explore the potential of interaction logs and code relations aiming at 100% precision.

To facilitate the usage of such fine-grained interaction logs we provide a trace link creation approach which we call *interaction link* (IL). We study the precision and recall of our approach in comparison with IR created trace links. The overall research question which we answer with our study is

Is there a difference between the application of IR and IL based trace link creation regarding precision and relative recall?

Since it is not possible to get a project from industry or open source which provides both, fine-grained interaction logs and a gold standard for trace links, we do not look at precision and recall of IR and IL wrt. a gold standard. Instead we directly evaluate the precision of IL and IR. Furthermore, we compute the relative recall of IR and IL. Relative recall compares the correct links found by one approach with the correct links found by both trace link creation approaches [13]. This kind of recall is well established in domains in which a gold standard creation and thus absolute recall calculation is not possible, e.g. in the field of search engine comparison [20].

For our study we use the interaction log data, requirements and source code from the Mylyn[1] development project. This interaction log data has also been used by others for different research purposes [18,21].

The results of the study show that IL has 100% precision and is better than the precision of IR. In addition we show that IL with code relations has also better relative recall than IR. The remainder of this paper is structured as follows. Section 2 gives a short introduction into IR, the creation of trace links, ITS as

---

[1] http://www.eclipse.org/mylyn.

data source for requirements, the evaluation of trace link creation approaches and interaction tracking. In Sect. 3 we discuss related work. Section 4 introduces our trace link creation approach. Section 5 states the research questions which are derived from the general research question introduced above and introduces the experimental design along with the selection of data sets for our study. In Sect. 6 we present the results of the study and answer the research questions including a discussion. Section 7 discusses the threats to validity of the study. Section 8 concludes the paper and discusses future work.

2 Background

This section introduces the background of our approach and the study.

2.1 IR and the Creation of Trace Links

IR is the computer based search for information within a set of artifacts. IR algorithms are used to execute search queries aiming to retrieve all relevant artifacts while minimizing the non-relevant artifacts [4]. When using IR for trace link creation the query concerns textual similarity between two artifacts. Textual similarity is determined by calculating the cosine similarity and defining a threshold for the calculated cosine similarity. Cosine similarity measures the similarity between the two term vectors representing the artifacts based on the cosine of the angle between the term vectors by a numerical value between 0 and 1 [5]. 0 indicates no similarity between two artifacts and 1 that two artifacts are identical. In order to define if two artifacts are related with each other and should be linked a threshold value for the cosine similarity is used [7]. Thus, varying this threshold value also varies the number of created trace link candidates.

In our study the artifacts are requirements issues and implementation artifacts. There are different IR algorithms. The most common IR algorithms used for trace link creation are vector space model (VSM) and latent semantic indexing (LSI) [5,14]. Thus, we used these two IR algorithms for comparison with our new trace link creation approach. The difference between VSM and LSI is that VSM uses a more strict term comparison than LSI. Whereas VSM measures the similarity based on terms, LSI measures the similarity based on concepts, which are high level abstractions of the used terms and can been seen as the topics of the artifacts [4]. Thus LSI enables similarity matches between artifacts which do not contain the exactly same terms.

The preprocessing of artifact is essential for the application of an IR algorithm. Typically, preprocessing consist of several steps. Some of them are fundamental and some are specific to the used data sources. In our study we applied the following common preprocessing steps [4,5,24]. First we used stop word removal to remove common words which have no impact on the similarity of artifacts (e.g. for, the, a, etc.). Then we performed stemming with the Porter Stemmer algorithm. And we removed punctuation characters. As a specific step we performed camel case identifier splitting (e.g. BugzillaTask becomes Bugzilla Task).

Since camel case notation is common in java source code while requirements use separate words [1,9], this splitting can significantly improve the similarity of source code and requirements artifacts.

2.2 ITS as Data Source for Requirements

ITS are a common platform for information exchange in software development projects [22]. Often ITS are used as a central information data source and thus also for the definition and management of requirements. Requirements are described as issues which at least consist of a title and a description. A basic feature of ITS is the discussion functionality of issues so that users can create comments for issues. These comments may contain requirement relevant content, e.g. a feature description.

2.3 Evaluation of IR Created Trace Links

Approaches on trace link creation, e.g. as described in the overview papers [5,14], by default use a gold standard to evaluate and compare the approach. Such a gold standard consists of the set of all correct trace links for a given set of artifacts. The creation of such a gold standard is labor intensive as it is necessary to manually check if trace links exist for each pair of artifacts. Therefore many approaches use data sets which are specifically created for the purpose of evaluation, e.g. within a student project [10]. We also plan to evaluate our approach in a student project where we can create the gold standard in parallel to the project. As a first step we wanted to explore the usefulness of interaction logs on existing data.

There are only few realistic data sets with interaction logs (cf. next Subsect. 2.4). The creation of a complete gold standard for such a project is not feasible. Therefore we only evaluate the precision of the links found by IR or IL and we compute the relative recall.

Precision (P) is the amount of correct links (true positives, TP) within all links found by an approach, i.e. the sum of TP and not correct (false positive, FP) links. Recall (R) is the amount of TP links found by an approach within all existing correct links, i.e. the sum of TP and false negative (FN) links:

$$P = \frac{TP}{TP + FP} \qquad R = \frac{TP}{TP + FN}$$

According to [15] values for P and R of IR for structured requirements can be categorized in three quality levels. *Acceptable* values for R are between 60 and 69% and for P between 20 and 29%. *Good* values for R are between 70 and 79% and for P between 30 and 49% and *excellent* values for R are between 80 and 100% and for P between 50 and 100%. Merten et al. [27] reported varying results for using IR on unstructured requirements data from ITS, i.e. they tried to achieve a 100% for R with different IR algorithms and different preprocessing steps. Then their best values for P were up to 11%. Considering other approaches for link creation between code and requirements using open source projects as data source Ali et al. also used VSM for trace link creation [2] and achieved similar but also very project specific results for P (between 15 and 77%). De Lucia et al. [10] report values of 90% for R and 25% for P for link creation between structured requirements and source code by using LSI in combination with categorization.

To evaluate our trace link creation approach we use the relative recall measure [13] as we do not have a gold standard. Relative recall is used if it is not possible to get all correct values for a data set due to the size of the data set. It is a well-established standard measure in the domain of web search engine performance and quality measuring [20]. Relative recall uses all correct links available as comparison measure for calculating the recall of a single approach. Therefore the relative recall for IL (RR_{IL}) and for IR (RR_{IR}) are defined as:

$$RR_{IR} = \frac{TP_{IR}}{TP_{IR} + TP_{IL}} \qquad RR_{IL} = \frac{TP_{IL}}{TP_{IL} + TP_{IR}}$$

2.4 Interaction Logs and Code Structure

Interaction logs are all developer interactions with artifacts managed by an IDE. Common IDEs like Eclipse[2] provide the functionality to record these interactions [28]. For the development of our approach we used interactions recorded with the Eclipse Mylyn extension during the open source development of Mylyn. Mylyn logs edit, select and other events after a developer has selected an issue from an associated ITS and activated the recording. Interactions for an issue are recorded until the developer finishes working on the issue, e.g. by closing the issue, by switching to another issue or by explicitly stopping the recording of interactions. For the development of Mylyn the developers use Mylyn together with the ITS Bugzilla[3] which is also used for requirements capture. The Mylyn developers are encouraged to trigger recording when they work on the implementation of a requirement. These interaction logs are accessible as attachments of the issues in the Mylyn Bugzilla ITS.

Interaction logs can have different event types e.g. edit and select events triggered by a developer and system generated events like propagation, command and preference. An interaction log entry comprises the event type E touching the implementation artifact I while working on requirement A. Based on such an interaction log entry a trace links can be created between A and I. Interaction logs enable the link creation on class (file), method and attribute granularity level, i.e. all parts of the source code abstract syntax tree (AST) model.

We use the term code structure to denote the following relations between two classes in the Mylyn name space: a class implements an interface, a class extends another class or a class references other classes in its attributes. These relations can be used for link creation as follows: If a trace link ($A \rightarrow X$) from requirement A to class X has been created, for each class Y which is related

---

[2] http://www.eclipse.org.
[3] https://bugs.eclipse.org/bugs/describecomponents.cgi?product=Mylyn.

with X also a trace link to the requirement A is created $(A \rightarrow Y)$. These related classes are likely relevant to the implementation of A. Clearly, this can be applied transitively and in consequence it is theoretically possible that from a single class all existing classes are linked. Therefore we explored different nesting levels in our study.

3   Related Work

In the following we first discuss related work on IR-based trace link creation approaches for structured and unstructured requirements and for considering code structure. Then we discuss related work on the usage of interaction logs. Borg et al. [5] present a current overview of IR based trace link creation approaches based on a systematic literature review. 46 of the 79 analyzed approaches deal with trace link creation between source code and requirements. In contrast to our study most of the approaches use laboratory settings (i.e. student projects) instead of real (open source) projects. We used the assessment of IR algorithms presented by Borg to select VSM and LSI as comparison algorithms for our approach. De Lucia et al. [10] is an example for such a study in which the usage of LSI and VSM are compared. As a result this study reports about possible improvements when using LSI. Our study setup is similar to theirs, since we share the research goal of improving trace link creation. McMillan et al. [25] use source code structure information to improve results of trace links created by VSM. We adapt the use of source code structure in our approach. Instead of using the structure only for verification of already created links by IR we use the source code structure to create additional new links.

Merten et al. [26] have evaluated the application of IR-based trace link creation algorithms in ITS and thus on unstructured requirements data. One of their findings was that preprocessing of the unstructured data is essential for reasonable application of IR. Another finding was that it is not possible to achieve good results for both, precision and recall. In our study we create links between (requirements) issues and source code instead of links between issues.

To identify related work using interaction data we completely explored the Mining Software Repositories conference proceedings, but did not find any approaches using interactions for trace link creation. In consequence we also partly searched in the ICSE and RE proceedings and identified the following relevant publications.

Kersten et al. [17] describe the initial version of Mylyn called Mylar. The basic idea of Mylyn is to reduce the information overload in an IDE by exploiting the interactions of a developer. To do so Mylyn provides the functionality to associate interactions to issues from an ITS within the IDE. With our approach we use these interaction logs available in Mylyn by filtering and aggregating the logs on different levels of granularity and directly providing links in the ITS to the code.

Konopka et al. [19] show that interaction logs are helpful to derive links between development artifacts. They also use Mylyn generated interaction logs

and data from the Mylyn project for development and evaluation of their approach. We adopt interaction based link creation for our trace link creation approach, but in contrast to their focus on code relations we derive links between
unstructured requirements and source code. Omoronyia et al. [30] capture interactions between source code and structured requirements specified as use cases
to infer trace links based on statistical evaluation of the interactions. We adopt
their approach using select and edit events for trace link creation. In contrast to
our goal their tool support focuses on visualizing the trace links after a task has
been performed and not on direct availability and usage of trace links. Asuncion and Taylor [3] describe the principle of recording interaction for trace link
creation, but do not provide a tool. In contrast to our approach their focus has
been trace link creation between structured requirements and design oriented
artifacts. In our earlier work we used VCS based changed logs, a coarse-grained
form of interaction logs, using work items as intermediate elements to create
trace links between source code and requirements [11]. Our actual approach
improves this earlier work. With more fine grained interactions more detailed
trace links can be created.

4   Interaction Log Trace Link Creation Approach

Figure 1 shows the overview of our IL approach. After the capture of the interaction logs in Mylyn there are two steps to create links. In the first step links
are created based solely on interaction logs. In the second step the source code
structure is used to create further trace links between requirements and code. We
implemented both trace link creation steps in a Python and Java based tool. The
NLTK library[4] is used to create the trace links. In the second step Eclipse JDT
library[5] is used to create the code structure considered for trace link creation.
The used interaction logs are based on the selected requirement in the ITS and
the implementation artifacts managed within a VCS. In our approach we only
use edit and select events, since these are directly triggered by a developer and
indicate relations between the affected artifacts and the processed requirement
(filtering). Trace links are created between a requirement and all source code
artifacts touched by select or edit interaction events. We support aggregation of
links, e.g. if trace links are created to multiple methods of a class, these links are
aggregated to a single link on file level. In our tool the granularity level of the
created trace links is configurable. To be comparable with IR created trace links,
which only support file granularity we configure our approach in the study to
aggregate interaction log created links to file level. Also the usage of source code
structure is configurable wrt. the nesting level of source code relations. E.g. if
there are classes A, B, C and D with the relations $A \rightarrow B \rightarrow C \rightarrow D$ and there
is a trace link, created by interaction logs, between requirement R and class A
($R \rightarrow A$), then the nesting level two will result in the creation of two additional
trace links $R \rightarrow B$ and $R \rightarrow C$.

---

[4] http://www.nltk.org/, Python Natural Language Toolkit.
[5] http://www.eclipse.org/jdt/, Eclipse Java development tools.

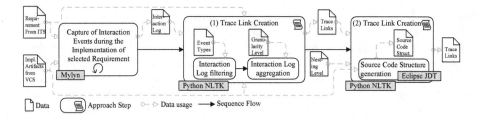

Fig. 1. IL approach overview

5   Experiment Design

In this section we describe the design of our evaluation experiment. Figure 2 shows the overview of the activities for the experimental design of our study. It is guided by the detailed research questions stated in the following Sect. 5.1. In the experiment we evaluate two different data sets both taken from the Mylyn project. The detailed characteristics of the data sets and our process to select the two data sets are described in Sect. 5.2. For each of the two data sets the experiment steps are:

Link Creation. Creation of trace links with our IL approach and the two selected IR algorithms VSM and LSI (cf. 5.3) and consideration of the source code structure. We apply this to both IR and IL.

Evaluation. Manual evaluation of trace links created with IL followed by manual evaluation of trace links created with IR. In the evaluation of IR trace links we could use the links already verified in the manual evaluation of IL trace links (cf. 5.4).

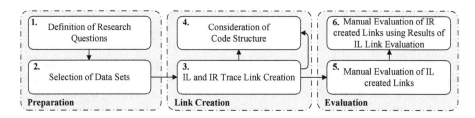

Fig. 2. Experimental design: Overview of performed activities

5.1   Research Questions

Our overall research question is **Is there a difference between the application of IR and IL based trace link creation regarding precision and relative recall?** We divide this into three sub-questions:

RQ₁: *What is the precision of IR and IL created trace links?* Our hypothesis is that the precision of IL is better than IR, since link creation in IL is based on developers' expert knowledge.

RQ$_2$: *What is the relative recall of IR and IL created trace links?* Our hypothesis is that the relative recall of IL is at least as good as the relative recall of IR. On the one hand IL can find links between artifacts which are not textual similar. On the other hand artifacts found by IR are also covered by interactions.

RQ$_3$: *What is the impact of using code structure?* Our hypothesis is that using the code structure in addition to IL and IR improves the relative recall of both trace link creation approaches.

5.2   Selection of Data Sets

The data sets used in our study consist of data from the Bugzilla ITS for requirements and interaction logs and from the Git VCS for implementation artifacts. For trace link creation with our IL approach we used all three data sources (requirements, implementation artifacts, interaction logs) whereas for IR-based trace link creation only requirements and implementation artifacts have been used. Issues in the Mylyn project have been created starting from early 2005, however the open source development of Mylyn really started at the beginning of 2007 when its source code first was made publicly available. The development activity of Mylyn decreased in the last years but is still ongoing. A reason for this is that the major features are already implemented and development efforts mostly concern bug fixing.

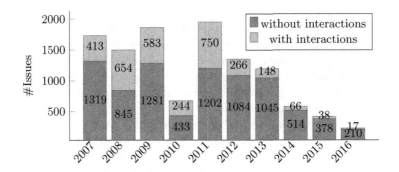

Fig. 3. Issue in the Mylyn Bugzilla ITS per year

Figure 3 shows the number of issues with and without interaction per year until mid of June 2016 when we fetched the data for our study. Till then there were a total of 11490 issues from which 3179 (27.7%) have interaction logs attached and therefore are suitable for our study. In total the 3179 issues have over 3 million interaction log entries attached. Based on these general data characteristics we decided to evaluate only a subset of the existing interaction logs by selecting a suitable subset of requirements issues. We used the following criteria for the requirements selection:

C_1: There should be two distinct data sets from different project phases, i.e. from early phase and later phase. Thereby we want to check whether IL trace link creation is applicable for different project circumstances.

C_2: The number of interactions in the two sets should be as similar as possible to ensure the comparability of the two data sets. Due to the data characteristics this criteria could only be fulfilled up to a certain extent, since also the number of interactions by issue decreases during the years.

These criteria resulted in the creation of two data sets. The *first data set R_{2007}* consists of the first 50 requirements issues in 2007 (and the corresponding interaction log and code) and the *second data set R_{2012}* consists of the first 50 requirements issues in 2012 (and the corresponding interaction logs and code). We used the first requirements of the years, as the Mylyn project employs an annual release cycle with a major release every June. Therefore, new requirements are mostly created at the beginning of a year whereas around the release date more bugs are created. Requirements are described as natural language text using the Bugzilla issue format, i.e. a title, a description text and technical meta-data like the affected components and the assignee. For each data set requirement issues including the comments and interaction logs have been downloaded from Bugzilla. Comments have been included, since they often contain requirement relevant information, e.g. changes to the functionality initially stated in the description. Since there is no explicit classification of the issues as requirement or as bug, we performed this classification for the issues by ourselves. First we fetched an overview list with all issue titles and then manually performed the classification of the issues by reading their title. If classification was not possible by only using the title, we also read the issues description. The two requirements sets have slightly different characteristics. In the first phase of the Mylyn project more complex requirements concerning the basic functionality and in the later phase of the project more requirements concerning small and advanced functionality have been implemented.

To identify the code related to the requirements we used a specific VCS version tag. For each data set we sorted all interaction log entries of the interaction logs in chronological order and then used the first version tag after the last interaction log entry. We assume the so selected VCS version comprises the implementation of the 50 requirements. From these implementation artifacts we removed all artifacts which are not textual and cannot be processed with IR such as pictures or binaries.

Table 1 shows the overview of both data sets. As expected there are much more implementation artifacts in the second (later) data set than in the first data set. In contrast, the amount of interaction log entries, overall and also for each requirement, in the second data set is lower than in the first data set. Therefore, only a minor part of all implementation artifacts are directly touched by interactions.

Table 1. Study data sets overview

Data set	#Requirements	#Int. Log entries	VCS version tag	#Impl. Artifacts		
				All	*Textual*	*Touched by IL*
R_{2007}	50	7687	*R_2_0_RC1*	1103	756	585
R_{2012}	50	1660	*R_3_8_3*	3451	2119	172

5.3 IR-based Trace Link Creation

For IR-based trace link creation we applied both IR algorithms VSM and LSI to the two data sets R_{2007} and R_{2012}. Upfront we applied the preprocessing steps as described in Sect. 2.1 to all used artifacts. We restricted the trace link candidate generation to links from requirements to implementation artifacts.

Table 2. Thresholds and number of candidate links for IR algorithms

Thresholds*	0.9	0.8	0.7	0.6	0.5	0.4	0.3
R_{2007} VSM	0	50	596	2347	6419	13798	24040
R_{2007} LSI	0	3	8	40	142	354	1058
R_{2012} VSM	185	2268	6431	12333	22397	39434	64284
R_{2012} LSI	1	14	86	297	920	2424	6014

*Selected values are highlighted

To determine a reasonable threshold for the IR algorithms we initially used approved threshold values of 0.7 for VSM [8] and 0.3 for LSI [10]. While this worked well for R_{2007}, we had to choose different thresholds for R_{2012}. As can be seen from Table 2, which shows the number of candidate links for different IR thresholds, for the second data set the number of generated links increases very quickly with lowering the threshold. To limit the effort for the verification of the links, we used thresholds with less than 1000 links. Clearly, the results for R_{2012} can only be seen as a first indication and can be improved with lower thresholds.

5.4 Data Evaluation

To evaluate the trace links created with our IL approach we compared the created links from both data sets (R_{2007} and R_{2012}) with links created by IR. We used two settings for trace link creation: one with code structure and one without. We performed the following steps to determine TP and FP for these link sets. We manually verified links created by IL in R_{2007} and R_{2012}. Subsequently, we removed these verified links from the IR trace link candidate sets. This resulted in sets of link candidates only found by IR. We also manually verified these links.

Finally, we use the verified IR links and the verified IL links to determine the set of links only found by IL.

6   Results

In the following subsections we answer the research questions of our study and discuss the results. In Sect. 6.1 we answer RQ_1 and RQ_2 concerning precision and relative recall of IL and IR created trace links. This is followed by the answer to RQ_3 concerning the consideration of code structure in Sect. 6.2.

6.1   Precision (RQ_1) and Relative Recall (RQ_2)

Table 3 shows the overview of the number of created trace link candidates, used implementation artifacts, used requirements, correct trace links, implementation artifacts involved in correct trace links, requirements involved in correct trace links, sum of correct trace links created by all approaches together, precision and relative recall for both data sets. Thus, we can answer our research questions as follows.

Table 3. Comparison of IR and IL trace link creation

	R_{2007}			R_{2012}		
	IL	IR ($VSM_{0.7}$)	IR ($LSI_{0.3}$)	IL	IR ($VSM_{0.9}$)	IR ($LSI_{0.5}$)
#Link cand. (LC)	1148	596	1058	240	185	920
#Impl. Artifact$_{LC}$	585	203	384	172	171	444
#Requirements$_{LC}$	50	23	46	37	4	34
#True positive (TP)	1148	204	328	240	25	274
Trace links		$(118_{IL} + 17_{LSI} + 69)$	$(184_{IL} + 37_{VSM} + 107)$		$(6_{IL}+24_{LSI}+1)$	$(41_{IL} + 24_{VSM} + 250)$
#Impl. Artifact$_{TP}$	585	126	200	240	24	169
#Requirements$_{TP}$	50	19	41	172	3	28
#Trace links$_{TP}$ by	1324			491		
all Approaches	$(1148_{IL} + 69_{VSM} + 107_{LSI})$			$(240_{IL} + 1_{VSM} 250_{LSI})$		
Precision	1	0.341	0.310	1	0.135	0.298
Relative recall	0.867	0.154	0.247	0.418	0.051	0.534

RQ_1: What is the precision of IR and IL created trace links? For both data sets all links created with our IL approach were correct (100% precision). For IR precision values vary between 13% and 34% with little difference between VSM and LSI for the standard thresholds in the first data sets and big difference for the higher thresholds in the second data set. Thus, IL clearly outperforms IR. Moreover, IL is independent from setting a threshold and finds more correct links than IR for the R_{2007} data set. Nevertheless, there are also links only discovered by IR in this data set.

For our R_{2012} data set the situation is different due to the smaller number of IL created trace links and much larger amount of used implementation artifacts for IR. Note that not all requirements are involved in interaction links in this set. This is due to the fact that some interactions concerned code outside of the VCS tag (e.g. used framework). LSI finds in total more correct trace links for the second data set than IL. This can be explained by the amount of considered requirements and implementation artifacts, i.e. IL considered 37 requirements and 172 implementation artifacts whereas LSI considered 34 and 444. In comparison with the values achieved by current approaches as discussed in Sect. 2.3 we can state that the 100% precision of IL in a real world setup is unique. The precision of IR is acceptable for the first and good for the second data set. The values for precision are in the range reported by DeLucia [10] (LSI), Ali [2](VSM) and Merten [27] (LSI, VSM, ITS as data source).

RQ_2: *What is the relative recall of IR and IL created trace links?* The used setting in our experiment resulted in relative recall rates between 5% and 53% (cf. Table 3) for IR and in relative recall rates of 86% and almost 42% for IL. As expected and reported by others [7,14], IR creates a lot of false positive trace links even with the moderate threshold setting we used for the second data set in our experiment. The difference in relative recall rates between the R_{2007} and R_{2012} data sets in our IL approach can be explained by the characteristics of the data sets which resulted in a lower number of interactions for the second R_{2012} data set (cf. Sect. 5.2, Table 1: R_{2007} has 7687 interactions on 756 used implementation artifacts, R_{2012} has 1660 interactions on 2119 used implementation artifacts).

6.2 Using Code Structure (RQ3)

As mentioned in Sect. 2.4 the first results concern the setting of an appropriate nesting level. Table 4 shows the differences according to the number of created links and their precision for considering code structure with different nesting levels for the R_{2007} data sets. $R_{2007}IL$ refers to links generated by our IL approach and $R_{2007}IR$ to links generated by IR. Since precision for IL drops when considering a nesting level of code relations greater than four, we used this nesting level for the answer of RQ3. It also can be seen that precision of IR only drops for nesting level 10. As our current focus is to maximize the precision of the IL approach, we choose level 4. Clearly, the results for IR could be improved with higher nesting level. We also performed this analysis for our second data set. Since the results are quite similar, we skip their detailed report here.

RQ_3: *What is the impact of using code structure?* As shown in Table 5 for both data sets all links created with our IL approach were also correct (100% precision) when considering code structure. Furthermore, relative recall was increased considerably for the second data set. Comparing Tables 3 and 5 we can see that the code structure consideration for IL results in five times more trace links for the second data set and twice as much links for the first data set. This can be explained by the more complex code structure due to the maturity of the project in the second data set.

Both IL and IR considered about 1/3 more implementation artifacts when using code structure. For VSM and LSI in the R_{2007} data set this resulted in an

Table 4. Trace links for different code nesting levels

Nesting level	$R_{2007}IL$			$R_{2007}IR$					
	#Link cand.	#TP links	Precision	#Link cand.		#TP Links[a]		Precision	
				$VSM_{0.7}$	$LSI_{0.3}$	$VSM_{0.7}$	$LSI_{0.3}$	$VSM_{0.7}$	$LSI_{0.3}$
0	1148	1148	1.000	596	1058	120	184	0.201	0.174
1	1446	1446	1.000	858	1718	234	338	0.273	0.197
2	1831	1831	1.000	1108	2181	363	562	0.328	0.258
3	2204	2204	1.000	1382	2706	499	805	0.361	0.297
4	2565	2565	1.000	1624	3214	639	1083	0.393	0.337
5	3027	2854	0.943	1915	3927	781	1349	0.408	0.344
6	3531	3202	0.907	2253	4510	947	1612	0.420	0.357
10	5805	3639	0.627	3374	5488	1258	1779	0.373	0.324

[a] Compared to IL

Table 5. IR and IL trace links considering code structure

	R_{2007}			R_{2012}		
	IL	IR ($VSM_{0.7}$)	IR ($LSI_{0.3}$)	IL	IR ($VSM_{0.9}$)	IR ($LSI_{0.5}$)
#Link Cand. (LC)	2565	1624	3143	1126	458	2766
#Impl. Artifact$_{LC}$	627	333	516	363	343	702
#Requirements$_{LC}$	50	23	46	37	4	34
#TP trace links of Trace links	2565	698 (581_{IL} + 63_{LSI} + 54)	1214 (1010_{IL} + 62_{VSM} + 142)	1126	108 (91_{IL} + 17_{LSI} + 0)	784 (491_{IL} + 11_{VSM} + 282)
#Impl. Artifact$_{TP}$	627	229	308	363	73	354
#Requirements (TP)	50	22	41	37	4	35
#Trace links$_{TP}$ by all Approaches	2761 (2565_{IL} + 54_{VSM} + 142_{LSI})			1408 (1126_{IL} + 0_{VSM} + 282_{LSI})		
Precision	1	0.425	0.386	1	0.236	0.283
Relative recall	0.929	0.253	0.440	0.800	0.077	0.557

increase of precision and relative recall. This is also true for the R_{2012} data set, except for the precision value of LSI which slightly drops.

In our experiments we could reduce the number of links only found by IR to almost zero by increasing the nesting levels of code relations. However, this also resulted in false positive links for IL which is contrary to our research goal to create trace links with 100% precision. Altogether, we can see that by using code structure we could achieve our research goal of 100% precision and excellent relative recall and that IL outperforms IR for both Mylyn project data sets.

7   Threats to Validity

In this section we discuss the threats to validity of our study. The internal validity is threatened as manual validation of trace links was only performed by one researcher. However, this researcher is very familiar with the Mylyn project in general, its source code, the used development infrastructure, and has Mylyn specific development experience for almost ten years.

When comparing the results achieved with our approach to IR the setup of the IR algorithms is a crucial factor. Wrt. preprocessing we performed all common steps including the identifier splitting which is specific to our used data set. However, the higher threshold for the second data set and the nesting level restriction impairs the results for IR. Thus, further comparison of IL and IR for data sets with few interactions is necessary.

Clearly, the external validity depends on the availability of interaction logs and respective tooling and usage of the tooling by developers. Up to now we have only studied one open source project retrospectively. While the generalizability based on one project is clearly limited, we think that using an open source project is not a limitation: Since IL performed quite well in the loosely organized and structured open source project, we expect even better results when applying the approach to a more strictly structured industry project.

8   Conclusion

The results for our IL approach are encouraging. With IL we could create trace links with 100% precision for two different data sets. Also our calculated relative recall values are excellent, i.e. almost 96% for the first and 80% for the second data set. Thus, the approach and the study show that trace link creation in practice can be supported with little extra effort for the developers. Clearly, the comparison with IR is only preliminary. We did not use the common thresholds for the second data set and we could only compute relative recall.

We already created a tool to assess created trace links in detail. The tool enables the automation of all steps necessary to compare two trace link sets on the basis of single requirements. The usage of this tool for detailed trace link evaluation and the determination of absolute recall values are part of our planed follow up study.

We will investigate the application of our approach including the evaluation of its practicability in a real project. The project started in Fall 2016 and lasts until Spring 2017. In this project we evaluate IL in a different context (Scrum, IntelliJ, Jira) where we can create both, interaction logs and a gold standard, and thus compute recall and provide a full comparison with IR. Furthermore, we evaluate the usage of IL created trace links by incorporating them into the ITS. To improve our approach further, we will investigate the use of existing trace links in combination with IL [16].

Acknowledgment. We thank the open source community for providing the data for our research.

References

1. Ali, N., Gueheneuc, Y.G., Antoniol, G.: Requirements traceability for object oriented systems by partitioning source code. In: Conference on Reverse Engineering, pp. 45–54. IEEE, October 2011
2. Ali, N., Gueheneuc, Y.G., Antoniol, G.: Trustrace: mining software repositories to improve the accuracy of requirement traceability links. IEEE TSE **39**(5), 725–741 (2013)
3. Asuncion, H.U., Taylor, R.N.: Automated techniques for capturing custom traceability links across heterogeneous artifacts. In: Cleland-Huang, J., Gotel, O., Zisman, A. (eds.) Software and Systems Traceability, pp. 129–146. Springer, London (2012)
4. Baeza-Yates, R., Ribeiro-Neto, B.: Modern Information Retrieval, 2nd edn. Pearson, Addison-Wesley, Harlow, Munich (2011)
5. Borg, M., Runeson, P., Ardö, A.: Recovering from a decade: a systematic mapping of information retrieval approaches to software traceability. Empir. Softw. Eng. **19**(6), 1–52 (2013)
6. Briand, L., Falessi, D., Nejati, S., Sabetzadeh, M., Yue, T.: Traceability and SysML design slices to support safety inspections. ACM ToSEM **23**(1), 1–43 (2014)
7. Cleland-Huang, J., Berenbach, B., Clark, S., Settimi, R., Romanova, E.: Best practices for automated traceability. Computer **40**(6), 27–35 (2007)
8. De Lucia, A., Fasano, F., Oliveto, R., Tortora, G.: Enhancing an artefact management system with traceability recovery features. In: ICSM, pp. 306–315. IEEE (2004)
9. De Lucia, A., Di Penta, M., Oliveto, R.: Improving source code lexicon via traceability and information retrieval. IEEE TSE **37**(2), 205–227 (2011)
10. De Lucia, A., Fasano, F., Oliveto, R., Tortora, G.: Recovering traceability links in software artifact management systems using information retrieval methods. ACM ToSEM **16**(4), 1–50 (2007)
11. Delater, A., Paech, B.: Tracing requirements and source code during software development: an empirical study. In: International Symposium on Empirical Software Engineering and Measurement, pp. 25–34. IEEE/ACM, Baltimore, October 2013
12. Falessi, D., Di Penta, M., Canfora, G., Cantone, G.: Estimating the number of remaining links in traceability recovery. Empir. Softw. Eng. (2016)
13. Fricke, M.: Measuring recall. J. Inf. Sci. **24**(6), 409–417 (1998)
14. Gotel, O., Cleland-Huang, J., Hayes, J.H., Zisman, A., Egyed, A., Grunbacher, P., Antoniol, G.: The quest for ubiquity: a roadmap for software and systems traceability research. In: RE, pp. 71–80. IEEE, September 2012
15. Hayes, J., Dekhtyar, A., Sundaram, S.: Advancing candidate link generation for requirements tracing: the study of methods. IEEE TSE **32**(1), 4–19 (2006)
16. Hübner, P.: Quality improvements for trace links between source code and requirements. In: Joint Proceedings of REFSQ Workshops, Doctoral Symposium, Research Method Track, and Poster Track. CEUR-WS, Gothenburg, Sweden (2016)
17. Kersten, M., Murphy, G.C.: Using task context to improve programmer productivity. In: Proceedings of the 14th ACM SIGSOFT International Symposium on Foundations of Software Engineering - SIGSOFT 2006/FSE 2014, pp. 1–11. ACM, New York, November 2006
18. Konopka, M., Navrat, P.: Untangling development tasks with software developer's activity. In: International Workshop on Context for Software Development, pp. 13–14. IEEE/ACM, May 2015

19. Konopka, M., Navrat, P., Bielikova, M.: Poster: discovering code dependencies by harnessing developer's activity. In: ICSE, pp. 801–802. IEEE/ACM, May 2015

20. Kumar, B., Prakash, J.: Precision and relative recall of search engines: a comparative study of Google and Yahoo. Singap. J. Libr. Inf. Manag. **38**(1), 124–137 (2009)

21. Maalej, W., Ellmann, M.: On the similarity of task contexts. In: International Workshop on Context for Software Development, pp. 8–12. IEEE/ACM, May 2015

22. Maalej, W., Kurtanovic, Z., Felfernig, A.: What stakeholders need to know about requirements. In: EmpiRE, pp. 64–71. IEEE, August 2014

23. Mäder, P., Egyed, A.: Do developers benefit from requirements traceability when evolving and maintaining a software system? Empir. Softw. Eng. **20**(2), 413–441 (2015)

24. Manning, C.D., Raghavan, P., Schütze, H.: Introduction to Information Retrieval, 1st edn. Cambridge University Press, Cambridge (2008)

25. McMillan, C., Poshyvanyk, D., Revelle, M.: Combining textual and structural analysis of software artifacts for traceability link recovery. In: ICSE Workshop on Traceability in Emerging Forms of SE, pp. 41–48. IEEE, May 2009

26. Merten, T., Falisy, M., Hübner, P., Quirchmayr, T., Bürsner, S., Paech, B.: Software feature request detection in issue tracking systems. In: RE, IEEE, September 2016

27. Merten, T., Krämer, D., Mager, B., Schell, P., Bürsner, S., Paech, B.: Do information retrieval algorithms for automated traceability perform effectively on issue tracking system data? In: Daneva, M., Pastor, O. (eds.) REFSQ 2016. LNCS, vol. 9619, pp. 45–62. Springer, Heidelberg (2016). doi:10.1007/978-3-319-30282-9_4

28. Murphy, G., Kersten, M., Findlater, L.: How are Java software developers using the elipse IDE? IEEE Softw. **23**(4), 76–83 (2006)

29. Niu, N., Mahmoud, A.: Enhancing candidate link generation for requirements tracing: the cluster hypothesis revisited. In: RE, pp. 81–90. IEEE, September 2012

30. Omoronyia, I., Sindre, G., Roper, M., Ferguson, J., Wood, M.: Use case to source code traceability: the developer navigation view point. In: RE, pp. 237–242. IEEE, Los Alamitos, August 2009

A Requirements Traceability Approach
to Support Mission Assurance
and Configurability in the Military

James Lockerbie[1(✉)], Neil Maiden[1], Chris Williams[2],
and Leigh Chase[3]

[1] City, University of London, London, UK
{James.Lockerbie.1, N.A.M.Maiden}@city.ac.uk
[2] Dstl Porton Down, Salisbury, UK
cwilliams@dstl.gov.uk
[3] IBM UK Ltd., Winchester, UK
Leigh_chase@uk.ibm.com

Abstract. *Context & motivation*: A challenge facing military mission planning is how to relate high-level mission objectives down to available human and technical assets. Understanding how changes in requirements affect the objectives, and how requirements can be revised to meet changing objectives, is critical to the design and implementation of mission configurable systems. *Question/problem*: Whilst current toolsets provide support for static requirements approaches, there is a need for a new approach to meet the dynamic nature of operational mission assurance and configuration. *Principal ideas/results*: Therefore, we have developed a new mission aware approach based on requirements traceability and metric measurements to enable the propagation of system performance to goal impacts. The approach is delivered through REDEPEND, an *i** goal modelling tool, underpinned with a controlled natural language reasoning engine, CEStore. *Contribution*: We report the approach and provide lessons learned from applying it to a real-world military scenario.

Keywords: Requirements traceability · Goal modelling · Controlled english · Mission assurance · Mission configurability

1 Introduction

Mission planning in the military involves the definition of mission objectives, the processes that deliver the objectives, and the capabilities and assets required to enable them. Relating high-level mission objectives down to available assets is a significant challenge facing the military – a challenge which can be viewed from two perspectives. First, *mission assurance* considers how changes in the performance and behaviors of a given configuration of human and technical assets impacts the mission objectives. In practical terms, mission assurance could provide military commanders and operators with prior warning of asset degradation to afford them more time to mitigate risks. Second, *mission configurability* considers how the available personnel, processes and

© Springer International Publishing AG 2017
P. Grünbacher and A. Perini (Eds.): REFSQ 2017, LNCS 10153, pp. 308–323, 2017.
DOI: 10.1007/978-3-319-54045-0_22

technologies need to be reconfigured to deliver changes in mission objectives. In practice, commanders and operators could be provided with greater scope for assessing the impact of reconfigurations prior to asset redistributions being carried out.

Existing work has sought to model the elements of a mission thread, from objectives down to assets, an example being the System of Systems Metamodel [1]. Whilst this model provides an architectural view of the layers in the system and how they connect, it lacks any notion of the required quality levels and any subsequent indications of risk to the overall system. Although an approach such as the NATO model [2] provides an example of traceability with quality measures across a mission thread, it does not support the writing of requirements. Whilst commercial toolsets support static requirements capture, they do not provide the support needed in a dynamic military environment. Through a static approach a system may deliver against the original design requirements, but as mission objectives change and evolve, or assets are taken into environments not foreseen as part of the original requirements capture, there is a lack of support for military personnel to handle this. Therefore, our work sought to provide solution ideas for these needs by drawing upon research in the areas of requirements engineering and conceptual modeling. The result was a new approach called MANGO, which integrates goal modelling, rich traceability and measurable requirements with a conceptual model that supports machine reasoning and automated deduction capability. This proof of concept approach was applied to a real-world military scenario and implemented though an integrated software prototype.

In this paper, we report project work undertaken for the Defence Science and Technology Laboratory (Dstl), an agency of the UK Ministry of Defence (MOD) that provides science and technology advice to MOD and wider Government. The next section of the paper outlines the requirements problem and describes the current military approach. Section 3 describes our development approach and Sect. 4 presents our method, called MANGO, in detail. In Sect. 5 we present a case study and show a worked example of our approach. Section 6 provides lessons learned and the paper ends with our plans for future development of our approach and tool support.

2 The Requirements Problem

Changes to the dynamics of the military environment and technology landscape have led to changes in the needs of military stakeholders over recent decades. Requirements include the need to shift towards more agile operations and to improve situational awareness whilst dealing with the resulting increases in infrastructure demands.

The background to our mission assurance and configurability problem has been well documented within the military, and three clearly defined aims were presented to us to address in our project work:

1. To enable modelling of a mission covering objectives, process, capabilities and assets, along with more complex dependencies between requirements.
2. To provide support for rich traceability to justify the requirements and how sub-requirements are combined to meet a higher level requirement.
3. To provide the means to show impacts on goals through automated reasoning.

Along with these three requirements, we also needed to consider how the overall approach would be delivered to users through a new toolset.

As mentioned earlier, the System of Systems Metamodel [1] provides us with a conceptual model of mission awareness across a complex system in its broadest context, shown in Fig. 1. The model illustrates the system layers from mission objectives down to assets.

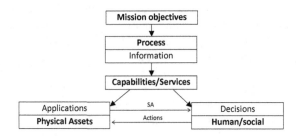

Fig. 1. System of systems conceptual model of a mission

Mission objectives captures the high level strategic objective that the commander seeks to attain. A single top level objective may be defined along with a number of sub-objectives that may require coordination/deconfliction during an operation. *Process/information* shows a mission task, or a unified series of tasks, from a logical perspective rather than relating to any physical implementation. The process views enable critical processes to be identified and show how they contribute to the mission, and provide a mapping to the capabilities that enable their implementation. *Capabilities* refers to the services or functions required to enable the process to be carried out in practice – they are not particular systems or equipment. In this model, capabilities are delivered through packages that link operational outcomes (mission objectives) to assets. At this layer, Systems of Sytems (SoS) are created, bringing together individual systems that are designed to operate autonomously. *Assets* are the means to implement capability in practice. The *Physical assets* element represents data exchanges between assets that support information flows identified by the Process element. The *Human/social* element includes knowledge, such as experience and situational awareness (SA), which is stored and used in context towards decision making.

However, this conventional architectural view only shows how elements are connected in the system and does not give any indication of the required levels of performance. It fails to provide support for answering important questions concerning what quality levels are acceptable and what are the risks. Whilst individual systems and their behaviors are typically well understood, combining such systems at the capability layer adds uncertainty, compounded by the limited time available for testing operational systems, particularly in a coalition arrangement. Therefore, there is a need to capture functional requirements of the subsystems and their metrics.

An example of metrics traceability within a military context is provided by the NATO model [2] which shows a hierarchy of measures covering policy at the mission objective layer, measures of effectiveness at the process and capability layers, and performance measures at the asset layer. However, the NATO model does not provide the necessary framework for writing requirements and providing traceability in a dynamic environment. Moreover at present, performance metrics are usually communicated in very different ways at each level of the system hierarchy. There is a need for a whole system view which presents performance in a meaningful way from the lower levels through to command levels, not least to avoid information overload for the commander. In simple terms, requirements and metrics need to be captured at each level, along with traceability between the architectural layers.

3 Development of a New Approach

Our research method followed a design cycle, iterating over design and investigation as described in [3]. We undertook three distinct project phases, each of which investigated the problem, considered treatments for the problem and presented the results to stakeholders for validation. First, we undertook a scoping study to determine whether requirements traceability could be a solution to the problems of mission assurance and mission configurability. Our study, reported in [1], investigated research in requirements engineering and conceptual modeling, including $i*$ goal modelling [4] Goal Structuring Notation (GSN) [5], satisfaction arguments [6] and Controlled English [7]. Our findings were reported to Dstl and presented to a wider military audience of stakeholders including commanders in the armed forces. It was concluded that the problems of mission assurance and configurability could be addressed by a combination of $i*$ goal modelling backed by a conceptual model implemented using Controlled English (CE). The second phase focused on requirements definition and semantic processing through the integration of $i*$ and CE. Formative evaluation was undertaken during the project and stakeholder feedback and lessons learned informed further development of the tool-based approach during the third phase of our project. We report our approach in the next section.

4 The MANGO Approach

The MANGO (Mission Assurance aNd Goal Orientation) approach is based on goal-oriented requirements engineering and a core conceptual model for Mission Assurance and Configuration. The approach is delivered through a goal modelling tool that provides visualizations to users and interoperates with a reasoning engine to demonstrate goal propagation outcomes. We describe each aspect of our approach as follows.

4.1 Goal-Based Modelling with Hierarchical $i*$

Goal modelling is a well-established requirements engineering technique with reported advantages that include the ability to show vertical traceability, from high-level strategic concerns to low-level technical details, and to provide a comprehensible structure to requirements in one single framework [8]. These advantages, amongst others, allow for a richer description of relationships than the existing model-based approaches used by the military [e.g. 2].

For our approach, we adopted the *i** framework [4, 9] supported in a new version of our Microsoft Visio based *i** modelling tool, REDEPEND [10]. Unlike other goal modelling approaches, such as KAOS [11], *i** contains a vivid visual representation of actor boundaries, useful for representing responsibilities and identifying vulnerabilities in socio-technical systems. Indeed, a primary aim of using *i** was to provide a one model visualization with usable viewpoints for presenting complex systems and concepts to military stakeholders. Our previous work in this area, for example in Air Traffic Management [12] proved its effectiveness as a communication tool and suitable for complex analysis through tool support. Despite the advantages of *i** and REDEPEND, there was a need to adapt the modeling for the needs of the stakeholders in the military domain.

We integrated the actor-based approach with the architectural view of the mission thread to enable responsibilities and complex dependencies to be presented within a context familiar to the users. The use of actors enables the users to specify and view requirements and associated concepts on a specific area of the model whilst being aware of dependencies to other actors. In addition to the mission layers, we implemented organizational boundaries for the divisions of the Permanent Joint Headquarters (PJHQ) in which to group actors. These Joint Functions, J1 to J9, are well understood by military users and useful tool for communicating our approach visually.

Following the presentation of our original scoping study we received a recommendation to simplify the number of constructs and relationships provided from the traditional *i** approach. A key requirement was that stakeholders, with limited time, could receive the benefits of the analysis without the overhead of learning a raft of modelling syntax. For example, rather than modelling tasks we model the goal state the task function achieves. Furthermore, the military already model tasks using Business Process Modelling Notation (BPMN) [13] which capture temporality that is unavailable in traditional *i** modelling. Figure 2 shows the organizational constructs and relationships of our adapted *i** modelling notation, as drawn in the REDEPEND tool.

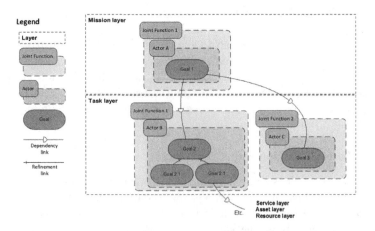

Fig. 2. Organizational constructs of the *i** model adapted for use in the military

4.2 Rich Traceability Through *i** Modelling

Requirements capture and system design for missions are not independent processes in the military and thus dependencies and assumptions need to be captured to provide an audit trail of how the design was developed [1]. Therefore, the MANGO approach includes concepts for capturing rich traceability that lie behind the *i** goal model. Rich traceability, defined by Hull et al. [14], concerns capturing the rationale associated with relationships, and can be applied in the form of a satisfaction argument [15]. Whilst satisfaction arguments have been applied to goal models before, for example KAOS [16] and GSN [6], our approach introduces actor ownership and provides traceability for metrics classes and non-functional requirements types typical of the military domain – shown in the schema in Fig. 3. We look at the main aspects of our schema in turn.

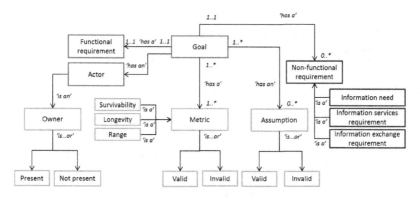

Fig. 3. Schema that relates goals to underlying requirements concepts

Requirements. Each goal is associated with a functional requirement that provides a realization of the goal's intent, and a set of non-functional requirements (NFRs) with a range of quality attributes that need to be met. Our treatment of the NFRs applies the military taxonomy for information requirements [17], from which 3 classifications of information types can be derived:

1. Information Needs.
2. Information Service Flow Requirements.
3. Information Exchange Requirements.

Taking this taxonomy, our approach aligns these requirement classes with our layered goal model to provide structure and ownership by allocating requirements to actors (also described as owners that are present/not present in our conceptual model). Another driver for us using a goal-based approach is the need for a Commander and their staff to express their information needs rather than the processes and/or systems they are familiar with, as mentioned in [17]. Starting with the task layer, the information needs (INs) specified by the Commander are associated with specific tasks.

These INs include the quality attributes of timelines, integrity, availability and confidentiality. The INs are then translated through an architecture of core services to derive the information service flow requirements (ISFRs) that capture information flows within and between services. The ISFRs have an additional set of quality attributes relating to throughput (shown later in Sect. 5). Once the information flows between services have been defined, it is possible to identify where the detailed information exchange requirements (IERs) exist in the asset layer e.g. between operational nodes.

The requirements are stored in an Excel spreadsheet, taken from an original Dstl source and embedded within REDEPEND. As these requirements are traced through our conceptual model we were able implement a requirements tree view in the REDEPEND tool, as shown in Fig. 4. This particular example shows a simple trace from the IN derived from the selected *C2* goal to an ISFR, and then onto an IER. The form also shows the goal's details and the non-functional requirements' attributes.

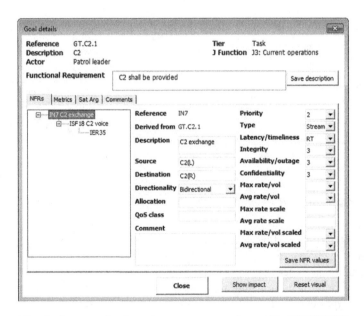

Fig. 4. An example of requirements presentation within REDEPEND

Metrics. A metricated approach is important for military planning as along with specifying requirements on the services and assets (what is needed) there needs to be a way of identifying whether the requirements are being met (have we got it?). In the MANGO approach, metrics are defined with values to determine whether a goal is achieved or not, with an invalid metric leading to the non-achievement of the goal. Each metric falls within one of three metric categories – survivability, longevity or range. These are typical categories used by the military, along with other metric types like security and resilience. In our study, survivability concerns measures such as bandwidth, longevity includes the time of unsupported mission duration, and range features various distances expressed within the location of the mission.

The metrics are stored and presented in a similar way to the requirements. Figure 5 shows metrics in the Excel worksheet, along with their attributes, including the metrics classes and units of measure mentioned above.

1	Ref	Trace	Owner	Description	Class	Threshold value	Threshold unit	Comment
79	MS.SRC.1	None	GS.SRC.1	Support aggregated ISFRs as defined on ISFR sheet	Survivability	As defined by ISFRs	Mbps	None
80	MS.SRC.2	MT.CIS.3	GS.SRC.1	Maintain information protection	Survivability	As defined by ISFRs	n/a	None
81	MS.SRC.3	Policy	GS.SRC.1	Shape traffic according to prioritisation	Survivability	As defined by ISFRs	n/a	None
82	MS.SRC.4	MT.L.1	GS.SRC.1	SRC comms duration	Longevity	5	Hours	None
83	MS.SRC.5	MT.C2.5	GS.SRC.1	SRC comms range (within patrol)	Range	1	km square	None

Fig. 5. Metrics captured in an excel spreadsheet embedded within REDEPEND

Assumptions. As mentioned earlier, there is a need to capture assumptions during the process so that the rationale behind certain decisions can be retrieved if needed in the future. Therefore, policy or domain assumptions are captured that validate or invalidate goal achievement.

The user form enables assumptions to be captured, along with a strategy to form a GSN satisfaction argument [6], as shown in Fig. 6. The satisfaction arguments provide rich traceability and rationale for the goal and its refinement into sub-goals. For example, there are a number of policy assumptions that must hold true for the goal *Urban area clearance of red force* to be achieved, along with some domain assumptions such as the urban area is hostile. The strategy behind this satisfaction argument is to identify the key military tasks to meet the objective. These tasks are represented by sub-goals that need to be sufficiently achieved for the mission objective to be met.

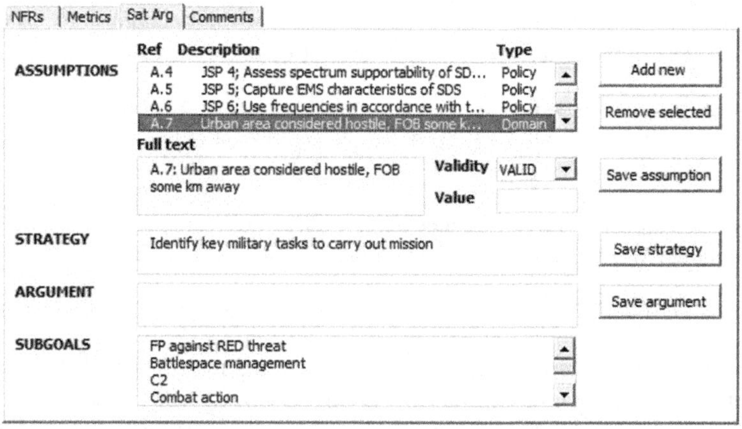

Fig. 6. Satisfaction argument for the mission objective, displayed in REDEPEND

4.3 Core Conceptual Model

In parallel with the *i** model development we also implemented the underlying semantic conceptual model using ITA Controlled English (CE). CE is a Controlled Natural Language within which formal statements can be made that enable model-based reasoning [18]. Based on first-order predicate logic [7], it provides an unambiguous representation of information for machine processing that is also readable by humans [18]. Indeed, a main reason for using CE in the MANGO approach is that the CE syntax is fundamentally motivated by human understandability [7], unlike many other semantic modelling approaches, for example ontologies such as OWL [19]. CE is directly targeted at non-technical domain-specialist users such as military planners [18], providing them with a simple and understandable syntax, rather than a computer language, for interacting with machine reasoning capabilities.

The CE language is implemented in a standalone, self-contained environment called CEStore, which comprises the following components:

The *domain model* – a natural language model containing concepts, relationships and properties, for example:

```
conceptualise a ~ goal ~ G that
  has the value D as ~ descriptive text.
conceptualise the actor A
  ~ owns ~ the goal G.
conceptualise the goal G
  ~ is an objective of ~ the actor A.
```

A set of *rules* – the logic governing the interaction of entities, relationships and outcome/output, for example:

```
if
  ( the goal G is an objective of the actor A )
then
  ( the actor A owns the goal G ).
```

A set of *facts* – describes the instantiation of entities and relationships, as defined within the domain model and governed by the set of rules, for example:

```
there is a goal named '{goalUID}' that is an objective of the actor
  '{actorUID}' and has 'Urban area clearance of red force' as
  descriptive text.
```

When the rules are run they generate new facts that were not necessarily stated when the model was instantiated, for example:

```
the actor {actorUID} owns the goal {goalUID}.
```

These three artefacts are intuitive to both humans and machines – the former being important in driving the user experience and ensuring knowledge is accurately represented. The fundamental value of using CE in this context is three-fold: (i) the domain model forces unambiguous definition of the scenario, its entities and relations – only the words defined by the analyst as part of a conceptual model are used; (ii) it provides objective, deductive machine reasoning about the scenario; and (iii) abstracts the user (and model definition processes) away from the reasoning functions – consistent with sound architectural practices for functional separation. The importance of CE herein is found in its capacity to make meaningful deductions within a multi-faceted, dynamic and complex problem domain. This is brought into sharp focus when considering the difficulty experienced by humans in making decisions and fully comprehending their impact within a high-dimension decision space. Here the CEStore is able to both model and reason within this environment, serving to supplement and support human analysis. Furthermore the CEStore provides the reasoning applied and logic as to what is behind the deductions it makes – for instance:

```
The goal 'C2' has the achievability 'UNACHIEVABLE' because
   The goal 'C2' is dependent on the goal 'Local C2' and
   The goal 'Local C2' has the achievability 'UNACHIEVABLE'
```

In this instance the CEStore reasons that 'C2' cannot be achieved because it depends on second goal ('Local C2') that is itself unachievable. From this example we can infer the rule which relates these concepts – viz. that a goals achievement is predicated upon the achievement of those goals on which it depends. Whilst a trivial example, one can consider how complexity could grow quickly as a scenario becomes more detailed and comprehensively modeled. CE applies this logic recursively in both the *upward* and *downward* direction; meaning any change in the status of the scenario will see the reasoning propagated in both directions. The statement of reasoning is specifically important in this context, where human analysts must be able to fully understand and account for the deductions made within the decision space.

4.4   Combining *i** and Controlled English – REDEPEND:CEStore

Although REDEPEND includes the syntax of *i** modelling it lacks an underlying semantic representation of the graphical model, unlike some of the other *i** tools. An example is OpenOME [20], which includes a metamodel of the *i** concepts and relationships along with a formal representation that uses propositional logic to capture the semantics for enabling reasoning [21]. Therefore, we needed to extend REDE-PEND to enable its integration with the underlying CE conceptual model in the CEStore, as described above. A requirement for our approach was to implement the goal model and conceptual model as separate concerns, as REDEPEND would remain a graphical interface providing visualizations to users, while CEStore would contain the core conceptual model and handle semantic concepts, rules and inferences.

The integration between the 2 tools is enabled through the CEStore API which allows for RESTful HTTP requests. The REDEPEND:CEStore interface is asynchronous and therefore non-blocking, meaning the approach works well within multiple network settings and configurations. Using Visual Basic for Applications (VBA) program code, REDEPEND sends data to the CEStore via HTTP POST requests and receives data via HTTP GET requests. As the CEStore is not persistent, all data concerned with the *i** model is stored within REDEPEND. This includes not only the *i** constructs and attributes but also all the requirements, assumptions and metrics. To begin any analysis, REDEPEND loads the conceptual model in the CEStore and posts *facts* to instantiate the relevant aspects of the conceptual model. It also calls for the rules to be run to trigger the automated reasoning within the CEStore. Responses are sent back to REDEPEND in JSON format and parsed to provide feedback to the user, for example which goals are no longer achieved due to an invalid metric, as shown later in Fig. 8(b).

5 Case Study on a Network-Enabled System

For our case study, proof of concept of the process and tool support was investigated using a network-enabled system scenario. The study was undertaken with Dstl, and we applied our MANGO approach to existing Dstl work on specifying requirements and modelling mission threads.

5.1 Overview of the Military Scenario

Our scenario focused on connectivity, as complex military systems require connectivity between disparate systems to support a range of military stakeholders. Whilst connectivity can provide beneficial support to personnel, processes and technologies, it can also introduce unexpected interactions between systems and the propagation of vulnerabilities. As described earlier, understanding how high level mission objectives can be related down to the technical and human assets available is critical to the design and implementation of such a system. We describe the scenario as follows:

The mission objective of Blue Force is the clearance of an urban area largely controlled by Red Force, the opposition force. Blue Force is stationed in a Forward Operating Base (FOB) 10 km away from the urban area. It needs to patrol the urban area to take over control of it by sending in patrols of 8 personnel for 4 h at a time. The patrol is supported by a video feed from an Unmanned Airborne Vehicle (UAV). There are threats to the work of the patrols including congestion and conflict in the use of the electromagnetic spectrum, such as from other patrols or between communication and electronic warfare (EW) equipment. The patrols use policy based radio, and a Communication Information System (CIS) management function creates the policies and sends them to the radios. In the event of a resource requirement conflict for the radio spectrum, a decision needs to be made on which traffic stream should be stopped.

Given this scenario, our aim was to demonstrate requirements traceability in the context of a mission thread featuring communications systems, policy based radio and radio spectrum.

5.2 Applying the MANGO Approach to the Case Study

Our first task was to model the scenario using the *i** framework in REDEPEND. An informal system model created in MS Visio was provided by Dstl as the baseline for the *i** model development. The *i** model was developed in REDEPEND iteratively over a 4-month period which included 4 half-day meetings with a Dstl analyst to refine and validate the latest model. The completed *i** model reflected the complexity of the scenario, including 1 actor at the mission layer, 10 actors in the task layer, 13 actors in the capability/service layer, and 15 actors in the asset layer. Given the scale of the model, shown in Fig. 7, we highlight some of its important elements below.

Starting with the mission layer, the mission objective *Urban area clearance of red force* is owned by the *Mission Commander* actor as part of *J3: Current operations*. From this high-level objective the tasks are defined in the next layer, covering the areas of current operations (J3), operational intelligence (J2), communication and information systems (J6), Policy, legal and media operations (J9), and logistics/medical (J4). The next layer details the services required to carry out the military tasks, such as Command & Control (C2), Situational Awareness (SA), medical support, Communication and Information Systems (CIS), Short Range Communication (SRC) and Medium Range Communication (MRC) services. In the asset layer, the SRC and DSA radio system are of particular importance in the described scenario. Finally, the radio spectrum is modelled as a resource in the resource layer.

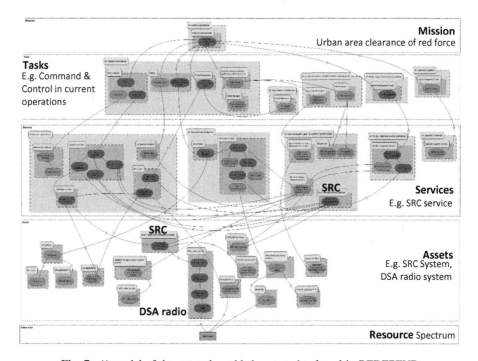

Fig. 7. *i** model of the network-enabled system developed in REDEPEND

Alongside the development of the *i** model, we refined the underlying CE conceptual model and cross-checked the concepts to ensure consistency. To complete the full picture, requirements, assumptions and metrics were captured and documented by a Dstl domain expert. We focused on a detailed example from the scenario based on the Short Range Communications (SRC) service in order to demonstrate the MANGO approach. The example covered the full scope of the *i** model, looking at the requirements trace from the top down to the radio and from the bottom up through goal propagation, as described in detail below.

320   J. Lockerbie et al.

The SRC service is required to carry aggregated short range traffic, as per the allocation defined in the information service flow requirements. These ISFRs are derived from information needs from tasks such as spectrum battlespace management and CIS provision. Associated with the SRC goal is the metric *MS.SRC.1*, shown earlier in Fig. 5, which measures the aggregated ISFRs. An underlying calculation behind this metric computes a traffic threshold value based on bespoke Quality of Service (QoS) class values. The logic applied aggregates average rate/volume data transfer rates for near real-time and best effort service provision, and adds maximum max rate/volume data transfer rates for real-time services. In our example, the design time requirement is a threshold of 2.3 megabits per second (Mbps). This requirement is met by the spectrum resource that is specified to have 3 channels with channel bandwidth of 1 MHz and spectrum efficiency of 1 bps/Hz. However, needs can change during the course of a mission resulting in greater demands on the spectrum. In this case, we can change the values of one or more ISFRs accordingly and run a propagation to discover the impacts on goal achievement across the whole model.

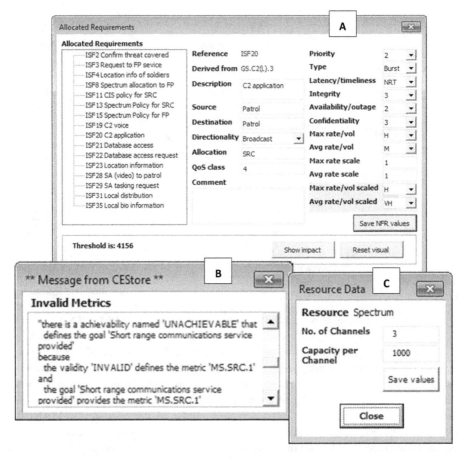

Fig. 8. User interfaces in REDEPEND for propagation analysis

Figure 8(a) shows an increase in the spectrum demand of the Command and Control (C2) application and a new calculated threshold of 4.2 Mbps which exceeds the capacity of the spectrum resource. The user receives feedback from the CEStore, in Fig. 8(b), informing them that the invalid metric has made the SRC service goal unachievable, along with the metrics that trace down from this goal through the DSA radio system, in turn making these system goals unachievable. Figure 7 shows how this example is propagated across the wider model, with the unachieved goals represented in a darker shade of orange. It shows upwards propagation through goal dependencies to the mission objective and downwards propagation via the metrics trace through the DSA radio and down to the spectrum resource. Finally, it is then possible for the user to reset the visualization and make further changes to the ISFRs or change the capacity of the spectrum resource via a simple form, shown in Fig. 8(c).

6 Lessons Learned

Following the completion of this case study we presented our tool-based approach to Dstl stakeholders and received formative feedback. Based on this feedback, and our own experiences, we outline the main lessons learned.

Our specialized use of $i*$, with a layered hierarchy and simplified syntax, was well received by the Dstl stakeholders, certainly in comparison to the traditional $i*$ representation presented in our original scoping study. Not only was the actor-based representation seen as useful for determining and displaying ownership, but the introduction of the J Functions gave an additional dimension for representing responsibilities within a mission thread. Furthermore, it was stated that the approach may also be useful at a micro level by, for example, modelling individual teams. In terms of syntax, it has been widely reported that $i*$ would benefit from a simplified notation, for example in [22].

The explicit modelling of metrics with traces across the whole mission was seen to have potential for encouraging military stakeholders to take a more metricated approach to designing mission configurable systems. For example, it is not only the users at the network layer that can see the benefits of a metricated approach, but through the propagation of goal impacts it is possible for at the top of the command chain to see tangible benefits. It was stated that defining metrics is currently a difficult challenge for users, but MANGO providing metrics classes and exemplars to follow should be a useful tool.

There was a concern expressed relating to the real-time capability of the approach. Whilst we demonstrated the design time analysis of ISFRs and the potential for run-time propagation of goal impacts, it was felt that extending this example to the IERs in the asset layer would be too challenging. The next step for us is to look into existing research on runtime goal modeling, for example the work of Dalpiaz et al. [23], who provide a framework for bridging across from design-time goal models to runtime behavior. We also acknowledge the relevance of work on requirements montors such as Robinson's requirements monitoring framework [24] and also work on awareness requirements, as defined by Souza et al. [25] as those requirements which refer to other requirements or domain assumptions and their success or failure at runtime.

7 Conclusion and Future Work

This paper reports the design and implementation of a new approach delivered through an integrated software prototype and applied to the problems of mission assurance and mission configurability in the military domain. Whilst we have demonstrated the potential benefits of the approach through our case study with Dstl, we need to further develop and validate the approach with military stakeholders.

The successful integration of REDEPEND and the CEStore provides huge potential for the development of further analytical capabilities. For example, we need to introduce prioritization information into our spectrum resource example to provide the user with resource reallocation solutions. To further support the user, we plan to further exploit the advantages of the CE interface – that is, to enable the user to provide CE input into the model and receive feedback from the CEStore during system design, for example warnings of missing traces. This feeds into collaborative working. Whilst our work to date suggests that the MANGO approach is useful for capturing domain expertise, we have not researched how the approach would work when the requirements, assumptions and metrics are being defined by multiple individuals. There is a need to consider how owners of different parts of the system interact – how should we facilitate ownership, coordination and the resolution of conflict in the development process?

From a visual perspective, work is needed on the REDEPEND user interface. The software needs greater requirements management capabilities supported by more user-friendly forms and analysis functions. REDEPEND also needs improved visualizations to support the collaborate working mentioned above, for example, allowing for different user perspectives through visual layers and collapsing actor boundaries. Also, given the simplified goal-based nature of our use of *i**, a plan for future work is to integrate BPMN with the task layer of the model.

Finally, despite the upfront modelling effort needed in the MANGO approach, along with the capture of domain knowledge, the utility of such rich models suggests that they have a future role as mission templates to be reused in multiple projects to analyse systems for mission assurance and configurability.

References

1. Williams, C., Ibbotson, J., Lockerbie, J., Attwood, K.: Mission assurance through requirements traceability. In: IEEE Military Communications Conference, pp. 1645–1650 (2014)
2. NATO Code of Best Practice for Command and Control Assessment, RTO TR-081 (2004)
3. Wieringa, R.J.: Design Science Methodology for Information Systems and Software Engineering. Springer, Heidelberg (2014)
4. Yu, E.: Modelling strategic relationships for process engineering, Ph.D. thesis, University of Toronto (1995)
5. Goal Structuring Notation. http://www.goalstructuringnotation.info/. Accessed 04 Oct 2016
6. Attwood, K., Kelly, T., McDermid, J.: The use of satisfaction arguments for traceability in requirements reuse for system families: position paper. In: Proceedings of the International Workshop Requirements Reuse in System Family Engineering, Eighth International Conference on Software Reuse, pp. 18–21 (2004)

7. Mott, D.: Summary of Controlled English, ITACS. http://nis-ita.org/science-library/paper/doc-1411a. Accessed 04 Oct 2016
8. van Lamsweerde, A.: Goal-oriented requirements engineering: a guided tour. In: Proceedings of the Fifth IEEE International Symposium on Requirements Engineering (RE 2001), pp. 249–263. IEEE Computer Society, Washington (2001)
9. iStar Language. https://sites.google.com/site/istarlanguage/home. Accessed 04 Oct 2016
10. Lockerbie, J., Maiden, N.A.M.: Extending i* modeling into requirements processes. In: Proceedings of 14th IEEE International Conference on Requirements Engineering, pp. 361–362. IEEE Computer Science Press (2006)
11. Dardenne, A., van Lamsweerde, A., Fickas, S.: Goal-directed requirements acquisition. Sci. Comput. Program. **20**, 3–50 (1993)
12. Lockerbie, J., Maiden, N.A.M., Engmann, J., Randall, D., Jones, S., Bush, D.: Exploring the impact of software requirements on system-wide goals: a method using satisfaction arguments and i* goal modelling. Requir. Eng. **17**(3), 227–254 (2012)
13. Business Process Model and Notation. http://www.bpmn.org/. Accessed 04 Oct 2016
14. Hull, E., Jackson, K., Dick, J.: Requirements Engineering. Springer-Verlag, London (2002)
15. Dick, J.: Design traceability. IEEE Softw. **22**(6), 14–16 (2005). IEEE Computer Society
16. van Lamsweerde, A.: Engineering requirements for system reliability and security. In: Software System Reliability and Security. NATO Security Through Science Series - D: Information and Communication Security, vol. 9, pp. 196–238. IOS Press, (2007)
17. JDP6-00, Communications and Information Systems Support to Joint Operations, Joint Doctrine Publication 6-00, Third Edition, Ministry of Defence (MOD) (2008)
18. Ibbotson, J., Braines, D., Mott, D., Arunkumar, S., Srivatsa, M.: Documenting Provenance with a Controlled Natural Language, IBM United Kingdom Ltd., Hursley Park. Whitepaper
19. Web Ontology Language (OWL). https://www.w3.org/OWL/. Accessed 04 Oct 2016
20. Horkoff, J., Yu, Y., Yu, E.: OpenOME: an open-source goal and agent-oriented model drawing and analysis tool. In: Proceedings of the 5th International i* Workshop (iStar 2011), pp. 154–156 (2011)
21. Horkoff, J., Yu, E.: Interactive goal model analysis for early requirements engineering. Requir. Eng. **21**(1), 29–61 (2016)
22. Moody, D.L., Heymans, P., Matulevicius, R.: Visual syntax does matter: improving the cognitive effectiveness of the i* visual notation. Requir. Eng. **15**(2), 141–175 (2010)
23. Dalpiaz, F., Borgida, A., Horkoff, J., Mylopoulos, J.: Runtime goal models: keynote. In: Proceedings RCIS 2013, pp. 1–11 (2013)
24. Robinson, W.: A roadmap for comprehensive requirements monitoring. IEEE Comput. **43** (5), 64–72 (2010)
25. Souza, V., Lapouchnian, A., Robinson, W., Mylopoulos, J.: Awareness requirements for adaptive systems. In: Proceedings of the 6th International Symposium on Software Engineering for Adaptive and Self-Managing Systems (SEAMS), pp. 60–69. ACM (2011)

Quality of Natural Language Requirements

On the Ability of Lightweight Checks to Detect Ambiguity in Requirements Documentation

Martin Wilmink[1] and Christoph Bockisch[2(✉)]

[1] Open Universiteit, Heerlen, The Netherlands
m.wilmink67@kpnmail.nl
[2] Philipps-Universität Marburg, Marburg, Germany
bockisch@mathematik.uni-marburg.de

Abstract. *Context & motivation*: The quality of requirements documentation, which is often written in natural language, directly influences the quality of subsequent software engineering tasks. Ambiguity is one of the main quality risks, but unfortunately natural language has a natural tendency towards ambiguity.

Question/problem: Precisely identifying ambiguity in specifications is virtually impossible fully automatically due the complexity and variability of natural language. Ignoring grammar and context in the analysis, on the other hand, makes an implementation and application feasible, but also reduces the accuracy. The question researched in this paper is whether such a lightweight check can still sufficiently accurately detect which requirements are formulated ambiguously or certainly.

Principal ideas/results: To investigate this research question, we have implemented a lightweight analysis tool based on a finite dictionary combining different results from the literature. The tool, called *tactile check*, adds annotations to phrases in requirements documents, which are weak respectively strong with regard to non-ambiguity. Within an embedded single case study, *tactile check* is applied to two real requirements documents (totaling 293 requirements) from KLM Engineering & Maintenance and the results (454 annotations in total) are assessed by three expert business analysts. In our study, the tool achieved a precision and recall of at least 77% respectively 59%. Annotations of weak phrases have prevalently been perceived as helpful for reducing ambiguity.

Contribution: In this paper, we establish that simple textual analyses with low overhead can detect ambiguity in requirements with significant accuracy. Our experts assessed the analysis' findings as helpful input to reducing the ambiguity. The tool and dictionary used in our study are provided for download to support repeatability of the study. Furthermore, we provide an extended dictionary for download that incorporates suggestions by our experts.

Keywords: Requirements engineering · Business requirements · Natural language · Ambiguity · Software quality · Context-insensitive analysis · *tactile check*

© Springer International Publishing AG 2017
P. Grünbacher and A. Perini (Eds.): REFSQ 2017, LNCS 10153, pp. 327–343, 2017.
DOI: 10.1007/978-3-319-54045-0_23

1   Introduction

The requirements engineering process covers all elements, from business requirements elicitation to detailed baseline build definition. Requirement documentation forms one of the important artifacts of this process. Requirements describe
the product services within its given boundaries [15,16]. They are initially specified at a very high level of abstraction and subsequently refined by adding
technical details. In this paper, we focus on requirements documents at the first
level of this process, which is called *business requirements*.

One key quality attribute of requirements is non-ambiguity, since ambiguity
easily leads to misinterpretation and thus failing to satisfy the expectations of the
business [2,10,11,13]. In practice, the business requirements are typically written
in natural language. However, natural language is inherently ambiguous.

In the context of this study, we mean by *ambiguity* (or *level of ambiguousness*)
of requirements whether (or to which degree) a requirement has the potential
to be interpreted differently by different readers targeted by the requirements
document. Thus, if, e.g., all members of the development team and the customer
understand the requirement in the same way, we consider it to be *certain* even if
the phrasing potentially also has multiple meanings. Referring to the Ambiguity
Handbook [1], the kind of ambiguity considered in our study intersects with the
categories *semantic ambiguity, pragmatic ambiguity* and *vagueness*.

Several studies [3,4,6,9,18] describe attributes, indicators and metrics for
quality characteristics including non-ambiguity. The studies are typically accompanied by a tool to identify these indicators. Often, ambiguity is caused by the
unintended usage of words or phrases that induce ambiguity in the text. The
tools developed in the aforementioned studies, therefore, use finite dictionaries
and complex techniques from natural language processing to determine the quality. However, the validation presented in these papers primarily takes place in an
academic context. From our experience, one reason could be that existing tools
are perceived as too heavy-weight by practitioners.

The first author of this paper is a functional application manager at KLM
Engineering & Maintenance for various IT related projects, and is deeply
involved in the definition of requirements. The study on which we report in this
paper is thus carried out in an industrial context. In our study *we investigate if
a simple and practical tool, only based on a finite dictionary, has the potential
to improve the ambiguity-awareness* of the analyst writing the document and
by doing so improving the overall quality of the specification document. Besides
performing the study in an *industrial environment*, another contribution of our
work is the combination of the concepts of two previously conducted studies:

- The NASA ARM tool [18] and its reconstruction [3] check for ambiguity in
  the form of *weak and strong phrases using a finite dictionary* approach. Additionally it checks the document structure, including cross references.
- The tool SMELL [6] detects various subjective and non-verifiable terms as
  ambiguity forms *without the objective of being 100% correct*. Advanced text
  analytics is used to recognize inflections of predefined words.

We adopt the approach of using a finite dictionary, ignoring context and grammar from the ARM tool and the incentive that 100% accuracy is unnecessary from the SMELL tool, into a lightweight analysis tool, which we call *tactile check*. We take over the dictionary of ARM as well as most inflections of words recognized by SMELL, but we omit context analyses like structural checks or text analytics. *Tactile check* is implemented as a macro for Microsoft Word and adds annotations to phrases in requirements documents, which are weak respectively strong with regard to non-ambiguity. It is very lightweight as it ignores context and grammar, which may reduce the precision of annotations and impact the usefulness in practice. We therefore investigate in our study the research question: *How do business analysts perceive the effectiveness of the* tactile check *in accurately detecting which requirements are formulated ambiguously or certainly?*

We apply *tactile check* in an embedded single case study to two actual requirements documents from KLM E & M with 199 respectively 94 requirements. A total of 454 phrase annotations are inspected by three expert requirements analysts from KLM E & M. For one of the documents, the experts affirmed a precision of at least 96% and a recall of at least 89%. For the other, they affirmed a precision of 77% and a recall of at least 59%. The weak annotations were predominantly perceived as helpful for reducing ambiguity, while annotations of strong phrases were considered not helpful. This paper is based on the first author's master thesis [17], where additional information can be found. We summarize the contributions of our work as follows:

- We establish that simple textual analyses with low overhead can accurately detect ambiguity in requirements.
- To make our study repeatable, we make the *tactile check* tool as well as the collected data available for download.[1]

2   Research Design

We split our general question into three sub-questions:

RQ-Weak. To what extent does the annotation of *weak* phrases with *tactile check* accurately detect ambiguous requirements?

RQ-Strong. To what extent does the annotation of *strong* phrases with *tactile check* accurately detect certain requirements?

RQ-Helpful. To what extent are the presented *tactile check* annotations perceived as helpful by business analysts to reduce the overall ambiguousness?

To answer these questions, we follow an approach [14] where the proposed *tactile check* tool is evaluated with the use of existing requirement documents as input data. The annotated phrases in the requirements document are the starting point for the assessment by three expert requirements analysts. This

---

[1] See the Tactile Check homepage: https://github.com/mwmk67/TactileCheck.

relates to an *interpretivism* research philosophy where data samples are limited but analyzed with in-depth knowledge. The expert assessment is based on a set of categories to be assigned to each annotated phrase. This follows an *abduction* research method where a new model is formed based on the collected data, which is a natural fit with the interpretivism philosophy.

In line with the research method and philosophy an *embedded single case study* is performed, where the case subject will be KLM Engineering & Maintenance and two different Business IT related projects as subject to analysis. From both projects the business requirements chapters are included for usage in this research. There is only one limitation on the document usage: No financial information may be disclosed.

- e-EGS (field loadable software solution to support Boeing 787). The requirements are written in natural language using the business stakeholder's vocabulary. The document revision state is "Approved".
- CMS-plus (logistics solution for aircraft maintenance execution and administration). The document is written in partially structured natural language as use cases/user stories. The document revision state is "Approved".

2.1 The *Tactile Check* Tool

First of all, we have developed a tool, called *tactile check*, to perform the lightweight, dictionary-based annotation of phrases in the requirements documents. This is to make the annotation process reliable and repeatable. To allow other researchers to re-assess our method with other requirements documents and other analysts, we make the tool and the dictionary available for download.[2]

Tactile check essentially combines the approaches of the NASA ARM tool [18] and the SMELL tool [6]. Both tools use dictionaries to identify weak and strong phrases, but they also both perform additional complex analyses, e.g., of the document structure or using text analytics. We limit our implementation to the dictionary-based analysis combining the dictionaries of ARM and SMELL. Instead of performing text analytics, we have extended the dictionary with inflections of its words.

Since requirements documents are written in MS Word at KLM E & M, we have developed the *tactile check* tool as a Visual Basic for Applications (VBA) macro. The dictionary is placed in a separate file to enable amendments to the dictionary without changing the VBA code. Annotations are represented by changing the phrase's font presentation, italic for weak, bold for strong phrases. The name of the quality indicator as defined by the loaded dictionary and a unique identification (sequence) number of the finding are added in the form of a comment. An example annotation of a weak as well as a strong phrase annotation is shown in Fig. 1.

Our tool it is provided as a Word macro and can thus be executed in the same environment as is used to write the requirements document. The results are

---

[2] See the Tactile Check homepage: https://github.com/mwmk67/TactileCheck.

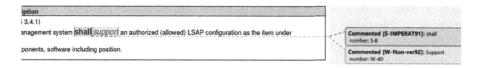

Fig. 1. Example of the annotation output.

also immediately displayed in the Word document. Annotations are provided as regular comment, a presentation format well known to requirements engineers. We therefore envision that requirements engineers can apply our tool very frequently, e.g., right after a new requirement has been specified or at the end of each day.

2.2 Data Collection

A detailed description of the data and data collection process for each research question can be found in annex 2 to the thesis of the first author [17]. In the following we give an overview of this process.

Accuracy of Weak and Strong Phrase Annotation. In research questions RQ-Weak and RQ-Strong, we address the reliability of the *tactile check* annotation of weak and strong phrases. To investigate these questions, the experts assess all[3] phrases in the requirements documents and their annotations by taking the context of the phrase into account.

Following the binary classification diagram shown in Fig. 2, they determine a label for each annotated phrase. These labels (cf. Table 1) indicate to which degree the expert agrees that the identified phrase is formulated ambiguously (for weak phrase annotations) or non-ambiguously (for strong phrase annotations). The table is based on Femmer et al. [6], extended with labels for strong phrases. For each label we specify the type of result (true or false positive) and whether a such annotated phrase influences ambiguity (A-Y) or not (A-N).

For requirements that are not annotated with weak or strong phrases, we determine together with the experts, whether the requirement is ambiguous or certain, and, thus, should have contained an annotated phrase. These "missed phrases" form the false negatives. Since our expert analysts only have limited time available for this project, we can only investigate samples of the requirements to identify missed phrases.

Perceived Helpfulness. In research question RQ-Helpful, we address whether the annotations actually have the potential to improve the non-ambiguity of requirements. To determine the perceived helpfulness, the experts perform a

---

[3] The strong phrases "and" and "should" occur extremely frequently in similar sentence patterns. To save the limited time of our expert analysts, we asked them to only assess 15 occurrences of these two phrases. All assessments are almost identical.

Table 1. Weak (based on [6]) and strong labels and associated attributes. (true: true positive, false: false positive, A-Y: influencing ambiguity, A-N: not influencing ambiguity)

Label code		Description	Type	Infl. ambig.	
Weak	Strong			Weak	Strong
W-1	–	This finding revealed a potential problem	true	A-Y	–
W-2	–	This requirement needs a review	true	A-Y	–
W-3	–	There is some explicit knowledge, which should be written down	true	A-Y	–
W-4	–	There should be a reference at this point	true	A-Y	–
W-5	–	This is a major issue that must be addressed	true	A-Y	–
W-6	S-1	While this is not an issue here, it must be further explained and refined at a different point	true	A-N	A-Y
W-7	S-2	This could be problematic, but this part of the specification is not so important	true	A-N	A-N
W-8	S-3	This finding seems problematic, but is clear to a domain expert	true	A-N	A-Y
W-9	S-4	This is not a problem here	true	A-N	A-N
W-10	S-5	The *tactile check* did not work correct	false	A-N	A-N

critical review of each assessed phrase within its context and determine whether the phrase annotation is helpful to "trigger" the expert to further clarify or enhance the requirement.

Interviews. When experts complete the analysis of both requirement data sets, they are interviewed to elaborate on their experience using the *tactile check*. This interview is semi-structured and includes the following questions:

- What is the view on the chosen approach?
- What is the view on the usefulness of weak phrase annotations?
- What is the view on the usefulness of strong phrase annotations?
- Would the *tactile check* be useful as additional method to assist a business requirements author to reduce the overall ambiguity of business requirements?

2.3 Reliability and Internal Validity Aspects

To ensure that the research outcome is valid it is important to identify possible threats to the validity. Reliability relates to the ability to repeat the

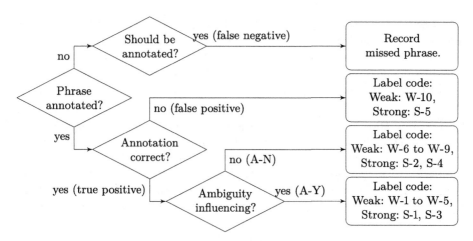

Fig. 2. Phrase classification diagram.

measurements and yield the same results. Saunders et al. [14] identify the threats to reliability and validity, which we discuss below.

Participant Error. Time pressure, distraction and knowledge influence our judgment and can lead to false assessment. To mitigate the influence of time pressure and distraction the experts are requested perform the classification and assessment in a time slot with a minimum of 2 h. Preferably the assessment is carried out at a distraction free office location.

The "knowledge" element is elusive to quantification. As minimum requirement, the expert must work at least 5 years with KLM E & M and a minimum of 3 years as business analyst. Nevertheless, this will not eliminate the risk of different knowledge levels between the individual domain specialists. Therefore it is to be expected that variations in classification will occur. To counter this effect three domain experts will perform the assessment. In case that a participant provides an extreme different interpretation, an additional review and argumentation can possibly clarify the differences. Additionally, we use the Fleiss' Kappa measure to determine inter-rater reliability.

Participant Bias. The result of this research has no direct impact on the daily activities of the domain specialist. And, as assessment will be performed on an individual basis, no deliberation between the participants is expected. There is no foreseen incentive to develop *tactile check* as a supported method in their daily work routines. Therefore, it is not expected that the analysts will consciously steer the interpretation and classification to a perceived favorable outcome.

Each data set (e-EGS and CMS-plus) is analyzed by one expert who participated in the analyzed project. This holds the risk of bias, as one expert is validating work in which he was previously involved.

Researcher Error. Due to the nature of the first author's curriculum (part-time student), there is a risk that the time frame in which the research is performed becomes fragmented. To mitigate this risk, a research project plan including detailed and realistic time schedules is used to measure the progress and identify at an early stage deviations from the planning.

Researcher Bias. In this research, the researcher is part of the organization where the research is conducted (internal researcher, cf. [14]). While the advantages are for example easy access to data and resources, the disadvantage is familiarity with the organization. In this research setting it is not anticipated as influential, as the researcher is *not* part of the business analyst team that will perform the assessments. During the assessment it is envisioned that only minimal assistance from the researcher is required hence limiting the risk of influencing the assessor. When evaluating the acquired data using the *nominal* measuring level limits the complexity of the applicable calculations and risk of interpretation bias.

Construct Validity. For this research setup the following elements that influence the construct validity are identified:

Consistency of Input Data. To create a consistent annotation of phrases from the finite dictionary an automated tool is developed. The automated approach ensures that annotation of the weak and strong phrases as defined in the dictionary is consistent and repeatable.

Measurement Scale. The measurement level at which the data is classified is nominal. This suits the objective of classifying the different findings and counting totals for weak and strong categories. Measurement at the nominal level accommodates basic counting of elements.

Consistency of Data Collection. Each domain specialist performs the assessment based on his own level of experience and proficiency, i. e., while the results can be arithmetically correct, there is room for variance in the outcome. All data of each assessment is used to compare and evaluate the influence of this variance.

Triangulation. To be able to value the findings of the assessment and classification a semi-structured interview is conducted with each participating analyst. The results of the semi-structured interviews are to be compared with the results of assessment analyses.

External Validity. The used single case study research strategy limits the ability to generalize the outcome of this result. The result may be specific to the domain and the context of the data used. Based on the small and domain-specific data set and limited group of domain specialists who evaluate the annotated data the external validity is uncertain.

3   Data Analysis

Each data item contains the unique phrase identifier, an identifier of the analyst whose assessment is recorded, the classification label assigned by the analyst and whether the analyst perceives the annotation as helpful. The classification label is further split up into its characteristics, namely the type (true/false positive/negative) and whether it influences ambiguity (A-Y or A-N).

Table 2 shows the generic breakdown of the analyzed requirements and phrases. It can be seen that volume of the requirements and annotated phrases in the e-EGS data set is considerable bigger than in the CMS-plus data set.

Table 2. Overall count of requirements and phrases.

Description	e-EGS	CMS-plus
$\sum$ Requirements in document	199	94
$\sum$ Requirements annotated	188	40
$\sum$ Requirements with weak phrases annotated	55	10
$\sum$ Requirements with strong phrases annotated	187	37
$\sum$ Phrases annotated	367	87
$\sum$ weak phrases annotated	67	20
$\sum$ strong phrases annotated	300	67

For e-EGS, the sum of requirements with weak phrases and requirements with strong phrases is larger than the total number of requirements. The reason is that requirements can contain phrases with weak annotations and phrases with strong annotations at the same time. The data shows that the number of weak annotations is relatively low and much smaller than the number of strong annotations. This is not surprising, considering that both requirements documents already have finalized status.

Generally, a requirement contains multiple phrases and we have collected and analyzed the data per requirement as well as per phrase. Both approaches have yielded almost identical results with at most 2% variation. Therefore, we only discuss the results at the granularity of requirements in the following. The full data sets can be found in [17].

To discuss the research questions RQ-Weak and RQ-Strong, we analyze the correctness of the annotations as seen by the expert analysts. The questions revolve around the accuracy of the weak and strong annotations. Important components of accuracy are the *precision* and *recall*, this is the percentage of correctly annotated requirements and the percentage of missing requirements annotations, respectively. Both measures can be combined, equally weighted, using the *balanced F-score* (F_1-*score*). To calculate these measures, we determine the values of *true* and *false positives* as well as *false negatives* (cf. Sect. 2.2). The formulas of for precision, recall and the F_1-score are given below. Other measures such as *miss rate* or *specificity* can also be calculated from the data presented in this paper. This can answer additional questions such as the likelihood of missing ambiguous requirements, which are however not the objective of the study presented here.

$$precision = \frac{true\ positives}{true\ positives + false\ positives} \tag{1}$$

$$recall = \frac{true\ positives}{true\ positives + false\ negatives} \tag{2}$$

$$F_1 = 2 \cdot \frac{precision \cdot recall}{precision + recall} \tag{3}$$

The data analysis presented in this section is based on the classification of items (i.e., the annotations provided by *tactile check*) by three different experts to increase the reliability of the classifications. To assess this reliability, we use Fleiss' Kappa measure [7] to determine the agreement between our raters. Generally, a positive κ value means that there is agreement between raters beyond what would be expected by chance; a value of 1 means complete agreement. We are limited to this instrument for assessing the inter-rater agreement, since we use a *nominal scale* for the classification.

Some annotations have not been rated by all experts due to time constraints. For the inter-rater reliability test we only considered those annotations rated by all three experts (this are 20 annotations for the CMS-plus data set and 43 for e-EGS). In both cases the confidence level was set to 95%, and in both cases we have a very low p-value ($9.687 \cdot 10^{-13}$, respectively $3.379 \cdot 10^{-5}$); this means that the statistical significance of our results is very high. Finally, the κ values of 0.586 (CMS-plus) and 0.202 (e-EGS) show that there is agreement between our experts, in the case of CMS-plus even largely so.

In the remainder of this section, we first discuss the data analysis from the perspective of our three research questions and finally combine the results obtained for the accuracy-related research questions (RQ-Weak and RQ-String) with the results of the perceived helpfulness (RQ-Helpful).

3.1   Accuracy of Weak Phrase Annotations

Our first research question, RQ-Weak, was: *To what extent does the annotation of weak phrases accurately detect ambiguous requirements?* To answer this question, we first need to establish whether the precision and recall values indicate that our method is usable with respect to weak phrase annotations. For each document and for each analyst Table 3 shows the number of annotations that were identified as true and false positives, and the number of false negatives found by the analyst for weak phrase annotations.

For the evaluated weak phrases in the e-EGS data set, the values for precision and recall are close to 90% or above. This indicates that most results are considered relevant and that most relevant results are shown. The F_1-score of 92% and above confirms a good accuracy for detecting weak phrases.

Table 3. Collected data from e-EGS and CMS-plus with regard to *weak* phrases.

	Analyst #1		Analyst #2		Analyst #3	
	e-EGS	CMS-plus	e-EGS	CMS-plus	e-EGS	CMS-plus
$\sum$ true positives	55	10	55	10	38	10
$\sum$ false positives	2	3	1	3	1	3
$\sum$ false negatives	7	6	7	7	4	0
Precision	96%	77%	98%	77%	97%	77%
Recall	89%	63%	89%	59%	90%	100%
F_1-score	92%	69%	93%	67%	94%	87%

For the CMS-plus data set, the values are considerably lower than those gathered from the e-EGS data set. But at least the value for precision is still relatively high with 77%, meaning that only one out of four annotations is wrong. For analysts #1 and #2, the recall drops to 59%, indicating that according to them almost half the weak phrases are left out. Analyst #3 did not identify any false negatives, leading to a recall of 100%. This result should be considered an outlier. The accuracy calculated by the F_1-score is therefore between 67% and 69%, which can still be considered good.

The low recall for CMS-plus is partially caused by phrases deemed weak by the assessors that are not explicitly listed in the dictionary and therefore not annotated in the text. Investigation shows that synonyms of these phrases are in the dictionary.[4] Analyst #3, however, classifies these additional phrases as W-10 ("not a problem") and thus not as "missed", hence his 100% score.

When discussing the lower recall values for the CMS-plus data set, the analysts indicate that despite the lower score, the values are sufficient to use the *tactile check* to annotate weak phrases. The overall experience by the experts is that annotating the weak phrases is consistent and precise enough to be valuable.

3.2   Accuracy of Strong Phrase Annotations

The second research question we want to investigate is RQ-Strong: *To what extent does the annotation of* strong *phrases accurately detect certain requirements?* We investigate this analogously to Sect. 3.1. Table 4 shows the number of annotations that were identified as true and false positives, and the number of false negatives.

For the evaluated strong phrases in both the e-EGS and CMS-plus data sets, the values for precision and recall are close to 90% or above. score of 88% and above shows that the accuracy with regard to detecting strong phrases is very good.

---

[4] An extended dictionary containing the additional phrases can be found at https://github.com/mwmk67/TactileCheck.

Table 4. Collected data from e-EGS and CMS-plus with regard to *strong* phrases.

	Analyst #1		Analyst #2		Analyst #3	
	e-EGS	CMS-plus	e-EGS	CMS-plus	e-EGS	CMS-plus
$\sum$ true positives	59	19	59	16	25	22
$\sum$ false positives	4	0	4	0	3	0
$\sum$ false negatives	2	4	5	0	4	1
Precision	94%	100%	94%	100%	89%	100%
Recall	97%	83%	92%	100%	86%	96%
F_1-score	95%	90%	93%	100%	88%	98%

3.3   Helpfulness of Annotations

The last research question is RQ-Helpful: *To what extent are the presented* tactile check *annotations perceived as helpful by business analysts in order to reduce the overall ambiguousness?*

For each label, the experts are asked to rate whether they consider it helpful or not with regard to reducing the ambiguousness level of the requirements document. Figures 3 and 4 show the distribution of the answers of each expert per requirements document.

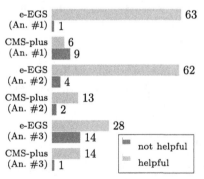

Fig. 3. Weak phrases helpful or not.

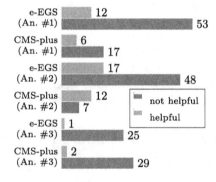

Fig. 4. Strong phrases helpful or not.

For the weak phrases, only analyst #1 ranks the annotations predominantly not helpful for the CMS-plus document. He explains that although the phrase "all" (which occurs multiple times) is indicated as weak, in his opinion it does not influence the overall ambiguity of the given requirements. In all other cases, the weak annotations are mostly rated helpful.

The strong annotations are predominantly rated not helpful more often than helpful with only one exception: The annotations in the CMS-plus document as rated by analyst #2. When asked to elaborate on this exceptional ranking, this is related to the combination of the used strong phrases in combination with the adjacent weak phrases and that the requirement could be further improved by also rephrasing the strong phrase.

3.4 Effectiveness of a Lightweight Tactile Check

To answer the main research question, the results from our research sub-question are combined and further analyzed. The classification label assigned to each annotated requirement by the experts encodes whether the annotation really indicates an impact on ambiguousness (A-Y) or not (A-N). Furthermore, the experts specify for each annotation whether they perceive it as helpful (Y) or not (N) to improve the requirement. The ratings for the requirements can be plotted in a four-quadrant matrix as shown in Fig. 5.

	A-Y	A-N
Y	helpful & influencing ambiguity	helpful & not influencing ambiguity
N	not helpful & influencing ambiguity	not helpful & not influencing ambiguity

Fig. 5. Four-quadrant evaluation matrix.

For the different data sets we determine the number of annotations, which fall in the different categories of each quadrant. Figure 6 shows this matrix for each data set whereby the number of weak annotations falling in the different categories are written in the respective quadrant. The quadrant with the largest count is highlighted.

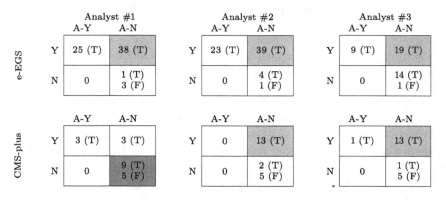

Fig. 6. Four quadrant evaluation for *weak* phrases. (T: true positive, F: false positive)

The matrices show that annotations are predominantly ranked as helpful, although not (seriously) influencing the ambiguity. Nevertheless, for the e-EGS case, still a significant number of weak annotations are regarded as helpful *and* influencing ambiguity. Only analyst #1 classifies most weak phrases of CMS-plus as not helpful.

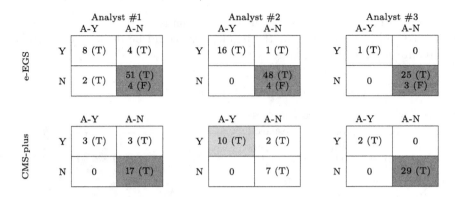

Fig. 7. Four quadrant evaluation for *strong* phrases. (T: true positive, F: false positive)

Figure 7 shows the same analysis for strong annotations. The strong phrases are predominantly ranked as not helpful and not influencing ambiguousness—in the e-EGS case even unanimously.

3.5   Discussion

To further elaborate on the perceived effectiveness of the lightweight ambiguity analysis of requirements, the analysts are asked for their expert opinion on several questions in a semi-structured interview. All three analysts are skeptical about the usefulness of annotating strong phrases, i. e., of marking requirements that are already perceived as good. In general, all experts express that the chosen approach is useful and applicable in practice, although it should be limited to annotating weak phrases.

Already during the assessments of the weak phrases, the analysts were indicating that the annotation made them "rethink" the formulation of single requirements. Even if a requirement has not been seen as severely ambiguous, options to clarify and simplify the requirement often become apparent. The annotations give an additional opportunity to reflect on the written requirements and can even provide the incentive to discuss this further with the stakeholders.

An important remark made by two analysts is that using the proposed *tactile check* would be more beneficial during the initial phase of compilation of the requirements. A critical note is that a consequence of applying the approach could be that requirements engineers (involuntarily) adapt to avoiding the usage of known weak phrases defined in the finite dictionary. Another consequence may be that requirements engineers are lead to not reviewing requirements without weak annotations, although these may still be ambiguous.

4   Related Work

There are several studies concerned with automatic quality assessment for requirements documents, of which we only present a few here. Gleich et al. [8]

detection ambiguity based on Part-Of-Speech tagging (POS), which is a technique from computational linguistics to identify for each word in a sentence, which syntactic role it plays. Patterns are defined that match sentences of tagged words to recognize lexical, syntactic, semantic, pragmatic or vagueness ambiguity. When a pattern matches, this also gives a short explanation in how far the sentence may be ambiguous.

The tool SMELLS introduced by Femmer et al. [5,6] further refines and employs techniques from Natural Language Processing (NLP): POS tagging, morphological analysis, finite dictionaries and lemmatization to identify possible ambiguous language usage. The tool is validated in an academic and industrial setting. Like in our study the specialists indicate that lightweight feedback early in the requirements specification cycle is seen as very beneficial.

These works and others [3,4,6,9,18] commonly describe some quality indicators together with analyses (sometimes supported by a tool) to determine the quality of requirements. In contrast to the approach evaluated in this study, these works apply relatively heavy-weight analyses using natural language processing or structural analyses of the whole document. In our study, we showed in an industrial context that a significantly simpler approach, i.e., purely dictionary-based, can also be employed to good effect.

5   Conclusions and Future Work

In this study, we analyzed whether a lightweight *tactile check* to detect weak and strong phrases with respect to non-ambiguity can effectively improve the quality of requirements documents. To ensure a consistent annotation of such phrases, we have developed a tool performing the checks as macro for MS Word together with a finite dictionary. To make our study repeatable, we provide both the tool and the dictionary, as well as an extended dictionary for download.[5] Within the study, we have applied this check to two actual requirements documents from KLM Engineering & Maintenance. Analyzing a total of 293 requirements with the *tactile check* resulted in 454 annotated phrases, which were assessed by three business analysts from KLM E & M. The analysts generally perceived the approach as effective in practice. The gathered data shows, in line with the qualitative assessment of the experts, that annotations for ambiguous requirements could be identified with a high precision and recall of 92% respectively 87% on average. For the annotated weak phrases, 58% were valued as helpful and 28% as helpful and positively influencing the overall ambiguity level.

The analysts confirmed that annotating the *weak* phrases is beneficial in reducing the ambiguousness level in the written business requirements. During the interviews, the analysts indicated that using the *tactile check* method to identify the weak phrases early during the initial phase of the requirements specification would be most beneficial. This would provide an additional incentive to discuss the annotated requirements with the stakeholders to clarify the requirements.

---

[5] See https://github.com/mwmk67/TactileCheck.

For the *strong* phrases, the analyzed data show that the *tactile check* method is not perceived as beneficial in reducing ambiguity influences of requirements written in natural language. The reason is that the attention is drawn to requirements, which are already identified as non-ambiguous. Thus, it is expected that no action needs to be taken on these requirements and therefore the annotation does not lead to a reduction in the ambiguousness level. Also the quantitative analysis has shown that there is no perceived benefit to annotating strong phrases. A better alternative could be to annotate requirements that lack strong phrases.

The difference in build-up of the two requirements documents used in this case study was visible in the phrases annotated and in the assessment. The e-EGS requirements are stated in plain natural language, and showed more variety in the annotations than the CMS-plus requirements that are written using a use case/user story structure. This difference in writing styles was not taken into account when the documents were selected. The CMS-plus document did not show a high number of strong phrases that are part of the strong dictionary and the annotated weak phrases showed little variation. We believe that this shows that the *tactile check* method is less effective on semi-structured documents.

During the interviews the experts also mentioned potential risks of the approach. A consequence of applying the approach could be that requirements engineers (involuntarily) adapt to avoiding the usage of known weak phrases defined in the finite dictionary. Another consequence may be that requirements engineers are lead to not reviewing requirements without weak annotations, although these may still be ambiguous.

As future work, we would like to adapt our approach according to the conclusions above and to repeat the study. In particular, it should be assessed whether the identified risks actually materialize. And the hypothesis should be investigated that the lightweight *tactile check* approach is even more advantageous for documents in an early stage of the requirements engineering process.

The ISO standard 29148 [12] includes natural language criteria for requirements specifications including weak and strong phrases. We did not consider the standard in our study, but will collate the phrases from there and our finite dictionary.

References

1. Berry, D.M., Kamsties, E., Krieger, M.M.: From contract drafting to software specification: linguistic sources of ambiguity. In: A Handbook (2003). http://cs.uwaterloo.ca/~dberry/handbook/ambiguityHandbook.pdf. Accessed 31 Dec 2016
2. Boehm, B., Basili, V.R.: Software Defect Reduction Top 10 List. Computer **34**(1), 135–137 (2001)
3. Carlson, N., Laplante, P.: The NASA automated requirements measurement tool: a reconstruction. Innov. Syst. Softw. Eng. **10**(2), 77–91 (2014). http://dx.doi.org/10.1007/s11334-013-0225-8

4. Davis, A., Overmyer, S., Jordan, K., Caruso, J., Dandashi, F., Dinh, A., Kincaid, G., Ledeboer, G., Reynolds, P., Sitaram, P., Ta, A., Theofanos, M.: Identifying and measuring quality in a software requirements specification. In: Proceedings First International Software Metrics Symposium, pp. 141–152. IEEE (1993)

5. Femmer, H., Fernández, D.M., Wagner, S., Eder, S.: Rapid quality assurance with requirements smells. J. Syst. Softw. **123**, 190–213 (2017)

6. Femmer, H., Fernández, D.M., Juergens, E., Klose, M., Zimmer, I., Zimmer, J.: Rapid requirements checks with requirements smells: two case studies. In: Proceedings of the 1st International Workshop on Rapid Continuous Software Engineering, pp. 10–19 (2014). http://doi.acm.org/10.1145/2593812.2593817

7. Fleiss, J., et al.: Measuring nominal scale agreement among many raters. Psychol. Bull. **76**(5), 378–382 (1971)

8. Gleich, B., Creighton, O., Kof, L.: Ambiguity detection: towards a tool explaining ambiguity sources. In: Wieringa, R., Persson, A. (eds.) REFSQ 2010. LNCS, vol. 6182, pp. 218–232. Springer, Heidelberg (2010). doi:10.1007/978-3-642-14192-8_20

9. Gnesi, S., Lami, G., Trentanni, G., Fabbrini, F., Fusani, M.: An automatic tool for the analysis of natural language requirements. Int. J. Comput. Syst. Sci. Eng. **20**(1), 53–62 (2005)

10. Hairul, M., Nasir, N., Sahibuddin, S.: Critical success factors for software projects : a comparative study. Sci. Res. essays **6**, 2174–2186 (2011)

11. Hofmann, H.F., Lehner, F.: Requirements engineering as a success factor in software projects. IEEE Softw. **18**(4), 58–66 (2001)

12. IEEE: ISO/IEC/IEEE 29148: 2011 Systems and software engineering - Life cycle processes - Requirements engineering, pp. 1–94. ISO (2011)

13. Kamata, M.I., Tamai, T.: How does requirements quality relate to project success or failure?. In: 15th IEEE International Requirements Engineering Conference (RE 2007), pp. 69–78. IEEE, October 2007

14. Saunders, M., Lewis, P., Thornhill, A.: Research Methodes for Business Students, 6th edn. Pearson Benelux, London (2012)

15. Sommerville, I.: Software Engineering, 10th edn. Pearson Education Limmited, Harlow (2016)

16. Wiegers, K., Beatty, J.: Software Requirements, 3rd edn. Microsoft Corporation, Redmont (2013)

17. Wilmink, M.: Requirements ambiguousness pitfalls. Master's thesis, Open Universiteit Nederland (2016)

18. Wilson, W.M., Rosenberg, L.H., Hyatt, L.E.: Automated analysis of requirement specifications. In: Proceedings of ICSE, pp. 161–171. ACM Press, New York, USA, May 1997

Using NLP to Detect Requirements Defects: An Industrial Experience in the Railway Domain

Benedetta Rosadini[1], Alessio Ferrari[3(✉)], Gloria Gori[2], Alessandro Fantechi[2], Stefania Gnesi[3], Iacopo Trotta[1], and Stefano Bacherini[1]

[1] Alstom Ferroviaria S.p.A., Florence, Italy
{benedetta.rosadini,iacopo.trotta,
stefano.bacherini}@transport.alstom.com
[2] University of Florence, DINFO, Florence, Italy
{gloria.gori,alessandro.fantechi}@unifi.it
[3] ISTI-CNR, Pisa, Italy
{alessio.ferrari,stefania.gnesi}@isti.cnr.it

Abstract. *Context and motivation*: In the railway safety-critical domain requirements documents have to abide to strict quality criteria. Rule-based natural language processing (NLP) techniques have been developed to automatically identify quality defects in natural language requirements. However, the literature is lacking empirical studies on the application of these techniques in industrial settings. *Question/problem*: Our goal is to investigate to which extent NLP can be practically applied to detect defects in the requirements documents of a railway signalling manufacturer. *Principal idea/results*: To address this goal, we first identified a set of typical defects classes, and, for each class, an engineer of the company implemented a set of defect-detection patterns by means of the GATE tool for text processing. After a preliminary analysis, we applied the patterns to a large set of 1866 requirements previously annotated for defects. The output of the patterns was further inspected by two domain experts to check the false positive cases. *Contribution*: This is one of the first works in which defect detection NLP techniques are applied on a very large set of industrial requirements annotated by domain experts. We contribute with a comparison between traditional manual techniques used in industry for requirements analysis, and analysis performed with NLP. Our experience tells that several discrepancies can be observed between the two approaches. The analysis of the discrepancies offers hints to improve the capabilities of NLP techniques with *company specific* solutions, and suggests that also company practices need to be modified to effectively exploit NLP tools.

Keywords: NLP · Requirements · Ambiguity · Defect detection · Quality

1 Introduction

The CENELEC norms provide standards for the development of railway safety-critical systems in Europe. The CENELEC EN 50128:2011 [6], specific for

© Springer International Publishing AG 2017
P. Grünbacher and A. Perini (Eds.): REFSQ 2017, LNCS 10153, pp. 344–360, 2017.
DOI: 10.1007/978-3-319-54045-0_24

software, asks requirements documents for railway systems to be *complete, clear, precise, unequivocal, verifiable, testable, maintainable, and feasible.* To ensure that these quality attributes are met, companies developing railway products have a Verification Engineer (VE) who reviews for defects any requirements document produced along the development process. This review activity is time consuming and error prone, and an automated review assistant might help VEs in their task. As well known, requirements are normally edited in natural language (NL) [19], and the railway domain makes no exception. Several natural language processing (NLP) approaches have been developed to assist requirements review. Part of these works focuses on the identification of typical defective terms and constructions [2,4,11,14,15,20], while other focus on artificial intelligence techniques [7,13,21]. However, the literature is lacking large-scale case studies concerning industrial applications of NLP approaches for defect detection [11]. This papers aims at filling this research gap, by providing the experience done within a collaboration between a world-leading railway signalling company, the University of Florence, and ISTI-CNR to investigate the feasibility of using NLP for defect identification in the requirements documents of the company. This experience, which involved three professional VEs and a large-scale experimentation on 1866 requirements, shows that NLP technologies can be used to develop *in-house* tools for defect identification. The internal development of the tools can enable the VEs of the company to tune the tools to account for part of the discrepancies that occur between manual reviews and automated ones.

The remainder of the paper is structured as follows. Section 2 summarises related works. In Sect. 3, we provide an overview of the current work. In Sect. 4 we describe the patterns adopted for defect detection. Sections 5 and 6 provide the results of a preliminary and a large-scale study, respectively, on the application of the patterns. In Sect. 7 we provide an analysis of the false positive cases performed on the large-scale study. Section 8 highlights the lessons learned.

2 Related Works

The literature counts several contributions concerning the application of NLP techniques to detect defects in NL requirements. These works can be categorised into those that use rule-based approaches [2,4,11,14,15,20] and those that leverage artificial intelligence approaches [7,13,21]. Our contribution falls into the first category, which collects all the works in which defects are identified based on linguistic patterns. Hence, we briefly discuss relevant works in this category.

The Ambiguity Handbook of Berry *et al.* [4] includes one of the most influential classification of ambiguity-related defects in requirements, and provides a large set of examples of typically dangerous words and constructions. Gnesi *et al.* [15] present QuARS, a tool for defect detection based on a quality model developed by the authors. Similarly, Gleich *et al.* [14] implemented a grep-like, pattern-based technique to detect defects, supported by statistical NLP techniques such as POS tagging. Tjong and Berry [20] developed SREE, a tool that identifies defects based on a pre-defined list of dangerous terms. Arora *et al.* [2] use patterns of linguistic defects as the other works, and, in addition, checks the conformance of the requirements to a given template. All these works were used as fundamental references to define the defect detection patterns of our study. On the other hand, all the listed works provide limited validation in real industrial contexts, as noted also by Femmer *et al.* [11]. In some cases, e.g., Gleich *et al.* [14], validation datasets are limited, while in other cases, e.g., Tjong and Berry [20], datasets are annotated for defects by one of the authors instead of domain experts. Large data-sets annotated by experts were considered by Falessi *et al.* [10]. However, their focus is solely on redundancy defects (i.e., equivalent requirements), detected by means of information retrieval techniques. The task of finding couples of equivalent requirements is radically different from the one we are dealing with in our study, in which multiple linguistic defects occurring in single requirements are considered. To our knowledge, the more general industrial work on defect detection is the one presented by Femmer *et al.* [11], who experimented their tool named *Smella* on several datasets belonging to three companies. Although domain experts were interviewed to assess the effectiveness of the tool, analysis of the results was performed by two researchers.

Compared to these studies, in the current work the validation of the approach is performed on a large set of industrial requirements annotated by domain experts. Another novelty is that defect detection NLP techniques are implemented *in-house* by a domain expert.

3   Overview

To experiment the feasibility of using defect detection NLP techniques, the company allocated one VE (VE1, 1st author) dedicated to the task, ISTI-CNR provided an Expert in defect detection through NLP (NLP-E, 2nd author), and the University of Florence provided a second VE (VE2, 3rd author), who worked at the company as VE, and then moved to the academia. NLP-E considered that assessing the effectiveness of a domain-generic tool for defect detection (e.g., QuARS [15]) would have required a strong *expertise* in the domain of the requirements documents. In addition, he considered that, if the tool would have provided too many false positive cases, e.g., *innocuous ambiguities* [7], the company would not have considered the tool as appropriate for its needs. Hence, it was decided to let VE1 develop the tool *in-house*, with the support of NLP-E. VE1 was initially required to study the papers of Berry *et al.* [4], Gnesi *et al.* [15], Gleich *et al.* [14], Tjong and Berry [20] and Arora *et al.* [2]. Then, she was required to perform the tutorials provided by GATE (General Architecture for Text Engineering [8]), which was the generic NLP tool selected to be tailored to support defect detection. The tool was chosen since it was considered sufficiently easy to use for an engineer, and sufficiently powerful for the task. After this autonomous training, VE1 and NLP-E met to define the defect classes on which to focus (Sect. 4). Priority was given to those defect classes that were considered more relevant from the point of view of VE1, and whose identification was considered feasible by NLP-E. For each defect class, VE1 used GATE to define a set of *patterns* for identification of defects. The patterns were experimented on a dataset annotated by VE1 herself, with the objective of maximizing recall, as suggested by Berry *et al.* [3] (Sect. 5). After the first encouraging results, a large-scale experiment was conducted on 1866 requirements, previously annotated by another VE of the company (VE3, 6th author) (Sect. 6). In this case, the results appeared particularly poor in terms of precision. Hence, VE1 and VE2 decided to analyse the false positive cases (Sect. 7). This analysis showed that many *true* linguistics defects were not considered in the validation performed by VE3. After marking these cases as *true positives*, several false positive cases remained, which could be in principle addressed by further tailoring the patterns to the specific language of the company. At the end of the experience, *all* the authors discussed about the lessons learned from the case study (Sect. 8).

4   A Rule-Based Approach to Predict Defects

4.1   NLP Technologies

Before describing the patterns that we defined to identify the defects, it is useful to list the natural language processing (NLP) technologies included in the tool GATE [8] that was adopted to define the patterns:

- **Tokenization:** This technology partitions a document into separate *tokens*, e.g., words, numbers, spaces, and punctuation.
- **Part-of-Speech (POS) Tagging:** This technology associates to each token a Part-of-Speech, e.g., noun (NN), verb (VB), adjective (JJ), *etc.* Common POS taggers are statistical in nature, i.e., they are trained to predict the POS of a token based on a manually annotated corpus.
- **Shallow Parsing:** This technology identifies noun phrases (NP) – in this case we speak about Noun Chunking – and verb phrases (VP) – in this case we speak about Verb Chunking – in sentences. For example, given the sentence *Messages are received by the system*, a shallow parser identifies {*Messages, the system*} as NP, and {*are received*} as VP.
- **Gazetteer:** This technology searches for occurrences of terms defined in a list of terms. In our case, we used it to check the presence of vague terms.
- **JAPE Rules:** This technology allows defining rules (i.e., high-level regular expressions) over tokens and other elements in a text [8]. A rule identifies sequences of elements that match the rule. Rules are expressed in the intuitive JAPE grammar, which is similar to regular expressions. JAPE rules can be rather long to report. In this paper, for the sake of space, to describe JAPE rules we will use a more concise and intuitive pseudo-code inspired to the JAPE grammar. In JAPE, and in our rules, the following symbols are used: "|" indicates logical or; "," indicates logical and; "!" indicates logical not; "$<expr>+$" indicates one or more elements matching the preceding expression *expr*; "$<expr>*$" indicates zero or more elements; "$<expr>?$" indicates zero or one elements. When we use a term in capital letters, this indicates a form of *macro* that identifies terms of the specific type, e.g., NUMBER identifies

numbers, while ELSE identifies the term *else* in its various orthographic forms. Although these macros differ in terms of semantics, we expect that the reader can infer their meaning.

Table 1. Pattern adopted for each defect class.

Defect class	Pattern
Anaphoric ambiguity	$P_{ANA} = (NP)(NP)+$ $(Split)[0,1]$ $(Token.POS == PP \mid Token.POS =\sim PR^*)$
Coordination ambiguity	$P_{CO_1} = ((Token)+ (Token.string == AND \mid OR))\ [2]$ $P_{CO_2} = (Token.POS == JJ) (Token.POS == NN \mid NNS)$ $(Token.string == AND \mid OR) (Token.POS == NN \mid NNS)$
Vague terms	$P_{VAG} = (Token.string \in Vague)$
Modal adverbs	$P_{ADV} = (Token.POS == RB \mid RBR),$ $(Token.string =\sim\ "[.]^*ly\$")$
Passive voice	$P_{PV} = (AUXVERB)(NOT)?(Token.POS == RB \mid RBR)?$ $(Token.POS == VBN)$
Excessive length	$P_{LEN} = Sentence.len > 60$
Missing condition	$P_{MC} = (IF)(Token, !Token.kind == punctuation)^*$ $(Token.kind == punctuation)(!(ELSE \mid OTHERWISE))$
Missing unit of measurement	$P_{MU_1} = (NUMBER)((Token)[0, 1](NUMBER))?(!MEASUREMENT)$ $P_{MU_2} = (NUMBER)((Token)[0, 1](NUMBER))?(!PERCENT)$
Missing reference	$P_{MR} = (Token.string == "Ref")(Token.string == ".")$ $(SpaceToken)?(NUMBER)$
Undefined term	$P_{UT} = (Token.kind == word, Token.orth == mixedCaps)$

4.2 Patterns for Defect Prediction

This section lists the classes of language defects considered, together with the patterns (i.e., JAPE rules) defined to identify them. Patterns are defined in terms of sequences of tokens to be matched within a requirement. Hence, the output produced by one pattern when applied to a requirement is zero or n requirement fragments (i.e., contiguous sequences of tokens in the requirement) that match the pattern. The patterns were defined by VE1 with the idea of identifying the defects that she perceived as more relevant for her job, and taking into account the defect classes provided by Berry *et al.* [4], and by the other papers she had studied [2,14,15,20]. In Table 1 we report the patterns in a compact version. The JAPE implementation of the patterns is available in our public repository[1]. Below, we describe the defect classes addressed by each pattern.

---

[1] https://github.com/BenedettaRosadini/QuARS-/tree/master/jape.

- **Anaphoric ambiguity.** Anaphora occurs in a text whenever a pronoun (e.g., *he, it, that, this, which*, etc.) refers to a previous part of the text. The referred part of the text is normally called *antecedent*. An anaphoric ambiguity occurs if the text offers more than one antecedent options [21], either in the same sentence (e.g., *The system shall send a message to the receiver, and **it** provides an acknowledge message - it = system* or *receiver?*) or in previous sentences. The potential antecedents for the pronouns are noun phrases (NP), which can be detected by means of a shallow parser. The pattern P_{ANA} matches any sequence of two or more noun phrases (NP), followed by zero or one sentence separators (Split), followed by a personal pronoun (PP), or other types of pronouns (PR*).

- **Coordination ambiguity.** Coordination ambiguity occurs when the use of coordinating conjunctions (e.g., *and* or *or*) leads to multiple potential interpretations of a sentence [7]. Two types of coordination ambiguity are considered here. The first type includes sentences in which more than one coordinating conjunction is used in the same sentence (e.g., *There is a 90° phase shift between sensor 1 **and** sensor 2 **and** sensor 3 shall have a 45° phase shift*). The second type includes sentences in which a coordinating conjunction is used with a modifier (e.g., *Structured approaches and platforms – Structured* can refer to *approaches* only, or also to *platforms*). The VE defined two patterns, one for each type. P_{CO_1} matches exactly two occurrences (notation "[2]") of one or more Tokens followed by a coordinating conjunction. P_{CO_2} matches cases in which an adjective (JJ) precedes a couple of singular (NN) or plural nouns (NNS), joined by *and* or *or*.

- **Vague terms.** Vagueness occurs whenever a sentence admits borderline cases, i.e., cases in which the truth value of the sentence cannot be decided [4]. Vagueness is associated with the usage of terms without a precise semantics, such as *minimal, as much as possible, later, taking into account, based on, appropriate*, etc. In our context, we use the list of 446 vague terms provided by the QuARS tool [15]. The list includes single-word and multi-word terms that were collected as source of vagueness in requirements. P_{VAG} matches any term included in the set *Vague* of vague terms.

- **Modal adverbs.** Modal adverbs (e.g., *positively, permanently, clearly*) are modifiers that express a quality associated to a predicate. As noted by Gleich *et al.* [14], adverbs are discouraged in requirements as potential source of ambiguity. VE1 noticed that, in the requirements of the company, most of the adverbs causing ambiguity were modal adverbs ending with the suffix *-ly*. For this reason, P_{ADV} matches adverbs in normal form (RB) or in comparative form (RBR) that terminate ($ indicates string termination) with *-ly*.

- **Passive voice.** The use of passive voice is a defect of clarity in requirements, and can lead to ambiguous interpretations in those cases in which the passive verb is not followed by the subject that performs the action expressed by the verb (e.g., *The system shall be shut down* – by which actor?). Passive voice detection is also considered by Gelich *et al.* [14] and by Femmer *et al.* [12]. To identify passive voice expressions, P_{PV} matches auxiliary verbs followed by a verb in past participle (VBN), possibly with negations and adverbs.

- **Excessive length.** Longer sentences are typically harder to process than short sentences, and can be source of unclarity. The VE decided to identify all the sentences that are longer than 60 tokens. Although this is a rather weak threshold – for generic English texts, Cutts recommends not to exceed 40 tokens [9] –, the VE considered this value appropriate for the length of the sentences in her domain.
- **Missing condition.** To be considered complete, each requirement expressing a condition through the *if* clause, shall have a corresponding *else* or *otherwise* clause. P_{MC} checks whether an *if* clause is followed by an *else/otherwise* clause in the same sentence.
- **Missing unit of measurement.** Each number is required to have an associated unit of measurement, unless the number represents a reference (see below). Hence, the patterns check whether a number has an associated unit, or a percentage value associated to it.
- **Missing reference.** This defect occurs when a reference that appears in the text in the form *Ref. <X>* does not appear in the list of references of the requirements document. To detect this defect we leverage the pattern P_{MR} to extract references in the text, and then – through Java code not reported here – we check whether each number found appears in the list of references.
- **Undefined term.** This pattern searches all the terms that follow the textual form used in the company for defining glossary terms (e.g., *restrictiveAspect*), which are expressed in camelCase format. As for the *missing reference* case, we leverage the P_{UT} pattern to search for terms expressed in camelCase (i.e., *mixedcap* orthography), and then we automatically search the glossary to check whether the term is present or not.

5   Preliminary Study

After the definition and implementation of the patterns, we performed a first assessment of the patterns on a real-world dataset of the company. In this phase, the goal was to establish whether the patterns were able to achieve a value of recall close to 100%. As noted by Berry *et al.* [3], defect detection techniques shall favor recall over precision since the cost of undetected *true* defects is much higher than the cost of manually discarding false positive cases. To perform the evaluation, the dataset was first manually annotated by VE1, and then she compared the output of the patterns with her annotations. In the following, we describe the annotation process, the evaluation measures adopted, and the observation on the results obtained.

5.1   Dataset and Annotation

For the analysis, a dataset of 241 system requirements was considered. This dataset was randomly selected from the requirements document of a wayside Automatic Train Protection (ATP) system and from the requirements document of an interlocking system. VE1 annotated the dataset. The requirement was labeled as *accepted* if it appeared to fulfill the criteria normally adopted by the company. These criteria are derived from the more general guidelines provided by the CENELEC EN 50128:2011 norm [6]. In particular a requirement was labeled as *accepted* if it was: (a) *feasible*: what is required is physically and technologically possible, can be done with available resources and is not against laws and regulations; (b) *testable*: can be demonstrated through repeatable tests or is at least verifiable through inspection; (c) *complete*: stand-alone, no missing references, undefined terms, to-be-defined parts, or missing conditions; (d) *clear and unambiguous*; (e) *uniquely identifiable*; (f) *consistent*: no internal contradiction and no contradiction with other requirements. The requirement was labeled as *rejected* in case it did not fulfill one of the criteria. In case the requirement was marked as *rejected* for criterion (c) or criterion (d), VE1 stated whether the rejection was due to one or more linguistic defect classes associated to the patterns listed in Sect. 4.2. In this case, VE1 labelled as $defective(i)$ each requirement fragment that included the i-th defect. After this annotation activity, 120 requirements were marked as *rejected*, while 121 were marked as *accepted*[2].

5.2 Evaluation Measures

Evaluation Measures by Defect. To measure the effectiveness of the patterns, we first provide a set of measures that focus on single defective fragments identified by the patterns. Given the pattern associated to the i-th defect, we consider the amount of true positive tp^D as the number of requirements fragments labeled as $defective(i)$ and correctly identified by the pattern; the amount of false positive fp^D as the number of requirements fragments wrongly identified as defective by the pattern; the amount of false negative fn^D as the number of requirements fragments labeled as $defective(i)$ that are not discovered by the pattern. Based on these definitions, we define the measure of precision (p^D) and recall (r^D) as:

$$p^D = \frac{tp^D}{tp^D + fp^D} \quad r^D = \frac{tp^D}{tp^D + fn^D}$$

The precision p^D is negatively influenced by the amount of defects wrongly identified (fp^D). The recall r^D is negatively influenced by the amount of undetected defects (fn^D).

Evaluation Measures by Requirement. To have a view of the effectiveness of the patterns applied together, we provide a set of measures that focus on the number of requirements, instead of on the number of defective fragments.

Here, we consider the amount of true positive tp^R as the number of requirements labeled as *rejected* for which at least one of the patterns correctly identified a defective requirement fragment; the amount of false positive fp^R as the number of requirements wrongly identified as defective (i.e., at least one of the

---

[2] The dataset appears balanced since VE1 continued to select requirements until a balanced number of accepted and rejected requirements was obtained.

patterns triggered a defect while the requirement was marked as *accepted*); the amount of false negative fn^R as the number of requirements marked as *rejected* for which none of the patterns triggered a defect. The measures of precision p^R and recall r^R are defined as for p^D and r^D, but considering tp^R, fp^R, and fn^R.

5.3   Results and Observations

In Table 2 we report the different evaluation measures. We see that, although the patterns for *anaphoric ambiguity* and *coordination ambiguity* are both based on shallow parsing, which normally has an accuracy of 90–95% [16], we achieve the objective of 100% recall. Similarly, for *modal adverbs* and *passive voice*, we achieve 100% recall, although these patterns employ POS tagging, which has an accuracy around 97% [18]. Two of the patterns that employ only lexical-based pattern matching, namely *missing reference* and *undefined term*, also achieve 100% recall. Lower values of recall are instead achieved for the patterns associated to *vague terms* (67.74%), *excessive length* (60.06%), *missing unit of measurement* (50%) and *missing condition* (97.05%).

Table 2. Preliminary study results for single defects and requirements.

Defect Class	tp^D	fp^D	fn^D	p^D	r^D
Anaphoric ambiguity	22	8	0	73.33%	100%
Coordination ambiguity	16	8	0	66.66%	100%
Vague terms	21	16	10	56.75%	67.74%
Modal adverbs	28	14	0	66.66%	100%
Passive voice	343	60	0	85.11%	100%
Excessive length	200	30	133	86.95%	60.06%
Missing condition	66	14	2	82.5%	97.05%
Missing unit of measurement	2	2	2	50%	50%
Missing reference	10	0	0	100%	100%
Undefined term	208	76	0	73.23%	100%
Requirements	tp^R	fp^R	fn^R	p^R	r^R
	106	59	14	64.24%	88.33%

- *Vague terms.* By inspecting the ten false negative defects for vague terms, VE1 found that they were all due to the absence of the quantifier *some* in the list of vague terms provided by QuARS. Hence, requirements such as the following were not marked as defective by the pattern: *In case the boolean logic evaluates the permissive state, the system shall activate **some** redundant output* – which output shall be activated? VE1 resolved the problem by simply adding the term *some* to the list of vague terms. Since also p^D was particularly low (56.75%), VE1 inspected the false positives and saw that they were due to domain-specific terms, namely ***raw data**, **hard** disk, **short**-circuit, **logical** or, **logical** and, **green** LED*. These terms were added to a stop-list to discard false positives in future analysis.

- *Excessive length.* By inspecting the false negative cases for excessive length, VE1 saw that they were due to a limitation of the GATE Tokenizer. For nested bullet point lists, the Tokenizer considers each item as a separate sentence. Hence, very long and deeply nested bullet point lists were not considered as sentences of excessive length. However, VE1 also argued that the length of a sentence, and the hard readability due to complex nested lists are different kinds of defects. Hence, she decided not to change the pattern for excessive length, and to consider the problem of nested lists as a defect that, at the moment, was left uncovered.
- *Missing unit of measurement.* Concerning the two false negative cases for missing unit of measurement, VE1 observed that these were due to the presence of ranges of numerical values, e.g., *[4,20]*, without the specification of the unit of measurement. To address these cases, the pattern was adjusted.
- *Missing condition.* The two false negative cases for missing condition appeared to be due to the presence of multiple *if* statements in the same sentence, with one *else* statement only, as in the following case: ***If*** *the initialization starts,* ***if*** *the board is plugged in and* ***if*** *the operator has sent the running command the system shall start,* ***else*** *it shall go in failure mode.* For requirements as the one presented, it is difficult to understand which specific *if* is covered by the *else* statement. Since the majority of missing condition defects were identified (66 out of 68), and considering that a VE has to manually review the requirements anyway, as required by the norm [6], VE1 decided not to add additional rules for this defect class.

False Negative Requirements. It is also useful to look at the values of false negative cases fn^R and recall r^R for the requirements. These 14 false negative cases not only include those already discussed, but also cases of defective requirements that could not be identified with our patterns – but which were annotated by VE1 following the guidelines of the company. In particular, interesting cases are those in which we have *inconsistent requirements* (e.g., 1: *The system shall accept only read access to file X*; 2: *The system shall accept read and write access to file X.*) that violate guideline (f), which asks requirements to be *consistent*. Other cases are those for which we have problems of *testability* (guideline (b)), as in the case of *under-specified statements* (e.g., *The system shall go in error mode when an internal asynchronism has been detected*; asynchronism among which components?), or *incomplete statements* (e.g., *The system shall make available its internal status*; through which interface?). Finally, other cases are those associated to other defects of completeness of the requirements document, as in the case of requirements for which it is expressed only the best-case scenario, and not the worst-case (e.g., *The system shall go at runtime state from power off state in 3 min in the best case.*; which is the requirement for the worst case?). Although some false negative cases were found, the evaluation of the patterns was considered successful in terms of recall by VE1. Hence, we decided to experiment the use of the patterns on a larger requirements dataset.

6   Large-Scale Study

The objective of the second study was to perform an assessment of the patterns on a larger requirements set of the company, previously validated by another VE (i.e., VE3), to understand to which extent the approach could be applicable more widely within the company.

6.1   Dataset, Annotations and Evaluation Measures

For this study a dataset of 1866 requirements was considered. The requirements belonged to a requirements document concerning a system that includes an interlocking, an ATP, a CTC (Centralised Traffic Control) and an Axle Counter. The defects of the document were previously annotated by VE3, following the criteria of the company already outlined in Sect. 5.1, and employed by VE1 for the preliminary study. Since this task was performed before this work was conceived, the annotation of the defective fragments was not performed by VE3, who just marked requirements as *accepted* or *rejected*, and described the reasons for rejection in a specific requirements validation document. From the 1866 requirements, 1733 were marked as *accepted*, while 93 were marked as *rejected*.

For the annotations performed by VE3, the measures adopted for evaluating the effectiveness of the patterns in identifying defective requirements are tp^R, fp^R, fn^R, p^R and r^R as defined in Sect. 5.2. Intuitively, these measures indicate whether the application of the different patterns simultaneously allows to identify requirements that were marked as *rejected* by VE3. Since VE3 did not annotate fragments, for this analysis we do not consider evaluation measures for the single defects as in the first analysis.

6.2   Results and Observations

In Table 4 we report the output of the patterns on the dataset in terms of defects identified ($\mathbf{D}$), and in terms of defective requirements ($\mathbf{R}$) – the other columns of the table will be discussed in Sect. 7. We see that the majority of the defects are due to *passive voice*. This is in line with the results of Femmer *et al.* [12]. The use of passive voice appears to be a sort of writing style of these requirements, since 615 out of 1866 (33%) include this defect. However, the most interesting – and disappointing – aspect comes from the evaluation presented in Table 3. The number of false positive requirements is extremely high, and the precision is only 5.7%. This value is comparable with the precision obtained through a random predictor [1] (for which $p^R = r^R = 93/1866\% = 5\%$). Hence, it appears not acceptable if the tool needs to be used in a real-world setting. Furthermore, also the value of r^R (74.19%) is not too encouraging. Hence, let us first focus on false negative cases, which impact the value of r^R, and in Sect. 7 we will discuss the analysis performed on false positive cases, which impact on p^R.

Table 3. Large-scale analysis results: requirements.

tp^R	fp^R	fn^R	p^R	r^R
69	1148	24	5.7%	74.19%

False Negative Cases. As for the preliminary analysis, the false negative cases are due to requirements that include defects that were not considered by any of the patterns, but that violate one or more criteria adopted by the company. Interesting examples are requirements that do not fulfill the criterion of *testability* (guideline (b)), as e.g., *The system shall be in continuous operation for 24 h a day and 7 days a week*; requirements that are not *feasible* (guideline (a)), e.g., *The core of the system shall use TCP/IP protocol in order to communicate with peripheral boards* – in this case, this requirement was considered not feasible since the only communication protocol that was considered applicable was UDP; requirements that include *inconsistent* statements (guideline (f)), e.g., *The brake symbol shall be able to show the following colors: Green when the brake is not active, Grey when the brake is not active*. Overall, these cases show that there is a variety of defects that are hardly identifiable with NLP techniques, and hence require a human expert to accurately assess them.

7 False Positive Analysis

Given the poor results in terms of precision, VE1 inspected the output of the tool, and saw that part of the false positive requirements were, in her opinion, actually defective. For example, the following requirement marked as *accepted*, was evidently defective due to several vague terms (highlighted in bold): ***Depending on** the technical or functional solution selected, there shall be time parameters in the control system, that the Purchaser shall be able to adjust during operation in order for the registration/deregistration to be made **as effectively as possible**.*[3] In other terms, her opinion was that VE3, when evaluating the requirements, actually tolerated several linguistic defects, and marked as *rejected* only those requirements that appeared to include severe conceptual defects. To assess how many of the false positive cases could be considered as linguistic defects from the point of view of a more strict annotator, a second annotation process was performed to evaluate the false positive cases.

7.1 Annotation and Evaluation Measures

A second annotation process was performed on the requirements marked as defective by at least one of the patterns. In this annotation process, two VEs (VE1 and VE2) independently annotated the output of the patterns as follows. For each requirement fragment labelled as defective according to pattern i, each

---

[3] The requirement was not rejected since it was clarified by other subsequent requirements. This violates the guideline (c) that require requirements to be stand-alone, but the defect was not considered crucial.

VE annotated the fragment as $defective(i)$, if the VE considered the defect as a true defect. The annotator agreement was estimated with the Cohen's Kappa [17], resulting in $k = 0.8225$, indicating an almost perfect agreement. Overall, if a fragment was annotated as $defective(i)$ by at least one annotator, the fragment was marked as $defective(i)$ in the annotated set used for the evaluation. In this analysis, we use evaluation measures for single defects, and for entire requirements. Since in this analysis we focus solely on the output produced by the patterns, we consider neither the amount of false negative cases, nor the measure of recall (for this reason the structure of Table 4 differs from that of Table 2). Hence, we consider p^D (for each defect class i) and p^R as defined as in Sect. 5.2.

Table 4. Evaluation of the results for the large-scale study.

Defect class	D	R	tp^D	fp^D	p^D
Anaphoric ambiguity	387	327	258	129	66.6%
Coordination ambiguity	263	213	190	73	72.24%
Vague terms	496	306	290	206	58.46%
Modal adverbs	476	373	331	145	69.53%
Passive voice	1265	615	1242	23	98.1%
Excessive length	16	16	16	0	100%
Missing condition	188	148	129	59	68.61%
Missing unit of measurement	0	0	0	0	-
Missing reference	4	2	4	0	100%
Undefined term	54	49	43	11	79.62%
Average					**79.24%**
Requirements			tp^R	fp^R	p^R
			1042	175	**85.6%**

7.2   Results and Observations

Table 4 reports the results of this phase. For each defect class, the precision reaches an average value of **79.24%** for what concerns the number of defects (average of different p^D). Overall p^R resulting from the application of all the patterns together, raises from the 5.7% of Table 3, to **85.6%**. However, there is still a significant amount of false positive cases that should be noticed. For the sake of space, we will present examples for *vague terms*, since these are the defects for which the false positive cases had a major impact on the precision value ($p^D = 58.46\%$). False positive cases of anaphoric ambiguity are studied by Yang et al. [21], while Chantree et al. [7] studied false positive cases of coordination ambiguity. Our false positive cases for these defect classes are similar to those addressed by these studies. For modal adverbs, false positives occur when adverbs form domain-specific names, e.g., **normally** closed to refer to relay status.

Vague Terms. A large number of false positive cases (206) is identified for this defect. These cases are due to the fact that many of the vague terms are lexically ambiguous. For example, the term *light*, considered as adjective, is vague, but when playing the role of noun, as in the requirement *Yellow Stop **lights** do not have to be monitored*, is not vague. Cases such as the one in this example can be potentially detected by applying POS tagging, and considering a term as vague only if it plays the role of adjective. Other cases occur when a vague word is part of a domain-specific multi-word term, as for the term *distant* of the following example: *The operator shall use " **distant** signalling distance" to apply the brake.* To discard these cases, techniques for multi-word term identification [5] should be applied. Finally, many cases were due to the usage of the term *possible* in the phrase *It shall be **possible** [. . .]*, considered an accepted requirement preamble within the company. This phrase was included in a stop-phrase list, to discard false positives, and allowed to increase the precision p^D for vague terms from 58.46% to **78.37%** (about 20% increase). This shows that small adjustments to the patterns can radically improve the results in terms of precision, since requirements appear to present *systematic* sources of false positives.

8   Discussion and Conclusion

This paper presents the experience of a railway signalling manufacturer in implementing a set of NLP patterns to detect defects in NL requirements. From the experience, a set of lessons learned were discussed among the authors, and are reported below.

In-house NLP. Our experience shows that NLP technologies are available for requirements analysts with limited NLP training, and that these technologies can be proficiently used for the detection of several typical requirements defects. Rule-based NLP patterns tend to generate large numbers of false positives [7,21]. If the results come from a tool that the requirements analyst cannot control, the analyst is likely to distrust the tool. Instead, if the analyst understands the inherent principles of the tool – and implementing the tool is a proper way for understanding its principles –, s/he can understand its weaknesses and use it at its best. Furthermore, it is also important to internally develop the tools, since, to reduce the amount of false positive cases, tailoring the patterns for the specific needs of the company is required. If the VE implements the patterns, s/he can customise them according to the language used in the domain, as, e.g., to account for terms such as *raw data*, *hard disk* (Sect. 5.3), and phrases such as *it shall be possible*. This last customisation allowed to increase p^D for vague terms by 20% (Sect. 7.2).

Requirements Language Counts. Looking at the large number of passive voice defects in the large-scale analysis, it appeared that the use of passive voice was a form of writing style. As a consequence, the patterns generated a large number of detected defects (i.e., 1265). This tells us that, to effectively use NLP, one cannot simply implement appropriate defect detection patterns: one should change also the language adopted in the requirements, to make it more error free, so that the VE can focus on a smaller amount of defects. For this reason, we argue that NLP tools should be first used by the requirements editors, to limit the amount of poor writing style, and only *afterwards* by a VE. However, this is not always practicable, especially in those cases in which requirements are produced by the customer, and assessed by the company who has to develop the product.

Validation Criteria Count. Comparing the results of the preliminary analysis with those of the large-scale study, we saw that a large part of the false positive cases encountered in the second analysis could be associated with a weaker validation performed by VE3, who did not focus on linguistic defects, but more on severe conceptual defects. For this reason, the results obtained in terms of precision were extremely poor. When changing criteria (Sect. 7), p^R varied from 5.7% to 85.6%. Hence, to perform an appropriate validation of rule-based NLP patterns, it is advisable to start from an annotated dataset that has been defined *knowing* the classes of defects that will be checked by the patterns. Otherwise, the results might be misleading. This observation might appear counter-intuitive, since we suggest to adapt human operators to tools. However, when dealing with the complexity of NL, we argue that the adaptation between humans and NLP tools should be bi-directional.

NLP is Only a Part of the Answer. In our large-scale study, several false negative cases occurred, which can hardly be detected with NLP. These are examples of conceptual defects that require a human with knowledge of the domain and of the specific project. The amount of these cases – 24 out of 93 defects in total – is not negligible. Furthermore, it is worth noting that 69 out of 93 conceptual defects could be actually detected by looking at *linguistic* defects that can be identified with NLP. Although computing the correlation between linguistic defects and conceptual defects is out of the scope of this work, this result suggests that some form of relation between the two might exist, and this is an aspect that is worth further exploration.

Statistical NLP vs Lexical Techniques. Our patterns make use of POS tagging and shallow parsing, which are statistical techniques that can hamper the objective of 100% recall [3]. However, in Sect. 5, we showed that 100% recall was achieved for those patterns that used these techniques, while it was *not* achieved for the pattern adopted for *vague terms*, which uses a lexical based approach. Hence, we argue that the argument in favour of a "dumb" lexical-based defect detection approach instead of an approach that leverages statistics-based technique [3] should be partially revised. If one wants to use lexical-based detection approaches, then one should use only defect indicators belonging to closed word classes (e.g., pronouns, conjunctions). Instead, if one uses open word classes (e.g., adjective, adverbs), the problems are not different from those that *might* emerge with statistical techniques. As these latter may fail, also lists of dangerous adjectives and adverbs may fail, because they might not include words that were not considered until they appear in the requirements (as e.g., the word *some*, as noted in Sect. 5.3).

Overall, the experience was considered extremely useful by the company. In particular, VE1 says that, after studying the literature on defect identification, and implementing the patterns, also her way of judging requirements defects became more strict. This is also the reason why requirements marked as *accepted* by VE3, were afterwards *rejected* by VE1 and VE2. In future works, appropriate adjustments will be defined to address the false positives identified in this study. Concerning false negative cases, it is worth remarking that, unless the tool for defect detection is appropriately validated, a VE has to manually inspect the requirements anyway to produce the verification report, as required by the CENELEC EN 50128:2011 norm [6]. Although human review cannot be replaced, NLP support can help a VE in *prioritising* the requirements to be manually analysed for defects, or, as suggested by Berry *et al.* [3], to check for defects left behind after a manual analysis has been performed.

References

1. Alvarez, S.A.: An exact analytical relation among recall, precision, and classification accuracy in information retrieval. Technical report BCCS-02-01. Computer Science Department, Boston College (2002)
2. Arora, C., Sabetzadeh, M., Briand, L., Zimmer, F.: Automated checking of conformance to requirements templates using natural language processing. IEEE TSE **41**(10), 944–968 (2015)
3. Berry, D., Gacitua, R., Sawyer, P., Tjong, S.F.: The case for dumb requirements engineering tools. In: Regnell, B., Damian, D. (eds.) REFSQ 2012. LNCS, vol. 7195, pp. 211–217. Springer, Heidelberg (2012). doi:10.1007/978-3-642-28714-5_18
4. Berry, D.M., Kamsties, E., Krieger, M.M.: From contract drafting to software specification: linguistic sources of ambiguity (2003)
5. Bonin, F., Dell'Orletta, F., Montemagni, S., Venturi, G.: A contrastive approach to multi-word extraction from domain-specific corpora. In: LREC 2010 (2010)
6. CENELEC: EN 50128: 2011: Railway applications - communication, signalling and processing systems - software for railway control and protection systems. Technical report (2011)
7. Chantree, F., Nuseibeh, B., Roeck, A.N.D., Willis, A.: Identifying nocuous ambiguities in natural language requirements. In: RE 2006, pp. 56–65 (2006)
8. Cunningham, H.: GATE, a general architecture for text engineering. Comput. Humanit. **36**(2), 223–254 (2002)
9. Cutts, M.: The Plain English Guide. Oxford University Press, Oxford (1996)
10. Falessi, D., Cantone, G., Canfora, G.: Empirical principles and an industrial case study in retrieving equivalent requirements via natural language processing techniques. IEEE Trans. Softw. Eng. **39**(1), 18–44 (2013)
11. Femmer, H., Fernández, D.M., Wagner, S., Eder, S.: Rapid quality assurance with requirements smells. J. Syst. Softw. **123**, 190–213 (2017)
12. Femmer, H., Kučera, J., Vetrò, A.: On the impact of passive voice requirements on domain modelling. In: ESEM 2014, p. 21. ACM (2014)
13. Ferrari, A., Gnesi, S.: Using collective intelligence to detect pragmatic ambiguities. In: RE 2012, pp. 191–200 (2012)
14. Gleich, B., Creighton, O., Kof, L.: Ambiguity detection: towards a tool explaining ambiguity sources. In: Wieringa, R., Persson, A. (eds.) REFSQ 2010. LNCS, vol. 6182, pp. 218–232. Springer, Heidelberg (2010). doi:10.1007/978-3-642-14192-8_20
15. Gnesi, S., Lami, G., Trentanni, G.: An automatic tool for the analysis of natural language requirements. Comput. Syst. Sci. Eng. **20**(1), 53–62 (2005)

16. Kang, N., van Mulligen, E.M., Kors, J.A.: Comparing and combining chunkers of biomedical text. J. Biomed. Inform. **44**(2), 354–360 (2011)
17. Landis, J.R., Koch, G.G.: The measurement of observer agreement for categorical data. Biometrics **33**(1), 159–174 (1977)
18. Manning, C.D.: Part-of-speech tagging from 97% to 100%: is it time for some linguistics? In: Gelbukh, A.F. (ed.) CICLing 2011. LNCS, vol. 6608, pp. 171–189. Springer, Heidelberg (2011). doi:10.1007/978-3-642-19400-9_14
19. Mich, L., Franch, M., Inverardi, P.N.: Market research for requirements analysis using linguistic tools. REJ **9**(1), 40–56 (2004)
20. Tjong, S.F., Berry, D.M.: The design of SREE — a prototype potential ambiguity finder for requirements specifications and lessons learned. In: Doerr, J., Opdahl, A.L. (eds.) REFSQ 2013. LNCS, vol. 7830, pp. 80–95. Springer, Heidelberg (2013). doi:10.1007/978-3-642-37422-7_6
21. Yang, H., Roeck, A.N.D., Gervasi, V., Willis, A., Nuseibeh, B.: Analysing anaphoric ambiguity in natural language requirements. REJ **16**(3), 163–189 (2011)

Research Methodology in Requirements Engineering

Specifying Software Requirements
for Safety-Critical Railway Systems:
An Experience Report

Luciana Provenzano[1,2(✉)] and Kaj Hänninen[2]

[1] Bombardier Transportation, Västerås, Sweden
[2] Mälardalen University, Västerås, Sweden
{luciana.provenzano,kaj.hanninen}@mdh.se

Abstract. *Context and motivation*: Software safety requirements are fundamental in the definition of risk reduction measures for safety critical systems,
since they are developed to satisfy the system safety constraints as identified by
mandated safety analyses. It is therefore imperative that the requirements are
defined clearly and precisely. *Question/Problem*: We describe our experiences
in introducing a safety compliant method of writing safety software requirements for railway projects in a distributed organization. Our goal was twofold,
to develop requirements specifications that comply with the EN 50128 standard
and that are understandable by the persons involved in the software development. *Principal ideas/results*: We introduced methods to transform natural
language requirements to functional requirements described as scenarios,
sequence, use-case and state-machine diagrams. *Contribution*: Our experience
shows that new ways of expressing requirements, even if proper to solve
technical issues such as compliance with standards, bring other challenges to the
organization like people's reluctance to changes in working routines and process
updates.

Keyword: Software requirements · Safety critical system · Railway domain ·
Compliance with safety standards

1 Introduction

In large-scale distributed development organizations, projects are often executed by
people and teams from different working-sites and countries. Teams with specific
responsibilities and differences in safety cultures are cooperating and contributing with
their knowledge and resources to develop parts of products that will be integrated into a
final system. Assuring safety and compliance with a safety standard is often a challenge
in distributed organizations.

In this paper we describe our experiences of introducing new ways of specifying
safety requirements in a development organization. The aim of the work was to
transform the way requirements were expressed, from a natural language, to
semi-formal descriptions in the form of diagrams according to the EN 50128 railway
standard [1]. This implied that a new way of working and new processes, that affected
people dealing with requirements engineering, had to be introduced.

© Springer International Publishing AG 2017
P. Grünbacher and A. Perini (Eds.): REFSQ 2017, LNCS 10153, pp. 363–369, 2017.
DOI: 10.1007/978-3-319-54045-0_25

In modern safety critical systems, the software is a vital part of the risk reduction measures in the sense that software functions are used to control or reduce the risk of hazards that may cause a system to fail with catastrophic consequences for human life, the environment and facilities. For this reason, software safety requirements and design constraints are the fundamentals in the definition of risk reduction measures for these types of systems, since they are developed to satisfy the system safety constraints as identified by mandated safety analyses. It is therefore imperative that the software safety requirements are defined clearly and precisely so that difficulties and ambiguities in interpreting them are avoided. In the railway domain, the EN 50128 standard prescribes best practice processes to be followed when developing the software, so that it achieves the necessary level of safety, called safety integrity level (SIL). With regard to the software safety requirements, the standard addresses both the requirements content, by pointing out the need to define failure modes, and the software properties that shall be considered, such as safety, robustness, maintainability, and so on. Depending on the criticality of the system, the standard also suggests techniques and measures that have to be applied when structuring requirements. This should be done so that the resulting specifications are understandable, testable, realizable, consistent and complete.

In reality, techniques and descriptions used to specify requirements shall be understandable by all the persons involved in a software life-cycle. This implies that people from different teams and with different experiences of requirements have to be able to use them in their daily work. In this paper, we describe the approach used to comply with the standard. We discuss the impact of this approach on the current process through different stakeholder's feedback and we conclude with some lessons learned.

2   Software Safety Requirements

The software safety requirements subject of this report concern the Train Control Management System (TCMS) for a high-speed train. The TCMS is a real-time on-board system in charge of the execution of the train control functions, the transmission of data inside and outside the train, and the collection of diagnostic data.

Software safety requirements for the TCMS system are derived from the vehicle safety requirements that are identified during the system hazard analysis. These requirements together with design constraints constitute the mitigation measures that have to be implemented to reduce any risks with the product to acceptable levels.

2.1   The Project Context and the Need for Change

When we began to document and assess the TCMS safety requirements, the project had been running for approximately two years. The most of the non-safety critical requirements had been written in natural language. With this situation, both designers and testers of the TCMS system expressed their issues concerning the quality of the existing requirements for the following reasons:

- Some requirements were not testable, mainly because of conditions that contained many implicit assumptions due to the fact that they were written by the most experienced persons with deep domain knowledge. These assumptions resulted in ambiguities for the testers.
- The sources of the input conditions and the destinations of the output results were not defined for all the requirements. This made the integration test very difficult to perform. The testers had to check the details of the implementation to understand the overall functionality.
- Requirements were not complete with regard to failure cases definitions. So decisions on possible alternative behaviors were taken by the designers. The testers had little or no chance to discover the alternative behaviors when performing the functional test, without checking the actual implementation.
- Many of the software requirements had been purely copied from system requirements without refinement for their actual use.

2.2   The Approach Towards Safety Compliance

Based on the above observations, our choice was to introduce a safety compliant method of writing requirements that aimed at:

- Improving the requirements' content to obtain clear, precise, unambiguous, testable, and feasible requirements;
- Including in the requirements the description of the required failure modes according to the EN 50128 standard;
- Describing ways to express the requirements' properties required by the standard, such as safety, robustness, maintainability, performance, efficiency;
- Identifying and documenting the internal and external interfaces of the TCMS.

Our methodology to write and structure the TCMS software safety requirements was driven by the EN 50128 standard. To evaluate the applicability and feasibility of the new method within our organization, this approach was submitted for approval to the project leads and line managers.

Clear, Precise, Unambiguous, Testable and Feasible Requirements through Scenarios. We applied use cases to identify the functional safety requirements. Each use case was described by a success scenario (basic scenario) *"and a set of scenario fragments as extensions of it"* [5]. Even if scenarios are not directly suggested by the EN 50128 standard, we decided to use them due to the following reasons:

- The requirements expressed as scenarios were more precise and clearer than the ones written in natural language. In particular, each step of the scenario was specified according to a well-defined style. This contributed to reduce possible ambiguities caused by natural language sentences while keeping requirements easy to understand by the persons using them.
- The resulting requirements described the failure cases, due to the possibility of defining alternatives and exceptions for each step in scenarios.
- We were able to check the consistency and the completeness of the input requirements, by examining input requirements with the aim of writing scenarios.

In fact, by searching for use cases out of a set of input requirements we could discover the overall function/s, i.e. understand what the TCMS was supposed to offer with regard to a specific set of requirements. Then by building the steps in the scenario for a given use case, we could check if the input requirements were consistent according to the overall goal, and/or if some requirements were missing or incorrect.

Interfaces Through Sequence Diagrams. We described the interfaces of the safety functions by a sequence diagram for each basic scenario. The description of the interfaces covered both internal and external input/output to perform a particular function. Sequence diagrams are a "highly recommended" technique suggested by the EN 50128 standard when modeling is chosen to specify safety requirements. We used the sequence diagrams for interfaces description because we believed that a graphical representation was a more intuitive and concise way to show the interactions of a safety function, and particularly useful when performing the integration test. We intentionally kept the sequence diagrams simple, i.e. they were not used to design the function logic. We did it to reduce the need of extensive training of those using the requirements.

Non-functional Requirements. The EN 50128 standard requires non-functional requirements to be included in the safety requirements specification, but it does not suggest how they should be specified. Since functional safety requirements were written as scenarios, we tried to figure out how these non-functional properties (i.e. robustness, efficiency, etc.) could be specified by stating the following questions:

- Can scenarios also be used to describe some of the non-functional properties?
- If non-functional requirements cannot be specified by scenarios, what is the typical content of a non-functional requirement?
- Are non-functional requirements only applicable to specific functional requirements or generic for all requirements? Which of the non-functional properties can be considered generic for all requirements?

By doing a literature review of current state of art, see for example [2–4], we discovered that non-functional requirements generally consist of a requirement identifier, a title, a description, and a list of sources and standards for the traceability.

So we decided to create a specific section for the non-functional requirements, to include all software properties (such as performance) that were not specific for any particular safety function. These non-functional requirements were specified using the above-mentioned format that was based on state of art. Non-functional requirements that concerned a specific safety function were described as part of the functional requirement by extending the scenario of that function.

3 Outcomes and Impact on Users and Process

Based on our new approach, we reviewed and accepted approximately 140 system safety requirements, which corresponded to the 10% of the whole set of system requirements allocated to the TCMS. From the system safety requirements, we identified about 70 use cases and we described each use case through scenarios. The safety software requirements specification was assessed by the safety assessor.

An interesting question out of this work was to understand if this method could be employed to manage safety requirements within other projects and to which extent so as to establish a common process issued from this experience to be used in the organization. To address this question, we collected data by informal interviews with the different stakeholders, and discussed with the test, design, change management and quality assurance leads within the project. Informal interviews with team members working with this new method were performed throughout the duration of the project to adapt the approach to the users' feedback. We therefore discuss in this section the impact of this method on the current process and the feedback from the persons who experienced it.

3.1   Impact on the Current Process

To identify use cases and scenarios, we needed to review the input requirements in-depth to grasp the overall functional behavior for each set of safety requirements. The review process was an opportunity to discuss and clarify the safety functions with the customers at a very early stage. This resulted in a better quality of the input requirements and in more involvement of the customer in the software development.

However, a need for a well-defined acceptance process of the input requirements became fundamental as well as the definition of a new role of the requirements manager. Managing requirements with this new approach required more activities than the ones performed to manage the non-safety requirements. This implied that the project needed to invest more time and resources into the requirements phase, and new skills, especially in software engineering, became necessary.

3.2   How Did People Accept This Approach?

Eleven team members who worked at the same site adapted the new method in their daily work. The team members consisted of: one safety manager and a safety engineer, two requirements engineers, three designers, one test lead and two testers, and a software quality manager. Four internal customers from different sites of the company collaborated with the safety manager and the requirements engineer to clarify the input safety requirements using this method as basis for discussions. An independent safety assessor was in charge of the assessment of the safety requirements specified according to this new approach.

Independent Safety Assessor (ISA). The ISA found the safety software requirements very easy to assess since all the EN 50128 standard recommendations had been taken into account (see Sect. 2.2). We were able to provide the assessor with a clear explanation of how each clause had been fulfilled and where in the safety software requirements specification the corresponding information could be found.

Management. The management appreciated that the safety requirements were assessed, which resulted in time-saving and reduced cost for any reworking activities. However, they judged this new method expensive due to the need for additional training of the personnel involved.

Designers. According to the designers, the new way of expressing requirements was too much detailed and overworked. Moreover, they argued that the precise description of the function behavior through scenarios constrained their possible interpretation of the requirements. We think that this was due to the fact that designers were the most experienced engineers in the project (most of them had been working on the TCMS for more than 10 years). They stated that the new way of expressing the requirements constrained them from using their skills and domain knowledge in their daily work. However, designers appreciated the description of the failure cases.

Testers. Testers needed extensive discussions with the requirements engineers to understand how to use the new requirements in order to build the test cases. They were used to work with non-safety requirements which were written in natural language, i.e. they were not familiar with requirements specified as scenario. Initially they claimed that they did not derive any tangible benefit from the sequence diagrams to perform the integration test. We observed that they had difficulties in understanding the relationships among the different use cases and the sequence diagrams. A possible explanation to this may be the way in which the software safety requirements were structured in DOORS [7]. In fact, sequence diagrams were described through DOORS objects tagged as "Information". As a result, sequence diagrams were not considered as actual requirements but as descriptions and, as such, discarded. They also thought that the number of test cases was considerably increased since they were obliged to test all the alternatives and exceptions for each scenario.

Safety Manager. The safety manager found the modeling very useful in discovering potential errors, oversights and inconsistencies in the input requirements. The manager also observed that the number of undefined behaviors identified when performing a Failure Mode and Effects Analysis (FMEA) [8] was drastically reduced due to the failure modes described in the alternative and/or exceptions sections of the scenarios.

Stakeholders. The stakeholders from different sites in the distributed organization appreciated the use of semi-formal modeling with a clear and precise semantics. This provided the stakeholders with a common formalism for discussions. Modeling therefore became the primary means of communication and understanding of the safety requirements.

4   Conclusions and Lessons Learned

In this paper, we introduced a safety compliant method of writing software safety requirements for railway projects in a distributed organization. Our experience shows that dealing with safety requirements was a great challenge that went beyond the technical aspects of producing a requirements specification that complied with the EN 50128 standard. We observed that most of the time and effort was devoted to make this new approach accepted by the persons involved in the software development, rather than to interpret the standard and propose a suitable solution. The reasons behind people's reluctance to change the working routines are many. In the organization, the use of semi-formal models to specify requirements was the most difficult and perplexing change. Models were not understood as being part of the requirements. However, in the long term the sequence diagrams and the scenarios were used by the testers and the designers to reason about functions. This resulted in constructive discussions, especially during the review meetings, that contributed to a deeper and better understanding of the safety functions.

We believe that the introduction of new methods must be enforced by the top management to be effective, especially in large-scale organizations. Moreover, the working processes have to be updated accordingly for the new techniques to be efficiently adopted. In fact, changes in the way of writing requirements impact the project management in terms of new review processes, new change management routines, new roles and broadened skills, new tools set-up, etc.

This approach pushed the organization to further realize that requirements have *"a crucial importance ... in critical software systems engineering"* [6], and efforts are now made to further improve the requirements management.

References

1. CENELEC EN 50128 Railway applications – Communication, signaling and processing systems – Software for railway control and protection systems (2011)
2. Shahrokni, A., Feldt, R.: Towards a framework for specifying software robustness requirements based on patterns. In: Wieringa, R., Persson, A. (eds.) REFSQ 2010. LNCS, vol. 6182, pp. 79–84. Springer, Heidelberg (2010). doi:10.1007/978-3-642-14192-8_9
3. Gustavsson, J., Österlund, M.: Requirements on maintainability of software systems – an investigation of the state of the practice. In: SERPS 2005 5th Conference on Software Engineering and Practice in Sweden (2005)
4. Bondi, A.B.: Best practices for writing and managing performance requirements: A tutorial. In: ICPE 2012 Proceedings of the 3rd ACM/SPEC International Conference on Performance Engineering, pp. 1–8 (2012)
5. Cockburn, A.: Writing Effective Use Cases. Addison-Wesley, Boston (2011)
6. Larrucea, X., Combelles, A., Favaro, J.: Safety-critical software [Guest editors' introduction]. IEEE Softw. **30**(3), 25–27 (2013)
7. IBM Rational DOORS. http://www-03.ibm.com/software/products/en/ratidoor
8. FMEA. https://en.wikipedia.org/wiki/Failure_mode_and_effects_analysis

Usefulness of a Human Error Identification Tool for Requirements Inspection: An Experience Report

Vaibhav Anu[1(✉)], Gursimran Walia[1], Gary Bradshaw[2], Wenhua Hu[3], and Jeffrey C. Carver[3]

[1] North Dakota State University, Fargo, USA
vaibhav.anu@ndsu.edu
[2] Mississippi State University, Starkville, USA
[3] University of Alabama, Tuscaloosa, USA

Abstract. *Context and Motivation:* Our recent work leverages Cognitive Psychology research on human errors to improve the standard fault-based requirements inspections. *Question:* The empirical study presented in this paper investigates the effectiveness of a newly developed Human Error Abstraction Assist (HEAA) tool in helping inspectors identify human errors to guide the fault detection during the requirements inspection. *Results:* The results showed that the HEAA tool, though effective, presented challenges during the error abstraction process. *Contribution:* In this experience report, we present major challenges during the study execution and lessons learned for future replications.

1 Introduction

Designing and performing empirical studies to evaluate the effectiveness of a newly developed software method, tool or technique poses a number of unique challenges (e.g., selecting representative set of subjects and artifacts; preparing training material; variables selection). The challenges are even greater when the novel Software Engineering (SE) technique borrows concepts from disciplines other than SE (e.g., Psychology) because of the issues faced by subjects in successfully comprehending theories from the other discipline and applying them to SE experimental tasks.

On those lines, our recent work [1, 4] uses a *Cognitive Psychology* perspective on *human errors* to improve the practice of requirements inspections. *Human errors* are understood as purely mental events, failings of human cognition in the process of problem solving, planning, and acting. Errors, in turn, will produce faults, a physical manifestation of the error. In the context of this paper, it is important that the reader makes a clear distinction between *human errors (mental events)* vs *program errors* (related to coding or programmatic failures).

Traditional fault-based requirements inspection techniques (like Fault Checklist inspection) focus inspectors' attention on different type of faults (e.g., incorrect or incomplete or ambiguous requirements) [6]. Even a faithful application of validated fault-based techniques does not help inspectors in finding all faults. As a result, a larger

© Springer International Publishing AG 2017
P. Grünbacher and A. Perini (Eds.): REFSQ 2017, LNCS 10153, pp. 370–377, 2017.
DOI: 10.1007/978-3-319-54045-0_26

part (40–50%) of the development effort is spent fixing the issues that should have been fixed in an earlier phase. We propose that inspections focused on identifying *human errors* (i.e., the underlying cause of faults) are better at identifying requirements faults when compared to inspections focused on faults (which essentially are manifestation of human error). To that end, the proposed inspection approach extends the traditional fault-checklist (FC) inspection approach by adding the following steps: (1) assisting inspectors in abstracting human errors from the faults found during the FC inspection, and (2) using the abstracted errors to locate additional related faults.

To help inspectors in identifying human errors, the authors over the past two years, have worked on developing the Human Error Taxonomy (HET) that classifies most commonly occurring human errors during requirements engineering [2]. We have also developed a human error analysis framework called the *Human Error Abstraction Assist (HEAA)* tool that can guide inspectors in analyzing and abstracting (i.e., extracting) human error information from requirements faults, a process referred to as *Error Abstraction (EA)* by Psychologists. Description of HET and HEAA appears in Sect. 2.

This paper discusses an empirical study to evaluate the usefulness of the HEAA tool during the error-based inspection, the challenges faced when designing and conducting the empirical study, and lessons learned to help improve future replications.

2 Background

In this section, we briefly describe human error based inspections and tools that have been developed to support human error based inspections.

(1) **Human Error Based Requirements Inspections:** Error based inspections [5], include two main tasks: (1) Error Abstraction - EA, wherein inspectors identify and extract human errors from previously found faults, and (2) error-inspection, wherein inspectors use the abstracted human errors to guide the detection of remaining faults.

(2) **Human Error Taxonomy (HET):** HET was developed to support the Error Abstraction (EA) leg of human error based inspections. HET provides a list of most common human errors that occur during the requirements engineering phase. The motivation for creating the HET was that, without a tangible list of requirements phase human errors, the inspectors would have to rely on their creativity when abstracting human errors. Detailed information about HET development can be found in [2].

(3) **Human Error Abstraction Assist (HEAA):** Although the HET provides a concrete list of the most commonly occurring human errors, EA is still a subjective process that different people might perceive in different ways. In order to reduce the subjectivity and complexity of EA we developed the HEAA tool, which can be found in [2].

The HEAA tool was created after performing pilot empirical evaluation of human error based inspections with different set of subjects [1, 4]. During these empirical studies, subjects performed EA using an ad hoc process, wherein subjects used their creativity when abstracting human errors from faults. After the studies, the subjects provided feedback that EA can be improved by focusing the inspector's attention on various requirements engineering (RE) activities (elicitation, analysis, specification, and management). Hence, to create HEAA, we further distributed the 15 human error classes of HET across the various RE activities. We created HEAA (which can be found in [2]) to act as an intuitive frame-work to systematically guide inspectors during EA. Inspectors have to answer a set of questions to trace a fault to a human error. The current study evaluated the effectiveness of human error based inspections supported by the HEAA tool and how can it be effectively used by researchers for future investigations.

3   Empirical Study Design

The main goal of this study was to evaluate and improve the use of the EA process (supported by the HEAA tool) in helping inspectors find requirements faults that are left undetected when using the fault checklist (FC) inspection technique.

(1) **Research Questions:**

   RQ 1: Does the HEAA tool help inspectors detect significantly large number of faults during requirements inspection compared to the fault-checklist inspection technique?

   RQ 2: Are inspectors able to use the HEAA tool to accurately abstract and classify human errors that occurred during the requirements development process?

(2) **Subjects and Artifacts:**

   Subjects: Sixteen (16) graduate students enrolled in the *Software Requirements Engineering* course at NDSU participated in this study. The course was a breadth course on software requirements encompassing analysis, documentation, and verification.

   Artifacts: Two SRS documents were used during the course of this study. Initially, subjects were trained on the EA process (and the HEAA tool) using an SRS document that specified requirements for a Parking Garage Control System (PGCS). Post training, subjects applied their knowledge of EA (and used the HEAA tool) to inspect a document that specified requirements fora Restaurant Interactive Menu (RIM) system.

(3) **Experiment Procedure:** The experiment was designed as a quasi-experimental repeated measures investigation and conducted in two phases: *pre-test* and *post-test*. During *pre-test*, subjects were trained on how to use the HEAA tool to abstract errors from a subset of PGCS faults (that were provided to them), and use the identified error information to re-inspect PGCS SRS for remaining faults. During the *post-test phase*, subjects applied FC and used the HEAA tool to inspect RIM SRS for errors and faults. The experiment procedure is shown in Fig. 1 and the steps are described below:

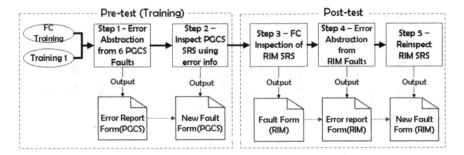

Fig. 1. Empirical study procedure

Fault checklist (FC) training: Subjects had been trained on FC inspections and had inspected SRS's using FC inspection prior to the beginning of this experiment.

Training 1 – Error abstraction (EA) training: During an in-class session, subjects were trained on human errors (via HET), and EA (supported by the HEAA tool).

Step 1 – Abstraction of human errors in PGCS SRS: Subjects were supplied with PGCS SRS along with 6 (out of 35 seeded) faults. Subjects used the HEAA tool to abstract and classify human errors from these 6 faults. The output of this step was **16 individual Error Report Forms** *(one per subject)*.

Step 2 – Inspection of PGCS SRS using error information: Subjects inspected PGCS for faults using the human error information contained in their own error report form (from Step 1). The output of this step was **16 individual New Fault Forms**.

Step 3 – FC inspection of RIM SRS: Subjects performed FC inspection of RIM SRS. The output of this step was **16 individual Fault Forms** (one per subject).

Step 4 – Abstraction of human errors in RIM SRS: Subjects abstracted human errors from the faults they found (during Step 3) using the HEAA tool. The output of this step was **16 individual Error Report Forms**.

Step 5 – Re-inspection of RIM SRS: Subjects re-inspected the RIM SRS for new faults using the human error information contained in their error report form (from Step 4). The output of this step was **16 individual New Fault Forms** (one per subject).

4   Data Analysis and Results

This section describes the analysis performed to answer RQs.

RQ1: Effectiveness of RIM Inspection guided by Faults vs. Errors

For each subject, Fig. 2 compares the effectiveness (# of faults found) during the *fault-based inspection of RIM (Step 3 in* Fig. 1*)* vs *the new faults found during the*

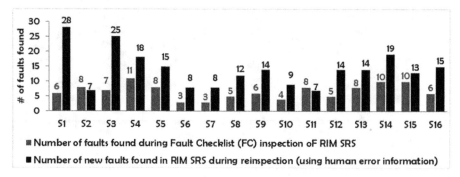

Fig. 2. Effectiveness of FC inspections vs human error based inspection

error guided inspection of RIM document (Step 5). As shown in Fig. 2, subjects were generally able to use underlying human errors to locate additional faults (that were either missed or undetected during FC inspection of RIM SRS). For example, subject S2 identified 8 faults during the FC inspection of RIM, then used the HEAA tool to abstract human errors (from 8 previously found faults) and reported 7 new faults during the re-inspection of RIM SRS using the identified error information.

A one-sample t-test was performed to evaluate whether the average number of *faults found in RIM using human error information* were significantly greater than the *average number of faults found in RIM using FC.* The result of the one-sample test ($p = 0.000221$) showed that the average number of faults found using underlying human error information (i.e., 14 faults) was significantly higher than the average number of faults found during FC (i.e., 6.75 faults).

RQ2: Error Abstraction and Classification using the HEAA Tool

To understand the usefulness of the HEAA tool, this section evaluates whether inspectors were correctly able to make a distinction between human error mechanisms (Slip, Lapse, and Mistake) and accurately classify the error into one of the 15 human error classes of HET. Using the error-report form for each subject (output at Step 4 in Fig. 1), EA accuracy was analyzed at two levels (Fig. 3) and described below:

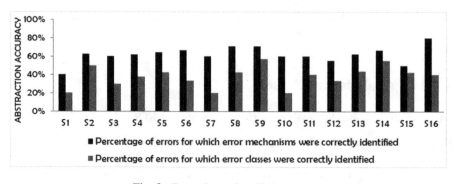

Fig. 3. Error abstraction (EA) accuracy

(1) *Error-Mechanism*: Accuracy with which subjects were able to distinguish between Slips, Lapses, and Mistakes (black colored columns in Fig. 3). To determine the EA accuracy when identifying the human error mechanisms, we calculated the percentage of total human errors for which human error mechanisms were correctly identified by each subject. Figure 3 shows the EA accuracies (when identifying error mechanisms) for 16 subjects. For example, subject S2 reported eight (8) human errors of which, five (5) were abstracted to the correct error mechanisms (i.e., 62.50% accuracy). The mean EA accuracy (when identifying error mechanisms) was found to be around 62%.

(2) *Error Class*: Accuracy with which subjects were able to identify the detailed human errors class (grey colored columns in Fig. 3). EA accuracy when identifying and classifying human error classes was calculated as the percentage of total human errors that were correctly classified into a human error class (from HET). The mean EA accuracy of abstracting *error classes* computed to be around 38%, considerably lower than the accuracy of abstracting *error mechanisms* (found to be 62%). This trend in the downgrade of EA accuracy going from *error mechanism* to *error classes* was evident across all the subjects, with an average difference of around 24% per subject. This trend showed that while the HEAA tool and EA training helped subjects identify errors that led to detection of faults, both the HEAA and the EA training needs to be improved in order to help subjects identify the right error classes.

5   Validity Threats and Lessons Learned

Validity Threats

(1) *External Validity*: Generalization of this study's results is limited by the facts that that it was conducted on a very small scale with only 16 participants and under classroom settings, rather than with requirements experts and professionals in real environment.

(2) *Internal Validity*: Owing to the comprehensiveness and length of the study, it is possible the participants became fatigued and did not perform certain tasks like EA properly, which might be the reason behind lower EA accuracy (Fig. 3) Another internal validity threat to a study likes ours is the effect of *intellectual maturation*. That is, subjects naturally performed better during error-informed reinspection of RIM SRS as they were inspecting/reviewing RIM for the second time (first inspection was FC inspection. See Fig. 2). We were able to control this threat to some extent by keeping the FC inspection and the error-informed reinspection 8 to 10 days apart from each other.

Lessons Learned: The lessons learned are discussed under five major headings:

(1) *Replicating the Study with Requirements Experts:* Although the study results were promising, in order to generalize the results, the study needs to be replicated with higher number of participants and also with requirements experts, who are likely to be able to perform important steps like EA with better accuracy.

(2) **Training Subjects on Cognitive Psychology Concepts:** EA required subjects to demonstrate some understanding of error patterns (i.e., inattentiveness, forgetfulness, knowledge-deficit, etc.) and make inferences in light of situational data (which is difficult when one was not involved during the requirements development). As results showed, subjects showed an understanding of the error mechanisms (slips, lapses, mistakes), but struggled to correctly identify the right human error classes. This motivated the development of new decision tree based error abstraction approach [2], with a simpler navigation method to help inspectors abstract and classify human errors.

(3) **Subjectivity of Tasks (During EA) Makes for Challenging Data Analysis:** Analyzing EA data provided by the subjects required careful attention to detail as subjects had varying accounts of human errors. A bigger challenge is to make a decision about the correctness of errors abstracted by subjects. For analyzing the EA data in the current study, we compared each subject's results of error abstraction with our error abstraction results (agreed upon by authors). This type of absolute analysis disregards a subject's reasoning behind why they selected a particular human error. In future, we intend to improve our data analysis process by using the concepts of Contextual Content Analysis [3], wherein the verbal or textual data is divided into small meaningful pieces that can be analyzed both qualitatively and quantitatively.

(4) **Challenge of Academic Environment:** An empirical study performed in academic environment poses certain challenges that are difficult to avoid. One of the important issues is the *lack of adequate time* during the class hours. We had to give a few important but time-consuming experimental tasks (Step 4 and Step 5 in Fig. 1) as homework assignments. This resulted in subjects not recording properly the time they took for completing these tasks. This caused the efficiency (number of faults found per unit time) data to be rather skewed. In future experiments, we intend to address this by having students perform experimental tasks during class hours or at predefined schedules.

(5) **Involvement of Domain Experts:** When performing a cross-disciplinary research, involvement of domain experts (from SE and Psychology fields) can allow interdisciplinary learning. The frequent communication between the domain specific accounts of SE errors and theories of human cognition in Psychology were integrated during the development of HET, the HEAA tool and during the planning of study. The psychology expert, Dr. Bradshaw provided timely and much needed advice throughout our study with real life examples of slips, lapses, and mistakes during the training (which can be found in [2] and can be used by other researchers).

6   Conclusions

A critical look at the empirical methodology followed to evaluate the performance of a newly developed human error based requirements inspection tool (HEAA) showed that both the *HEAA tool* and the EA *training*, even though effective, need tobe improved.

Major challenges we encountered and the lessons learned during the empirical study were portrayed for future replications and also for the benefit of other researchers.

Acknowledgment. This work was supported by NSF Awards 1423279 and 1421006. The authors would like to thank the students of the *Software Requirements* course at North Dakota State University for participating in this study.

References

1. Anu, V., Walia, G.S., Hu, W., Carver, J.C., Bradshaw, G.: Effectiveness of human error taxonomy during requirements inspection: an empirical investigation. In: Software Engineering and Knowledge Engineering, SEKE 2016 (2016)
2. Anu, V., Walia, G.S., Hu, W., Carver, J.C., Bradshaw, G.: The Human Error Abstraction Assist (HEAA) tool (2016). http://vaibhavanu.com/NDSU-CS-TP-2016-001.html
3. Hsieh, H.F., Shannon, S.E.: Three approaches to qualitative content analysis. Qual. Health Res. **15**(9), 1277–1288 (2005)
4. Hu, W., Carver, J.C., Anu, V., Walia, G.S., Bradshaw, G.: Detection of requirement errors and faults via a human error taxonomy: a feasibility study. In: 10th ACM/IEEE International Symposium on Empirical Software Engineering and Measurement, ESEM 2016 (2016)
5. Lanubile, F., Shull, F., Basili, V.R.: Experimenting with error abstraction in requirements documents. In: Proceedings of the 5th International Symposium on Software Metrics (1998)
6. Porter, A.A., Votta, L.G., Basili, V.R.: Comparing detection methods for software requirements inspections: a replicated experiment. IEEE Trans. Softw. Eng. **21**(6), 563–575 (1995)

Author Index